POWERING THE FUTURE

A Lawyer's Guide to Clean Energy

STEVEN FERREY

AMERICAN BAR ASSOCIATION
Environment, Energy, and Resources Section

Cover design by ABA Design

Printed in the United States of America.

28 27 26 25 24 5 4 3 2 1

A catalog record for this book is available from the Library of Congress.

Contents

PART IV

Looming Challenges

About the Author

Steven Ferrey is an experienced energy, environmental, and land-use attorney who has worked in the United States and internationally. He is Professor of Law at Suffolk University Law School and also served as Visiting Professor of Law at Harvard Law School and Visiting Professor of Law at Boston University Law School. He provided expert testimony on energy and environmental matters before seven different committees of the U.S. Senate and the U.S. House of Representatives and served as an expert witness in litigated matters.

He is a member of the California and Massachusetts bars. His work includes:

- Leading the team handling the first successful U.S. independent company purchase ($1.8 billion) of a utility's divested electric and gas energy assets
- Representing parties before various state PUCs and siting boards
- Representing parties in numerous environmental and land-use matters
- Permitting and siting large renewable field-mounted and rooftop solar projects, onshore and offshore wind projects, hydro projects, fossil fuel projects, and LFG projects
- Obtaining permits for power generation facilities; negotiating PPAs, interconnection agreements, and land leases and easements
- Obtaining/transferring state Renewable Energy Credits and net metering entitlements
- Advising on energy and climate matters in dozens of different countries on five continents

Professor Ferrey earned a juris doctor (JD), a master's degree in energy and environmental planning, and a BA in economics and between his two graduate degrees was awarded a Fulbright Fellowship at the University of London working on energy and environmental matters. He served as vice-chair of two different ABA section committees. He may be contacted by email at sferrey@suffolk.edu.

Preface

The Legal "Edge" Honed In This Book

This preface is brief, as a preface should be. This book promises up front to take each reader through multiple topics and for each to provide key analysis and information for every practicing lawyer and stakeholder. This book covers the once-in-a-century shift in key energy technology enacted through new laws to shift the entire U.S. economy off fossil fuels to electric power by 2035. Electric power is the most important invention in history, as well as legally subject in the United States to a unique state versus federal separation of power regulation. Now changing rapidly is the role of environmental, climate, and energy law practice. Current policy now rapidly redirects electric power to dominate all U.S. energy use. The following chapters each analyze emerging legal issues and share insights and strategies on changing law affecting legal practice. This book clearly repositions legal issues on the "radar screen."

This book is designed so you can move to any topic—each chapter is a self-contained analysis of separate major legal issues now bringing into play new environmental and land-use impacts. This book focuses on the fast-changing role of electricity, the most important invention in history now undergirding the entire U.S. economy. This book constructs a roadmap of how lawyers can successfully understand, navigate, and utilize key legal opportunities as this critical industry fundamentally is altered at unprecedented speed.

This is a forward-looking guide for those interested or involved in the future of electricity, environment, climate, and power—including those attorneys and others working for energy companies, state PUC and FERC regulators, lenders, venture capitalists, investors, and all electric industry stakeholders. Each chapter provides strategic workarounds for current and future challenging legal issues, applying policy tools to guide attorneys and clients.

Part I isolates what is unique and irreplaceable about electric energy, its impact on the environment and climate, and why and how it now operates as the most important invention in history.

Part II in separate chapters identifies new legal pressure points affecting the critical U.S. electric power sector, the environment, land use, and climate. Each chapter showcases how lawyers can strategically manage legal distinctions among state, federal, and local regulation of power. Profiled in detail are key opportunities created by the 2022 Inflation Reduction Act, the 2021 Infrastructure Investment and Jobs Act, changes in tax law, and changing state and federal electric power subsidies. Strategic state law distinctions and different opportunities in all 50 states are compared and highlighted—providing a roadmap successfully to navigate legal and technical challenges in this fast-changing environment.

Part III examines and creates the new business model that energy clients and their counsel will need and seek to utilize to navigate and maneuver in the changed legal and regulatory environment.

Part IV looks beyond the radar screen into the future to chart important legal changes for the power grid; new legal and legislative tripwires; and changing technology affecting the environment, land use, and energy.

Nothing contained in this educational book should be considered or relied on as legal or tax advice for specific matters or cases, and readers are responsible for obtaining such advice from their own legal counsel.

The author is happy to talk with any readers of this book. The author acknowledges the work of his research assistants Kiara Benac, Sydney Cramer, and Joe Ruggiero; the helpful editorial input of Professor Steven Weissman on behalf of the ABA SEER Committee and the Committee as a whole; and the staff at ABA Publishing.

I invite you to read on. Let's get started.

PART I

Unique, Inventive, Irreplaceable: Changing the World

CHAPTER 1

Electricity: Legally and Physically Unique

"The electric power sector is among the largest in the U.S. economy, with links to every other sector."

West Virginia v. EPA[1]

When asked whether the day that he won the presidency in 1976 was the most important and happy day of his life, our 39th president and Nobel Peace Prize recipient Jimmy Carter responded that neither that day, nor any other during his presidency, was the most important day. He recalled that the most important day in his life was the day in the 1930s when his boyhood home in Georgia first received electricity.[2] President Carter stated that electricity opened the world of reading in the evening to him and allowed him to listen to the radio, which connected him to the outside world from rural Georgia.[3] This is an important presidential reminder.

Before segueing in Part II of this book to a series of cutting-edge legal issues, this introductory chapter sets forth why electric power is

- The second most important invention in history (after the wheel).
- The essential input for more than a dozen of the 50 other most important inventions in history.
- The critical U.S. resource for all sectors protected by the U.S. Department of Homeland Security.
- A very large source of revenue in the country, with more money collected annually than collected from all U.S. corporate taxes (even before the corporate tax rate was reduced in 2017).
- The most legally regulated sector of the U.S. economy, occupying the time and efforts of a growing number of attorneys.

---

1. West Virginia. v. EPA, 597 U.S. 697 (2022).
2. Interview by Katie Couric with President Jimmy Carter, *Today Show*, NBC (Oct. 30, 2000).
3. *Id.*

Electricity is the most capital-intensive, and thus most significantly "legal," sector of the U.S., North American, and EU economies: with a delivered value in the United States of approximately $390 billion annually in 2010,[4] exceeding the total amount of all corporate income taxes collected in the United States,[5] and increasing to $488 billion in revenue in 2022,[6] the electric sector is substantial in breath and formative in its impact. Global electricity sales exceed $4.5 trillion per year, 50 percent more revenue annually than global automobile manufacturing. The International Energy Agency notes that global spending on the electric power sector now exceeds spending on fossil hydrocarbon fuels, where electric power plants have a lifetime of service that is among the longest of all infrastructure.[7] Lawyers now serve as the critical legal guides into the new electrified future.

This first chapter will examine how electricity is different than all other forms of energy used in the United States, before later chapters analyze how electric power sector law legally is treated differently by congressional statute and the courts than all other energy or any other sector of the U.S. economy (see Chapter 4). This distinct unique legal treatment of U.S. electric power is not found anywhere else in international law. The electric power sector and how it operates exert a disproportionate impact on the U.S. and world environment and the need now to control climate change—electric power is

- The most significant source of air pollution and a contributor to water pollution.
- Responsible for the largest share of climate warming emissions and climate change.
- Responsible in recent Biden administration laws for shouldering 67 to 75 percent of the reductions of greenhouse gases, even though contributing only about one-quarter of them.
- The legal target of three of the most important Supreme Court decisions in the last half century:

4. *See Electricity Sales Revenue in the U.S. 1970–2022*, Statista (Oct. 18, 2023), https://www.statista.com/statistics/190548/revenue-of-the-us-electric-power-industry-since-1970/.

5. Tax Pol'y Ctr., *Amount of Revenue by Source*, https://www.taxpolicycenter.org/statistics/amount-revenue-source.

6. *Electricity Sales Revenue in the U.S. 1970–2022*, *supra* note 4.

7. *World Energy Investment 2023*, Int'l Energy Agency, https://www.iea.org/reports/world-energy-investment-2023/overview-and-key-findings (last visited May 9, 2024).

- *Loper Bright v. Raimondo* in 2024 overturning 1984's *Chevron v. N.R.D.C.* decision
- *Michigan v. EPA*
- *West Virginia v. EPA*

Electric power: With so much money passing through it annually, as well as having the distinction of being more regulated at the federal, state, and local levels than any other sector of the U.S. economy and now subject to relatively radical change, it confronts a plethora of new and persistent legal challenges and roadblocks—some apparent and some under the legal radar screen. All these cutting-edge legal issues are analyzed in detail in Parts II, III, and IV of this book. And for each legal challenge and roadblock, the following chapters provide legal workarounds under existing U.S. law to navigate around the obstacles, while assessing which legal options are viable in which states or federal circuit courts.

Before the book embarks on Parts II, III, and IV, this chapter sets forth why electricity is different and unique in fact, as well as uniquely treated under U.S. law. Its singular importance will increase as the U.S. economy now addresses climate issues, with the complexity of legal issues multiplying.

The Critical Role of Electric Power

The importance of electricity is significantly underappreciated. Electricity has been recognized as one of the three most important technological breakthroughs in the history of humankind. It also is by far the most recent and the only modern one of the three. Moreover, it likely will prove to be the most important technological breakthrough going forward. Nevertheless, no book has analyzed the critical importance of electricity. Let's do it here.

James Fallows in the *Atlantic Monthly* researched and compiled a list of the 50 greatest technological breakthroughs since the wheel.[8] To compile the list, a panel of scientists, entrepreneurs, and engineers were asked to assess the innovations that have most shaped the nature of modern life. The panel places electricity at the second-highest position.[9] Fallows's research shows that electricity is essential, with no available substitute, to a number of other

8. James Fallows, *The 50 Greatest Breakthroughs Since the Wheel,* Atl. Monthly (Nov. 2013).
9. The movable type printing press took the No. 1 slot. *Id.*

highly ranked inventions on the list, such as air-conditioning and the internet.[10] As well, electricity had an even greater effect on all inventions that came later by improving our technological ability to develop those inventions and by enabling humankind to better share information about inventive endeavors.

For example, the semiconductor industry (No. 4 on the list) undoubtedly had a massive effect on the modern world by enabling the development of the transistor and thereby the development of modern computers. While the automobile (No. 18 on the list) does not require electricity per se in order to be manufactured or operated, it is hard to imagine today's automobile industry in the absence of electricity. Without electricity, mass assembly lines would have to operate without the benefit of electric motors, perhaps using hydraulic motors, which are slower and less effective at performing delicate tasks. Without electricity, automobiles themselves would have no lights to drive at night, dashboard displays, radios, or air-conditioning. While none of this would necessarily doom the nonelectric automobile industry, at the very least it would have greatly stunted its development compared with what we have observed in the past 100 years.

Indeed, while there are at least eight inventions on Fallows's list that directly depend on electricity (e.g., semiconductors, the internet, computers, etc.), there are another eight inventions whose growth would have been, as with the automobile industry, greatly hindered by a lack of electricity. Combined, these inventions represent the vast majority of the 19 postelectricity inventions on the top 50 list—our modern world would be almost unrecognizable in the absence of electricity.

The 16 entries connected to electricity directly or indirectly in Fallows's list are briefly highlighted in order next (dates provided are from the article). Ten of the top 25 inventions are enabled or perfected by electricity. Electricity itself also is included to lead the list.

- **Electricity (late 19th century).** Placed **No. 2.** Although several experimenters observed naturally occurring electrical effects throughout history, the recognition of electromagnetism, which led to inventions such as the electric motor and electrical circuits, occurred in the first half of the 19th century.[11]

---

10. *Id.*
11. Richard S. Kirby, Engineering in History (1990).

- **Semiconductor electronics (mid-20th century).** Placed **No. 4.** Semiconductors are materials that are neither electrical conductors (such as copper) nor electrical insulators (such as glass). An understanding of semiconductors led to the development of the transistor in 1948, which is a semiconductor device that acts like a switch in an electrical circuit and is the basis of all modern electronic devices, including computers, phones, and televisions. Naturally, the very function of a semiconductor is based entirely on the way it responds to electricity. The global market for semiconductors is massive, reaching $39.4 billion in sales for the month of November 2020 alone.[12]
- **The internal combustion engine (late 19th century), the automobile (late 19th century), and the combine harvester (1930s).** Placed **Nos. 7, 18, and 50**, respectively. First used for commercial drilling operations, the internal combustion engine became popular when, at the turn of the 20th century, the Ford Motor Company popularized the engine in its Model T car.[13] As discussed earlier, while the engine itself does not require electricity (other than a spark to ignite the fuel mixture), it is hard to imagine today's automobile industry in the absence of electricity. Certainly, the kind of mass production of these devices that is taken for granted today would be difficult or impossible without the use of electricity. And now, the Biden-Harris administration is moving the economy to electric vehicles.
- **The internet (1960s).** Placed **No. 9.** The internet grew out of a communications network created by the U.S. military called the ARPANET, which grew into what we think of as the modern internet in the early 1990s.[14] These types of network are called packet-switched networks. In contrast to a telephone network, where electrical cables are used to form a direct wired connection between the telephones, a packet-switched network routes packets of data through a network of computers by including routing information (e.g., an address) inside each packet. Each routing step along the path knows how to direct the

---

12. Semiconductor Indus. Ass'n, *Global Semiconductor Sales Increase 7 Percent Year-to-Year in November* (Jan. 4, 2021), https://www.semiconductors.org/global-semiconductor-sales-increase-7-percent-year-to-year-in-november/ [https://perma.cc/S3VL-CZAZ].

13. Richard Bak, Henry and Edsel: The Creation of the Ford Empire (2003).

14. *See* Barry Leiner et al., *A Brief History of the Internet*, Internet Soc'y (1997), https://www.internetsociety.org/internet/history-internet/brief-history-internet/ [https://perma.cc/7C6A-HL2Z].

packet based on the routing information so the packet gets to its destination. Each packet contains electrical signals that represent bits of data, and accordingly electricity is fundamental to the process of communication via the internet and indeed any such network. "Today we take this simplified browser technology for granted, but it actually was one of the most important inventions in modern history."[15]

- **Refrigeration (1850s) and air-conditioning (1902).** Placed **Nos. 13 and 44**, respectively. Both of these technologies depend on a cycle in which a circulating compound (Freon) undergoes repeated condensation and evaporation in such a way as to remove heat from the system. To perform this cycle, modern devices use compressors and valves that are powered by electricity. Nonelectric refrigeration is possible but inefficient. For example, a large tank of water may be cooled overnight by exposure to the air and then used to keep a refrigerator cool,[16] but it requires much more space than is typically available in a modern home. Moreover, this technique only works when the air has low humidity so it would not work well for air-conditioning in the summer.
- **The airplane (1903).** Placed **No. 15.** While the aerodynamic structure of wings and propellers (e.g., the airfoil shape) is necessary for flight, with few exceptions, airplanes rely on engine-driven propellers or internal combustion jet engines to generate sufficient propulsion for the aerodynamic structure to cause flight.[17] Either way, an engine is necessary to power the propulsive motion, and earlier comments regarding the internal combustion engine and electricity therefore apply.[18] In addition, the modern airline industry depends on radio, GPS, and other forms of electronic communication that would be impossible without electricity.
- **The personal computer (1970s).** Placed **No. 16**. As discussed earlier, the primary driving force that allowed the personal computer and other modern electronic devices to be small enough to fit inside

---

15. THOMAS FRIEDMAN, THE WORLD IS FLAT 64 (Farrar, Straus & Giroux, 3d ed. 2006).

16. Kazuko Kojima, *Life without Electricity,* OUR WORLD (Nov. 2, 2011), http://ourworld.unu.edu/en/life-without-electricity.

17. *See Aircraft Principles,* MIT DEP'T OF AERONAUTICS & ASTRONAUTICS (Mar. 17, 1997), http://web.mit.edu/16.00/www/aec/aircraft.html [https://perma.cc/NV5J-XGWC].

18. DAVID GREATRIX, POWERED FLIGHT: THE ENGINEERING OF AEROSPACE PROPULSION (2012).

the home was the development and miniaturization of the transistor. Without the transistor, a computer would have to utilize steam valves, gears, and/or some other nonelectronic means to move information around, which would hardly be practical. For instance, one of the first computers, the "Difference Engine" developed by Charles Babbage in the early 1800s, was purely mechanical but could only perform relatively simple calculations and would have filled a small room.[19]

- **Nuclear fission (1939).** Placed **No. 21**. Fission is a process in which the nucleus of an atom splits into smaller parts, releasing energy in the process.[20] The first atomic bombs produced energy by producing a runaway fission process called a chain reaction, and today nuclear power plants produce energy through a controlled form of fission. Typically, fission reactions are initiated by a particle accelerator, which requires electricity to run, and material for the reactions is enriched through centrifuge or laser techniques, which require electrical power to operate.[21]
- **The telephone (1876).** Placed **No. 24**. A telephone must convert sound into electronic signals that can be sent via transmission cables and then replayed in an audible form to a receiver. As such, use of electricity to send the signals is essential.[22]
- **The telegraph (1837).** Placed **No. 26**. The electrical telegraph was an important precursor to the telephone (indeed, early versions of the telephone were referred to as "speaking telegraphs").[23] Use of electrostatics or electromagnetism is essential to this technology.[24]
- **Radio (1906).** Placed **No. 28**. Radio, by definition, is electromagnetic radiation of a particular range of wavelengths (generally 3 kHz to 300 GHz). Transmitters and receivers of electromagnetic waves are essential to the production and reception of radio waves.[25]

---

19. Doron Swade, The Difference Engine: Charles Babbage and the Quest to Build the First Computer (2002).

20. *See Nuclear for Climate*, Eur. Nuclear Soc'y, https://www.euronuclear.org/nuclear-for-climate/ (last visited Apr. 11, 2024).

21. Maxwell Irvine, Nuclear Power: A Very Short Introduction (2011).

22. Improvement in Telegraphy, U.S. Patent No. 174,465 (issued Mar. 7, 1876).

23. *See* J. Munro, *Heroes of the Telegraph*, White Files, https://whitefiles.org/scm/telegraph/index.htm (last visited Apr. 11, 2024).

24. Samuel Morse, Examination of the Telegraphic Apparatus and the Processes in Telegraphy (1869).

25. Franklyn Branley, The Electromagnetic Spectrum (1980).

- **Photography (early 19th century).** Placed **No. 29**. Photography as an art can certainly exist in the absence of electricity: the filters, lenses, phosphors, and developing fluids needed to produce photographic images do not require it. However, digital photography could not exist without electricity. Modern cameras use charge-coupled devices or active pixel sensors to produce electrical signals from light.[26]
- **Television (early 20th century).** Placed **No. 45**. Aside from the fact that the medium of television is distributed through electromagnetic waves (either through wires or through the air), the television itself also needs electricity to produce an image, whether via an electron gun (as in older CRT devices) or by operating a liquid crystal (as in an LCD display).[27]
- **The assembly line (1913).** Placed **No. 49**. An assembly line process can be, and prior to the Ford Motor Company was, performed by people and/or by non–electrically powered machines (e.g., steam engines). However, in order to arrange machines and processes in an assembly line, the source of power must be extremely flexible, which was not the case in steam-driven factories. The further the steam was from its source, the less powerful it became. Such power is not practical in a complex assembly line process, and electrical power is needed to power the motors, conveyor belt, and so on.[28]

Why Electricity Is Even More Important among Most Important Inventions Than Its No. 2 Ranking

"I am convinced that the flattening of the world, if it continues, will be seen in time as one of those fundamental shifts or inflection points, like Gutenberg's invention of the printing press, the rise of the nation-state, or the Industrial Revolution."[29]

The role of electricity is expanding in scope. Some of the other technologies that were seen as so formative historically have more recently been taken over and subsumed by electrically driven replacements. For example, both

26. Junichi Nakamura, Image Sensors and Signal Processing for Digital Still Cameras (2005).
27. Albert Abramson, The History of Television (2009).
28. David Nye, America's Assembly Line (2013).
29. Friedman, *supra* note 15, at 49.

books and music have become digitally displayed, which requires and utilizes electricity to do so. In 2001, only 1 percent of music sales were digital music; by 2012, more than 50 percent of global music sales were digital.[30] In 2012, 31 percent of all books sold in the United States, excluding textbooks, were sold in digital form.[31] In 2012, more viewers watched movies online than on hard media such as DVDs, which five years before had all but 10 percent of home movie views.[32] There are substitutes for digital books and music: conventional paper books and records or tapes of music are alternative technologies for each medium.

Similarly, robotic technology has taken hold in the auto industry assembly line and elsewhere. Not existing before 1960, robots can provide precision welding and move heavy items. Electric mechanization can have shelves of products in an Amazon or other warehouse revolve to reach stationary employees who deploy or ship them, rather than the employee having to walk to the shelf to get a product.[33] Again, while human and other machine labor can substitute for this, robots are much safer and faster and reduce human injuries.[34] And the move to online shopping accelerated substantially during the 2020–2023 COVID-19 pandemic crisis.[35]

In the medical field, robotic procedures powered by electricity are used now in surgeries. In some cases, this is a mere substitute technology, but in others these robots can be guided to perform some surgeries too delicate for human hands alone.[36] Genetic sequencing and the revolution in biotechnology are largely driven by electric devices that can store millions of chemical sequences.[37] 3D printing modernizes and refines product design from

---

30. Michael Grothaus, *Streaming Hits New Milestone, Accounts for Nearly 80 Percent of US Music Revenue in 2019*, Fast Co. (Feb. 26, 2020), https://www.fastcompany.com/90468503/physical-and-digital-download-music-sales-continue-to-shrink-as-subscription-services-soar [https://perma.cc/DE4M-K7CP].

31. *See Ebook Industry News Feed*, About Ebooks (Nov. 29, 2023), https://about.ebooks.com/ebook-industry-news-feed/ [https://perma.cc/D4BU-2HHK].

32. *See* John Mauldin, *2012—The Most Important Year Yet in Technology*, Outside the Box (Sept. 30, 2012), https://ritholtz.com/2012/09/2012-the-most-important-year-yet-in-technology/.

33. *Id.*

34. *Id.*

35. *COVID-19 Has Changed Online Shopping Forever, Survey Shows*, UNCTAD (Oct. 8, 2020), https://unctad.org/news/covid-19-has-changed-online-shopping-forever-survey-shows [https://perma.cc/HW75-SNKY].

36. Mauldin, *supra* note 32.

37. *Id.*

aerospace to architecture to automobiles. This requires electricity, with no substitutes for necessary electric energy.

In military applications, electronic sensors are used in spy satellites, fighter planes, and night vision goggles.[38] Electrically guided drones are used extensively by the military.[39] Again, while there are conventional human equivalents, they pose more risk to humans.

Electricity was ranked No. 2 of the most important inventions in history, with the determination conceding that the wheel automatically was more important than any invention listed and first place going to the movable type printing press. Of note in terms of how quickly inventions mold society, "The introduction of printing happened over a period of decades, and for a long time affected only a relatively small part of the planet."[40] Today, with so much transfer of readable material occurring with electronically transmitted files and books, there is an argument that electricity is more important than the printing press, especially in a time of climate warming and efforts to reduce carbon emissions. See Chapter 2.

What Makes Electricity Unique

"We believe that electricity exists, because the electric company keeps sending us bills for it, but we cannot figure out how it travels inside wires."[41]

What electricity makes possible facilitates a semipermanent transformation of the economy and society. Although taken for granted and seldom analyzed, electricity is a unique energy form. Electricity is a formative technology reshaping society along a vertical spatial axis. This is true physically and virtually.

Electricity is a substitute, complementary, and unique-dimensional technology. Electricity is a *substitute* for other heating technologies as now required in some states and cities, lighting, and other transportation

38. *Id.*
39. *Id.*
40. *See* FRIEDMAN, *supra* note 15, at 49.
41. Dave Barry (Pulitzer Prize–winning humorist).

technologies.[42] Electricity is a *complementary* technology for computing, spacecrafts, military applications, and many others.[43]

Electric power is a technology that adds unique dimensions. Electric power, exploiting the electromagnetic spectrum, adds new dimensions that other technologies cannot. The internet is a dimension-changing technology allowing instantaneous access to common information worldwide.[44] Whereas energy technology formerly was integrated into culture, modern energy technologies shape and dominate the evolution of culture.[45]

Complementary vertical dimensions. In several dimensions, electricity is unique. First, while oil- and coal-powered transportation technology allowed society to disperse horizontally, electricity as a complementary power adds a high-rise vertical spatial dimension through uniquely being able to power modern elevators and air-conditioners to make possible tall buildings.

Exponential magnitude. Second, the impact of electric power is distinct from other major technological innovations in terms of its magnitude of impact on civilization. Where harnessing of domesticated animals or deployment of fossil fuels provided a tenfold or greater increase in work power or speed, electricity accelerated the amount and speed of work not tenfold or 100-fold but to the asymptotic physical maximum approaching the speed of light transferring information.

Space and time. Third, electric power adds the dimension of both space and time. Electricity "restacks" human interaction and communication through the internet, television, radio, telephone, and modern communications and information transfer. Electrically powered technologies provide a virtual proximity that counteracts the horizontal spatial dispersion created by industrial-age fossil fuel technologies across land and continents. In terms of quality of life, electric-powered communication media mediate the harsh

42. *See, e.g.*, *Electric Resistance Heating*, U.S. DEP'T OF ENERGY, https://www.energy.gov/energysaver/home-heating-systems/electric-resistance-heating (last visited Apr. 12, 2024).

43. *See, e.g.*, Tanya Bodell, *Integrating Energy Markets—How Substitutes, Complements Are Evolving*, POWERGRID INT'L (July 1, 2012), https://www.power-grid.com/smart-grid/integrating-energy-markets-how-substitutes-complements-are-evolving/#gref.

44. *See* Micha Kaufman, *The Internet Revolution Is the New Industrial Revolution*, FORBES (Oct. 5, 2012), https://www.forbes.com/sites/michakaufman/2012/10/05/the-internet-revolution-is-the-new-industrial-revolution/?sh=294b406347d5.

45. Friedrich Rapp, *The Material and Cultural Aspects of Technology*, PHIL. & TECH. 48 (Spring 1999).

edges of darkness, disconnection, and distance. While electricity is a substitute for fossil fuels as an energy source, it is a complement to and a socioevolutionary force on, and in, human society.

Velocity and speed. Fourth, energy changes speed as well as space. Electric energy transfer occurs instantaneously at +/–186,000 miles per second. While the Industrial Revolution accelerated scientific discovery and technology development, electricity has ramped up the pace of technology deployment:

> The introduction of printing happened over a period of decades, and for a long time affected only a relatively small part of the planet. Same with the Industrial Revolution. The flattening process is happening at warp speed and directly or indirectly touching a lot more people on the planet at once.[46]

Unique interface. Fifth, electricity and the electromagnetic spectrum are unique transmitters. Electricity can itself be the medium to transmit continuously millions of units or bits per second of information as audio, text, or other information at the speed of light for modern communications, computing, and advanced scientific research technologies: "Today we take this simplified browser technology for granted, but it actually was one of the most important inventions in modern history."[47]

For historical perspective, electricity was only harnessed commercially in the late 19th century and significantly deployed at scale in the last 100 years in the United States: "The light bulb 'burned like an evening star,' and we had the exact beginning of a new era for civilization: October 21, 1879."[48] Figure 1.1 illustrates energy use over the last 240 years.

---

46. Friedman, *supra* note 15, at 49.

47. *Id.* at 64.

48. Vaclav Smil, Energies: An Illustrated Guide to the Biosphere and Civilization 159 (MIT Press 1999). The filament has been coiled since 1934 to reduce heat loss from convection. Each stage in the evolution of electric lightbulbs increased their efficiency and luminosity, as well as increasing the expected life of mass-produced bulbs. Incandescent bulbs have not improved much since the 1930s.

Figure 1.1[49]

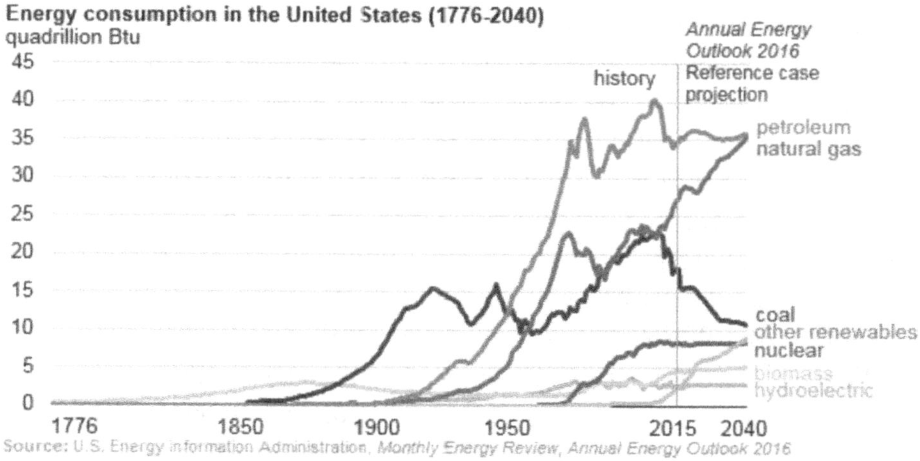

Law and courts in the United States now are recognizing the importance of electric power and its regulation:

> The discovery of fire was a significant event, creating for mankind warmth against the cold and light in the darkness . . . . The concept of electricity was first deduced by William Gilbert, a physician in the service of Elizabeth I of England (1533–1603). In 1752, Benjamin Franklin demonstrated the practical application of electricity by flying a kite carrying a key into a lightning storm. Today, electricity is a principal source of light and heat for the world and its people.
>
> As the importance of electricity has increased exponentially in human affairs, politicians and governments inevitably stepped up regulation of the generation and marketing of electrical energy.[50]

---

49. *Fossil Fuels Still Dominate U.S. Energy Consumption Despite Recent Market Share Decline*, ENERGY INFO. ADMIN. (July 1, 2016), https://www.eia.gov/todayinenergy/detail.cfm?id=26912.

50. Allco Fin., Ltd. v. Klee, Nos. 3:15-cv-603, 3:16-cv-508, 2016 WL 4414774, at *2 (D. Conn. Aug. 18, 2016).

Electricity and Security

Without access to reliable electric power, all critical modern infrastructure is at risk and significant economic value can be lost.[51] The United States now maintains a permanent Department of Homeland Security, whose security operation for the country significantly revolves around electric power. The Department of Homeland Security identifies 16 critical infrastructure sectors in the United States, including communications, emergency services, energy, food and agriculture, health care and public health, transportation, and water and wastewater sectors. All 16 of these critical infrastructure sectors depend on stable and reliable electric power in order to function.[52]

While government, through the Department of Homeland Security and several other agencies, is concerned about protecting the availability of electricity, the private sector owns most electric infrastructure in the United States supplying electricity to households and businesses. The U.S. electricity sector contains more than 6,413 power plants (this includes 3,273 traditional electric utilities and 1,738 nonutility power producers) collectively with approximately 1,075 gigawatts of installed generation capacity.[53]

As recently as 2014, coal generated 39.3 percent and natural gas generated 27.3 percent of U.S. electricity,[54] with coal declining by an additional 57.2 percent by 2023.[55] The composition of power generation is now rapidly shifting through recent government laws from fossil fuels to renewable power generation and from centralized to more distributed locations of generation not owned by U.S.-regulated utilities:

---

51. U.S. Dep't of Energy, Quadrennial Energy Review, Transforming the Nation's Electricity System: The Second Installment of the QER 2-57, at 1–7 (Jan. 2017).

52. *Critical Infrastructure Sectors*, Cybersec. & Infrastructure Sec. Agency, https://www.dhs.gov/critical-infrastructure-sectors (last visited Apr. 12, 2024).

53. *Energy Sector*, Cybersec. & Infrastructure Sec. Agency, https://www.dhs.gov/energy-sector (last visited Apr. 12, 2024).

54. Chris Mooney, *Why 2015 May Be Remembered as a Transformative Year for How We Get Energy*, Wash. Post (Dec. 24, 2015), https://www.washingtonpost.com/news/energy-environment/wp/2015/12/24/why-2015-may-be-remembered-as-a-transformative-year-for-how-we-get-energy/.

55. *Electric Power Monthly: Table 1.1 Net Generation by Energy Source: Total (All Sectors), 2014–February 2024*, U.S. Energy Info. Admin., https://www.eia.gov/electricity/monthly/epm_table_grapher.php?t=epmt_1_01 (last visited May 9, 2024).

"It is now possible for a customer in Vermont [to] purchase electricity from an environmentally friendly power producer in California or a cogeneration facility in Oklahoma."[56]

Starting with the next chapter of this book, we profile a series of cutting-edge legal issues and pressures involving electric power and the environment, as well as strategic alternatives and legal workarounds for new issues that now are arising. Fasten your seat belt before turning the page to the next chapter, as U.S. law will be leading attorneys and clients rapidly to diminish greenhouse gas emissions progressively by 2025, 2030, and 2050.

56. New York v. FERC, 535 U.S. 1, 8 (2002) (internal quotation marks omitted).

CHAPTER 2

Decarbonizing Electricity

"We're killing our planet. Let us face it. There is no Planet B."

—French President Emmanuel Macron, April 25, 2018, speech to joint session of U.S. Congress

The Calculations Underlying International Climate Pressure on the Electric Sector

Because international climate agreements have never been submitted to the Congress for ratification, federal policy on climate has changed with each presidential administration during the 21st century. The United States has been part of and then backed away from international climate commitments, tempered by changing executive branch regulations and court challenges to them. Energy and environmental law have now changed dramatically with the enactment of new U.S. statutes passed by the Congress targeting the generation of electricity and climate-warming emissions that will be the law for the next decade. "Climate" now becomes the new factor changing the practice of U.S. energy and environmental law.

U.S. policy in the Biden administration and recently passed laws now pursuing deep decarbonization are incentivizing and requiring a diverse portfolio of clean energy technologies, including firm dispatchable clean energy to satisfy much more demand for electric generation. Energy is a significant contributing source of greenhouse gas (GHG) emissions: more than 99 percent of human-made GHGs emanate from burning fossil fuels.[1] The electric power sector is now the key target for U.S. policy to limit future GHGs and is being targeted disproportionately to reduce a larger percentage

1. U.S. Dep't of Energy, Quadrennial Energy Review, Transforming the Nation's Electricity System: The Second Installment of the QER, at 3–5 (Jan. 2017).

of U.S. GHG emissions than it is responsible for, which demands and pressure will intensify for decades.[2]

Legal Obligations

In order to meet the goals of the 2015 Paris Agreement (discussed later), which aim to limit global temperature increase to below 1.5° Celsius (C) and as an absolute "stop" below 2°C, global GHG emissions must peak before 2025 at the latest and be reduced by 43 percent a few years later, by 2030. Since world temperature already has risen 1.2°C, trying to hold the increase below 1.5°C is an extreme challenge.

Because of the failure of the Kyoto Protocol a quarter century ago and the 2015 Paris Agreement to reduce world GHG emissions in order for temperature increase to remain below an additional 1.5°C, the world reduction in GHG emission from current emission levels would need to amount to at least 14 percent each and every year from now to 2030. World nations won't hold temperature rise below 1.5°C—and to have any chance to hold temperature rise below 2°C, the electric power sector will be asked to shoulder a very disproportionate share of the carbon reduction over the next quarter century. Discussed next is the science and the policy surrounding climate and electric power.

U.S. Carbon Policy Now

President Joe Biden explicitly made potential influence on climate from modern emissions a central principle of his domestic and foreign policy agendas with ambitious binding pledges, such as a net-zero carbon electricity grid in place by 2035. President Biden's 2021 bipartisan Infrastructure Act is designed to reduce U.S. carbon emissions to approximately 50 percent of 2005 levels by 2030, reach 100 percent carbon-free electric power nationwide by 2035, and achieve net-zero emissions by 2050.[3]

---

2. FULFILLING AMERICA'S PLEDGE, BLOOMBERG PHILANTHROPIES 5–6, 19 (2018), https://www.bbhub.io/dotorg/sites/28/2018/09/Fulfilling-Americas-Pledge-2018.pdf (the power sector responsible for less than one-third of GHG emissions is targeted to make more than half the reductions in global warming emissions); *Sources of Greenhouse Gas Emissions*, EPA (Apr. 11, 2024), https://www.epa.gov/ghgemissions/sources-greenhouse-gas-emissions [https://perma.cc/8YQ4-PW4E].

3. *See FACT SHEET: The Bipartisan Infrastructure Deal Boosts Clean Energy Jobs, Strengthens Resilience, and Advances Environmental Justice*, THE WHITE HOUSE (Nov. 8, 2021), https://www.whitehouse.gov/briefing-room/statements-releases/2021/11/08/fact-sheet-the-bipartisan

The Infrastructure Act will replace transit vehicles with "clean, zero emission vehicles" and school buses and the U.S. Postal Service fleet with electric vehicles, as well as investing in a substantial network of electric vehicle charging stations throughout the United States. Also, the law will incentivize investment in port infrastructure in part by encouraging electrification and other low-carbon technologies. The largest investment will be modernizing and expanding clean energy transmission lines to promote renewable energy production to support the growing electricity needs expected with the expansion and substitution of the use of electric power in the United States.

The 2022 Inflation Reduction Act changes the electric sector. See Chapter 6 and Chapter 13. The Department of Energy's (DoE) preliminary assessment finds that the Inflation Reduction Act of 2022 (IRA)[4] can help drive 2030 economy-wide GHG emissions to 40 percent below 2005 levels.[5] The DoE estimates that the clean energy provisions of the IRA, combined with the 2021 Bipartisan Infrastructure Investment and Jobs Act, could reduce GHG emissions by approximately 1,000 million metric tons (MMT) (a gigaton).[6] Along with other climate and energy provisions of these laws, the provisions raise the DoE-estimated total annual U.S. carbon reduction to nearly 1,150 MMT by 2030, which is equivalent to the combined annual carbon emissions from all U.S. homes.[7]

The IRA is estimated to facilitate a 37–41 percent potential reduction in U.S. GHG emissions from 2005 levels by 2030 by one assessment[8] and to potentially reduce U.S. GHG emissions 31–44 percent from 2005 levels by another assessment.[9] Note that maintaining business as usual with no

---

-infrastructure-deal-boosts-clean-energy-jobs-strengthens-resilience-and-advances-environmental-justice/.

4. Inflation Reduction Act of 2022, Pub. L. No. 117-169, 136 Stat. 1818, https://www.congress.gov/bill/117th-congress/house-bill/5376/text.

5. U.S. Dep't of Energy, *The Inflation Reduction Act Drives Significant Emissions Reductions and Positions America to Reach Our Climate Goals* 1 (Aug. 2022) [hereinafter *IRA Reductions*], https://www.energy.gov/sites/default/files/2022-08/8.18%20InflationReductionAct_Factsheet_Final.pdf.

6. *Id.*

7. *Id.*

8. Megan Mahajan et al., *Modeling the Inflation Reduction Act Using the Energy Policy Simulator* 1, Energy Innovation Pol'y & Tech. LLC (Aug. 2022), https://energyinnovation.org/wp-content/uploads/2022/08/Modeling-the-Inflation-Reduction-Act-with-the-US-Energy-Policy-Simulator_August.pdf.

9. Ben King et al., *A Congressional Climate Breakthrough*, Rhodium Grp. (July 28, 2022), https://rhg.com/research/inflation-reduction-act/.

additional federal action featured economic shifts from coal-fired power to renewable energy and was forecast to achieve a 27 percent reduction in annual GHG emissions from 2005 levels.[10] Business as usual realizes 61–87 percent of what the IRA is forecast to do, although the IRA is not expected to achieve the Biden-Harris administration's commitment to reduce emissions at least 50 percent from 2005 levels by 2030.[11]

Most of these dramatic potential reductions by 2030 are forecast to be achieved in the electric power sector. The DoE estimates that approximately two-thirds of the carbon reductions incentivized by the IRA and the Infrastructure Act will be in the power sector, dwarfing all of the other transportation, building space heating, and industry sectors combined.[12] Notable is that while the electric power sector is responsible for approximately one-quarter of GHG emissions, federal policy is targeting it to shoulder a disproportionate two-thirds of the intermediate-term reductions in carbon emissions.

The Biden administration's long-term strategy on climate itself states that a delayed transition would entail a "higher likelihood of reaching catastrophic damages or 'tipping points' and potentially irreversible economic impacts."[13] The current U.S. commitment: the United States submitted to the United Nations Framework Convention on Climate Change (UNFCCC) an intended nationally determined contribution of 17 percent reductions below 2005 levels by 2020 and 26–28 percent reductions by 2025.

Fitting U.S. Carbon Emissions into the World Carbon Puzzle

While the United States is a major contributor to world GHG emissions, by a large margin it is not close to the largest emitter, as shown in Table 2.1. Who is increasing GHG emissions: China and Indonesia increased their CO_2 emissions from 2017 to 2020, while the developed countries (the United States, Japan, Germany, and South Korea) decreased their emissions over

10. Alice C. Hill & Madeline Babin, *What the Historic U.S. Climate Bill Gets Right and Gets Wrong*, Council on Foreign Rels. (Aug. 17, 2022, 4:50 PM), https://www.cfr.org/in-brief/us-climate-bill-inflation-reduction-act-gets-right-wrong-emissions.

11. *Id.*

12. *IRA Reductions*, *supra* note 5, at 3.

13. The Long-Term Strategy of the United States: Pathways to Net-Zero Greenhouse Gas Emissions by 2050, U.S. Dep't of State & U.S. Exec. Off. of the President (Nov. 2021), https://unfccc.int/sites/default/files/resource/US_accessibleLTS2021.pdf.

those three years. Ten years ago, China produced less CO_2 emissions than the United States. Today, China is approaching three times U.S. CO_2 emissions, with China's emissions increasing rapidly and U.S. emissions decreasing.

Table 2.1 CO_2 Emissions of Top Countries in 2020 (CO_2 expressed in MT)[14]

1. China	11,680.42
2. United States	4,535.30
3. India	2,411.73
4. Russia	1,674.23
5. Japan	1,061.77
6. Iran	690.24
7. Germany	636.88
8. South Korea	621.47
9. Saudi Arabia	588.81
10. Indonesia	568.27

Although criticized as a large per capita emitter, placed in economic perspective, the United States also is by far not the largest per capita emitter of GHGs in the world. China and more than a dozen other countries are larger emitters per capita of carbon than is the United States.[15] With the United States being one of the three most populous countries and by a significant margin the largest producer of goods and services in the world (15 percent of gross GDP)—which contributes more than 20 percent of world income—the United States emits less than the global average amount of CO_2 per unit of goods and services produced and is reducing more quickly.[16]

The three predominant GHGs, CO_2, nitrous oxide, and methane, all of which are produced in the power sector, occur both naturally and as by-products of human activities. Methane is, by a large margin, the second most damaging GHG, after CO_2. See Chapter 16. The three minor-impact GHGs, HFCs, SF_6, and PFCs, all are synthetic chemicals manufactured and released only by humans.

---

14. *See Carbon Footprint by Country 2024*, World Population Rev., https://worldpopulationreview.com/country-rankings/carbon-footprint-by-country (last visited Apr. 12, 2024).

15. *See* Int'l Energy Agency, Global Energy Review: CO_2 Emissions in 2021 (Mar. 2022), https://www.iea.org/reports/global-energy-review-co2-emissions-in-2021-2.

16. *Id.*

Energy Sector Carbon Emissions

Context

Daily, 100,000,000 million tons of GHGs are released into the atmosphere. Each second, more than 100,000 tons of carbon dioxide are emitted into the environment from technologies. About three-quarters of all industrial CO_2 emissions in history have occurred since the 1960s, and more than half have occurred since the late 1980s.[17] These numbers constitute an unsustainable trend. As of 2024, the concentration of atmospheric carbon was measured at 429 parts per million (ppm),[18] approximately halfway to doubling preindustrial CO_2 levels, which doubling will likely increase the earth's temperature between 1.5° and 4.5°C.

The year 2023 was the warmest since global records began in 1850, rising 2.12°F (1.18°C) above the 20th-century average of 57.0°F (13.9°C), and was 2.43°F (1.35°C) above the preindustrial average (1850–1900).

Figure 2.1 Global Average Surface Temperature 1880-2023[19]

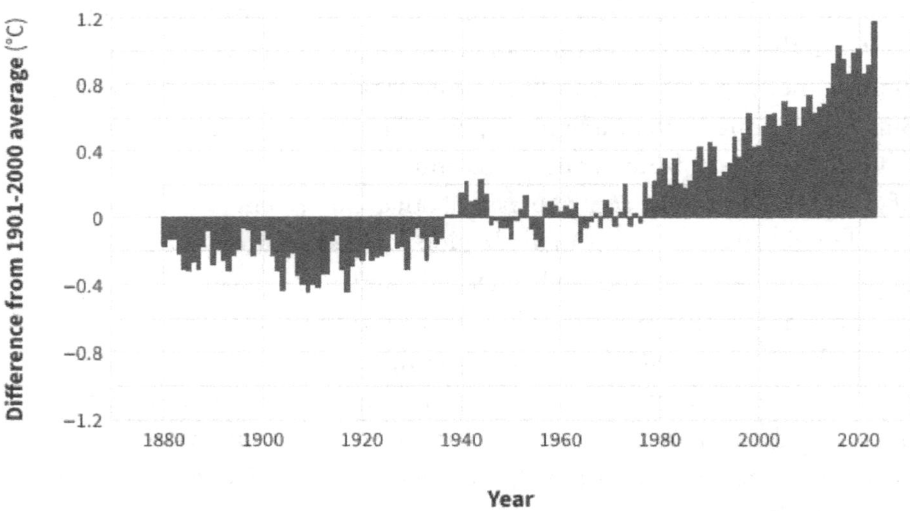

17. *Id.*

18. *See Daily CO2*, CO2 EARTH, https://www.co2.earth/daily-co2 (last visited May 9, 2024).

19. Rebecca Lindsey & Luann Dahlman, *Climate Change: Global Temperature*, CLIMATE.GOV (Jan. 18, 2024), https://www.climate.gov/news-features/understanding-climate/climate-change-global-temperature.

Limiting modern-era global warming to 4°F will require stabilizing CO_2 concentrations in Earth's atmosphere at no more than 450 ppm, achieved only if developed nations reduce CO_2 emissions by 80 to 95 percent by 2050. Within a century, if this reduction is not achieved, average global temperature could climb anywhere from 1.4° to 5.8°C (2.5–10°F).[20]

U.S. Energy Trends

In 1949, only 11 percent of global warming gases in the United States came from the generation of electricity; today, that percentage is more than 25 percent, roughly equivalent to the transportation sector emissions in the United States. The electric power sector is the first to be compelled to dramatically reduce emissions. The power sector also is involved in methane emissions, which molecule for molecule contribute even more to climate warming. See Chapter 16. It is the world electricity and heat sectors that increased carbon emissions by dramatically more in recent years than any other economic sector.[21]

Rapid Change; Lagging Impact on Carbon Emissions

The Intergovernmental Panel on Climate Change's Sixth Assessment Report emphasizes that meeting the temperature goals of the Paris Agreement will require both rapid decarbonization of the global economy and large-scale deployment of carbon dioxide removal approaches. Longevity of atmospheric carbon is an issue: it is now estimated that between 15 and 40 percent of the carbon dioxide emitted will remain in the atmosphere for up to a thousand years, with roughly 10–25 percent of it persisting for tens of thousands of years.[22] After 800 years of atmospheric GHG levels hovering between 175 and 250 ppm, they have now precipitously increased significantly above 420 ppm.[23] The high electrification scenario developed by the

---

20. Int'l Energy Agency, *supra* note 15.

21. *Id.*

22. *See Explainer: Carbon Removal*, Am. Univ., https://www.american.edu/sis/centers/carbon-removal/explaining-carbon-removal.cfm#:~:text=Carbon%20removal%2C%20also%20known%20as,long-%20lived%20products%20like%20cement (last visited Apr. 12, 2024).

23. Brian Clark Howard, *Northern Hemisphere Cracks 400 ppm CO_2 for Whole Month for First Time*, Nat'l Geo. (May 27, 2014), https://www.nationalgeographic.com/science/article/140527-400-ppm-carbon-dioxide-global-warming-climate-science. *See also Daily CO2*, *supra* note 18.

U.S. National Renewable Energy Laboratory for its Electrification Futures study predicted (even before Biden administration electrification legislation—see Chapter 6) that U.S. electricity consumption will increase by a factor of 1.6 by 2050 relative to the 2018 prepandemic level of approximately 4,000 terawatt-hours of total U.S. electric demand.

So past and current concentrations of carbon from the energy sector may need to be removed and sequestered to meet international or national targets on carbon. This is much more difficult and expensive than supposed: carbon removal is the process of capturing carbon (CO_2) from the atmosphere and sequestering it for decades or centuries in plants, soils, oceans, rocks, saline aquifers, depleted oil wells, or long-lived products such as cement. Carbon capture and storage captures carbon dioxide from a power plant smokestack or other industrial flue and sequesters it underground. All known and proposed methods of carbon removal are slow acting, limited in scope, and expensive such that they are not currently forecast to offset significant carbon dioxide emissions.

In the power sector, coal-fired electric power generation is accounting for about 70 percent of the emissions.[24] Despite a world consensus three decades ago at the 1992 UNFCCC agreement on climate that GHGs needed to be dramatically reduced, the world today emits approximately 60 percent more—not less—GHG emissions than were emitted in 1990.[25] Even in the most recent years this century, global increase in carbon emissions was a function of greater burning of coal. Global energy-related emissions are expected to increase 57 percent from 2005 to 2030.[26] The result according to NASA and to the Intergovernmental Panel on Climate Change: "The scientific evidence is unequivocal: climate change is a threat to human wellbeing

---

24. Joëlle de Sépibus, The Liberalisation of the Power Industry in the European Union and Its Impact on Climate Change: A Legal Analysis of the Internal Market in Electricity 2–4, Working Paper No. 2008/10, Swiss Nat'l Ctr. of Competence in Rsch. (2008), https://papers.ssrn.com/sol3/papers.cfm?abstract_id=1137823.

25. PBL Netherlands Env't Assessment Agency, Trends in Global CO_2 and Total Greenhouse Gas Emissions: 2019 Report 4 (The Hague 2020).

26. U.S. Gov't Accountability Off., GAO-09-151, International Climate Change Programs: Lessons Learned from the European Union's Emissions Trading Scheme and the Kyoto Protocol's Clean Development Mechanism 48 (2008), http://www.gao.gov/assets/290/283397.pdf.

and the health of the planet. Any further delay in concerted global action will miss the brief, rapidly closing window to secure a liveable future."[27]

Electric Power with a Target on Its Back

Four-fifths of the total energy-related CO_2 emissions permitted until 2035 in the International Energy Agency's 450 Scenario are already locked in by existing operating capital stock, including power stations, buildings, and factories.[28] The global fleet of power plants will emit an estimated 300 billion tons of carbon dioxide before they are retired, with coal-fired plants comprising about two-thirds of this total.[29] The electric power sector offers some of the most cost-effective opportunities to reduce CO_2 emissions, compared to transportation and other sectors. So where in the electric sector will reductions occur?

Nuclear power? Reductions in GHG emissions must be accomplished at a time when there is significant retirement of aging coal, nuclear, and gas-fired power generation facilities. Moreover, as shown in Figure 2.2, uranium fuel for U.S. civilian nuclear power plants is now almost entirely imported, including from Russia and two formerly Soviet-affiliated countries. In 2020, uranium supply was nearly 30 percent less than reactor fleet requirements for that year.[30]

In the most recent three decades, only four conventional nuclear power plants were under construction in the United States:

- Two in South Carolina under construction were canceled in 2017 after a $9 billion expenditure, which drove Westinghouse, its builder, into bankruptcy under the construction contract.
- Two in Georgia are at least seven years behind schedule, and their original $14 billion price tag has at least doubled to date.

27. *The Effects of Climate Change*, NASA, https://science.nasa.gov/climate-change/effects (last visited May 9, 2024).

28. Int'l Energy Agency, World Energy Outlook (November 9, 2011).

29. Andrew Childers, *300 Billion Tons of Carbon Dioxide Will Be Emitted by Power Plants Globally, Study Says*, Bloomberg BNA Env't Rep. (Aug. 28, 2014) (quoting Steven J. Davis & Robert H. Socolow, *Commitment Accounting of CO_2 Emissions*, Env't Rsch. Letters (2014), https://iopscience.iop.org/article/10.1088/1748-9326/9/8/084018/meta).

30. *See* The Nuclear Fuel Report, World Nuclear Ass'n, https://world-nuclear.org/our-association/publications/global-trends-reports/nuclear-fuel-report.aspx (last visited Apr. 12, 2024).

Figure 2.2[31] U.S. and Foreign Uranium Purchased by U.S. Nuclear Plants 2016–2021

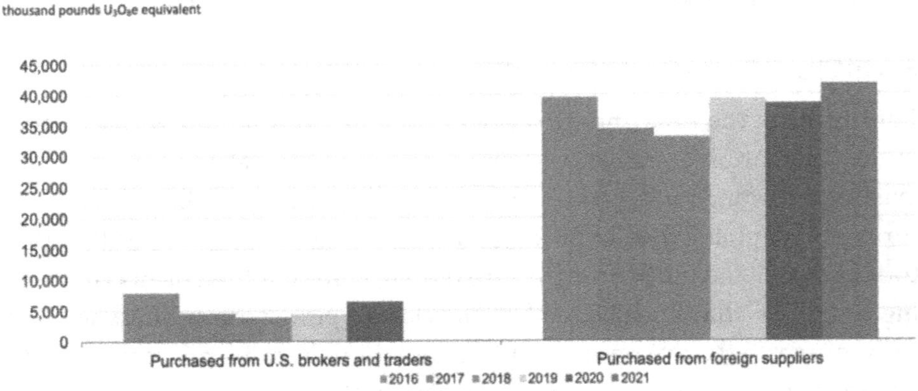

Source: U.S. Energy Information Administration, Form EIA-858, *Uranium Marketing Annual Survey* (2016–2021).

International U.S. Climate Commitments

A quick overview about legal requirements in place. According to the UNFCCC, in order to mitigate the most drastic effects of climate change, global temperature increase must be kept under 1.5°C with a rapid 45 percent reduction in global GHG emission from 2010 levels, and by 2050 global GHG emission must be net-zero.[32]

However, national leaders do not agree on legal policy to be employed. The president of the annual world climate conference COP28 in Dubai, Sultan Al Jaber, stated in December 2023, "There is no science out there, or no scenario out there, that says that the phase-out of fossil fuel is what's going to achieve 1.5C . . . . unless you want to take the world back into caves."[33] U.N. Secretary-General António Guterres told the COP28 conference, "The

31. Uranium Marketing Annual Report, U.S. Energy Info. Admin. (May 2022), https://perma.cc/BN5F-5GQX.

32. *The Paris Agreement*, United Nations Framework Convention on Climate Change, https://unfccc.int/process-and-meetings/the-paris-agreement/the-paris-agreement (last visited Apr. 12, 2024).

33. Damian Carrington & Ben Stockton, *Cop28 President Says There Is "No Science" behind Demands for Phase-Out of Fossil Fuels*, The Guardian (Dec. 3, 2023), the guardian.com/environment/2023/dec/03/back-into-caves-cop28-president-dismisses-phase-out-of-fossil-fuels (documenting these quoted statements).

science is clear: The 1.5C limit is only possible if we ultimately stop burning all fossil fuels. Not reduce, not abate. Phase out, with a clear timeframe."[34]

The United Nations agreed to and ratified three major international legal instruments addressing climate change: the UNFCCC, the Kyoto Protocol, and the Paris Agreement.

The Kyoto Protocol

The UNFCCC is the parent treaty that generated the 1997 Kyoto Protocol.[35] The UNFCCC was enacted in 1992 at the Rio Earth Summit "as a way for countries to work together to limit . . . climate change, and to cope with [its] impac[t]."[36] The Kyoto Protocol was adopted in 1997 by 192 ratified counties to achieve specific reductions in GHG emissions. Of note, the legally mandated targets were only applied to three dozen developed countries, omitting any requirement for more than 150 developing countries. Thirty-seven states, consisting of industrialized countries and the European community, have imposed GHG emission limitation and reduction commitments, while the remaining 155 developing countries among the 192 signatories, including the largest GHG emitter among all nations, have non-binding generic general undertakings to constrain emissions.[37] These Kyoto Protocol–covered countries represent less than 20 percent of all countries and less than 40 percent of world carbon emission sources.[38]

The Kyoto Protocol, prominently not ratified by the United States and, for a time, not ratified by Australia, required its three dozen covered developed nations by 2012 to reduce annual CO_2 emissions an average

34. *Id.*

35. *The Kyoto Protocol—Status of Ratification*, United Nations Framework Convention on Climate Change, http://unfccc.int/kyoto_protocol/status_of_ratification/items/2613.php (last visited Apr. 12, 2024).

36. *International Agreements on Climate Action*, Council of the Eur. Union (July 6, 2018), https://perma.cc/8D2Q-5YHK; *Climate Change*, United Nations (Nov. 30, 2019), https://perma.cc/HS72-P7CU.

37. *Kyoto Protocol—Targets for the First Commitment Period*, United Nations Framework Convention on Climate Change, http://unfccc.int/kyoto_protocol/items/2830.php (last visited Apr. 12, 2024).

38. *See GHG Data*, United Nations Framework Convention on Climate Change, https://unfccc.int/topics/mitigation/resources/registry-and-data/ghg-data-from-unfccc. There are 196 recognized countries in the world. *See The Number of Countries in the World*, ThoughtCo, http://geography.about.com/cs/countries/a/numbercountries.htm (last visited Apr. 12, 2024). Not recognized as independent countries are Taiwan, Puerto Rico, Bermuda, Greenland, and Palestine.

of 7 percent below 1990 baseline levels. GHGs other than CO_2 were to be reduced to 5 to 7 percent below either their 1990 or 1995 baseline levels between 2008 and 2012. Emission allowance trading is allowed under the Kyoto Protocol.

International climate agreements have operated poorly: the 1997 Kyoto Protocol concluded its operative phase in 2012, and three major and necessary covered world powers—Russia, Japan, and New Zealand—then refused to agree to any subsequent obligations.[39] Some of the failure of the Kyoto Protocol was carbon leakage that occurred from developing countries importing high-GHG products from countries not covered by the protocol. The E.U. approach now to carbon leakage is to implement a Carbon Border Adjustment Mechanism (CBAM), which applied border/leakage controls on imports to the E.U., replacing its traditional free allocation of emission credits to industries (which act as a subsidy).[40] It remains unclear whether the E.U. might exempt U.S. products from CBAM (it can only exempt countries that have carbon prices, which the United States doesn't have except for National Environmental Policy Act considerations).

The Paris Agreement: Repercussions in the United States

The world is already on a path to reach a temperature increase of perhaps 4°C. To ratchet up the effort 18 years after adoption of the Kyoto Protocol, the 2015 Paris Agreement included 186 participating countries that agreed to "mobilize stronger and more ambitious climate action" to hold "the increase in the global average temperature to well below 2°C above pre-industrial levels and to pursue efforts to limit the temperature increase to 1.5°C above pre-industrial levels, recognizing that this would significantly reduce the risks

39. Juliet Eilperin, *Kyoto Protocol Extended in Contentious U.N. Climate Talks*, Wash. Post (Dec. 8, 2012), http://www.washingtonpost.com/national/health-science/kyoto-protocol-extended-in-contentious-un-climate-talks/2012/12/08/f64a51c0-4178-11e2-ae43-cf491b837f7b_story.html; Michael Bastasch, *Only 37 Countries Willing to Back Kyoto Protocol Extension*, The Daily Caller (Dec. 10, 2012), http://dailycaller.com/2012/12/10/only-37-countries-willing-to-back-kyoto-protocol-extension/.

40. Key policy issues in border controls are what commodities are covered and what emissions will be covered, which can be targeted at emissions from each facility or emissions from carbon content. *See* Roberto Schaeffer, Resources for the Future webinar (Sept. 22, 2022).

and impacts of climate change."[41] The 2015 Paris Agreement requires countries to set annual, nationally determined contributions for GHG emission standards.

The Nationally Determined Contributions (NDCs) are gradually progressive, meaning countries are supposed to lower their GHG emissions progressively and continually from each year to the following year. The Paris Agreement NDCs don't require or incorporate any trade restrictions, in order not to violate World Trade Organization requirements by only having countries make commitments on a nationwide, not industry-wide, basis. A foundation of the Kyoto Protocol and the Paris Agreement is that there are "common differentiated responsibilities" where no country needs to meet a certain bar of GHG emissions—the interpretation of which is quite controversial.

During the Trump administration, the United States began the process of withdrawing from the Paris Agreement. In 2021, the Biden administration rejoined the Paris Agreement and enacted new laws and regulations to eliminate GHG emissions from all U.S. electric power generation by 2035, according to President Biden.[42] To meet Paris Agreement pledges, an unprecedented large Infrastructure Investment and Jobs Act was enacted to make what President Biden calls a "once-in-a-generation investment" to modernize the U.S. power sector with renewable power generation technology; the Inflation Reduction Act incentivizing renewable technologies was enacted as well. See Chapter 6 and Chapter 13 for more details on these laws. President Biden also announced the goals of having a zero-emissions power sector by 2035 and net zero emissions for the entire country by 2050.[43]

However, the Paris Agreement guidelines may have become moot before they are implemented. The world is already on track to reach a temperature increase of at least 4°C, far in excess of the Paris Agreement's 1.5–2°C increase limit. There are now atmospheric concentrations of GHGs

---

41. Paris Agreement to the United Nations Framework Convention on Climate Change (Jan. 29, 2016), FCCC/CP/2015.10/Add. 1 at 3, 22.

42. The United States of America, Nationally Determined Contribution, Reducing Greenhouse Gases in the United States: A 2030 Emissions Target 1 (2021), https://perma.cc/6KWB-WH5U.

43. The Long-Term Strategy of the United States, *supra* note 13, at 1, 5.

at levels that have not been seen for almost a million years.[44] Only some of the Paris Agreement provisions are legally binding, and the agreement does not include any binding emissions targets or financial commitments for any country.[45]

And with international climate agreements to date, what you see is not necessarily what the world gets. One of the problems plaguing international climate agreements has been transparency and verification. Many nations underreport their GHG emissions and exaggerate their mitigating actions, resulting in exaggerated data "equivalent to between the amount of emissions produced in a year by a major industrialized nation (8.5 billion metric tons of greenhouse gases) and on the upper end almost a quarter of humanity's total annual contribution to the climate crisis (13.3 billion metric tons)."[46]

Notwithstanding inaccurate claims of decarbonization, *even if* all announced country pledges were fully realized on time, the world would end up with at least a 2.1°C warmer climate by the end of the century, not achieving the Paris Agreement requirements, according to the International Energy Agency.[47] The dimension of the undertaking confronting the United States and the world circa 2022 was put in scale by energy expert Vaclav Smil:

> Now, according to COP 26, we should reduce our carbon dioxide emissions by 45 percent by 2030 as compared with 2010 levels. This is undoable because there's just eight years left, and emissions are still rising. People don't appreciate the magnitude of the task . . . .[48]

As with the Kyoto Protocol, the Paris Agreement contains no enforcement mechanism. Notwithstanding these three international arrangements and agreements, according to the Climate Action Network, as of 2018, "[n]o

---

44. Intergovernmental Panel on Climate Change, Climate Change 2013: The Physical Science Basis 9 (2013).

45. *Paris Climate Agreement Q&A*, Ctr. for Climate & Energy Sols. (Nov. 30, 2019), https://perma.cc/QQ2Z-ZWUY.

46. Zoya Teirstein, *Report Exposes the Shaky Data Undermining the World's Progress on Climate Change*, Grist (Nov. 8, 2021), https://grist.org/cop26/report-exposes-the-shaky-data-undermining-the-worlds-progress-on-climate-change/. A significant amount of underreporting was due to over-reporting CO_2-absorbing contributions of local forests and systemic underreporting of methane and fluorinated gas emission, each of which is a more powerful warming emission than CO_2. Regarding methane emissions, see Chapter 16.

47. *Id.*

48. David Marchese, *This Eminent Scientist Says Climate Activists Need to Get Real*, N.Y. Times (Apr. 22, 2022), https://www.nytimes.com/interactive/2022/04/25/magazine/vaclav-smil-interview.html.

single EU country [was] performing sufficiently in both ambition and progress in reducing carbon emissions."[49] A report by the Universal Ecological Fund also found that 75 percent of the 184 Paris Agreement NDC pledges were "insufficient to slow climate change," and some of the pledges had yet to be implemented.[50]

The Glasgow Agreement

More recently than the Paris Agreement in 2015, the Glasgow COP26 negotiations of all countries held in November 2021 did not commit to what was required to arrest destabilizing climate change in time, according to the leader of the United Nations.[51] The COP26 Glasgow Climate Pact did establish several soft agreements:

- An amendment sponsored by China and India replaced proposed language to "phase-*out*. . . . unabated coal power and inefficient subsidies for fossil fuels" with language about "phasing *down*" coal use.
- More than 40 of the world's 200 countries, including major coal users Poland, Vietnam, and Chile, agreed to shift away from coal use.
- One hundred twenty countries pledged to halt and reverse deforestation, but not until 2030.
- More than 100 countries agreed to cut emissions of methane by 2030 (see Chapter 16).

Where the United States Arrived: The Electric Power Sector

After three decades of world climate pacts since the original UNFCCC agreement on climate: unprecedented worldwide efforts to limit GHG emissions could lead to a more moderate increase in temperature of 1.6–1.8°C by 2040

49. *Off Target: Ranking of EU Countries' Ambition and Progress in Fighting Climate Change* 4, Climate Action Network Eur. (June 2018), https://perma.cc/5D5S-SMDY; Dave Keating, *Winners and Losers in the Race to Meet the Paris Climate Goals*, Deutsche Welle (June 16, 2018), https://perma.cc/3UMC-SU55 (quoting Climate Action Network director Wendel Trio as saying that "[w]hile all European Union countries signed up to the Paris Agreement, most are failing to work towards delivering on its objectives").

50. Stuart Braun, *Paris Climate Pledges "Far Too Little, Too Late,"* Deutsche Welle (Nov. 5, 2019), https://perma.cc/7HSK-J4JN.

51. Laura Quiñones, *COP26 Closes with "Compromise" Deal on Climate, but It's Not Enough, Says UN Chief*, UN News (Nov. 13, 2021), https://news.un.org/en/story/2021/11/1105792.

and then mitigating to a 1.4–1.75°C increase by 2100.[52] This could contain average world temperature increases to less than 2°C or perhaps 1.5°C as pledged in the Paris Agreement. However, without a Herculean effort that is not now evident, it is predicted that there will be an increase in temperatures over historic levels by 2040 of 1.75–2°C, growing to an increase of average temperature of 2.8–4.8°C by 2100. These higher levels are predicted to cause havoc with world systems.[53]

Biden Administration Federal Action on Carbon and Power

The electric power generation sector is now targeted for rapid change: more than 98 percent of anthropogenic GHG emissions result from fossil fuel use.[54] The electric power sector, because of its size, is targeted to make the carbon-mitigation changes. The DoE estimates that approximately two-thirds of the required carbon sector reductions incentivized with $430 billion by the Inflation Reduction Act of 2022 and the Infrastructure Act of 2021 must and will be in the power sector, dwarfing all of the other transportation, building space heating, and industry sectors combined, as shown in Figure 2.3.

Figure 2.3[55] Estimated Emissions Reductions in 2030 from Inflation Reduction Act and Bipartisan Infrastructure Law (2030, MMT CO_2e)

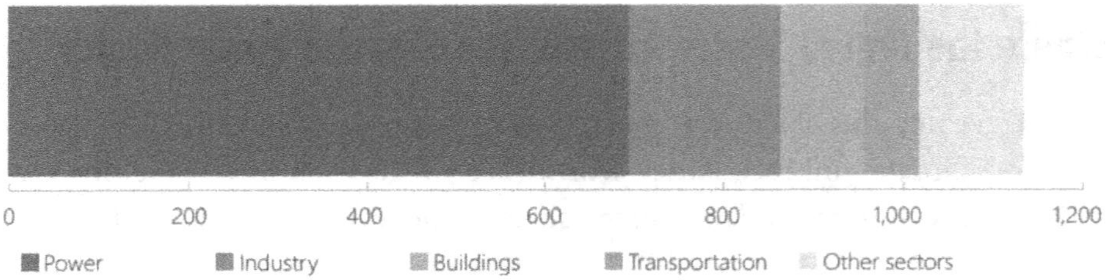

52. Intergovernmental Panel on Climate Change, Sixth Assessment Report, Climate Change 2022: Impacts, Adaptation and Vulnerability: Summary for Policymakers 16 (Feb. 28, 2022), https://www.ipcc.ch/report/ar6/wg2/downloads/report/IPCC_AR6_WGII_SummaryForPolicymakers.pdf.

53. *Id.*

54. U.S. Dep't of Energy, *supra* note 1.

55. *IRA Reductions, supra* note 5, at 3.

The DoE's preliminary assessment finds that the Inflation Reduction Act of 2022 can and will help drive 2030 economy-wide emissions to 40 percent below 2005 levels. The DoE estimates that the clean energy provisions of the Inflation Reduction Act, combined with the 2021 bipartisan Infrastructure Act, could reduce GHG emissions by approximately 1,000 MMT (a gigaton). Along with other climate and energy provisions of these laws, they raise the DoE-estimated total annual carbon reduction to nearly 1,150 MMT by 2030, which is equivalent to the combined annual carbon emissions from all U.S. homes.[56] The Inflation Reduction Act and the Infrastructure Act together represent historic investments in the nation's energy system, totaling more than $430 billion.[57]

To begin this transition to a carbon-neutral world, there has been a significant increase since 2010 in U.S. investment in, and production of, renewable energy, including a rapid threefold increase in wind power.[58] The importance of the electric sector to the modern corporate industrial economy and to climate change is reflected in its changing dominant role. In 1949, only 11 percent of global warming gases in the United States came from the electric sector; today it contributes more than one-quarter.[59] The U.S. Energy Information Administration (EIA) concluded that the electric power sector offered the most cost-effective opportunities to reduce CO_2 emissions, compared to transportation, the other largest GHG-emitting sector.

Electricity production accounts for less than 5 percent of U.S. economic activity yet is held responsible for about one-quarter of emissions of certain criteria air pollutants. Electric power derived from burning gaseous, liquid, and solid fossil fuels to create it releases large quantities of CO_2 into the environment.[60] Fossil fuel power generation results in 64 percent of total human-

---

56. *Id.*

57. *Id.*

58. Tik Root, *Renewable Energy Use Nearly Quadrupled in Past Decade, Report Finds,* Wash. Post (Nov. 9, 2021), https://www.washingtonpost.com/climate-solutions/2021/11/09/renewable-energy-solar-wind-biden/.

59. U.S. Energy Info. Admin., Annual Energy Review 2011, at 303, 309 (2012), https://www.eia.gov/totalenergy/data/annual/pdf/aer.pdf.

60. The amount of carbon released per unit of usable energy decreased each time as human populations moved from wood to coal as the dominant CO_2-releasing fuel in the late 19th century, again

made atmospheric CO_2, and this amount has increased significantly since 1990.[61] Electric power demand worldwide is continuing to increase dramatically.[62] The share of all burned fossil fuels converted to create electricity increased from 1 percent in 1900 to 25 percent in 1990.[63]

During the Obama administration, the EPA took a phased approach and chose only to regulate those sources whose GHG emissions exceeded 75,000 tpy (tons per year) (for modifications) or 100,000 tpy (for new construction), in order to apply only to 280 CO_2 emitters rather than 80,000 emitters had the EPA followed the written provisions in the U.S. Clean Air Act. When this approach was challenged, the Supreme Court struck such executive discretion and held in *UARG v. U.S. EPA* that

> EPA lacked authority to "tailor" the Act's unambiguous numerical thresholds of 100 or 250 tons per year to accommodate its greenhouse-gas-inclusive interpretation of the permitting triggers. Agencies must always "'give effect to the unambiguously expressed intent of Congress.'"[64]

The United States is now deploying in the Inflation Reduction Act of 2022 large amounts of subsidies that reduce prices (to make U.S. products more attractive), which is the flip side of border tariffs. On the flip side of that policy, the E.U. Carbon Border Adjustment Mechanisms (CBAM or similar U.S. measures if enacted) will impose a tariff/cost on more carbon-intensive imports often exported from less-developed countries using more environmentally damaging older production processes for goods; with a border tariff, the importing developed country realizes substantial additional revenue from that tariff. There is an option for the exporting (perhaps

---

moved from coal to oil in the mid-20th century, and will move toward natural gas in the future; *see generally* Peter A. O'Connor et al., *U.S. Energy Transitions 1780–2010*, 7 Energies 7955, 7963, 7969, 7972 (2014).

61. *See* U.S. Energy Info. Admin., Emissions of Greenhouse Gases in the United States 2009 (2011), https://www.eia.gov/environment/emissions/ghg_report/.

62. *See, e.g.*, Int'l Energy Agency, World Energy Outlook 2017, at 47, 49–50, https://www.iea.org/reports/world-energy-outlook-2017.

63. Steven Ferrey, *Power Future*, 15 Duke Env't L. & Pol'y F. 261, 267 (2005).

64. Util. Air Regul. Grp. v. EPA, 573 U.S. 302, 326 (2014) (quoting Nat'l Ass'n of Home Builders v. Defs. of Wildlife, 551 U.S. 644, 665 (2007)).

less-developed) country to impose a domestic carbon price or control on its internal industries in order to be exempt from paying a CBAM tariff, in which case the host exporting country realizes any revenue from this internal charge or tariff on its industry. A significant amount of wind and solar power equipment is of foreign manufacture. There are ongoing significant E.U. legal concerns about the greater tax credit subsidies for sourcing and use of domestic products for renewable energy power generation embedded in the U.S. Inflation Reduction Act (see Chapter 6) as violating the World Trade Organization prohibition on geographic location discrimination in trade, by which the United States is bound.

Carbon and Technology Change

Diminishing Reliance on Coal and Fossil Fuels for Power

The U.S. electric system has traditionally used coal-fired resources as its principal prime mover power generation technology since the first harnessing of electricity.[65] The dominance of coal use in the United States is in steep decline in recent years: coal for power generation has been rapidly decreasing during the 21st century, to where it now supplies less than one-fifth of U.S. electric power, with its share continuing to decrease. In 2007, coal supplied half of all power generation, and its share has declined by more than half since then, with additional declines forecast.[66] According to the EIA, coal will account for 85 percent of U.S. electric generating capacity retirements in 2022.[67] As of September 2021, there were no plans to install any new utility-scale coal-fired power plants in the United States. The recent sources of electric power generation in the United States are shown in Table 2.2.

---

65. *See* James G. Speight, The Chemistry and Technology of Coal 13 (3d ed. 2013).

66. Mario Parker & Naureen Malik, *Coal Confronting Bigger Threat than Obama's Rules for Clean Air*, Bloomberg Energy & Climate Rep. (June 10, 2015); *see also* Bloomberg Energy & Climate Rep. (June 2, 2015).

67. *Short-Term Energy Outlook*, U.S. Energy Info. Admin. (Apr. 9, 2024), https://www.eia.gov/outlooks/steo/report/electricity.php.

Table 2.2 U.S. Utility-Scale Electricity Generation by Source, Amount, and Share of Total in 2023[68]

Energy source	Billion kWh	Share of total
Total—all sources	4,178	
Fossil fuels (total)	2,505	60.0%
Natural gas	1,802	43.1%
Coal	675	16.2%
Petroleum (total)	16	0.4%
Petroleum liquids	12	0.3%
Petroleum coke	5	0.1%
Other gases	11	0.3%
Nuclear	775	18.6%
Renewables (total)	894	21.4%
Wind	425	10.2%
Hydropower	240	5.7%
Solar (total)	165	3.9%
Photovoltaic	162	3.9%
Solar thermal	3	0.1%
Biomass (total)	47	1.1%
Wood	31	0.8%
Landfill gas	8	0.2%
Municipal solid waste (biogenic)	6	0.1%
Other biomass waste	2	0.1%
Geothermal	16	0.4%
Pumped storage hydropower	-6	-0.1%
Other sources	10	0.2%

The DoE also forecasts a decline in natural gas generation, which is estimated to fall from a 37 percent share in 2021 to 35 percent in both 2022 and 2023, even though the government expected the cost of natural gas for power generation to fall from an average of $5.85/MMBtu in 2022 to an annual average of $4.21/million British thermal units (MMBtu) in 2023.[69] In September 2023, Michael Bloomberg announced that Bloomberg Philanthropies

68. U.S. Energy Info. Admin.: Frequently Asked Questions (2019), *What is U.S. Electricity Generation by Energy Source?*, https://www.eia.gov/tools/faqs/faq.php?id=427&t=3[https://perma.cc/Y7XG-NHUG].

69. *Id.*

would provide an additional $500 million to the Beyond Carbon campaign. This was accompanied by a press release announcing a goal to "shut down every last U.S. coal plant" and "slash gas plant capacity in half, and block all new gas plants."[70] According to the Statistical Review of World Energy, natural gas and coal supplied 59.8 percent of all U.S. electric generation in 2022.[71]

The legally applied "social cost of greenhouse gases" estimate is used in rulemaking processes, cost-benefit analysis (see Chapter 7), and environmental permitting decisions to approximate economic damages associated with burning fossil fuels in electric power generation, and this is controversial as it silently changes U.S. direction and policy. The Biden administration increased by 400 percent the cost of carbon emissions utilized by the Trump administration, to $51/ton from $10/ton, without going through a rulemaking process or allowing public comment.[72] The federal circuit court of appeals reversed the trial court, and subsequent to that, the U.S. Supreme Court in 2022 in a brief opinion upheld discretion of the president unilaterally to set the value of carbon emissions in determining costs and benefits of environmental regulation.[73]

Proposed by the Biden administration and currently undergoing public and scientific comment is a revised almost 400 percent increased cost of each ton of carbon emitted to $190/ton. A federal appellate court in 2022 upheld that the Federal Energy Regulatory Commission (FERC) must consider foreseeable indirect upstream and downstream GHG impacts of projects seeking FERC approval if the impacts are known.[74]

---

70. *See* Press Release, Michael R. Bloomberg Doubles Down with Additional $500M to Help End Fossil Fuels and Usher in a New Era of Clean Energy in the United States, Bloomberg Philanthropies (Sept. 20, 2023), https://www.bloomberg.org/press/michael-r-bloomberg-doubles-down-with-additional-500m-to-help-end-fossil-fuels-and-usher-in-a-new-era-of-clean-energy-in-the-united-states/; *see also* Robert Bryce, *Michael Bloomberg's $1 Billion Assault on the Electric Grid* (Oct. 18, 2023), https://robertbryce.substack.com/p/michael-bloombergs-1-billion-assault.

71. *Statistical Review of World Energy*, Energy Inst. (2022), https://www.energyinst.org/statistical-review.

72. Executive Order on Protecting Public Health and the Environment and Restoring Science to Tackle the Climate Crisis (Jan. 20, 2021), https://www.whitehouse.gov/briefing-room/presidential-actions/2021/01/20/executive-order-protecting-public-health-and-environment-and-restoring-science-to-tackle-climate-crisis/.

73. Louisiana v. Biden, 142 S. Ct. 2750 (2022).

74. Food & Water Watch & Berkshire Env't Action Team v. Fed. Energy Regulatory Comm'n, 28 F.4th 277 (D.C. Cir. 2022).

Renewable Energy Ascent

Historically. In 1800, the world obtained 94 percent of its energy from renewable sources.[75] That figure has declined since. In 1971, 13.12 percent of the world's energy came from renewable power; in 2011, 40 years later, renewable power's share had declined to 12.99 percent.[76] In the United States, renewable energy accounted for 9.3 percent of energy production in 1949 and was previously projected to be 10.8 percent by 2040, although it has already passed this mark. In China, renewable energy production dropped from 40 percent in 1971 to 11 percent two decades ago.[77]

While natural gas gets much credit for displacing more carbon-intensive coal use for power generation, recently renewable energy and energy efficiency were the primary source of the 4.2 percent decrease in power sector carbon emissions achieved in 2017.[78] In 2012, wind energy was the most installed new U.S. electricity generation source, at 43 percent of all new electric generation. Wind, along with natural gas, has dominated new sources of electric energy deployed since 2012.[79] During 2014–2019 and ongoing, in most of those years additions of renewable wind and solar power constituted the majority of total additions to power generation in the United States as shown in Figure 2.4. In the first ten months of 2022, U.S. solar output increased 26.23 percent year to date, according to the EIA. Renewable electric energy generation quickly is substituting for operation of coal generation since 2010 in the United States.

---

75. Bjørn Lomborg, *Green Energy Needs to Be Cheaper*, SLATE (Aug. 25, 2013), https://perma.cc/6QF2-8KUC; *see also* Todd Woody, *The Next Big Innovation in Renewable Energy Won't Be Technological*, ATL. MONTHLY (Nov. 11, 2013), https://perma.cc/8EUM-4AC5.

76. See Lomborg, *supra* note 75.

77. *Id.*

78. BLOOMBERG NEW ENERGY FIN., 2018 FACTBOOK, SUSTAINABLE ENERGY IN AMERICA.

79. *See Energy Dep't Reports: U.S. Wind Energy Production and Manufacturing Reaches Record Highs*, ENERGY.GOV (Aug. 6, 2013), www.geni.org/globalenergy/library/technical-articles/generation/energy.gov/Energy_Dept_Reports_US_Wind_Energy_Production_and_Manufacturing_Reaches_Record_Highs/index.shtml.

Figure 2.4[80]

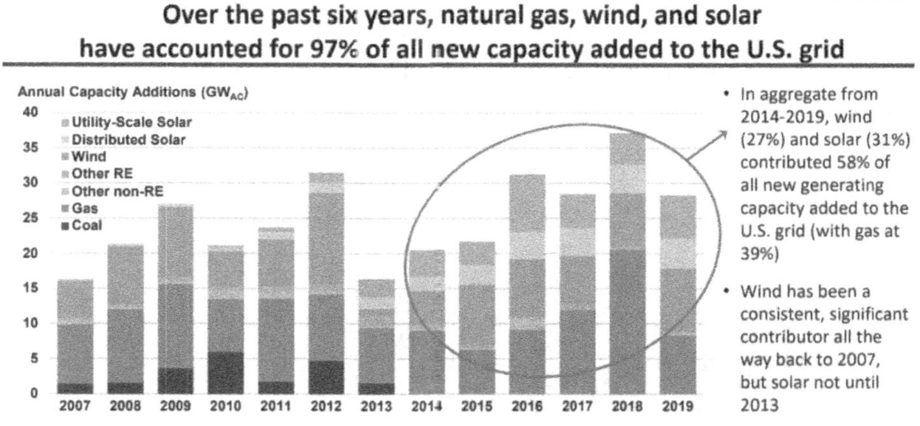

Declining Costs. In the U.S. economy and in the power sector business model, cost matters: the capital cost of wind power projects has decreased to be competitive with the cost of more traditional fossil fuel resources for electricity generation.[81] Wind projects in the United States generate electricity at an average cost of $45/megawatt-hour (MWh) for capacity and energy without other subsidies,[82] and some large wind power projects can produce power at the very low cost of $10–$20/MWh.[83] Between 1998 and 2021, the

---

80. Mark Bolinger, *Utility-Scale Wind and Solar in the U.S.: Comparative Trends in Deployment, Cost, Performance, Pricing, and Market Value* 5, Lawrence Berkeley Nat'l Lab'y (2020), https://perma.cc/QRU2-NAMV.

81. Tara Patel, *Fossil Fuels Losing Cost Advantage over Solar, Wind, IEA Says*, Bloomberg (Aug. 31, 2015), http://www.bloomberg.com/news/articles/2015-08-31/solar-wind-power-costs-drop-as-fossil-fuels-increase-iea-says [https://perma.cc/5UX4-RWRS]; *see also Advantages and Challenges of Wind Energy*, Off. of Energy Efficiency & Renewable Energy, https://www.energy.gov/eere/wind/advantages-and-challenges-wind-energy (last visited Apr. 15, 2024) [https://perma.cc/X5AJ-4YBU].

82. Jim Efstathiou Jr. & Brian K. Sullivan, *Smarter Wind Turbines Try to Squeeze More Power on Each Rotation*, Bloomberg Env't Rep. (May 9, 2018), https://www.bloomberg.com/news/articles/2018-05-09/smarter-wind-turbines-try-to-squeeze-more-power-on-each-rotation.

83. *Advantages and Challenges of Wind Energy*, *supra* note 81. While natural gas gets much credit for displacing more carbon-intensive coal use for power generation, recently renewable energy and energy efficiency were the primary source of the 4.2 percent decrease in power sector carbon emissions achieved in 2017.

levelized cost of wind energy in the United States decreased by 70 percent.[84] See Figure 2.5.

Figure 2.5[85] Estimated Levelized Cost of Wind Energy by Commercial Operation Date

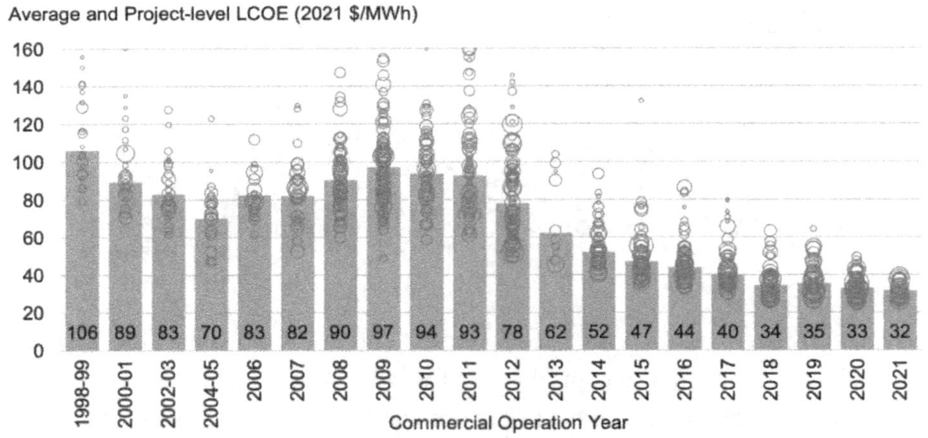

Note: Size of bubble reflects project capacity.

Source: Berkeley Lab

In a recent study, unsubsidized wind power and utility-scale solar projects came in at lower price ranges than any other analyzed resource, including gas, coal, and nuclear power.[86] The cost of unsubsidized wind ranges from $28 to $54 per MWh; factoring in subsidies, wind prices plunge to $11–$45/MWh. See Chapters 5 and 6 on federal subsidies and Chapters 8 and 9 on state renewable energy subsidies for electric power. Lazard illustrates the marginal cost of new renewable energy as generally comparable to that of existing fossil fuel generation, as shown in Figure 2.6.

---

84. U.S. Dep't of Energy, Revolution Now: The Future Arrives for Five Clean Energy Technologies—2016 Update 1; *see also* Int'l Energy Agency & Clean Energy Ministerial, Next Generation Wind and Solar Power: From Cost to Value 6 (2016); Silvio Marcacci, *Renewable Energy Prices Hit Record Lows: How Can Utilities Benefit from Unstoppable Solar and Wind?*, Forbes (Jan. 21, 2020), https://www.forbes.com/sites/energyinnovation/2020/01/21/renewable-energy-prices-hit-record-lows-how-can-utilities-benefit-from-unstoppable-solar-and-wind/?sh=577034ff2c84 [https://perma.cc/NE96-UHL3]

85. U.S. Dep't of Energy Off. of Energy Efficiency & Renewable Energy, Land-Based Wind Market Report: 2022 Edition 66, https://perma.cc/45V5-F7D7.

86. *See* Marcacci, *supra* note 84.

Figure 2.6[87]

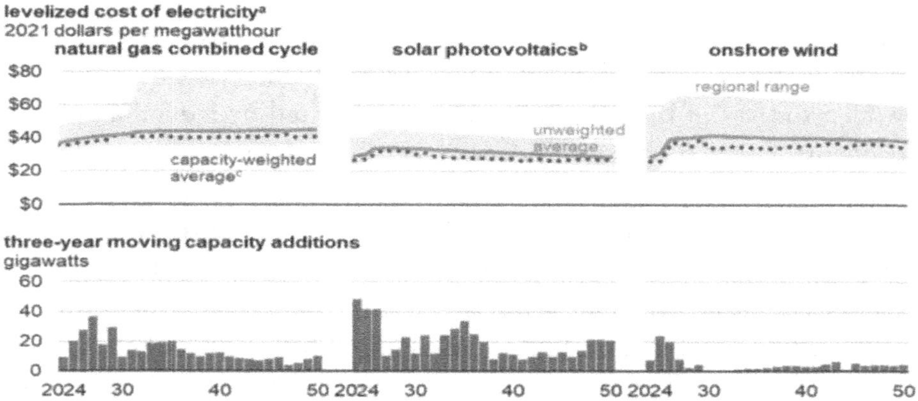

Source: U.S. Energy Information Administration, *Annual Energy Outlook 2022*
[a] Levelized cost includes tax credits available for plants entering service during the projection period.
[b] Technology is assumed to be photovoltaic with single-axis tracking. Costs are expressed in terms of net AC (alternating current) power available to the grid for the installed capacity.
[c] Capacity-weighted average is the average levelized cost per technology, weighted by the new capacity coming online in the previous three years in each region. For example, plants coming online in 2027 are based on additions from 2025 to 2027.

Wind power is forecast by the DoE to be cheaper than electricity produced from natural gas by 2025, even without a continuing federal production tax credit incentive, which will in fact be continuing due to the Inflation Reduction Act.[88] On the Inflation Reduction Act, see Chapter 6. There has been a lack of empirical data because wind generation data from existing turbines is considered proprietary and/or business secrets that are not in the public domain. Solar insolation data is more available. Wind and solar photovoltaic power generation costs decreased by double-digit amounts from 2020 to 2021.[89]

The cost to install photovoltaic solar panels has decreased in the decade between 2010 and 2021 across residential, commercial-rooftop, and utility-scale projects, with a 64 percent, 59 percent, and 82 percent reduction respectively; solar panel prices at the start of 2023 average $2.86/watt before

87. *Levelized Costs of New Generation Resources in the* Annual Energy Outlook 2022, at 14, U.S. Energy Info. Admin. (Mar. 2022), https://perma.cc/TT85-353X.

88. *See* Christopher Martin & Justin Doom, BNA Energy & Climate Report (Mar. 12, 2015); *U.S. Wind Energy Production Tax Credit Extended through 2021*, U.S. Energy Info. Admin. (Jan. 28, 2021), https://www.eia.gov/todayinenergy/detail.php?id=46576 [https://perma.cc/82AH-THH8].

89. Int'l Renewable Energy Agency, Renewable Power Generation Costs in 2021 (2022), https://www.irena.org/publications/2022/Jul/Renewable-Power-Generation-Costs-in-2021.

incentives.[90] Solar inverters constitute about $0.21/watt, or 8 percent, of the total installed cost of solar, with the price decreasing by about 50 percent since 2013.[91] The market size of the U.S. solar power industry grew almost 20 percent per year on average between 2018 and 2023.[92] See Chapter 12.

The success of the solar industry is augmented by federal and state tax credits, falling installation prices,[93] and the proliferation of net metering programs in 40 states. See Chapter 9. Solar electric energy is now cost-competitive with traditional fossil fuels due to substantial subsidies[94] and will expand in use in the next decade. The EIA forecasts that the annual share of U.S. electricity generation from renewable energy sources would rise from 20 percent in 2021 to 23 percent in 2023, as a result of continuing increases in solar and wind generating capacity, and it did in fact constitute 22 percent of U.S. power generation in 2023.[95]

The DoE estimated even before the Inflation Reduction Act of 2022 and Infrastructure Act of 2021 (discussed earlier) that the U.S. electric power sector added 14 gigawatts (GW) of new wind capacity in 2021, with a forecast of an additional 10 GW of new wind capacity online in 2022 and 4 GW in 2023. For solar, larger utility-scale solar capacity rose by 13 GW in 2021,

---

90. *See* Press Release, Nat'l Renewable Energy Lab'y, Documenting a Decade of Cost Declines for PV Systems (Feb. 10, 2021), https://perma.cc/VD7R-PH7D. NREL Senior Financial Analyst David Feldman explained that "[a] significant portion of the cost declines over the past decade can be attributed to an 85% cost decline in module price. A decade ago, the module alone cost around $2.50 per watt, and now an entire utility-scale PV system costs around $1 per watt." *Id. See How Much Do Solar Panels Cost in 2023?*, EnergySage (Feb. 2023), https://perma.cc/V2WW-MC9C (documenting the average cost of solar panels in 2023).

91. *See* Spencer Fields, *How Have Solar Equipment Costs Declined over Time?*, EnergySage (May 21, 2021), https://perma.cc/ZNY3-6UET.

92. *See Solar Power in the US—Market Size (2004–2029)*, IBIS World, (Oct. 12, 2023), https://www.ibisworld.com/industry-statistics/market-size/solar-power-united-states/#:~:text=Has%20the%20Solar%20Power%20industry,average%20between%202018%20and%202023.

93. *See Solar Industry Research Data*, Solar Energy Indus. Ass'n, http://www.seia.org/research-resources/solar-industry-data (last visited Apr. 15, 2024).

94. Int'l Renewable Energy Agency, Renewable Power Remains Cost-Competitive Amid Fossil Fuel Crisis (July 13, 2022), https://www.irena.org/news/pressreleases/2022/Jul/Renewable-Power-Remains-Cost-Competitive-amid-Fossil-Fuel-Crisis.

95. *Short-Term Energy Outlook*, *supra* note 67; *see also Solar and Wind to Lead Growth of U.S. Power Generation for the Next Two Years*, U.S. Energy Info. Admin. (Jan. 16, 2024), https://www.eia.gov/todayinenergy/detail.php?id=61242.

with a forecast for added utility-scale solar capacity of 20 GW for 2022 and 24 GW for 2023—these numbers would have solar additions account for nearly half of total new electric generating capacity in 2022. In 2021 small-scale solar increased by 5 GW to a total of 33 GW in the United States[96] and is projected to grow by 4 GW in 2022 and by almost 6 GW in 2023. In 2023, U.S. solar generation capacity increased by 51 percent compared to 2022 additions.[97]

State and Regional Carbon Regulation and Electrification

States and regions have their own low-carbon goals and laws that regulate the electric power sector. These states and regions also are encouraging the substitution of electric power for direct combustion of fossil fuels for building space conditioning and transportation. The state of New York has in place and is executing its policy path to achieve 70 percent renewable energy use by 2030 and 85 percent economy-wide GHG reductions by 2050.

RGGI and California Credits

RGGI. The Regional Greenhouse Gas Initiative (RGGI), now in 11 eastern states, regulates its cap-and-trade allowances only for CO_2 emissions from power plants with capacity larger than 25 MW. All RGGI states adopted virtually uniform state laws to implement the RGGI program, auctioning emission allowances to the highest bidders rather than freely allocating allowances.

The RGGI scheme also creates an offsets program, which excludes renewable energy generation as an eligible source but includes offsets created elsewhere from landfill methane capture, sulfur hexafluoride emission reduction, forestry or afforestation, end-use efficiency, and avoided agricultural methane emissions. Offsets purchased by and applied to RGGI sources reduce their required allowances for up to 3.3 percent of that regulated generator's total emissions per control period.[98] This creates business

96. *Id.* Small-scale solar is defined as systems with less than 1 megawatt (MW) installed capacity.

97. *U.S. Solar Market Insight*, Solar Energy Indus. Ass'n (Mar. 6, 2024), https://www.seia.org/us-solar-market-insight.

98. *See* Reg'l Greenhouse Gas Initiative, Inc., *Offsets*, https://www.rggi.org/allowance-tracking/offsets (last visited Apr. 15, 2024).

opportunities for creating such projects while earning tax credits (see Chapter 6), potential RPS RECs (see Chapter 8), and/or net metering credits (see Chapter 9) while creating and selling offsets in the RGGI market. Not participating in the award of offsets program for in-state facilities are Massachusetts, New Hampshire, Rhode Island, and Virginia; nonparticipation influences where and what offset projects might be undertaken.

California. California's Assembly Bill (A.B.) 32 regulates all carbon emissions from all major industries in the state and requires reduction of GHG emissions to 1990 levels by 2020, counting all in-state and out-of-state generation used to serve California's electric load.[99] Implementing A.B. 32, California adopted a plan to reduce emissions by 40 percent below 1990 levels by 2030. A 2020 executive order announced a plan that all new cars and passenger trucks sold must be zero-emission vehicles after 2035 but does not ban or impose a fine on the sale of gas-powered cars as part of the used car market. So far, 16 states have signed on to follow California's plan for only electric new car sales: New York, Massachusetts, Vermont, Maine, Washington, Connecticut, Oregon, New Jersey, Delaware, Colorado, Rhode Island, Minnesota, New Mexico, Virginia, Nevada, and Pennsylvania.

California recognized that low-carbon sources and carbon alternatives will cause increased electricity substitution and usage as industries switch to different energy sources—primarily electricity—for heating and transportation. As a result, in 2018, California adopted Senate Bill 100, which established a goal to achieve 100 percent carbon-free electricity by 2045.[100] A.B. 32 does not distinguish the geographic source of power generation and covers the liberal import of power into California from other states implementing AB 32.

Comparatively. These programs started with RGGI in January 2009 in ten northeastern states, now 11 states; Pennsylvania also is seeking to join RGGI.[101] CO_2 emissions from power plants in the region were capped at then-current levels, and after 2015 annual allowed CO_2 emissions were

99. *See* CAL. HEALTH & SAFETY CODE § 3850; *see also AB 32 Global Warming Solutions Act of 2006* (Sept. 28, 2018), CAL. AIR RES. BD., http://www.arb.ca.gov/cc/ab32/ab32.htm.

100. *See* Executive Order B-55-18 to Achieve Carbon Neutrality (Sept. 10, 2018), https://www.ca.gov/archive/gov39/wp-content/uploads/2018/09/9.10.18-Executive-Order.pdf.

101. *Elements of RGGI*, REG'L GREENHOUSE GAS INITIATIVE, https://www.rggi.org/program-overview-and-design/elements#:~:text=For%202021%2C%202022%2C%20and%202023,%2C%20Vermont%2C%20and%20Virginia (last visited May 9, 2024).

reduced.[102] Since coal produces approximately twice as many tons of CO_2 as natural gas per unit of electricity generated, this decreasing standard places financial pressure on coal unit operation, as well as other fossil fuel unit operation within the RGGI states.

RGGI is more limited in impact than California's A.B. 32 in covered entities and industries, the range of GHG chemical emissions controlled, and the amount of emissions targeted and controlled: RGGI controls only CO_2 while A.B. 32 controls all six GHGs; RGGI controls only larger electric generation facilities while A.B. 32 controls, in three phases, electric generation and all other larger industrial emitters of GHGs, including transportation fuels. Both RGGI and A.B. 32 carbon credits are tradable. More states are expected to either join or replicate the California or RGGI legal arrangements.

Under both California and RGGI programs, covered power generation sources must purchase their emission allowances at auction if they emit carbon; zero-carbon sources of generation are not required to purchase allowances. These programs act much like a tax at the wholesale level on carbon emissions during operations. The auction proceeds raise significant revenue for the states. Although the proceeds are required to be devoted to energy-related purposes, some of the states have siphoned some of these funds away for purposes unrelated to energy. For even the relatively modest-sized state of Massachusetts, this auction at only $5 per allowance would raise more than $100 million annually. The total amount of auction proceeds realized by the RGGI states was more than $5.3 billion as of mid-2022.[103]

State Electrification. One of the RGGI states, Massachusetts, plans to reduce GHG emissions by at least 85 percent by 2050 and ultimately achieve net-zero emissions.[104] The MA Decarbonization Roadmap features a plan to transfer existing home heating from natural gas and oil to electric. Combustion of fossil fuels in residential and commercial building subsectors was responsible for 27 percent of state GHG emissions in 2017; space heating

---

102. Steven Ferrey, *Courts Cap the "Trade": Regulation of Competitive Markets When Courts Overturn State and Federal Cap-and-Trade Regulation*, 117 W. Va. L. Rev. 681, 717–18 (2014); *see also* Memo. of Understanding from the Reg'l Greenhouse Gas Initiative 2–3 (Dec. 20, 2005), http://www.rggi.org/docs/mou_final_12_20_05.pdf; Rep. 1797 (BNA) (June 14, 2013).

103. *See* Reg'l Greenhouse Gas Initiative, Inc., *Auction Results*, https://www.rggi.org/auctions/auction-results (last visited Apr. 15, 2024).

104. *See* MA Decarbonization Roadmap, Exec. Off. of Energy & Env't Affairs, https://www.mass.gov/info-details/ma-decarbonization-roadmap (last visited Apr. 15, 2024) [https://perma.cc/F2WW-7ZUX].

was the primary contributor to emissions.[105] To make this transition, Massachusetts's goal is to convert 100,000 homes to electric heating per year starting in 2020 using electrified air source heat pumps. By 2030, the state hopes to have converted one million buildings; however, in 2021 less than 500 homes were converted to heat pumps.[106] These conversions for existing buildings are subsidized by rebates paid for by higher retail rates for remaining natural gas and electric resistance heating customers.

The renewable electric energy RPS targets of the six New England states over the next two decades range from 25 to 90 percent renewable energy by 2040.[107] These targets are planned to be achieved by solar photovoltaic (PV) incentives and by large amounts of offshore wind development. For example, Massachusetts plans 3,000 MW of additional solar power through the Solar Massachusetts Renewable Target program and 4,000 MW of offshore wind. Approximately 7,000 MW of power demand is what is used on a typical day in Massachusetts—although both solar and wind are intermittent suppliers of electricity (see Chapter 12, "Transitioning from Baseload Fossil and Nuclear Electric Power to Intermittent Renewable Power"). Massachusetts, Rhode Island, and Connecticut have procured 3.1 GW of offshore wind and are planning to procure an additional 5.8 GW of offshore wind by 2030.

In addition to building electric and space conditioning requirements, the other major sector responsible for GHG emissions is transportation. The MA Decarbonization Roadmap plans to electrify public transit within the next few decades.[108] Prior to 2040, the plan will require the greater Boston subway and bus authority, the MBTA, to electrify all buses.[109] To further support the state's efforts, Massachusetts is considering imposing a carbon fee

---

105. *See* MASSACHUSETTS 2050 DECARBONIZATION ROADMAP, EXEC. OFF. OF ENERGY & ENV'T AFFAIRS (2020), https://www.mass.gov/doc/ma-decarbonization-roadmap-lower-resolution/download.

106. *Id.*; *see* Sabrina Shankman, *Massachusetts Should Be Converting 100,000 Homes a Year to Electric Heat. The Actual Number: 461*, BOS. GLOBE (Aug. 21, 2021), https://www.bostonglobe.com/2021/08/21/science/massachusetts-should-be-converting-100000-homes-year-electric-heat-actual-number-461/?event=event12.

107. ISO-NE & ANALYSIS GRP., PATHWAYS STUDY (Apr. 2022).

108. *See* MASSACHUSETTS 2050 DECARBONIZATION ROADMAP, *supra* note 105, at 40.

109. *See* Matt Stout, *Senate Climate Bills Would Push State to Adopt Carbon Pricing*, BOS. GLOBE (Jan. 23, 2020), https://www.bostonglobe.com/2020/01/23/metro/senate-climate-bill-would-push-state-adopt-carbon-pricing/?p1=BGSearch_Overlay_Results.

extended to transportation and heating fossil fuel prices.[110] All of these state (i.e., California, Massachusetts, etc.) and regional (RGGI) laws will have the long-term effect over the next three decades of substantially increasing the demand for electricity, increasingly produced from renewable and zero-carbon resources. Several states have announced their own goals to enact legislation to have zero-carbon electricity sector emissions from their power generation in relatively short periods of time:

- New York, 100 percent by 2040[111]
- California, 100 percent by 2045[112]
- Virginia and New Jersey, 100 percent by 2050[113]

There is consideration of a Clean Heat Standard in Vermont and suspension of subsidies for new natural gas building hookups in Connecticut.

State and Local Government Litigation to Impose Liability on Fossil Fuel Companies

Cities and states already are initiating litigation against fossil fuel companies prior to the clean power targets that they have enacted. The Supreme Court unanimously held that the Clean Air Act, when coupled with the EPA's discretionary authority that the Court recognized in *Massachusetts v. EPA*, as well as the actions the EPA took to regulate GHGs, displaces federal common law causes of action addressing climate change.[114]

---

110. House Bill 3292 seeks to extend a current carbon fee on power plants to these additional sectors. *See Bill H. 3292*, https://malegislature.gov/Bills/192/HD1972 (last visited Apr. 15, 2024); *see also* Sarah Shemkus, *Massachusetts Groups Back Expanded Carbon Tax with Focus on Equity*, Energy News Network (Mar. 2, 2021), https://energynews.us/2021/03/02/massachusetts-groups-back-expanded-carbon-tax-with-focus-on-equity/.

111. *Climate Act*, N.Y. State, https://climate.ny.gov/ (last visited Apr. 15, 2024).

112. Press Release, Cal. Energy Comm'n, California Releases Report Charting Path to 100 Percent Clean Electricity (Mar. 15, 2021), https://www.energy.ca.gov/news/2021-03/california-releases-report-charting-path-100-percent-clean-electricity#:~:text=Modeling%20of%20the%20core%20scenario,percent%20renewable%20electricity%20by%202030.

113. *2020 Session: HB 1526 Electric Utility Regulation; Environmental Goals: Summary as Passed*, Va. Legis. Info. Sys., https://lis.virginia.gov/cgi-bin/legp604.exe?201+sum+HB1526 (last visited Apr. 15, 2024).

114. As held by the Supreme Court in *Am. Elec. Power Co. v. Connecticut*, 131 S. Ct. 2527 (2011).

San Francisco and Oakland, California, sued oil companies Chevron, ConocoPhillips, ExxonMobil, Royal Dutch Shell, and BP seeking financial compensation for their expenses in adapting to sea level rise, arguing that the GHGs emitted from burning oil they sold to consumers were a public nuisance under state common law. Preliminarily, the Court stated:

> Plaintiffs do not bring claims against emitters, but rather bring claims against defendants for having put fossil fuels into the flow of international commerce. Importantly . . . claims here attack behavior worldwide. While some of the fuel produced by defendants is certainly consumed in the United States (emissions from which are regulated by the Clean Air Act), greenhouse gases emanating from overseas sources are equally guilty (perhaps more so) of causing plaintiffs' harm . . . . Here, the Clean Air Act does not provide a sufficient legislative solution to the nuisance alleged to warrant a conclusion that this legislation has occupied the field to the exclusion of federal common law.[115]

Subsequently, in a final ruling, the federal court stated:

> The problem deserves a solution on a more vast scale than can be supplied by a district judge or jury in a public nuisance case . . . . [T]he problem at hand clearly deserves a solution best addressed by those branches . . . . All of us have benefited. Having reaped the benefit of that historic progress, would it really be fair to now ignore our own responsibility in the use of fossil fuels and place the blame for global warming on those who supplied what we demanded?[116]

A federal court in New York held that New York's federal and state common-law claims against five oil companies alleged to be responsible for more than 11 percent of all the atmospheric carbon and methane pollution since the Industrial Revolution from their marketing of fossil fuels contributing to climate change were preempted by the federal Clean Air Act and that global warming was an issue reserved for the Congress:

---

115. City of Oakland v. BP P.L.C., 969 F.3d 895 (9th Cir. 2020); *see also* Chevron Corp. v. City of Oakland, Cal., 141 S. Ct. 2776 (2021).

116. City of Oakland v. BP, 325 F. Supp. 3d 1017, 1029 (N.D. Cal. 2018); City of Oakland v. BP P.L.C., 969 F.3d 895 (9th Cir. 2020).

> The City's global-warming tort claims are based on Defendants' worldwide fossil fuel production and "the use of their fossil fuel products [that] continue[] to emit greenhouse gases and exacerbate global warming . . ." [seeking] an injunction to abate the public nuisance and trespass . . . . the Clean Air Act displaces such federal common law claims under *American Electric Power Co. v. Connecticut* . . . [B]ecause the Clean Air Act has spoken "directly to the question" of domestic greenhouse gas emissions, the City's claims are displaced. . . . Global warming and solutions thereto must be addressed by the two other branches of government . . . Such claims implicate countless foreign governments and their laws and policies. . . . [117]

Part II: Legal Strategy for Each Evolving Issue

Part II in each subsequent chapter creates a roadmap charting now-changing key legal guideposts and strategy to apply "best practices" for each energy and environmental legal and business challenge emerging under new U.S. law and climate policies in the fast-changing electric power sector.

---

117. City of N.Y. v. BP P.L.C., 325 F. Supp. 3d 466, 471, 474, 475 (S.D.N.Y. 2018).

PART II

Navigating Legal Changes in the Power Sector

Electricity is the most significantly government-regulated industry in the United States. It is regulated in ways that are unique compared to regulation of every other industry in the United States. All electric sector stakeholders and their counsel must understand the shape and operation of this distinct regulation and how it now is changing. Part II provides a roadmap of legal obstacles and strategic workarounds necessary in the next decade to successfully navigate the evolving electric sector as electricity substitutes for and dominates fossil fuels, changing the environment.

The starting point: wind and solar power will require an order of magnitude more land than traditional denser power generation technologies. Under the U.S. Constitution's Tenth Amendment separation of powers, that greater amount of needed land is under the control of cities and states, not federal agencies. This triggers multiple layers of additional legal and regulatory approvals and delays as well as legal challenges; each is covered in detail in this part regarding how to:

- Exercise effective control at the state and federal levels regarding new rules.
- Take best advantage of the new Inflation Reduction Act and the Infrastructure and Jobs Act.
- Understand and identify best locations/opportunities for siting each new power technology.
- Maximize use of federal PURPA, state RECs, and net metering, which differ in each state.
- Understand the Supreme Court's "new math" of required cost-benefit analysis.
- Identify and manage city, county, and state techniques now blocking new sustainable electric power transmission and generation facilities and that infrastructure.

Part II is an understandable roadmap to navigate strategically the changing electric sector.[1]

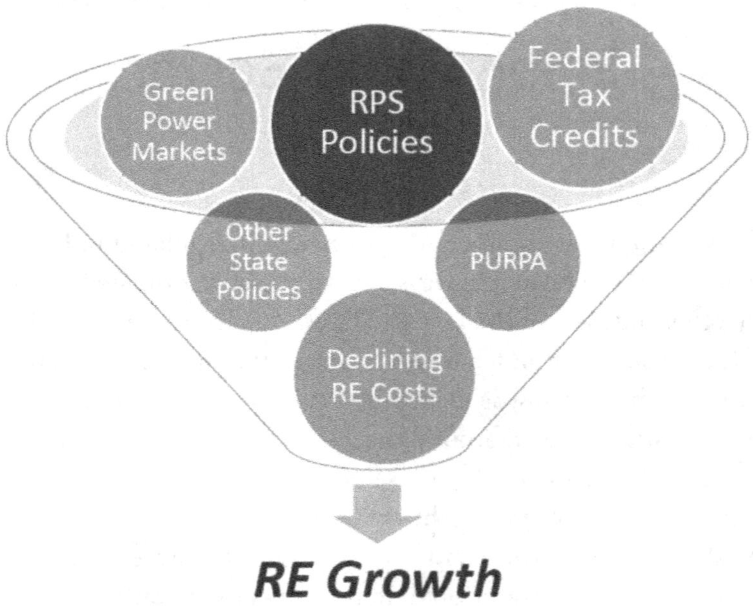

1. Galen Barbose, *U.S. State Renewables Portfolio & Clean Electricity Standards: 2023 Status Update*, U.S. Dep't of Energy, Lawrence Berkeley Nat'l Lab'y (June 2023), https://eta-publications.lbl.gov/sites/default/files/lbnl_rps_ces_status_report_2023_edition.pdf; *see also Solar Explained: Where Solar Is Found and Used*, U.S. Energy Info. Admin. (Apr. 25, 2023), https://www.eia.gov/energyexplained/solar/where-solar-is-found.php.

CHAPTER 3

Geographic and Regional Advantages

All U.S. States Are Not Equal in New Power Generation Capability

Up until now, fossil fuel or uranium (for nuclear power) was brought to where power was needed and power generation facilities were sited within reasonable transmission distance of the 332 million people in the United States. That now will change dramatically. With new laws to address climate on an expedited basis (see Chapter 2), sustainable wind and solar power within the next decade are pledged by the Biden administration to replace all fossil fuels generating electricity. This occurs during a short period of time where the demand for electricity is forecast to increase by 60 percent as electricity replaces fossil fuel furnaces for heat and powers electric vehicles.

However, the best wind and solar power locations are not near the bulk of the 332 million Americans. The best wind and solar power sources cannot be moved to where consumers are located, as are coal, oil, and natural gas generating electric power. This chapter parses where sustainable power, which will now enjoy significant subsidies for the indefinite future under now-current law (see Chapters 6, 12, and 13), is located in each region of the country. These locational variations trigger a host of legal concerns for counsel concerning local land-use and zoning permissions, new federal tax incentives and grants, exclusive state control over new transmission infrastructure to move power, and recent Supreme Court requirements to consider costs, as well as the Major Questions Doctrine restricting executive branch regulation.

All 50 U.S. states are *not* physically or legally equal regarding energy generation capabilities or options. The western states are different from the eastern states in three notable regards, although nearly 40 U.S. states have established some form of renewable or clean electricity standards to promote renewable energy, including renewable energy subsidy programs funded by system benefit charges.[1] This has locational implications: fossil fuels are transportable within the United States—by either pipeline or surface transport. Renewable energy is fixed in place and in its natural form is not transportable as are fossil fuels. While fossil fuels come to power plants near consumers, renewable energy is captured where it is and must be transmitted via expensive new infrastructure to consumers.

GHG Emissions in Different States

More GHG emissions come from the eastern portion of the United States than the West, with the limited exception of a few population centers on the West Coast in California, Oregon, and Washington.[2] GHG emission quantities are significantly related to population concentration and industrial activity. The two primary anthropomorphic sources of GHGs, CO_2 and CH_4 (see Chapter 16 on methane), are a function of human use of energy to power modern society. GHG emissions are directly correlated with population growth and with the use of fossil fuel energy in the last approximately 200 years for electricity production and other industrial and building heating applications.

If one reorients the map of GHG emissions in the United States to display emissions geographically in relationship to population, this illustrates whether a particular area of the country is producing more or less GHGs than average to serve the regional population. When GHG emissions are adjusted to per capita production, a very different map emerges. The concentration and location of carbon per capita switch around. The per capita map at this link[3] shows that the East Coast is more concentrated in population but is a less intensive emitter of GHGs adjusted for per capita population. Certain areas in the West, including Texas, the coastal states, and certain of the mountain states, are much more intensive emitters of GHGs when measured per capita.

---

1. *State Renewable Portfolio Standards and Goals,* Nat'l Conf. of State Legislatures (2020), https://www.ncsl.org/energy/state-renewable-portfolio-standards-and-goals.

2. *GHGRP Emissions by Location, Figure 1: Location and Total Reported Emissions from GHGRP Facilities (2021),* U.S. Env't Prot. Agency (Jan. 12, 2023), https://perma.cc/E9KF-CLAV.

3. Katharina Buchholz, *The States Producing the Most CO2 Per Capita,* Statista (Feb. 17, 2020), https://perma.cc/G4CH-4VN5.

Comparative Renewable Energy Potential by State

The western states have a comparative advantage in two regards applied to both newly harnessed renewable energy and traditional baseload renewable resources. First, western states have better access to solar power. Second, the western states have a disproportionate amount of nonintermittent baseload renewable resources to tap.

Intermittent Renewable Resource Potential

The amount of wind power available every single day is different across the 24 hours of the day.[4] There is a lack of empirical data on wind reliability because wind generation data from existing turbines is considered proprietary and/or business secrets that are not in the public domain. There is significant, uncontrollable variation in intermittent renewable energy output, which must be carefully managed by power grid managers.

Solar power resources are not equally distributed across the United States or the world. Latitude matters. Local climate matters. Logically, the closer a region is to the equator, the more direct and intense solar radiation it would experience.[5] There would be more uniform and intense annual insolation, with less variation in seasonal hours of sunshine. The 90° angle of insolation to fixed solar photovoltaic (PV) panels produces more electric power than if sited at more northern latitudes of the United States where there is more seasonal variation from the arc of motion of the sun resulting in not maintaining a 90° angle to a fixed PV panel.[6] Figure 3.1, illustrating available solar resources, shows a distinct advantage to the southwestern United States to produce and utilize solar power.

---

4. Stanislas Gillet, *Qualifying the Intermittency of Different Sources of Electricity Production*, LinkedIn (Aug. 3, 2023), https://www.linkedin.com/pulse/qualifying-intermittency-different-sources-production-gillet/.

5. Gerardo R. Ayala Gonzalez, *Solar Energy Potential at Different Latitudes*, Altenergy Mag (Aug. 1, 2005), http://www.altenergymag.com/article/2005/08/solar-energy-potential-at-different-latitudes/120/.

6. *Id.*

Figure 3.1[7]

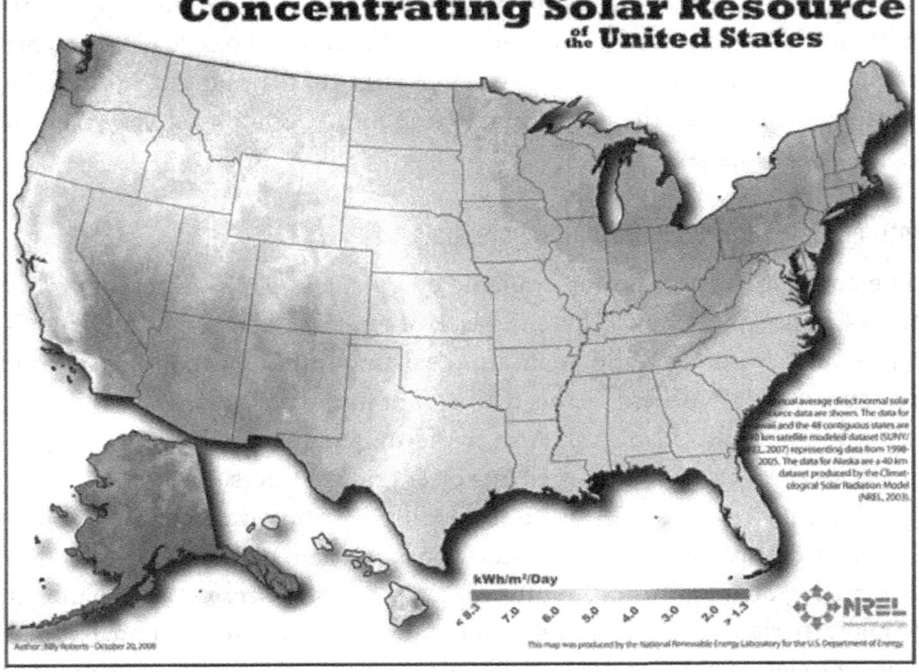

Location in the United States matters in other critical ways—as to legal and regulatory differences that affect subsidies and business models in each state. Certain states allow third-party ownership by development companies of, or by third-party investors in, residential roof solar PV systems.[8] Not all states do this. This third-party ownership has been an important business model, constituting almost half of residential solar installations nationwide and more than half of residential installations in Massachusetts, Maryland, Arizona, and California.[9]

---

7. *Solar Explained: Where Solar Is Found and Used*, *supra* note 1; *Concentrating Solar Resource of the United States*, NAT'L RENEWABLE ENERGY LAB'Y (2008), https://perma.cc/MQ5Y-SY2R.

8. Marie Donahue, *States Agree: Third-Party Ownership Enables Distributed Solar, but What's Next?*, INST. FOR LOCAL SELF-RELIANCE (Mar. 23, 2018), https://perma.cc/RC37-NLN8.

9. *See* Christian Roselund, *44% of U.S. Residential Solar Is Owned by Third Parties*, PV MAG. (Dec. 9, 2016), https://pv-magazine-usa.com/2016/12/09/44-of-u-s-residential-solar-is-owned-by-third

Because of unobstructed strong winds often reaching over ten meters per second, the waters off the American western and northeastern coastlines and the Great Lakes are prime locations for offshore wind development.[10] The eastern continental shelf and parts of the Great Lakes also feature some relatively shallow depths to which to attach offshore wind turbines. UNCLOS, the Law of the Sea, outlines that a nation's "contiguous zone" extends 24 nautical miles from the coastline.[11] In 1953, the U.S. Congress passed the Submerged Land Act, which granted states some control over the land beneath coastal waters out to three miles from the coastline and nine miles in other areas.[12]

Solar development has grown continually in the United States during the 21st century with its price falling by approximately 75 percent.[13] Renewable energy is projected to draw almost two-thirds of the spending on new power plants over the next 25 years, dwarfing spending on fossil fuels.[14] The prices for solar panels and solar PV installation costs are expected to decline 4–6 percent per year, or a total of 40–60 percent between 2015 and 2025.[15]

PV generation experiences differing rates of degradation of operational generation capacity. This affects operation and maintenance expenses and output reliability over time. The following data indicates that the scale of solar power development makes a difference (perhaps because large field-mounted projects undergo more prophylactic maintenance). Evaluating data from a single state regarding more than 90,000 solar PV facilities in operation

---

-parties/; GTM Rsch. & Solar Energy Indus. Ass'n, Solar Market Insight Report 2013 Q2, https://www.seia.org/research-resources/solar-market-insight-report-2013-q2 (last visited May 9, 2024).

10. *See* U.S. Dep't of Energy, Off. of Energy Efficiency & Renewable Energy, Computing America's Offshore Wind Energy Potential (Sept. 9, 2016).

11. U.N. Convention on the Law of the Sea, 1833 U.N.T.S. 397 (Dec. 10, 1982, entered into force Nov. 1, 1994).

12. 43 U.S.C. §§ 1301 *et seq.*

13. Mark Bolinger et al., *Utility-Scale Solar, 2022 Edition* 33, Lawrence Berkeley Nat'l Lab'y (Sept. 2022), https://perma.cc/L3EV-DBPZ.

14. Ehren Goossens, *Renewable Energy Expected to Draw Bulk of Spending for New Power Plants,* BNA Env't Rep. (June 23, 2016).

15. Alex Morales, *Distributed Solar Power Revenues May More Than Triple in Decade,* Bloomberg BNA Energy & Climate Rep. (July 21, 2015).

between 2010 and 2019 shows the following solar PV degradation rates[16] for different sizes/scales of PV units:

Size	Nameplate Capacity	Average Annual Output Degradation (%)
Small	< 25 kW	-1.51%
Medium	25 kW–1 MW	-1.08%
Large	> 1 MW	-0.56%

Small roof units experienced approximately triple the capacity degradation rates of larger field-mounted units greater than 1 MW. This indicates the importance of obtaining warranties regarding PV unit performance and degradation. This data would indicate that after 25 years of operation,

- Small-sized projects with a generating capacity of less than 25 kW would be at only 62 percent of their original generating capacity.
- Medium-sized projects with a generating capacity between 25 kW and 1 MW would be at 75 percent of their original generating capacity.
- Large-sized projects with a generating capacity exceeding 1 MW would be at 86 percent of their original generating capacity.

Regarding the other primary intermittent renewable energy source, wind power, Figure 3.2 shows the amount of potential usable wind power and its location. The amount of wind power is greater in the western states than in the eastern states.

16. Sustainable Energy Advantage, *Where Did the Sun Go? A Quick Look at Solar Panel Degradation in Massachusetts* (May 2022), https://www.seadvantage.com/blog-post/where-did-the-sun-go/. This uses Massachusetts's Department of Energy Resources data. For these calculations, production in years that had 10 percent less sunshine (i.e., irradiance) versus the 20-year average were given a 10 percent upward adjustment to their production to ensure that the analysis was "weather neutral" and was not biased by especially sunny or cloudy years.

Figure 3.2[17]

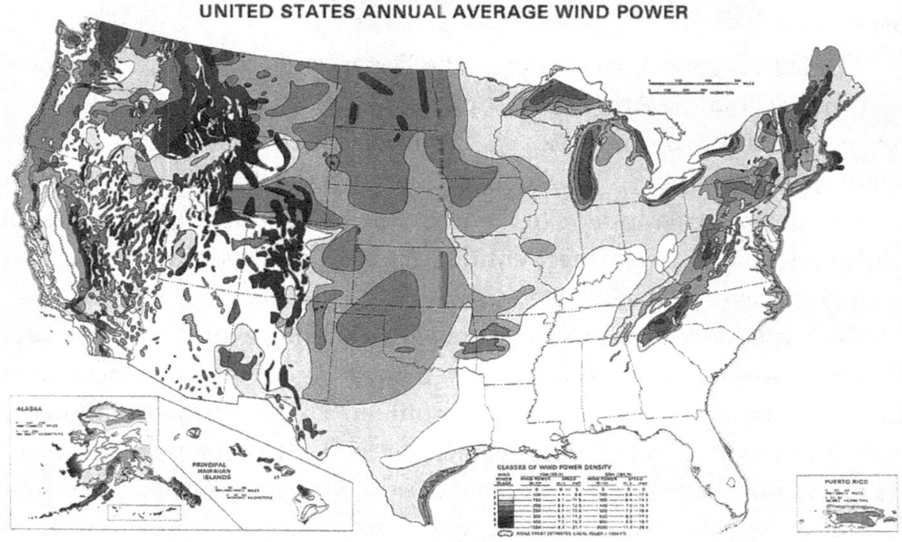

Baseload Renewable Resource Potential

The western states also are better endowed with nonintermittent, baseload renewable energy resource potential than other parts of the United States.

Hydroelectric Baseload Power

After Edison harnessed electricity in the second half of the 1870s, in 1882, the Vulcan Street Plant was the first hydropower plant to operate in the United States.[18] By the early 1900s, hydroelectric power accounted for more than 40 percent of the U.S. supply of electricity.[19] Today, more than 2,200 hydropower plants in the United States provide the country with almost

17. *United States Annual Average Wind Power*, Nat'l Renewable Energy Lab'y, https://perma.cc/44FU-GPKA (last visited Apr. 16, 2024).

18. *Hydropower Program: The History of Hydropower Development in the United States*, Bureau of Reclamation (Feb. 3, 2016), http://www.usbr.gov/power/edu/history.html.

19. *Id.*

100,000 MW of reliable hydropower capacity.[20] Hydropower is generated through run-of-river energy, stored hydro, pumped storage, or offshore hydropower.[21]

The federal government, through the Department of Interior's Bureau of Reclamation and the Army Corps of Engineers, owns 52 percent of hydropower generation and operates 133 hydroelectric power plants.[22] Private utilities, public utilities, and municipalities own the remaining 48 percent of hydropower generation. The Federal Energy Regulatory Commission (FERC) documents that "these entities operate 1,623 hydropower facilities in every region in the United States."[23]

The western states have a fair share of this existing hydropower that supplies state power resources. What is even more important is the location of the remaining available hydropower resources. The Department of Energy analyzed every two-mile stream segment in the United States for its potential for hydropower development and identified almost 500,000 sites suitable for small-scale hydropower developments, capable of providing more than 100,000 MW of power.[24] This would represent nearly 10 percent of the nation's total electric power generation capacity and approximately 80 percent of the nation's supply of renewable energy generation as of the early part of the 21st century.[25] If developed, it would more than double the contribution of hydroelectric capacity to U.S. power supply.

In incentives for new electric power supply, not all states are equal. State Renewable Portfolio Standards (RPS) programs require electric utilities and other retail electric providers to include in their retail sales a specified percentage of electricity supply annually from eligible renewable energy sources as dictated by state law. These acquisitions are evidenced by state Renewable

20. *See* Colin M. Sasthav & Gbadebo A. Oladosu, *Environmental Design of Low-Head Run-of-River Hydropower in the United States: A Review of Facility Design Models* 3, Off. of Sci. & Tech. Info. (Mar. 4, 2022), https://www.osti.gov/servlets/purl/1854486#:~:text=Over%20the%20last%20two%20centuries,of%20about%2081GW%20%5B2%5D.

21. *See Hydroelectric Power: How It Works*, U.S. Geological Surv. (June 6, 2018), https://www.usgs.gov/special-topics/water-science-school/science/hydroelectric-power-how-it-works.

22. *See All about Hydropower*, Nat'l Hydropower Ass'n, http://www.hydro.org/tech-and-policy/faq/#723 (last visited Apr. 16, 2024).

23. *See id.*

24. *See* Lea Kosnik, *The Potential for Small Scale Hydropower Development in the US*, 38 Energy Pol'y 5512 (2010).

25. *Id.* at 5512.

Energy Credits (RECs) associated with production of each megawatt-hour of generation from an eligible renewable energy facility. Chapter 8 covers RPS programs in detail. RECs exist as a separate commodity to be traded and transferred, if allowed by the state. The RPS programs in the 29 states that utilize them are very different in terms of what technologies qualify. Most of the 29 RPS states allow some form of hydropower to be eligible in their RPS programs, but almost always with environmental conditions imposed. The top ten hydropower-generating states allow hydropower facilities to qualify for their RPS REC incentives.[26]

Only two U.S. states do not have hydro-generated power: Mississippi and Delaware. The U.S. Bureau of Reclamation operates 53 power plants and is the largest wholesaler of water in the country. Coastal western states are the leading hydropower states: Washington and California. Washington leads the nation in electricity generation from hydroelectric resources and is among the top ten in electricity generation from renewable resources.[27] The Grand Coulee Dam on Washington's Columbia River has a total generating capacity of 6,809 MW and is the largest hydroelectric power producer in the United States.[28] Washington state's RPS mandates that utilities generate 15 percent of electricity from renewables by 2020 and 100 percent by 2045.[29] Hydropower projects are eligible if "incremental electricity produced as a result of efficiency improvements completed after March 31, 1999, meets certain specifications."[30] In 2013, Washington supplied a total of 29 percent of the nation's net hydroelectricity generation.[31]

---

26. *See Hydro in the States*, NAT'L HYDROPOWER ASS'N, http://www.hydro.org/why-hydro/available/hydro-in-the-states/ (last visited Apr. 16, 2024) (the top ten hydropower generation states are Alabama, Arizona, California, Idaho, Montana, New York, South Dakota, Oregon, Tennessee, and Washington).

27. *See Washington: Profile Analysis*, U.S. ENERGY INFO. ADMIN. (Mar. 16, 2023), https://www.eia.gov/state/analysis.cfm?sid=WA.

28. *Id.* (the Grand Coulee Dam is the largest generating facility of any kind in the United States measured by capacity).

29. *See Programs: Washington Renewable Energy and Energy Efficiency*, DATABASE OF STATE INCENTIVES FOR RENEWABLES & EFFICIENCY, https://programs.dsireusa.org/system/program/wa (last visited May 9, 2024).

30. *See id.*; *Renewable Energy Standard*, DATABASE OF STATE INCENTIVES FOR RENEWABLES & EFFICIENCY (Nov. 27, 2023), https://programs.dsireusa.org/system/program/detail/2350/renewable-energy-standard

31. *See id.*

California is the second-largest producer of electricity from hydropower in the United States.[32] California is also a leader in net electricity generation from several renewable energy sources, including geothermal, solar, wind, and biomass.[33] California's RPS was originally established by legislation in 2002[34] and requires California's electric utilities to increase procurement from eligible renewable resources to 33 percent by 2020, 60 percent by 2030, and 100 percent by 2045.

California has about 26,000 MW of hydropower facilities, located mostly in its eastern mountain ranges.[35] However, California's RPS limits eligible hydropower facilities to only small- and medium-scale facilities of under 30 MW each to qualify as renewable energy.[36] If a small hydropower facility causes adverse impact on in-stream beneficial uses or causes change in stream flow, it will not qualify as an eligible RPS renewable facility.[37] Besides California, 25 other states among the 29 states with RPS incentive systems allow only small hydroelectric power facilities of between 5 and 30 MW maximum size per facility to qualify for their state RPS program financial incentives.[38]

---

32. *See id.* (also noting that The Geysers facility, located in the Mayacamas Mountains, is the largest complex of geothermal power plants in the world, with more than 700 MW of installed capacity).

33. *See California: Profile Analysis*, U.S. ENERGY INFO. ADMIN. (Apr. 20, 2023), http://www.eia.gov/state/analysis.cfm?sid=CA.

34. *See RPS Program Overview*, tbl. 1 & sec. II, CAL. PUB. UTIL. COMM'N, https://www.cpuc.ca.gov/industries-and-topics/electrical-energy/electric-power-procurement/rps/rps-program-overview#:~:text=In%202002%2C%20Senate%20Bill%201078,the%20accelerated%20deadline%20into%20law (last visited May 9, 2024) (describing California's RPS program and eligible requirements); *see also Renewables Portfolio Standard (RPS) Program*, CAL. PUB. UTIL. COMM'N https://www.cpuc.ca.gov/industries-and-topics/electrical-energy/electric-power-procurement/rps (last visited May 9, 2024).

35. FERC v. Elec. Power Supply Ass'n, 136 S. Ct. 760, 767 (2016); *Hydroelectric Power*, CAL. ENERGY COMM'N, http://www.energy.ca.gov/hydroelectric/ (last visited Apr. 16, 2024).

36. *See Hydroelectric Power*, *supra* note 21; CAL. ENERGY COMM'N, RENEWABLES PORTFOLIO STANDARD ELIGIBILITY 19, tbl. 1 (5th ed. 2012), https://www.energy.ca.gov/sites/default/files/2021-07/CEC-300-2012-002-CMF.pdf.

37. *See* CAL. ENERGY COMM'N, *supra* note 35.

38. *See* Patrick Donnelly-Shores, *Will RPS Statutes Be Watered Down by Hydro?*, BERKELEY ENERGY & RESOURCE COLLABORATIVE (Apr. 3, 2013), https://web.archive.org/web/20130720071537/http://berc.berkeley.edu:80/will-rps-statutes-be-watered-down-by-hydro/.

Over a decade, California shifted to much more abundant use of non-hydro renewable resources, particularly solar power.[39] Several midcontinent states shifted to much greater use of wind power. U.S. states are shifting to more use of intermittent, rather than baseload hydro, renewable resources. This affects grid reliability. The Federal Power Act requires a FERC-issued license "to operate a hydroelectric facility on a body of water that is within Congress' jurisdiction to regulate interstate commerce."[40] Courts hold that FERC regulation preempts state and local regulation of hydro facilities in the United States.

Geothermal Baseload Renewable Resources

Geothermal is a baseload power generation resource that can be managed to produce power around the clock or at specific designated times, rather than in an intermittent pattern like generation from wind and solar power. Figure 3.3 illustrates where geothermal power resources are located in the United States, primarily in a handful of the western states and not in the eastern states. However, recently developed technology employs energy waves to melt rock to go as far as 12 miles underground—three to five times deeper than typical oil and gas drilling—reaching a layer of rock across the United States that has heat at more than 700°F, which would allow that heat to produce geothermal power in many more locations anywhere on the planet.[41]

---

39. *Nonhydro Renewables Now Routinely Surpass Hydropower Generation*, U.S. Energy Info. Admin. (July 31, 2014), https://www.eia.gov/todayinenergy/detail.php?id=17351 [https://perma.cc/HDS5-TJNQ].

40. 16 U.S.C. § 799.

41. Adele Peters, *These 12-Mile-Deep Holes Could Convert Power Plants from Fossil Fuel to Geothermal*, Fast Co. (Feb. 8, 2022), https://www.fastcompany.com/90717968/these-12-mile-deep-holes-could-convert-power-plants-from-fossil-fuel-to-geothermal.

Figure 3.3[42]

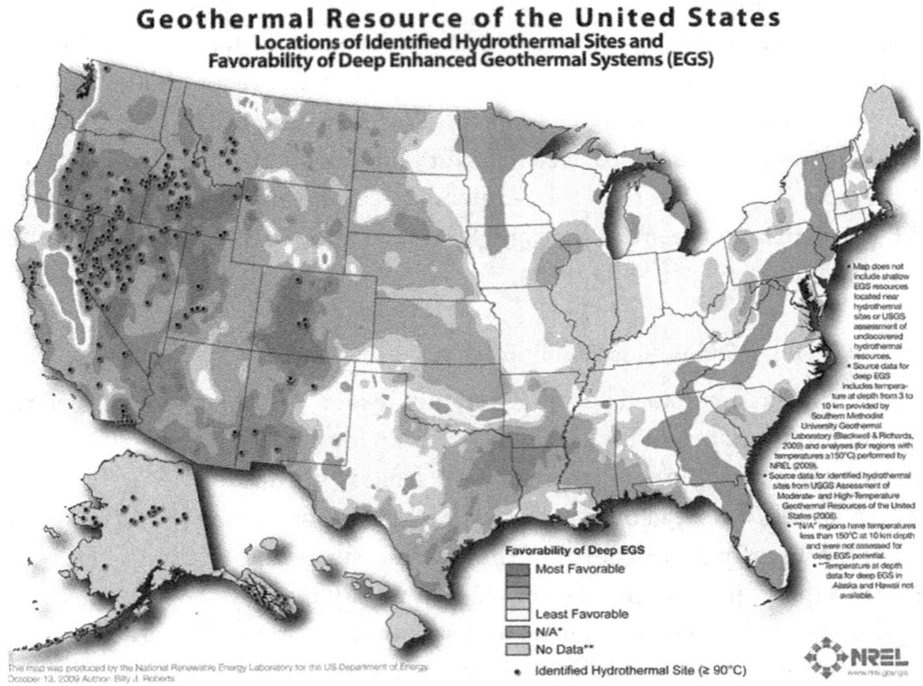

Figure 3.4 illustrates that as of 2011 California and Nevada were unique in that their major nonhydro renewable energy source was baseload geothermal energy, unlike other states, whose primary nonhydro renewable energy source was intermittent wind power in the West and Midwest and biomass power in the East. As shown in Figure 3.1, California and Nevada also have abundant non-GHG-emitting solar resources to develop. Figure 3.4 illustrates that in 2011 solar and geothermal resources, combined at approximately 0.5 percent of all electric power resources in the United States, were less than 20 percent of the contribution of wind resources and less than 10 percent of the contribution of hydroelectric resources.

42. *Geothermal Resource Data, Tools, and Maps*, Nat'l Renewable Energy Lab'y, https://www.nrel.gov/gis/geothermal.html (last visited Apr. 16, 2024) [https://perma.cc/X2F2-5HV2].

Figure 3.4[43]

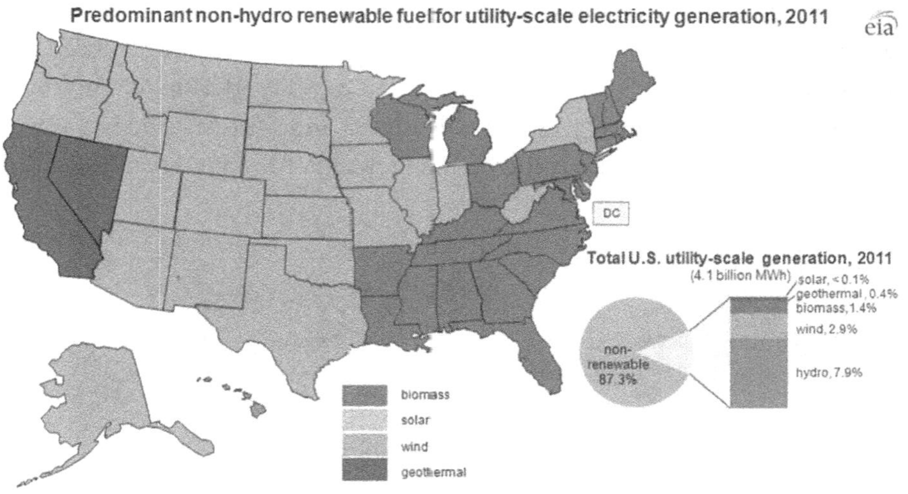

Going forward, to satisfy the ambitious push for electricity from renewable energy, the western states are the only states with both great quantities of efficient solar and hydro or geothermal power capabilities still to exploit.[44] Having the two resources combined, potential development of both intermittent and baseload renewable power is available going forward. Figure 3.5 illustrates the rapid increase in nonhydro power generation in different regions of the United States during the 21st century.[45] As of 2021, a decade later than shown in Figure 3.4, California had one-third of its power generation provided by renewable sources: 19.9 percent from solar, 8.7 percent from large and small hydro, 6.9 percent from wind, 5.5 percent from geothermal, and 2.6 percent from biomass.[46] Counting nuclear power, more than half of all California power generation was from zero-carbon generation technologies in 2021.

---

43. *Renewable Utility-Scale Electricity Production Differs by Fuel among States*, U.S. Energy Info. Admin. (May 3, 2012), https://perma.cc/9XA2-C5XG.

44. Boualem Hadjerioua et al., An Assessment of Energy Potential at Non-Powered Dams in the United States, U.S Dep't of Energy Wind & Water Power Program (2012), https://www.eere.energy.gov/water/pdfs/npd_report.pdf [https://perma.cc/C98J-U46C].

45. Barbose, *supra* note 1, at 15.

46. *2021 Total System Electric Generation*, Cal. Energy Comm'n, https://www.energy.ca.gov/data-reports/energy-almanac/california-electricity-data/2021-total-system-electric-generation (last visited Apr. 16, 2024).

As shown in Figure 3.5, the West, Midwest, and Texas had increased nonhydro electric power generation far exceeding their states' RPS goals for renewable energy based upon significant growth in solar and wind energy (see Chapter 8 on RPS). The Southeast had developed a small amount of additional renewable energy, and the Northeast and Mid-Atlantic had lagged behind their RPS standards as shown in Figure 3.5. All states are not equal.

Figure 3.5[47]

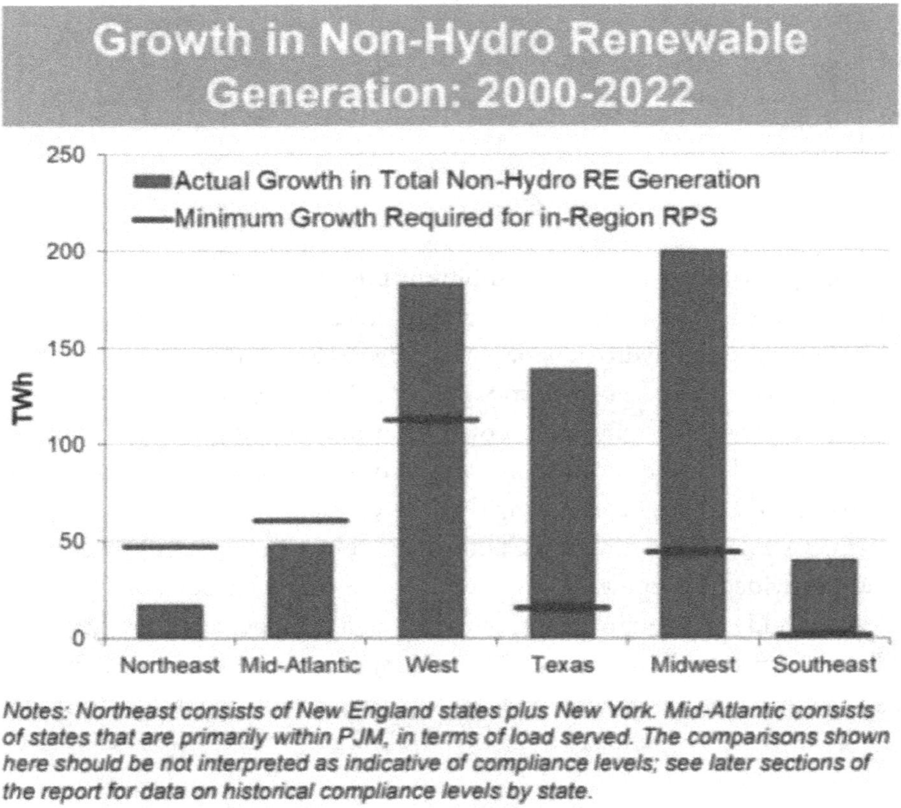

Regional Electric Regulatory Differences

States are different in terms of energy law that affects electric utility stakeholders:

47. Barbose, *supra* note 1, at 15.

- Different regional renewable energy endowments, costs of decarbonization, and difficulty in financing a lower-carbon power sector.
- State utility participation in a multistate independent system operator (ISO) wholesale energy/capacity power market.
- Different precedent in different federal circuit courts of appeals on energy decisions—notably in the 9th Circuit (covering nine western states) relaxing constitutional limitation on state energy regulatory authority.

Zero-Carbon Energy

The high electrification scenario developed by the National Renewable Energy Laboratory for its 2018 Electrification Futures study predicts that U.S. electricity consumption will increase by a factor of 1.6 by 2050 relative to the 2018 prepandemic level of approximately 4,000 terawatt-hours of electric demand. This is a substantial increase in power generation in the next generation and requires changing technologies to decarbonize power generation accomplished at a time when there is significant retirement of aging coal, nuclear, and gas-fired baseload power generation facilities—making more complex the maintenance of grid reliability.

Nuclear power operation also does not emit carbon to the atmosphere. There are approximately 93 still-operating nuclear power plants in the United States at 554 different power plant locations in 28 states with a generation capacity of 95,492 MW. See Figure 3.6. The Inflation Reduction Act also will subsidize new nuclear power plants. However, there are 12 states that currently have restrictions on the construction of new nuclear power plants: California, Connecticut, Hawaii, Illinois, Maine, Massachusetts, Minnesota, New Jersey, New York, Oregon, Rhode Island, and Vermont. While nuclear power is sometimes considered "zero carbon" in operation, even though not a renewable resource, its future remains to be determined. In the most recent three decades, only four conventional nuclear power plants were under construction in the United States:

- Two in South Carolina under construction were canceled in 2017 after a $9 billion expenditure, which drove Westinghouse, its builder, into bankruptcy under the construction contract.
- Two in Georgia are at least seven years behind schedule, and their original $14 billion price tag has at least doubled to date.

Figure 3.6[48]

U.S. Operating Commercial Nuclear Power Reactors

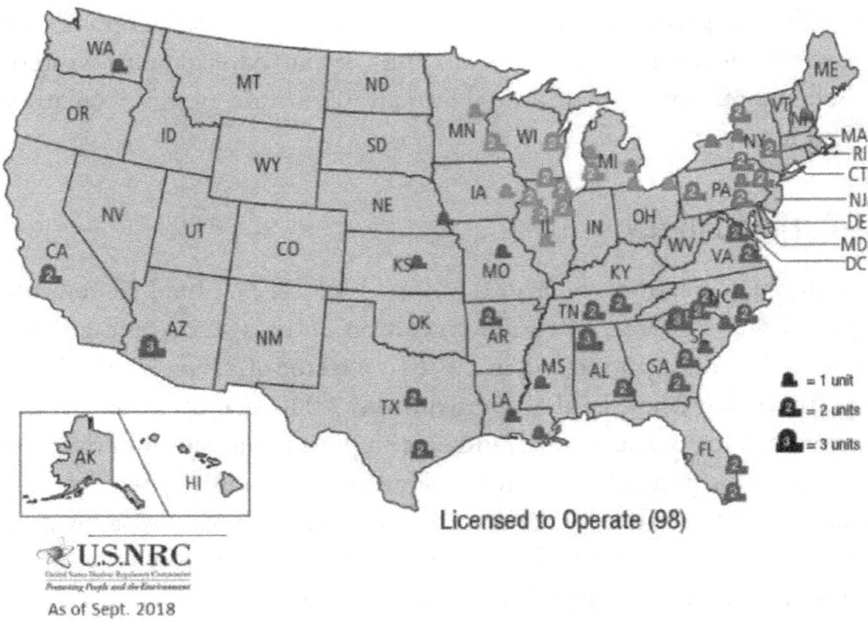

The earlier sections illustrate that regions of the country vary significantly in their extent and technologies of decarbonized power generation resources of different types to move to zero CO_2 emissions in the power sector:[49]

- The Northeast United States has the lowest-quality variable renewable energy resources and the highest CO_2 emissions and will experience the highest system average electricity cost passed on to consumers to achieve a given CO_2 emissions goal; the Northeast also is one of the most transmission-constrained regions of the country in terms of access to interregional transmission of power.

48. Cong. Rsch. Serv., 21st Century U.S. Energy Sources: A Primer 30, fig. 7 (Nov. 5, 2018), https://crsreports.congress.gov/product/pdf/R/R44854.

49. Cristian Junge et al., *Properties of Deeply Decarbonized Electric Power Systems with Storage* 52, WP 2022-003, M.I.T. Ctr. for Energy & Env't Pol'y Rsch. (Feb. 2022), https://ceepr.mit.edu/wp-content/uploads/2022/02/2022-003.pdf.

- Texas, due to its excellent wind and solar resources, anticipates a significant "natural" reduction in CO_2 per kWh generated.
- The Southeast has factors not matching the Northeast or Texas in resource challenges.

Decarbonization using intermittent variable resources will result in many hours of very low or zero marginal energy generation value along with a small number of daily hours with very high-value generation. Energy storage technologies offer a new opportunity to shift renewable power to on-peak usage when its value is highest. Due to the increased complexity of actual power system dispatch with significant storage deployment, the cost-optimal dispatch of storage, unlike the cost-optimal dispatch of generation resources, cannot be reduced to a simplistic merit-order or time-invariant economic dispatch protocol.

Ancillary energy markets are unpredictable for hybrid projects with storage, yielding additional revenue from $1 to $33/MWh.[50] 30 percent of all U.S. battery storage capacity installed through 2020 was distributed behind the meter, much of that paired with solar PV. Only 6 percent of residential and 2 percent of nonresidential PV systems included storage. Adding storage increases total installation cost by $1,000/kWh of storage on average.[51]

ISO and Federal Circuit Location Distinctions

No state or its utilities are compelled to participate in a multistate ISO or regional transmission organization (RTO). A state or its utilities electing to do so shift power from state energy regulatory discretion to exclusive federal control over all involved wholesale power sales. If a particular state and its utilities elect to participate in an ISO or RTO, either of which is subject to federal jurisdiction and oversight by FERC, a federal authority, rather than state regulators, governs legal rules. All national ISOs and RTOs are shown in Figure 3.7. Approximately 60 percent of U.S. consumers are served by a utility whose wholesale transactions and transmission tariffs are governed by an ISO or RTO. Western and southern states are not in ISOs with the exception

---

50. Joachim Seel et al., *Batteries Included: Top 10 Findings from Berkeley Lab Research on the Growth of Hybrid Power Plants in the United States*, Energy Markets & Pol'y, Berkeley Lab (Apr. 2022), https://emp.lbl.gov/publications/batteries-included-top-10-findings.

51. *Id.*

of California, which is a member of one of only two single-state ISOs in the United States (the other state is New York). Where one locates geographically in the U.S. power sector matters in terms of by whom one is regulated.

Figure 3.7[52]

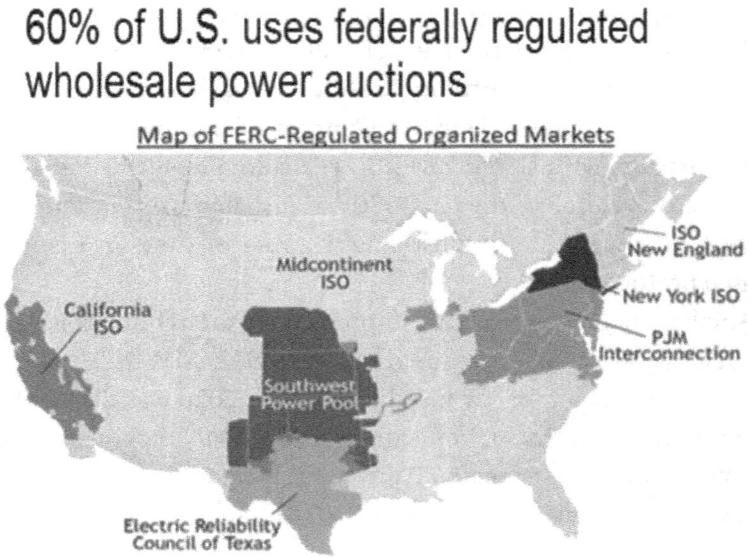

There is a growing number of power generators that are not regulated utilities but are independent less-regulated "merchant" companies as "independent power producers."[53] More than 40 percent of all power first goes through a wholesale sale before being delivered to consumers, with that percentage climbing almost 400 percent from less than 10 percent two decades earlier.[54] As noted by the Supreme Court:

> When combined with federal preemption law, one crucial result of these energy market regulatory reforms has been "a massive shift in regulatory jurisdiction from the states to FERC." . . . The upshot of

52. *Regional Transmission Organizations*, FED. ENERGY REGUL. COMM'N (Nov. 2015), https://www.ferc.gov/industries/electric/indus-act/rto/elec-ovr-rto-map.pdf [https://perma.cc/LSB2-HMVY].

53. U.S. Energy Info. Admin., *Electric Power Monthly with Data for June 2015*, at tbls. 1.2, 1.3, 1.4 & 1.5 (Aug. 2015), https://www.eia.gov/electricity/monthly/archive/august2015.pdf.

54. Fed. Energy Regul. Comm'n, Order No. 888, 61 Fed. Reg. 21,540, 21,549 (1996).

> these federal and state innovations in electricity regulation is that state regulators, despite their continued authority over rates charged directly to consumers, have much less actual authority over those rates than they did [earlier].[55]

FERC approves all RTO and ISO terms of service and the financial tariffs. In the 2016 *Hughes* matter, which was upheld unanimously by the Supreme Court, the affirmed circuit court decision notes that in recent times, the role of federal regulation has become increasingly prominent.[56] The circuit court stressed that the state of Maryland chose to abandon its prior state model "and throw in its lot with the federal interstate market," effectively compelling obedient state participation in the interstate market.[57] The Federal Power Act applies federal authority over these wholesale power transactions, preempting state authority. As held by the federal court of appeals and affirmed by the Supreme Court:

> Local utilities now obtain power largely through wholesale contracts subject to FERC's exclusive regulation, rather than through self-generated and transmitted power. . . . Although state regulators formerly took an extremely active role so as to ensure the just and reasonable retail power rates, FERC has exclusive jurisdiction over the wholesale rates that now drive the electric power market and, as a practical matter, largely determine the rates ultimately charged to the public.[58]

In addition, there are 12 separate federal circuit courts of appeals handling legal disputes concerning energy in different areas of the country.[59] None of the nine western states in the federal 9th Circuit Court of Appeals is within a multistate ISO. Moreover, the western states are not interconnected electrically to the eastern two-thirds of the United States, to Texas,

---

55. Pub. Util. Dist. No. 1 of Snohomish Cnty., Wash. v. FERC, 471 F.3d 1053, 1066–67, *aff'd in part and rev'd in part sub nom.* Morgan Stanley Cap. Grp., Inc. v. Pub. Util. Dist. No. 1, 554 U.S. 527 (2008).

56. PPL Energyplus, LLC v. Nazarian, 974 F. Supp. 2d 790 (D. Md. 2013); PPL Energyplus, LLC, v. Hanna, 977 F. Supp. 2d 372 (D.N.J. 2013) (citing New York v. FERC, 535 U.S. 1 (2002)).

57. *PPL Energyplus, LLC*, 977 F. Supp. 2d at 473.

58. *Pub. Util. Dist. No. 1 of Snohomish Cnty.*, 471 F.3d at 1066–67; *see also* Entergy v. Shumlin, 733 F.3d 393 (2d Cir. 2013).

59. *You Are Here*, U.S. DIST. CT. MIDDLE DIST. OF FLA., https://www.flmd.uscourts.gov/you-are-here (last visited Apr. 16, 2024).

or to Hawaii or Alaska in the 9th Circuit. There is a legal nonacquiescence doctrine in which a decision of one federal circuit court of appeals need not be recognized as nationally binding law outside the geographic area of states served by that particular circuit court of appeals. So each of these 11 geographic areas of the United States can be bound by different legal precedent determining electric energy law.

Texas is segregated electrically from all states as shown in Figure 3.8 (see Chapter 4 regarding Texas ERCOT). The Western Interconnection is an entire semi-isolated electric transmission system not operating pursuant to orders or tariffs of any interstate ISO as shown by comparing Figures 3.6 and 3.7.

Figure 3.8[60] U.S. Electric Transmission Grid

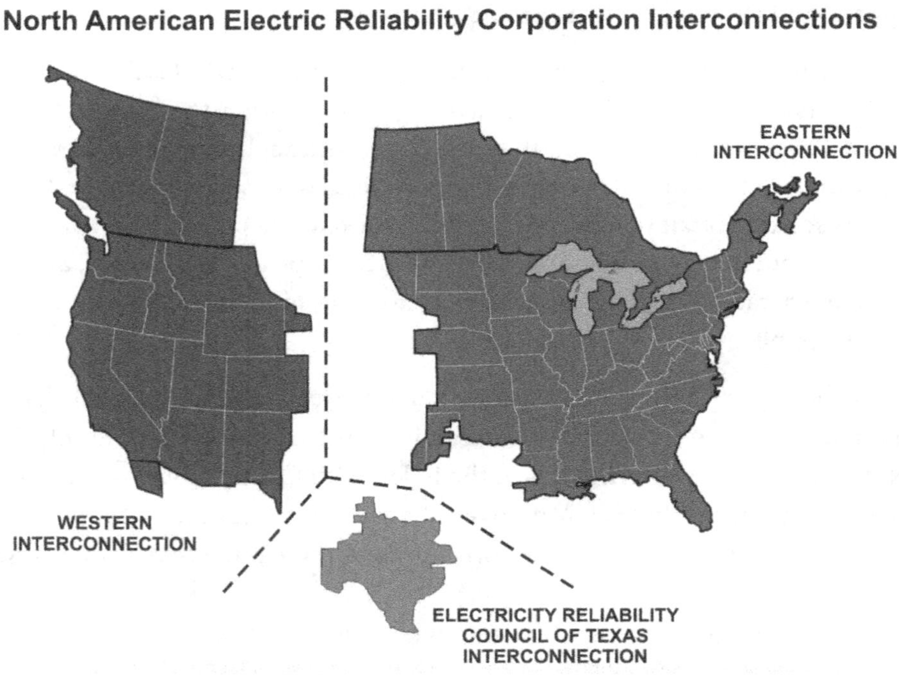

60. *Recovery Act Interconnection Transmission Planning*, Off. of Electricity (2023), https://perma.cc/J8CG-BXHE.

State Legal and Regulatory Differences regarding Electricity

Massachusetts, Rhode Island, and Connecticut have procured 3.1 GW of offshore wind and are planning to procure an additional 5.8 GW of offshore wind by 2030. For example, Massachusetts plans 3,000 MW of additional solar power through the Solar Massachusetts Renewable Target program and 4,000 MW of new offshore wind. To scale how much power this is, in the vicinity of 7,000 MW of power demand is what is used on a typical day in Massachusetts—although both solar and wind are intermittent suppliers of electricity and operate sporadically and not necessarily when demanded.

Relevant to future generation choice, during the Biden administration, FERC intensified its policy of considering and vetting natural gas fossil fuel impacts before considering and possibly approving additional natural gas projects in the United States. In 2022, FERC issued two policy statements to provide revised guidance for its review of pending and future natural gas infrastructure projects in the United States.[61] FERC stated that it will hereafter consider a more wide-ranging suite of environmental and social (negative) impacts associated with proposed natural gas projects covered by section 3 and section 7 of the Natural Gas Act and/or the National Environmental Policy Act, including foreseeable GHG emissions.[62] FERC will now examine whether a project will displace a more carbon-intensive energy source or will enhance renewable energy integration for jurisdictional natural gas infrastructure projects. This policy adds more layers for future approval of additional natural gas infrastructure not so comprehensively applied to renewable electric generation alternatives.

---

61. Updated Policy Statement on Certification of New Interstate Natural Gas Facilities, 178 FERC ¶ 61,107 (2022); Consideration of Greenhouse Gas Emissions in Natural Gas Infrastructure Project Reviews, 178 FERC ¶ 61,108 (2022).

62. A project's reasonable foreseeable GHG emissions will be based on the projected amount of capacity that will be actually used and a "100% utilization or 'full burn' rate for the proposed project's emissions" for purposes of determining whether an Environmental Assessment or Environmental Impact Statement (EIS) is required under NEPA. *Consideration of Greenhouse Gas Emissions in Natural Gas Infrastructure Project Reviews: Interim Policy Statement*, Fed. Energy Regul. Comm'n (Mar. 11, 2022), https://www.federalregister.gov/documents/2022/03/11/2022-04536/consideration-of-greenhouse-gas-emissions-in-natural-gas-infrastructure-project-reviews. See Chapter 6, "NEPA Review." There will be a rebuttable presumption that projects with 100,000 metric tons per year of emissions of carbon dioxide equivalents (CO_2e) will be deemed to have significant impact on climate change and will thus require an EIS.

Going forward, FERC is exercising greater power over electricity because of the greater number of wholesale generators supplying a much larger percentage of electricity now, the growing extent of state retail deregulation, and the greater ISO and RTO participation in wholesale power markets. The next chapter maps the key legal distinctions between federal and state legal power over electricity in 21st-century America— a fast-changing legal regulatory divide that is essential for electric stakeholders and their counsel to understand along with the most recent Supreme Court decisions interpreting it.

CHAPTER 4

The Major Questions Doctrine and Power

"In the early 20th century, state and local agencies oversaw nearly all generation, transmission, and distribution of electricity."[1]

—U.S. Supreme Court

Telescoping climate challenges (Chapter 2) and recent changes to address climate in the National Environmental Protection Act and IRS and environmental laws (Chapter 6) change what needs to be in the legal toolbox to practice energy, environmental, and land-use law. Electric power is regulated uniquely and differently than everything else in the U.S. economy. There has now surfaced a distinct Tenth Amendment tension pitting reserved state law against federal law regarding electric power. The uniqueness of electric power law and the Supreme Court's "bright line" separation of (state/local/federal) powers regarding electricity, coupled with recent new laws, alter the legal challenges confronting federal and state (Public Utility Commission) energy regulatory officials and legal counsel serving the 2,200 U.S. electric utilities, co-ops, and municipal power providers in the United States, as well as counsel for "merchant" unregulated power generators. This chapter brings all these stakeholders current on how electric power will be legally regulated.

Electricity is distinct and different than every other form of energy, and not coincidentally, it is legally regulated uniquely in the United States compared to every other energy source or item: nothing else in the U.S. economy is regulated exclusively by completely different levels of government depending on whether individual transactions related to it are deemed wholesale transactions or retail transactions. There is exclusively bifurcated government regulation of U.S. electric power.

1. Allco Fin. Ltd. v. Klee, 861 F.3d 82, 98 (2d Cir. 2017) (quoting FERC v. Elec. Power Supply Ass'n, 136 S. Ct. 760, 767 (2016)).

Every electricity stakeholder and their counsel need to understand the legal nuances of these distinctions. The U.S. system regulates electric power distinctly from how oil and gas are regulated or, for that matter, how electric power is regulated in any of the other 197 nations in the world: the federal government exercises exclusive regulatory authority over certain essential power activities, while states exercise exclusive authority over other essential aspects.

The "Bright Line" between Federal and State Legal Power over Electricity

Sales of Wholesale Power

For more than eight decades, the Federal Power Act of 1935 has separated state and federal authority over the electric power market.[2] The act provides that the Federal Energy Regulatory Commission (FERC) has jurisdiction over interstate and wholesale power sales; however, its authority does not extend to "any other sale of electric energy."[3] Sections 205 and 206 of the act[4] empower FERC exclusively to regulate the commerce and rates for the interstate and wholesale sale and transmission of electricity in the United States.[5]

While the Federal Power Act grants FERC exclusive jurisdiction over transmission of electric energy in interstate commerce and sales of electricity in wholesale transactions, as well as rates, terms, and conditions of jurisdictional service, this contrasts with the Natural Gas Act,[6] which vests FERC comprehensively with exclusive jurisdiction over transportation of natural gas in interstate commerce; sales or resale of natural gas; and rates, terms, and conditions of jurisdictional service. Sections 4 and 5 of the Natural Gas Act grant FERC exclusive authority to ensure that the rates, charges, practices, rules, and regulations governing interstate natural gas sales and transportation are "just and reasonable" and nondiscriminatory, authorizing FERC to grant certificates for the construction and operation of interstate natural gas

2. Federal Power Act, 16 U.S.C. § 824 (2012).

3. *Id.* § 824(b)(1).

4. *Id.* § 824(d)–(e).

5. Pub. Util. Dist. No. 1 of Snohomish Cty. v. FERC, 471 F.3d 1053, 1058 (9th Cir. 2006), *aff'd in part, rev'd in part sub nom.* Morgan Stanley Cap. Grp., Inc. v. Pub. Util. Dist. No. 1, 554 U.S. 527 (2008).

6. 15 U.S.C. §§ 717 *et seq.*

pipelines. The Filed Rate doctrine, applying both to natural gas and to electric power contracts and tariffs, requires that lawful, just, and reasonable rates for jurisdictional service must be on file with and approved by FERC and not countermanded by states.

The U.S. Supreme Court established what the court called a "bright line" between federal and state jurisdiction. The Court held that "Congress meant to draw a bright line, easily ascertained and" not requiring case-by-case analysis "between state and federal jurisdiction."[7] The rates, terms, and provisions of any wholesale sale or transmission of electricity in interstate commerce are solely within federal jurisdiction and control, not state authority:[8] "FERC has exclusive authority to set and to determine the reasonableness of wholesale rates."[9]

Three U.S. States Are Exceptions Not Subject to the Supreme Court's "Bright Line" of Power Separation

As to exceptions where FERC does not exercise this authority: Alaska and Hawaii are not subject to FERC's authority because they do not engage in interstate commerce in electricity due to their geographic isolation from all other states. In addition, there is one exception to FERC authority in the continental United States: Texas enjoys a unique exception. Texas is regulated by the Electric Reliability Council of Texas (ERCOT) and has repeatedly fought against its physical or deemed interconnection to interstate commerce.

In 1935, with the intent to avoid Federal Power Act regulation, Texas opted to isolate its electricity from interstate commerce. ERCOT operates the only major U.S. grid that does not have a capacity market—a system that provides payments to operators to be on standby to supply power during severe capacity shortages; Texas is the only state to rely almost completely on market price to achieve resource adequacy. The Energy Policy Act of 2005 included exemptions specifically for ERCOT from additional requirements imposed by the Federal Power Act:

---

7. Fed. Power Comm'n v. S. Cal. Edison Co., 376 U.S. 205, 215–16 (1964).

8. New England Power Co. v. New Hampshire, 455 U.S. 331, 340 (1982).

9. Miss. Power & Light Co. v. Mississippi *ex rel.* Moore, 487 U.S. 354, 371 (1988) ("FERC has exclusive authority to determine the reasonableness of wholesale rates."); *accord Pub. Util. Dist. No. 1 of Snohomish Cty.*, 471 F.3d at 1058, 1066–67.

- An explicit exemption from FERC authority.[10]
- An explicit exemption from the native load service obligation or long-term contracts to supply electricity.[11]
- An exemption from price transparency in markets for the sale and transmission of electric energy in interstate commerce.[12]

Reserved State Authority over Electricity

Section 201(a) of the Federal Power Act provides that federal regulation "only extend[s] to those matters which are not subject to regulation by the States."[13] So what are those state-regulated areas? FERC lacks jurisdiction over the siting, construction, and ownership of generation or transmission facilities, which remain exclusively within state jurisdiction.[14] That construction of facilities subject to state control is analyzed in Chapter 10. There is a brewing and still percolating jurisdictional conflict over exactly where the state versus federal jurisdictional "bright line" begins and ends:

- FERC orders for the last three decades inject competition and regionalization through independent system operator (ISO) and regional transmission organization (RTO) orders into wholesale power dispatch and transmission to operate electric systems most efficiently and to minimize consumer costs of power.
- Several states have subsidized with Renewable Energy Credits (RECs) and ZECs (see Chapter 8) and/or ordered their utilities to purchase certain wholesale power that is not currently at lowest consumer cost.
- ISOs and RTOs have explored a carbon price in the wholesale energy market, a Forward Clean Energy Market, and an Integrated Clean Capacity Market to incorporate state preferences to purchase certain electric power output not minimizing consumer cost.

---

10. 16 U.S.C. § 824p(k).
11. *Id.* § 824q(h).
12. *Id.* § 824t.
13. *Id.* §§ 819 (repealed 1935), § 824(a) (2015).
14. Piedmont Env't Council v. FERC, 558 F.3d 304, 309–10, 313 (4th Cir. 2009); *see* Transmission Planning and Cost Allocation by Transmission Owning and Operating Public Utilities, FERC Order No. 1000, 76 Fed. Reg. 49,842 (Aug. 11, 2011), 136 FERC ¶ 61,051 at para. 287 (2011).

Supreme Court Federal/State Legal "Bright Line"

Supreme Court decisions repeatedly have upheld these unique regulatory distinctions between the federal and state levels of U.S. government:[15]

- "[I]t is difficult to conceive of a more basic element of interstate commerce than electric energy, a product used in virtually every home and every commercial or manufacturing facility. No State relies solely on its own resources in this respect."[16]
- "FERC has exclusive authority to set and to determine the reasonableness of wholesale rates."[17] Sale of electric energy at wholesale is any sale to any person for resale,[18] which is beyond any state authority.[19]
- "It is common ground that if FERC has jurisdiction over a subject, the States cannot have jurisdiction over the same subject."[20]
- "'FERC is a creature of statute' and thus 'has no power to act unless and until Congress confers power upon it.'"[21]

When a transaction is subject to exclusive federal jurisdiction and FERC regulation, state regulation is preempted as a matter of federal law and the U.S. Constitution's Supremacy Clause, according to a long-standing and consistent line of rulings by the U.S. Supreme Court.[22] The Supreme Court in 1986,[23] 1988,[24] 2003,[25] and 2008[26] reaffirmed the Constitution's Supremacy

15. New England Power Co. v. New Hampshire, 455 U.S. 331, 340 (1982).

16. FERC v. Mississippi, 456 U.S. 742, 757 (1982).

17. Miss. Power & Light Co. v. Mississippi *ex rel.* Moore, 487 U.S. 354, 371 (1988); *accord* Pub. Util. Dist. No. 1 of Snohomish Cty. v. FERC, 471 F.3d 1053, 1066 (9th Cir. 2006); *aff'd in part and rev'd in part sub nom.* Morgan Stanley Cap. Grp., Inc. v. Pub. Util. Dist. No. 1, 554 U.S. 527 (2008).

18. 16 U.S.C. § 824(d) (2012).

19. Fed. Power Comm'n v. S. Cal. Edison Co., 376 U.S. 205, 214 (1964); Indep. Energy Producers Ass'n v. Cal. Pub. Util. Comm'n, 36 F.3d 848 (9th Cir. 1994); S. Cal. Edison Co., 70 FERC ¶ 61,215, 61,675 (1995).

20. *Miss. Power & Light Co.*, 487 U.S at 377 (Scalia, J., concurring).

21. E.P.S.A. v. FERC, 753 F.3d 216, 220 (2015).

22. *See, e.g.*, New England Power Co. v. New Hampshire, 455 U.S. 331, 338–44 (1982). *See also* Montana-Dakota Utils. Co. v. Nw. Pub. Serv. Co., 341 U.S. 246, 251 (1951); Nantahala Power & Light Co. v. Thornburg, 476 U.S. 953 (1986); *Miss. Power & Light Co.*, 487 U.S. 354; Entergy La., Inc. v. La. Pub. Serv. Comm'n, 539 U.S. 39 (2003).

23. *Nantahala Power & Light Co.*, 476 U.S. at 966.

24. *Miss. Power & Light Co.*, 487 U.S. at 370.

25. *Entergy La., Inc.*, 539 U.S. at 49–50.

26. *See* Morgan Stanley Cap. Grp., Inc. v. Pub Util. Dist. No. 1, 554 U.S. 527, 531 (2008).

Clause applied to negate state energy regulation over wholesale transactions otherwise subject to FERC's exclusive authority. Where a state imposes a wholesale contract rate different than that set by FERC by either "law or policy," those state "contracts will be considered to be void *ab initio*."[27]

Expanded Federal Authority Due to State Market Restructuring

The Supreme Court found that now with markets partially deregulated, regulating "practices" is accomplished by more general rules of market operation.[28] With fewer utility-specific tariffs, FERC's role has shifted from reviewing whether an individual firm's action is an unjust, unreasonable, or discriminatory practice to overseeing the elements and results of wholesale markets' operations.[29] The Supreme Court noted in 2002 that "[s]ince 1935, and especially beginning in the 1970s and 1980s . . . . the number of electricity suppliers has increased dramatically."[30]

Deregulation

There has been a significant change on which level of government regulates what, resulting from state retail deregulation. Thirteen states have deregulated their retail power systems, and an additional five states have partially deregulated systems, allowing competition in their power markets (see Chapter 13). Several of these 13 deregulating states compelled their regulated electric utilities to divest their power generation facilities to the highest bidders, in an effort to encourage competition[31] (see Chapter 13, "The Changing Checkerboard, Stakeholders, Assets in Deregulated Electric Markets in the U.S."). This divestiture causes utilities in these states to purchase their power through a wholesale transaction, greatly increasing the number

---

27. Conn. Light & Power Co., 70 FERC ¶ 61,012, 61,029–30 (1995).

28. Global Crossing Telecommc'ns, Inc. v. Metrophones Telecommc'ns, Inc., 550 U.S. 45, 56–58 (2007).

29. *See generally Morgan Stanley Cap. Grp., Inc.*, 554 U.S. 527; New York v. FERC, 535 U.S. 1 (2002).

30. *New York*, 535 U.S. at 7.

31. *See* John Kwoka et al., *Divestiture Policy and Operating Efficiency in U.S. Electric Power Distribution*, 38 J. Regul. Econ. 86–109 (2010), https://www.researchgate.net/publication/225652262_Divestiture_policy_and_operating_efficiency_in_US_electric_power_distribution. The paper establishes that 28 of the 73 electric utilities in the database underwent a major divestiture during the sample period ending in 2003, while 45 of them did not. Of the 28 divesting utilities, eight involved mandatory divestitures; the remaining 20 were nonmandatory divestitures of power generation facilities. In this limited period, this represented 22 percent of all generation capacity in the United States.

of wholesale transactions that automatically become subject to exclusive federal authority. As noted by the federal courts and affirmed by the Supreme Court, these independent market participants are the new competitive reality in power and energy markets:

> When combined with federal preemption law, one crucial result of these energy market regulatory reforms has been "a massive shift in regulatory jurisdiction from the states to FERC." . . . The upshot of these federal and state innovations in electricity regulation is that state regulators, despite their continued authority over rates charged directly to consumers, have much less actual authority over those rates than they did [earlier].[32]

State Clean Energy Targets

Figure 4.1[33]

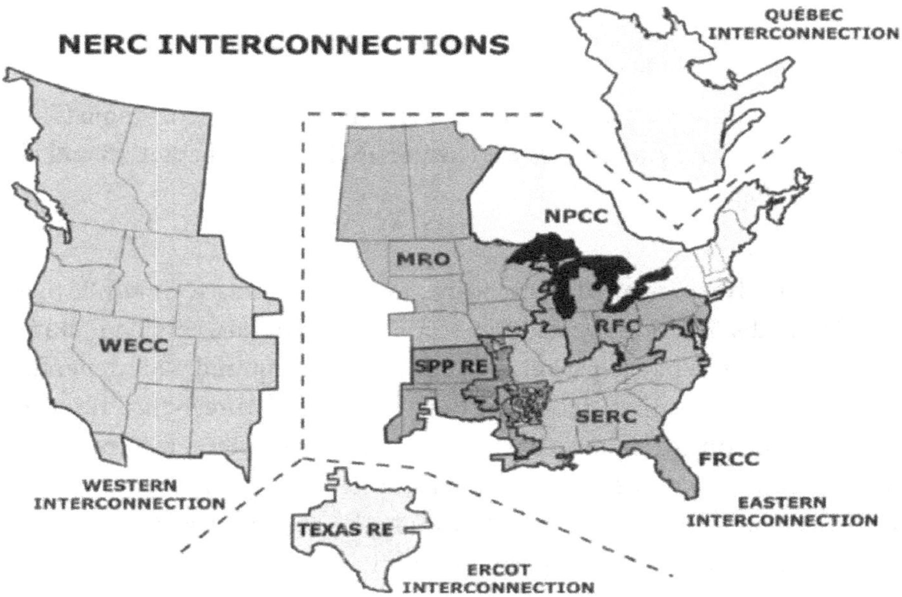

32. Pub. Util. Dist. No. 1 of Snohomish Cty. v. FERC, 471 F.3d 1053, 1066–67 (9th Cir. 2006).

33. U.S. Dep't of Energy, Annual U.S. Transmission Data Review (2018), https://www.energy.gov/sites/prod/files/2018/03/f49/2018%20Transmission%20Data%20Review%20FINAL.pdf.

By December 2020, ten U.S. states, along with Washington, DC, and Puerto Rico, had committed to the goal of attaining 100 percent carbon-free clean electric energy by the year 2050.[34] See Chapter 13, "Independent 'Merchant' Owners and Distributed Generation." In 2022, Rhode Island established the earliest total clean electricity target in the country, requiring that 100 percent of the state's electricity demand be met with renewable energy by 2033. Many of these states also obtain all wholesale power through their participation in a multistate ISO, regulated by FERC, which dispatches wholesale power daily based on lowest cost. ISOs are required to comply with the rules and regulations of FERC and the North American Electric Reliability Corporation (NERC) regions shown in Figure 4.1.

FERC Orders Promoting Electric Sector Competition

Next, we place in context key FERC orders promoting electric sector competition.

Power Generation Markets

The power sale markets are different depending on which geographic ISO or RTO a stakeholder participates in (covered in detail in Chapter 13 and also mapped in Figure 3.7).

Demand Response

FERC initially sanctioned demand-response programs formally in 2008 with its Order No. 719, years after some wholesale markets had allowed demand-response participation.[35] Order No. 719 required all independent system-operator markets to accept bids from demand-response resources in a manner comparable to other resources, to permit aggregators to bid demand response on behalf of retail customers, to modify market rules as needed to maintain reliability, and to study the need for further reforms to eliminate barriers to demand-response participation. FERC Order No. 745

34. "In addition to the ten states, plus Washington D.C. and Puerto Rico, who have committed to clean energy by 2050, another ten states also have 100% clean energy goals including nineteen large utilities, approximately 210 cities, and more than 150 businesses pledging to achieve 100% clean energy or net-zero emissions." Sophia Ptacek, *Race to 100% Clean*, NAT. RES. DEF. COUNCIL (Dec. 2, 2020), https://www.nrdc.org/resources/race-100-clean.

35. *See* Wholesale Competition in Regions with Organized Electric Markets, 125 FERC ¶ 61,071 (Oct. 28, 2008) (codified at 18 C.F.R. pt. 35).

requires ISOs to pay the same price to owners of demand-response resources responding in times of power system need as to suppliers of conventional power.[36] The Supreme Court upheld FERC authority to issue Order No. 745.[37]

Power Transmission Markets

The U.S. "grid" is composed not only of the approximately 4,800 interconnected power generation resources in the United States but also of wire cable to connect them with consumers and the hardware to manage them in an energized instantaneous network.[38] The high-voltage transmission network at 230 kV and higher comprises 167,000 miles of transmission lines in America.[39] The transmission system operates at 15 different voltage levels.

Competition

FERC fostered greater wholesale competition in a series of orders:

- **Order No. 888**[40] established the foundation for nondiscriminatory open access transmission service by electric utilities. All regulated public utilities that own, control, or operate jurisdictional transmission facilities are required by FERC Order No. 888 to have open access transmission tariffs, which must track the FERC-mandated pro

36. Demand Response Compensation in Organized Wholesale Energy Markets, FERC Order No. 745, 134 FERC ¶ 61,187, at para. 2 (2011). FERC's rules defined demand response as "a reduction in the consumption of electric energy by customers from their expected consumption in response to an increase in the price of electricity" as an incentive designed to induce lower consumption of electric energy. 18 C.F.R. § 35.28(b)(4).

37. FERC v. E.P.S.A., 136 S. Ct. 760 (2016).

38. *Glossary*, U.S. Energy Info. Admin., http://www.eia.doe.gov/glossary/glossary_e.htm#electr_pow_grid (last visited Apr. 17, 2024).

39. Stan Mark Kaplan, *Electric Power Transmission: Background and Policy Issues* 1–5, n.3, Cong. Rsch. Serv. (Apr. 14, 2009), https://digital.library.unt.edu/ark:/67531/metadc700834/.

40. Promoting Wholesale Competition through Open Access Non-Discriminatory Transmission Services by Public Utilities; Recovery of Stranded Costs by Public Utilities and Transmitting Utilities, Order No. 888, FERC Stats. & Regs. ¶ 31,036, 61 Fed. Reg. 21,540 (May 10, 1996), *clarified*, 76 FERC ¶ 61,009 (1996) and 76 FERC ¶ 61,347 (1996), *reh'g*, Order No. 888-A, FERC Stats. & Regs. ¶ 31,048, 62 Fed. Reg. 12,274 (Mar. 14, 1997), *clarified*, 79 FERC ¶ 61,182 (1997), *reh'g*, Order No. 888-B, 81 FERC ¶ 61,248, 62 Fed. Reg. 64,688 (Dec. 9, 1997), *reh'g*, Order No. 888-C, 82 FERC ¶ 61,046 (1998), *aff'd*, Transmission Access Pol'y Study Grp. v. FERC, 225 F.3d 667 (D.C. Cir. 2000), *aff'd*, New York v. FERC, 535 U.S. 1 (2002).

forma open access transmission tariff.[41] The pro forma tariff requires that the transmission provider plan and construct additional transmission facilities so as to be able to serve network customers "on a basis comparable to the Transmission Provider's delivery of its own generating and purchased resources to its Native Load Customers."[42]

- **Order No. 888-A**[43] promulgated a revised pro forma open access transmission tariff (OATT) providing an incumbent customer with a right of first refusal (ROFR) to match the duration offered by a new customer at a full OATT rate.
- **Order No. 890**[44] amended the Order No. 888 pro forma tariff to require transmission providers to plan for the needs of their customers on a comparable basis to planning for their own needs.[45]
- **Order No. 2000**[46] encouraged the development of RTOs to form "competitive wholesale electric [] markets,"[47] which were required to incorporate nondiscriminatory transmission service.[48]

Renewable Power Integration

Hourly scheduling of resources for transmission service was the norm. Subsequently:

---

41. 18 C.F.R. § 35.28(a), (c) (2011); *New York*, 535 U.S. at 36 ("The Court also relies on FERC's explanation that the prospect of unbundling retail transmission and generation 'raises numerous difficult jurisdictional issues that we believe are more appropriately considered when the Commission reviews unbundled retail transmission tariffs that may come before us in the context of a state retail wheeling program.' Order No. 888, at 31,699.") (ratifying core provisions of Order No. 888).

42. Preventing Undue Discrimination and Preference in Transmission Service, 72 Fed. Reg. 12,266, 12,521 (Mar. 15, 2007) (to be codified at 18 C.F.R. pts. 35, 37).

43. Idaho Power Co. v. FERC, 312 F.3d 454, 457 (D.C. Cir. 2003); *see also* Promoting Wholesale Competition through Open Access Non-Discriminatory Transmission Services by Public Utilities; Recovery of Stranded Costs by Public Utilities and Transmitting Utilities, 62 Fed. Reg. 12,274, 12,274 (Mar. 14, 1997) (to be codified at 18 C.F.R. pt. 35).

44. 72 Fed. Reg. 12,266 (Mar. 15, 2007) (to be codified at 18 C.F.R. pts. 35, 37), *reh'g*, Order No. 890-A, 73 Fed. Reg. 2,984 (Jan. 16, 2008), *reh'g*, Order No. 890-B, 123 FERC ¶ 61,299 (2008), *reh'g*, Order No. 890-C, 126 FERC ¶ 61,228 (2009).

45. N.Y. Reg'l Interconnect, Inc. v. FERC, 634 F.3d 581, 584 (D.C. Cir. 2011).

46. Regional Transmission Organizations, Order No. 2000, FERC Stats. & Regs. ¶ 31,089 (1999), *order on reh'g*, Order No. 2000-A, FERC Stats. & Regs. ¶ 31,092 (2000), *petitions for review dismissed*, Pub. Util. Dist. No. 1 of Snohomish Cty. v. FERC, 272 F.3d 607 (D.C. Cir. 2001).

47. Maine Pub. Utils. Comm'n v. FERC, 454 F.3d 278, 280–81 (D.C. Cir. 2006).

48. *See* 18 C.F.R. § 35.34(k)(7).

- **Order No. 764**[49] required that every transmission customer moving power be given the ability to adjust its schedule at 15-minute intervals to reflect changing conditions and to accommodate intermittent renewable power.
- **Order No. 792**[50] amended FERC's pro forma Small Generator Interconnection Agreement and Small Generator Interconnection Procedures to include small energy storage resources.
- **Order No. 819**[51] allows energy storage resources to provide further ancillary services, including primary frequency response service.
- **Order No. 1000**[52] creates obligations for transmission system owners to engage in regional and interregional transmission planning and requires incumbent transmission providers, utilities, and the RTOs that manage regional multistate transmission access to the grid to remove ROFRs from FERC-approved transmission tariffs.

Transmission Queues

Despite the previous transmission reform orders issued by FERC, in 2022, more than 1,400 gigawatts of generation and storage were waiting to connect in interconnection queues nationwide, still unaware about the costs and timing of interconnecting projects—creating a critical path barrier to new distributed power. There could be an average four-year wait for additional NEPA Environmental Impact Statement compliance, as well as a multilayered multiyear wait while transmissions providers/utilities conduct studies on the impacts of individual interconnection requests for distributed power resources and any transmission upgrades they necessitate.

In 2023, FERC issued Order No. 2023 to address these backlog and delay issues by implementing a "first-ready, first-served" cluster interconnection study process as deployed in various ISOs and state markets to replace

---

49. Integration of Variable Energy Resources, Order No. 764, FERC Stats. & Regs. ¶ 61,246, at paras. 2, 21, 97 (2012). FERC Order No. 764 requires that interconnecting distributed generators pay for any incremental generation required, subject to reimbursement for generators who later interconnect to the increased transmission capacity.

50. Small Generator Interconnection Agreements and Procedures, 78 Fed. Reg. 73,240, 73,241 (Dec. 5, 2013) (to be codified at 15 C.F.R. pt. 35). The Small Generator Interconnection Procedures rules apply to facilities and resources that produce or store less than 20 MW.

51. Third-Party Provision of Primary Frequency Response Service, 80 Fed. Reg. 73,965, 73,966 (Nov. 27, 2015) (to be codified at 18 C.F.R. pt. 35).

52. Transmission Planning and Cost Allocation by Transmission Owning and Operating Public Utilities, Order No. 1000, FERC Stats. & Regs. ¶ 61,051, at paras. 7, 313 (July 21, 2011).

the "first-come, first-served" approach. This "first-ready, first-served" protocol will require each applicant to move quickly and pay significant sums of money to hold its priority position for interconnection. Deposits to pay for interconnection study costs were proposed as follows:

- For projects 20–80 MW, $35,000 + $1,000 per MW
- For projects 80–200 MW, $150,000
- For projects greater than 200 MW, $250,000

Transmission providers would be required to allow more than one resource to colocate on a shared site behind a single point of interconnection and share a single interconnection request. Of note regarding federal-state conflicts, Massachusetts limits the capacity of renewable energy projects that want to net meter their output to no more than a cumulative 2 MW, which must be placed at a single site, through a single point of interconnection, and with a single meter, which is not consistent with this proposal. See Chapter 9. Under the FERC order, interconnection customers would be able to add additional generating facilities to an existing interconnection request in the queue under certain circumstances without automatically losing their position in the interconnection queue. New customers joining a cluster study would also need to demonstrate that they have obtained 100 percent site control for their proposed generating facility and continue demonstrating commercial readiness, with transmission providers determining appropriate acreage requirements for each technology.

In Order No. 2023, FERC dispenses with the prior first stage of feasibility studies as part of an interconnection application and instead requires transmission operators to provide accessible, updated "heat maps" that show graphically where there is transmission system congestion that would require system upgrades to accommodate more power generation using the grid. This creates an initiative-oriented, proactive role for lawyers/stakeholders utilizing these additional tools accessing this critical path transmission interconnection obstacle.

State Control of Generation Technology

States have enacted statutes mandating the technology of energy generation to be procured by their regulated electric utilities apart from least-cost competitive wholesale electricity markets. These state procurements of wholesale power are not based on FERC's least cost of power principles and are not technology neutral. Such individual state mandates for a particular type of power when the state participates in a multistate federally regulated ISO or RTO (see Chapter 13 and Figure 3.7) can cause conflicts and raise jurisdictional questions for state regulatory commissions and FERC.

Supreme Court's Recent Restrictions on Federal Electric Power Regulation

Next, this chapter concisely highlights what every stakeholder needs to know regarding what the U.S. Supreme Court has done since 2014 to erode and undercut the discretion of the president and the EPA to regulate the electric power sector or its choice of dispatch of electric power or to impose restrictions on emission of carbon from power plants.

The Most Cited Supreme Court Decision in the Last Half Century Concerns Regulation of Electric Power—Now Overruled

Chevron v. Natural Resources Defense Council is the Supreme Court's most cited administrative law precedent year after year[53] and is one of the seven most cited Supreme Court cases in the history of the Court.[54] As of the beginning of the 2020s, the *Chevron* case had been cited since its issuance in 1984 by a total of 18,256 subsequent U.S. court decisions.

So-called *Chevron* deference by courts to EPA or FERC decisions involves a two-part test: first, has Congress spoken to the precise issue at hand? If yes, then any additional deference to the executive branch ends there; if no, then the court must not substitute its own judgment; it must determine if the agency has made a permissible interpretation of the statute and, if so, defer to the executive branch as long as the action is not "arbitrary and capricious."[55]

---

53. Christopher J. Walker, *Most Cited Supreme Court Administrative Law Decisions*, YALE J. REGUL. & ABA SECTION OF ADMIN. L. & REGUL. PRAC.: NOTICE & COMMENT (Oct. 9, 2014), http://yalejreg.com/nc/most-cited-supreme-court-administrative-law-decisions-by-chris-walker/.

54. Lauren Mattiuzzo,, *Most-Cited U.S. Supreme Court Cases in HeinOnline: Part III*, HEIN ONLINE BLOG (Sept.. 26, 2018), https://home.heinonline.org/blog/2018/09/most-cited-u-s-supreme-court-cases-in-heinonline-part-iii/.

55. Chevron U.S.A., Inc. v. NRDC, Inc., 467 U.S. 837 (1984); Burlington Truck Lines v. United States, 371 U.S. 156 (1962); Motor Vehicle Mfrs. Ass'n v. State Farm Mut., 463 U.S. 29 (1983) (applying the "hard look" doctrine).

In a 6-3 decision in two cases, *Loper Bright Enterprises, et al. v. Raimondo* consolidated with *Relentless Inc. v. Department of Commerce,* in 2024 the Supreme Court majority opinion written by the Chief Justice held that:

> "*Chevron* defies the command of the APA that 'the reviewing court'—not the agency whose action it reviews—is to 'decide all relevant questions of law' and 'interpret . . . statutory provisions. . . . We have instead expected Congress to delegate such authority 'expressly' if at all, ibid., for '[e]xtraordinary grants of regulatory authority are rarely accomplished through 'modest words,' 'vague terms,' or 'subtle device[s],' *West Virginia v. EPA*, 597 U. S. 697, 723 (2022).

In concurring, Justice Thomas expressed that:

> "*Chevron* deference also violates our Constitution's separation of powers, as I have previously explained at length. . . . *Michigan v. EPA*, 576 U. S. 743, 761–763 (2015) (concurring opinion) . . . It allows 'the Executive . . . to dictate the outcome of cases through erroneous interpretations.' (citation omitted). . . . *Michigan*, 576 U. S., at 763, n. 1 (opinion of Thomas, J.) . . . by allowing agencies to definitively interpret laws so long as they are ambiguous, Chevron 'transfer[s]' the Judiciary's 'interpretive judgment to the agency.' . . . see also . . . *Michigan*, 576 U. S., at 761–762 (opinion of Thomas, J.)."

The dissent notes that "As if it did not have enough on its plate, the majority turns itself into the country's administrative czar." Kagan, J, dissenting, (joined by Sotomayor, J. and Jackson, J.). A concurring opinion in a footnote by Justice Gorsuch rebuts this dissent for not noting that two members of the Supreme Court authored books or articles allegedly noting that the *Chevron* decision conflicts with Section 706 of the Administrative Procedure Act:

> "Nor is the dissent's list of Harvard's finest administrative law scholars entirely complete. See [Justice] S. Breyer et al., Administrative Law and Regulatory Policy 288 (7th ed. 2011) (acknowledging that *Chevron* deference 'seems in conflict with . . . the apparently contrary language of 706); [Justice] Kagan 212 (likewise acknowledging *Chevron* deference rests upon a 'fictionalized statement of legislative desire'"

Along with the *Loper* decision, the earlier ensemble of Supreme Court opinions below substantially changes the future of energy, land-use, and environmental law and practice. While different presidential administrations can influence federal agencies' regulatory interpretations once every four or more years, *Loper* speeds up and multiplies potential changes in law. *Loper* now shifts to more than 800 different Article III federal judges the task to determine *de nova* what Congress meant or intended in statutes, potentially leading to different or contradictory decisions in federal circuits and district courts. Since *Loper* held that *Chevron* was incorrect based on the Administrative Procedure Act rather than based on the Constitution, Congress and the President also could amend or change the APA statute's delegation or reinstate *Chevron*.

The Supreme Court beginning in 2014 with regard to electricity and the electric power sector of the economy perhaps less noticeably pivoted away from its traditional *Chevron* deference to federal agency regulations and rules through a series of three decisions that weakened the past four decades of court deference to EPA decisions regarding electric power, especially regarding climate change issues. The following three Supreme Court decisions announced in 2014, 2015, and 2016 set the stage for the Supreme Court in 2024 in *Loper* overturning the 1984 *Chevron* decision in a 6-3 majority/dissent split of Justices resembling the 6-3 Supreme Court split in 2022 that created the "Major Questions Doctrine" limiting federal executive branch regulation of the electric power sector of the U.S. economy.

No Federal Presidential Legal "Tailoring" for the Electric Sector

In 2010, the Obama administration implemented its greenhouse gas (GHG) "Tailoring Rule," which provided for a phasing in of federal Clean Air Act monitoring and permitting requirements for CO_2 emissions from U.S. electric power plants.[56] The EPA refused to apply this requirement to all sources emitting more than 250 or 100 tons per year (tpy)—the congressional

56. Prevention of Significant Deterioration and Title V Greenhouse Gas Tailoring Rule (Final Rule), 75 Fed. Reg. 31,514 (June 3, 2010); James E. McCarthy, EPA Regulation of Greenhouse Gases: Congressional Responses and Options, 7-5700, R41212, Cong. Rsch. Serv. (Feb. 5, 2015); Justice Scalia's dissenting opinion in *Massachusetts v. EPA*, 549 U.S. 497, 558 (2007), noting that under such an interpretation of what could be regulated, "[i]t follows that everything airborne, from Frisbees to flatulence, qualifies as an 'air pollutant.'"

threshold standards provided in the Clean Air Act—but rather elected to regulate only sources emitting more than 75,000 tpy (for existing facility modifications) or 100,000 tpy (for new facility construction).[57] Following the Congress's tonnage threshold would have increased the number of covered sources under just this one program from 280 CO_2-emitting sources to what EPA characterized as the "absurd result" of affecting and regulating as many as six million sources of GHG emissions.[58] This is a disparity of 400:1. The EPA's regulatory preamble asserted that literally following the Clean Air Act statutory provisions was

> so severe that they bring the judicial doctrines of "absurd results," "administrative necessity," and "one-step-at-a-time" into the Chevron two-step analytical framework for statutes administered by agencies .... Under the "administrative necessity" doctrine ... an agency may depart from statutory requirements that, by their terms, are impossible to administer .... Under the "one-step-at-a-time" doctrine, Congress is presumed ... to have intended to allow the agency to administer the statutory requirements on a step-by-step basis .... Each of these doctrines supports our action separately .... Therefore, we conclude that under the "absurd results" doctrine ... the approach we take in this Tailoring Rule ... is also justifiable under the "administrative necessity" and "one-step-at-a-time" doctrines.[59]

In doing so, EPA elected to unpack and unload every argument and doctrine in its legal arsenal to justify executive branch discretionary variation from specific provisions in statutory law. This rule expanded executive discretion because

- It changed congressionally specified quantitative thresholds.
- It applied to CO_2 in a federal statute at that time that hardly mentioned CO_2.
- Congress had never ratified the Kyoto Treaty regarding carbon emissions.

57. 75 Fed. Reg. 31,523 (pmbl.) (June 3, 2010).

58. "The 'absurd results' doctrine, which authorizes agencies to apply statutory requirements differently than a literal reading would indicate, as necessary to ... avoid absurd results ...." 75 Fed. Reg. 31,516, 31,536 (pmbl.) (June 3, 2010).

59. 75 Fed. Reg. 31,514, 35,317–18 (pmbl.) (June 3, 2010).

It is debatable whether this was the federal rule—dealing only with reporting emissions—with the best facts to test the boundaries of separation of powers, as the Obama administration attempted then to do. For environmental, land-use, and environmental lawyers, their areas of law are the ones that most incorporate and rely on

- Quantitative values (tons per year, parts per million, cost per kWh, etc.)
- Measurable metrics (minimum required land areas, feet of setbacks, degrees of warming impact, measurable costs and benefits, etc.)
- Warming impacts affecting the whole world, with U.S. law only local
- Unclear redressable injury remedy costs and benefits from any judicial decisions.

The U.S. Supreme Court declared in *Utility Air Regulatory Group v. EPA* that this unilateral agency "tailoring" of the Congress's specified quantitative value was not permissible:

> EPA lacked authority to "tailor" the Act's unambiguous numerical thresholds of 100 or 250 tons per year to accommodate its greenhouse-gas-inclusive interpretation of the permitting triggers. Agencies must always "give effect to the unambiguously expressed intent of Congress." . . . The power to execute the laws does not include a power to revise clear statutory terms that turn out not to work in practice.[60]

The U.S. Supreme Court held that "EPA's interpretation was unreasonable because it would bring about an enormous and transformative expansion in EPA's regulatory authority without clear congressional authorization," where a court should demand "clear congressional authorization."[61] By invoking this entire arsenal of legal doctrines that could support creative executive discretion, on these facts the EPA emptied the legal arsenal of justifications for liberal exercise of executive deference. There followed after this 2014 decision in sequence additional Supreme Court declarations, in 2015 requiring more economic consideration and support for environmental/energy/climate regulations (*Michigan v. EPA*), in 2016 enjoining entirely environmental/energy/

60. Util. Air Regul. Grp. v. EPA, 573 U.S. 302 (2014).
61. *Id.* (citing FDA v. Brown & Williamson Tobacco Corp., 529 U.S. 120, 160 (2000)).

climate regulations rather than only enjoining their challenged provisions (*West Virginia v. EPA*), and in 2022 the Major Questions Doctrine blocking environmental/energy/climate regulations (*West Virginia v. EPA*). This suite of decisions significantly changed the practice of environmental, land-use, climate, and energy law, as analyzed in the following sections of this chapter and detailed further in Part II of this book.

Costs Imposed on the Electric Power Sector Must Be Analyzed

EPA imposed regulations for Maximum Achievable Control Technology (MACT) Mercury Air Toxics (MATS) standards for mercury emissions where "[t]he final rule sets standards for all hazardous air pollutants . . . emitted by coal- and oil-fired electric generating units . . . with a capacity of 25 megawatts or greater."[62] The MATS standards promulgated by EPA were estimated to avert up to 11,000 premature deaths, 4,700 heart attacks, and 130,000 asthma attacks every year.[63] However, virtually none of this was related to what the rule regulated directly: more than 99 percent of the value of estimated avoided deaths and monetized benefits would come from the rule's effect on emissions of particulate matter (PM) and not mercury, which PM reductions were characterized as so-called cobenefits, rather than from identified reduction of mercury and other air toxic chemical exposure. EPA already regulates PM as a criteria pollutant under other provisions of the Clean Air Act and other EPA regulations.[64]

EPA could quantify only $4–6 million in benefits attributed to reductions of hazardous air pollutants such as mercury, a fraction of 1 percent of the EPA-claimed total long-term benefits of $37–90 billion annually; EPA provided no statistical basis or medical proof.[65] EPA was found by the Supreme Court to have exercised authority beyond the bounds of reasonable interpretation and was "capricious" regarding what was "appropriate and necessary."[66] Chief Justice Roberts called it an "end-run" around the statutory language, which "raises the red flag" regarding counting as much as

62. *Basic Information about Mercury and Air Toxics Standards*, U.S. Env't Prot. Agency (Jan. 8, 2024), https://www.epa.gov/mats/basic-information-about-mercury-and-air-toxics-standards; National Emission Standards for Hazardous Air Pollutants, 77 Fed. Reg. 9304 (2012).

63. *Healthier Americans*, U.S. Env't Prot. Agency (Jan. 25, 2024), https://www.epa.gov/mats/healthier-americans.

64. 40 C.F.R. pt. 50.

65. *Id.*

66. Michigan v. EPA, 576 U.S. 743 (2015).

$90 billion of benefits under the MATS rule from reductions of pollutants that are regulated under other sections of the Clean Air Act. The Supreme Court thereafter overturned MATS because

> EPA must consider cost—including cost of compliance—before deciding whether regulation is appropriate and necessary . . . . One would not say that it is even rational, never mind "appropriate," to impose billions of dollars in economic costs in return for a few dollars in health or environmental benefits.[67]

The *Michigan* Court made clear that "it will be up to the agency to decide . . . how to account for cost."[68]

Federal Agencies May Not Reorganize Power Dispatch or Regulate Power Sector Carbon Emissions

The Supreme Court issued a major decision in 2022 on federal regulatory power over the electric sector in *West Virginia v. EPA*[69] that changed fundamental separation of powers in U.S. regulation of the power sector:

- Diminishing U.S. executive branch discretion in enacting programs
- Causing the courts to defer less to unilateral executive branch decision-making
- Increasing the power of the 50 states vis-à-vis the federal government regarding climate change and Clean Air Act implementation

The Court found that the Clean Air Act forbids EPA, which the act directs to regulate major pollution sources employing Best System of Emission Reduction, to accomplish that by regulating emissions only from those sources. In the Obama administration Clean Power Plan regulation, EPA had stated that area-wide or regional initiatives to reduce emissions could utilize a statewide system of emissions reduction for purposes of Clean Air Act section 111 New Source Performance Standards Best System of Emission Reduction regulation.

The concurring opinion by Justice Gorsuch reinforces state "sovereign immunity" to make these clean air power plant decisions that cannot be abrogated by the federal EPA by "unintentional, oblique, or otherwise

67. *Id.*
68. *Id.*
69. West Virginia v. EPA, 142 S. Ct. 2587 (2022).

unlikely" intrusions on these interests[70] without clear statements by the Congress for the EPA to do so:

> "The importance of the issue," along with the fact that the same basic scheme EPA adopted "has been the subject of an earnest and profound debate across the country, . . . makes the oblique form of the claimed delegation all the more suspect."

Importantly linking this case on power plant emissions to larger issues of federal agencies affecting industry dispatch of electric power, the Court declared that "precedent counsels skepticism toward EPA's claim" that the statutory provision authorizes it to adopt "a [power] generation shifting approach." The majority opinion noted that the Congress did not grant EPA any authority to change the U.S. energy delivery system, and EPA admitted that it had no expertise in this energy area. The dissenting opinion written by Justice Kagan calls the majority opinion's exercise of judicial control to restrain the executive branch regulation of fossil-fuel-fired power plants "frightening." In contrast, the concurring opinion penned by Justice Gorsuch and joined by Justice Alito restricts executive branch power.

Major Questions Doctrine Limits Future Presidential Regulation of Electric Power Generation

The majority 6–3 opinion in the 2022 *West Virginia* opinion relies heavily on recent prior application of the relatively new Major Questions Doctrine to restrict executive branch discretion and deference when the EPA acts without clear congressional instruction on matters on which "[t]he electric power sector is among the largest in the U.S. economy, with links to every other sector." [71] The concurrence finds that the "agency seeks to "intrud[e] into an area that is the particular domain of state law"—where there is extensive state control over electric power.[72]

In the year before the *West Virginia* decision, the Major Questions Doctrine was utilized to strike federal exercise of authority in two other major

70. *Id.* at 2620 (quoting NFIB v. OSHA, 142 S. Ct. 661, 669 (2022) (Gorsuch, J., concurring).

71. *Id.* at 2622 (quoting Nathan Richardson, *Keeping Big Cases from Making Bad Law: The Resurgent "Major Questions" Doctrine*, 49 CONN. L. REV. 355, 388 (2016)).

72. *Id.* at 2621 (referencing FDA v. Brown & Williamson Tobacco Corp., 529 U.S. 120, 160 (2000); MCI Telecommc'ns Corp. v. Am. Telephone & Telegraph Co., 512 U.S. 218, 231 (1994); Util. Air Regul. Grp. v. EPA, 573 U.S. 302, 324 (2014); Ala. Ass'n of Realtors v. Dep't of Health & Hum. Servs., 141 S. Ct. 2485, 2488–89 (2021)).

realms almost as pervasive as electric power. In 2021, the Supreme Court granted an emergency motion to end the nationwide temporary renter eviction moratorium for nonpayment of rent imposed by the Centers for Disease Control and Prevention (CDC). The Supreme Court explained that the CDC's action was of major national significance because it covered 80 percent or more of the nation; created an estimated economic impact of tens of billions of dollars; and interfered with the landlord-tenant relationship, which the Court declared as "the particular domain of state law."[73]

A few months before the *West Virginia* decision, the Supreme Court halted the enforcement of the Department of Labor Occupational Safety and Health Administration's (OSHA's) COVID-19 masking or vaccination and testing emergency temporary standard applying to all employers with 100 or more employees, quoting its 2021 decision discussed in the previous paragraph: "There can be little doubt that OSHA's mandate qualifies as an exercise" of "powers of vast economic and political significance."[74] The concurring opinion by Justice Gorsuch (joined by Justices Thomas and Alito) states that the Major Questions Doctrine is a key element of the separation of powers in the Constitution.

Both of these Major Questions Doctrine case opinions rendered less than a year before the *West Virginia* opinion were cited again multiple times in the majority opinion, the dissent, and the concurring opinion in the landmark *West Virginia* decision. Perhaps the most relied-on precedent in *West Virginia* is the Supreme Court decision in *Utility Air Regulatory Group v. EPA*, discussed earlier.[75] The implications of this Supreme Court decision will have significant impacts on the electric power sector and stakeholders. Attorneys general from one-third of the U.S. states recently filed an opposition to the FERC Rulemaking on Regional Transmission Planning and Cost Allocation[76] stating that such "national scale energy grid regulation" is a Major Question given the massive economic consequences from revamping the electric generation mix of the grid.

This decision also raises questions about EPA use of so-called cap-and-trade Clean Air Act regulations imposed on power plants where regulated

73. Ala. Ass'n of Realtors v. Dep't of Health & Hum. Servs., 141 S. Ct. 2485 (2021).

74. Nat'l Fed. of Indep. Bus. v. Dep't of Labor, Occupational Safety & Health Admin., 142 S. Ct. 661 (2022).

75. Util. Air Regul. Grp. v. EPA, 573 U.S. 302 (2014) ("agency has no power to 'tailor' legislation to bureaucratic policy goals by rewriting unambiguous statutory term").

76. FERC Docket RM 21-17 (2021).

sources can purchase credits from other entities making the reductions to their source site emissions. Similar cap-and-trade regulatory mechanisms employed in the 21st century by the environmental agencies of both the federal and state governments have been the subject of consistent challenges, and courts have found fault with cap-and-trade programs affecting the generation of electricity.

Supreme Court Reinforces the Federal/State Split of Authority

In the *Hughes v. Talen Energy* case, the Supreme Court unanimously upheld FERC's exclusive federal authority to control electric wholesale markets in the United States. Even indirect interference of states in these markets is not within state powers. The Supreme Court *Hughes* opinion notes that "[o]ver the past few decades, many states, including Maryland, have deregulated their energy markets" and utilities "purchase that electricity from independent power generators."[77] The Court notes that the electricity market has evolved to become a "competitive interstate business and FERC's role has evolved accordingly."

Discriminatory State Energy Regulation Is Constitutionally Prohibited

> *"[I]t is difficult to conceive of a more basic element of interstate commerce than electric energy, a product used in virtually every home and every commercial or manufacturing facility. No State relies solely on its own resources in this respect."*[78]

State discrimination against electric sector stakeholders in different geographic locations is outlawed by the Constitution. Here is a brief overview, and readers are urged to also read coverage of this applied to renewable electric power in Chapter 8, where this topic is more fully analyzed. States or localities are not permitted to favor their own in-locality sources of electric power while denying such benefits to out-of-region power. The Supreme Court in its opinion quoted before the start of this paragraph declared that electricity, to a degree not affecting other items in commerce, is in interstate commerce.[79]

---

77. Hughes v. Talen Energy Mktg., LLC, 136 S. Ct. 1288, 1291–92 (2016).
78. FERC v. Mississippi, 456 U.S. 742, 757 (1982).
79. *See id.*; *see also* New York v. Fed. Energy Regul. Comm'n, 535 U.S. 1, 16 (2002).

Geographically discriminatory legal provisions are reviewed under a separate provision of the Constitution, the Dormant Commerce Clause, subject to judicial "strict scrutiny," and a state must establish that the statute or regulations serve a compelling state interest through the least restrictive means affecting interstate commerce to achieve that interest.[80] According to the Supreme Court, "even if environmental preservation were the central purpose of the pricing order, that would not be sufficient to uphold a discriminatory regulation."[81]

States cannot regulate in ways where the practical effect is to control conduct in other states. States may also not "provid[e] a direct commercial advantage to local business."[82] "Statutes that discriminate by 'practical effect and design,' rather than explicitly on the face of the regulation, are similarly subjected to heightened constitutional scrutiny."[83] A state cannot regulate to favor, or require use of, its own in-state energy resources,[84] nor can it, by regulation, harbor beneficial energy-related resources originating in the state.[85] For example, an Oklahoma energy statute overturned by the Supreme Court involved only a 10 percent allocation of the market to in-state energy producers, where the market changed its use of almost all out-of-state coal to "[in-state] Oklahoma coal in amounts ranging from 3.4% to 7.4% of their annual needs, with a necessarily corresponding reduction in purchases of Wyoming coal."[86] So even a small or de minimis degree of discriminatory impact or effect of geographic discrimination is still unconstitutional.

A state regulatory order cannot require the use of in-state fuels even for the rationale to satisfy federal Clean Air Act environmental requirements.[87] States cannot give income tax credits solely to in-state producers.[88] A law that

---

80. *See* Entergy v. Shumlin, 733 F.3d 393 (2d Cir. 2013); Gade v. Nat'l Solid Wastes Mgmt. Ass'n, 505 U.S. 88, 105 (1992); Norris v. Lumbermen's Mut. Cas. Co., 881 F.2d 1144, 1150 (1st Cir. 1989).

81. West Lynn Creamery v. Healy, 512 U.S. 186, 202 n.20 (1994).

82. NW States Portland Cement Co. v. Minnesota, 358 U.S. 450, 458 (1959); Rocky Mountain Farmers Union v. Goldstene, 843 F. Supp. 2d 1071, 1099 (E.D. Cal. 2011).

83. Tri-M Grp., LLC v. Sharp, 638 F.3d 406, 427 n.28 (3d Cir. 2011).

84. Wyoming v. Oklahoma, 502 U.S. 437, 454–56 (1992); Alliance for Clean Coal v. Craig, 840 F. Supp. 554, 560 (N.D. Ill. 1993).

85. New England Power Co. v. New Hampshire, 455 U.S. 331, 339 (1982).

86. *Wyoming*, 502 U.S. at 455. *See also* Alliance for Clean Coal v. Miller, 44 F.3d 591, 596 (7th Cir. 1995).

87. *Alliance for Clean Coal v. Miller*, 44 F.3d at 596–97.

88. New Energy Co. of Ind. v. Limbach, 486 U.S. 269, 271, 278–80 (1988). *See also* Or. Waste Sys., Inc. v. Dep't of Env't Quality of Or., 511 U.S. 93, 99–100 (1994).

is geographically discriminatory is "virtually per se invalid."[89] The Supreme Court held that statutes that establish regional barriers (not necessarily just a state-based barrier) and discriminate only against some states rather than all states violate the Commerce Clause.[90] The Supreme Court repeatedly held that state regulation does not need to "be drafted explicitly along state lines in order to demonstrate its discriminatory design."[91]

State statutes or regulations found to discriminate against out-of-state interests based on geography or favoring local interests are found to be per se invalid.[92] Subsidy of in-state businesses, even if the taxes to raise the subsidies are imposed on all commerce, can be stricken under strict scrutiny.[93] Even where a statute is drafted in a fashion that is facially neutral rather than expressly discriminatory, for example by not mentioning or in any other way distinguishing the geographic location of the commerce but otherwise employing terms that result in a geographic preference, a court may apply a strict scrutiny standard where the purpose or effect of a state law is discriminatory.[94]

Continue with us in the next chapter to dig deeper to analyze the current impact of a law from a half century ago, twice upheld by the U.S. Supreme Court, which started and continues the most fundamental change in the electric power sector and its environmental impact. It contains and continues legal obligations, rights, and opportunities that after the 2022 enactment of the Inflation Reduction Act (covered in Chapter 6) now combine to become the primary engine propelling future power development.

---

89. Dep't of Revenue of Ky. v. Davis, 553 U.S. 328, 338–39 (2008).

90. *See* Hunt v. Wash. Apple Advertising Comm'n, 432 U.S. 333, 350–52 (1977).

91. Rocky Mountain Farmers Union v. Corey, 730 F.3d 1070, 1097 (2013) (quoting Amerada Hess Corp. v. N.J. Dep't of Treasury, 490 U.S. 66, 76 (1989)). *See also* C & A Carbone, Inc. v. Town of Clarkstown, 511 U.S. 383, 391 (1984); Fort Gratiot Sanitary Landfill v. Mich. Dep't of Res., 504 U.S. 353 (192); Dean Milk v. Madison, 340 U.S. at 349 (1951).

92. *See* City of Philadelphia v. New Jersey, 437 U.S. 617, 624 (1978) (noting that if a statute is facially discriminatory, it is virtually per se invalid); Gen. Motors Corp. v. Tracy, 519 U.S. 278, 287 (1997); *Dep't of Revenue of Ky.*, 553 U.S. at 338–39.

93. West Lynn Creamery, Inc. v. Healy, 512 U.S. 186 (1994); Alliance for Clean Coal v. Miller, 44 F.3d 591, 596 (7th Cir. 1995).

94. *Carbone*, 511 U.S. at 391 (1994) ("[O]rdinance is no less discriminatory because in-state or in-town processors are also covered by the prohibition."); *Hunt*, 432 U.S. at 352–53; S.-Cent. Timber Dev., Inc. v. Wunnicke, 467 U.S. 82, 145 (1984).

CHAPTER 5

Legal Foundations of Power Regulation

There is a statute that supported renewable power from the Carter presidency that many have assumed is no longer still the law. It remains in place, and with the federal shift indefinitely into the future to renewable energy to replace traditional energy, "past is prologue." That key statute remains in place and now becomes even more central as the legal fulcrum leveraging the elevation of sustainable power to replace fossil-fuel energy in the U.S. economy. This chapter reassesses that legal fulcrum.

Here we dig a level deeper: since Edison first harnessed electricity less than 150 years ago—major parts of the United States were only electrified in the 20th century—the Federal Power Act establishes the foundation of the electric energy industry. The act is occasionally amended, and the Public Utility Regulatory Policies Act of 1978 (PURPA) amendments to it have been U.S. law for almost a half century.[1] PURPA has been upheld by the Supreme Court on several recent occasions. Now moving forward, PURPA looms even larger given two recent scientific and policy concerns regarding our energy supply now taking center stage in the 21st century:

- Climate change and warming, compelling pledges by both the United States and other developed nations to reduce greenhouse gas (GHG) emissions of the power sector
- Policy to electrify major sectors of the U.S. infrastructure and the entire economy, thus substantially increasing future demand for power:
  - Electrification of built space conditioning, supplanting gas and oil heating
  - Electrification of the transportation sector, supplanting gasoline and diesel fuel
  - Research to electrify aviation

1. 16 U.S.C. §§ 824a–w.

For more on the penetration of electrification into key U.S. industries, see Chapter 1. For more on lower levels of state government control over key renewable infrastructure, see Chapters 10 and 11.

PURPA remains the key federal fulcrum for how electricity going forward will be sited, produced, delivered, and consumed. Since 1978 the primary incentive for competitive renewable power development has been PURPA, which was "designed to combat the nationwide energy crisis."[2] PURPA permitted new renewable electric power generation projects to operate separately and independently from state-regulated utilities as well as removed conventional "utility-type" regulation by the states of eligible PURPA Qualifying Facilities (QFs).[3] PURPA requires utilities to purchase all of the renewable power produced by these projects at a favorable "Avoided Cost" price.[4] PURPA is still in full force and is something that everyone in the electric industry needs to understand.

Benefits of PURPA QF Status

Under PURPA, if a power generation project satisfies specified federal legal requirements in place since its enactment in 1978, that project and its developer, owner, and operator receive certain regulatory exemptions and benefits. For a renewable or waste-fueled generation project to be a QF under PURPA, it must produce electric energy solely by the use of biomass, waste, renewable resources, geothermal resources, or any combination thereof and must not be greater in gross capacity than 80 megawatts (MW). This 80 MW size limit for so-called Small Power Producers is eliminated if the generation project also cogenerates sequentially two sources of energy, for example electricity and useful heat.[5] In the original regulations, QF status was lost if more than 50 percent of a project was owned by an electric utility or its subsidiary (not including gas or telephone utilities). This 50 percent ownership limitation was eliminated by Energy Policy Act (EPAct) 2005 amendments to PURPA.

2. FERC v. Mississippi, 456 U.S. 742, 745 (1982).
3. 16 U.S.C. § 796.
4. Am. Paper Inst. v. Am. Elec. Power Serv. Corp., 461 U.S. 402 (1983).
5. 16 U.S.C. § 796 (2015).

QF status is available to two types of generation technologies, cogenerators and Small Power Producers.[6] The benefits of QF status principally apply to generation projects that sell their power to other utilities or other electric power consumers, as listed in Table 5.1.

Table 5.1: Benefits of QF Status

Benefit	Description
Federal exemption	The QF is exempt from regulation under the Federal Power Act.
Local exemption	The QF is exempt from any state or local regulation of entities as utilities or energy producers—that is, no "utility-type" regulation.
Power sale	The QF can sell any or all of its power output to the local electric utility or to any other utility it can reach with its electric power.
Avoided Cost	The price that the utility must pay for power purchased from a QF is equal to the utility's full Avoided Cost of generating or purchasing an equivalent amount of energy and capacity.
Interconnection	Utilities must interconnect their transmission grids with the QF to facilitate purchases and sales.
Backup power	The utility must supply necessary backup and supplemental power to the QF at nondiscriminatory and fair prices.

Where distributed generators use fossil-fuel technologies without cogenerating thermal energy and thus are not eligible to become QFs under PURPA, they have no right under federal law to sell or barter wholesale power back to the utility unless the state has adopted a net metering credit or similar requirement, which in many states is limited to certain renewable distributed generators of a particular small size. See Chapter 9. Important to note is that both cogeneration and Small Power Producer QFs are distributed technologies that use their own power and/or sell some or all of their electricity through the electric grid. When PURPA was first enacted, the majority of new QFs were cogeneration facilities; the majority later shifted to being Small Power Producer QFs.[7]

6. A Small Power Producer is not a cogenerator; it produces only electricity (not useful thermal energy) and employs waste or a renewable resource as its fuel for power generation. A waste fuel is defined as any by-product fuel source that is unessential to the overall goal of an economic process and currently of little or no commercial value.

7. *See generally Renewable Energy*, CTR. FOR CLIMATE & ENERGY SOLS., https://www.c2es.org/content/renewable-energy/ (last visited Apr. 18, 2024) [https://perma.cc/3R95-DQVN].

There is a net reduction in central system generation demand with distributed generation. One kW of distributed generation used on-site with no transmission losses displaces more than 1 kW of centralized generation, which must account for line losses in transmission and distribution.[8] While average line losses may approximate 5 percent, marginal line losses can be up to 20 percent.[9] Load pockets, which exhibit limited transmission capacity, are likely to be areas where there are high line losses and where distributed generation or cogeneration is economic.[10] A systems analysis might find that on-site cogeneration displaces 120 percent of the central station power otherwise used to serve consumers in a load pocket. Following is a guide to specific provisions to qualify as a QF, maintain that status, and enjoy the benefits set forth in Table 5.1.

Cogenerators: "Useful" Thermal Energy

A cogenerator sequentially produces at least two physically distinct useful forms of energy in the same process from the same facility—typically electric and thermal energy. The thermal energy (typically in the form of steam or hot water, which conventional steam-cycle power generating equipment otherwise would release to the environment as thermal or water pollution) is captured and used to heat a building or for industrial processes that require heat.

The heat recovered from a total energy system cogenerating heat and electricity can be used for direct application heat, for industrial process heat, or for preheating the combustion air for a utility boiler.[11] By capturing waste heat in the process of electric generation, more useful energy as a usable

---

8. *See* Jim Lazar & Xavier Baldwin, *Valuing the Contribution of Energy Efficiency to Avoided Marginal Line Losses and Reserve Requirements*, Regul. Assistance Proj. (2011), https://perma.cc/N4Y3-LTCA.

9. Nathaniel Greene & R. Hammerschlag, *Small and Clean Is Beautiful: Exploring the Emissions of Distributed Generation and Pollution Prevention Policies*, 13 Elec. J. 57 (2000).

10. *See* Richard Benjamin, *Generation, Transmission, and the Load Pocket Problem*, Int'l Ass'n for Energy Econ. 23 (2008), https://www.google.com/url?sa=t&rct=j&q=&esrc=s&source=web&cd=&ved=2ahUKEwjuj_GqhdLvAhVPJt8KHT4nDP4QFjAAegQIBBAD&url=https%3A%2F%2Fwww.iaee.org%2Fen%2Fpublications%2Fnewsletterdl.aspx%3Fid%3D42&usg=AOvVaw1dDqvNJ8UOpBtaSE3WVjvy [https://perma.cc/9SPR-UZBE].

11. *See generally* Hussam Jouhara et al., *Waste Heat Recovery Technologies and Applications*, 6 Thermal Sci. & Eng'g Progress 268 (2018), https://reader.elsevier.com/reader/sd/pii/S2451904918300015?token=1C97D5423A2A35592799960F7FC5082524AFBFF351A40E29B7CEA3B8CE36946C3BFBEC877B3D4A7B01BF5D6E573629FF [https://perma.cc/22VV-GBF5].

percentage of the fossil fuel input can be utilized while generating less environmental pollutants and emissions. Thus, cogeneration facilities operate at overall thermal efficiencies as great as 250–300 percent higher than conventional electric steam turbine generating technologies.[12]

Thermodynamically, the advantage of cogeneration technologies compared to conventional steam-cycle electric generating technologies is that they can raise efficiency under the First Law of Thermodynamics.[13] This first-law efficiency for electricity production increases from about 33 percent for conventional steam generators to as high as 85 percent or more with cogeneration.[14] Cogeneration technologies can raise efficiencies under the Second Law of Thermodynamics[15] from 35 percent to as high as 49 percent.[16]

Generators that recover waste heat and produce electricity can achieve efficiencies from 60 to 80 percent, which is very high compared to noncogenerating fossil-fuel technologies.[17] With optimum full implementation of distributed energy systems with heat recapture, 40 percent of building primary energy consumption could be conserved if distributed energy systems were installed in lieu of centralized electricity production.[18] With very

---

12. *See id.* at 268.

13. The efficiency of a heat engine, which is a device that converts chemical energy to mechanical or electric energy, is governed by the First and Second Laws of Thermodynamics. The First Law of Thermodynamics simply measures the percentage of chemical energy input that is converted to useful thermal and electric energy. It reflects the efficiency of energy originally in a chemical form converted to other forms.

14. *See* Marc H. Ross & Robert H. Williams, Our Energy: Regaining Control 156 (1981).

15. The Second Law of Thermodynamics reflects the quality of energy produced. Electric energy is of much higher quality than thermal energy. The Carnot efficiency expresses the ratio of the useful (electric and heat) output of an engine as a fraction of the total energy input. In essence, the Carnot efficiency predicts the maximum potential usable energy output that can be generated by different engine technologies.

16. Ross & Williams, *supra* note 14; *see also* Robert H. Williams, *Industrial Cogeneration*, 3 Ann. Rev. Energy 313 (1978).

17. *See Combined Heat and Power (CHP) Partnership: CHP Benefits*, U.S. Env't Prot. Agency (Nov. 13, 2023), https://www.epa.gov/chp/chp-benefits [https://perma.cc/P3RV-5SYT].

18. A. Jalalzadeh-Azar, *Quantifying Potential of Integrated Energy Systems with a Varying Level of Nationwide Deployment* 7, NREL/TP-550-32754, Nat'l Renewable Energy Lab'y (Nov. 2002). Even with only 60 percent of recoverable thermal energy from on-site distributed generation utilized, the research concludes that this result conserves more energy than even advanced central system energy generation and reduces emissions to the environment. *Id.*

efficient cogeneration technology, the CO_2 emissions can actually be less per unit of usable energy than for large central station combined-cycle generation, and NO_x emissions can be comparable.[19]

A key regulatory distinction compared to the Small Power Producer QF category, discussed later, is that a cogenerator may be of any size, large or small, and can use any fuel to produce its electric power. However, it is required that the cogeneration facility meet certain minimum production efficiency criteria for its output and at least 5 percent of the total energy output of the cogeneration facility be in the form of "useful" thermal energy.

This "useful" concept has been tightened by FERC over time. When a cogeneration QF filed with FERC for QF status under the FERC rules in place from 1978 to 2006, there was a rebuttable presumption favoring the project developer that the thermal output was "useful."[20] "Usefulness" was determined by use of the heat for any common industrial or commercial application. If the heat use was not common, a more exacting test was applied. If the entity that used the thermal energy of the cogenerator was legally related to the QF, a more careful examination without presumption of legitimacy was applied by FERC reviewing the actual contracts for thermal energy use.[21] To be "useful," a cogeneration thermal energy use needs to demonstrate an independent business justification for its use.[22]

FERC regulations were tightened in 2006 and became more demanding to require that the thermal output be used in a "productive and beneficial manner," determined by a case-by-case analysis demonstrated by the project developer and determined by FERC. If over 50 percent of the total energy output of the QF cogeneration facility is used for "industrial, commercial, residential or institutional purposes," it is now presumed used for an allowed

---

19. Greene & Hammerschlag, *supra* note 9, at 57.

20. Kamine/Besicorp Allegheny L.P., 63 FERC ¶ 61,320 (1993).

21. EG&G, Inc., 16 FERC ¶ 61,060 (1981) (an aquaculture facility would not burn natural gas to heat pond water but for the desire to achieve QF status for the facility). Thermal applications that would not be undertaken except for the by-product availability of inexpensive thermal energy may not necessarily be "useful" thermal applications. Where there is a close sizing of the cogeneration facility output to the *thermal* needs of the cogeneration facility itself, rather than sizing to the maximum *electric* output for a cogeneration facility, an aquaculture use of the thermal output can be deemed "useful." *In re* Savage, 28 FERC ¶ 61,273 (1984).

22. Electrodyne Rsch. Corp., 32 FERC ¶ 61,102, 61,279 (1985).

"safe harbor" purpose.[23] FERC may waive any of the requirements upon a showing that the facility will produce significant energy savings.[24]

Small Power Producers

The second type of eligible PURPA QF is a Small Power Producer. A Small Power Producer commercially produces only electricity (it need not produce useful thermal energy) and does so by using defined waste materials or a defined renewable resource. A Small Power Producer is limited in size, typically to a maximum of 80 MW of generation capacity. Certain types of waste-fueled QF projects can be no more than 30 MW in capacity. A waste fuel is defined as any by-product fuel source that is unessential to the overall goal of an economic process and currently of little or no commercial value.

Small Power Producer waste fuel has been defined to include such unconventional fuels as small unproductive deposits of fossil fuels, as well as facilities that turn solid waste into energy.[25] Users of renewable energy technologies, including hydroelectric, solar, wind, and wood-based technologies, qualify as Small Power Producers. In any given year, not more than 25 percent of the fuel input into a Small Power Producer can come from traditional fossil fuels.

At the inception of PURPA, the state of Mississippi challenged the constitutionality of a different section of PURPA than its section II establishing QFs described earlier for interfering with state rights over retail power sales and for the federal agency exceeding its administrative discretion in rulemakings under PURPA.[26] A federal district court in Mississippi held that the PURPA scheme was an impermissible transgression on states' rights under the Federal Power Act and the Commerce Clause of the Constitution. On appeal, PURPA was narrowly upheld, 5–4, by the U.S. Supreme Court.[27]

---

23. 18 C.F.R. § 292.205(d)(3); Chugach Elec. Ass'n, Matanuska Elec. Ass'n, 121 FERC ¶ 61,287, 2007 WL 4472021, ¶ 42 (Dec. 21, 2007) ("the Commission created a safe harbor").

24. 18 C.F.R. § 292.205(c) (2007).

25. Am. Lignite Prods. Co., 25 FERC ¶ 61,054 (1983); Gabriel Mills Energy Co., 41 FERC ¶ 62,288 (1987).

26. Mississippi challenged the constitutionality of Title I, Title III, and § 210 of Title II of PURPA.

27. FERC v. Mississippi, 456 U.S. 742 (1982).

The Price Earned for PURPA QF Power

Under PURPA, QFs are allowed to sell their excess energy and capacity to utilities at the utility's Avoided Cost of power. PURPA specifies that the rates established by FERC for purchases of power from QFs may not exceed the "incremental cost" to the utility of purchasing alternative electric energy.[28] The incremental or Avoided Cost is defined as "'the cost to the electric utility of the electric energy which, but for the purchase from such QF, such utility would generate or purchase from another source.'"[29] PURPA requires the payment by a purchasing utility for this QF wholesale power at the Avoided Cost.

Pursuant to PURPA, FERC issued its Orders Nos. 69 and 70, which establish rules requiring electric utilities to offer to purchase electric energy and capacity from QFs at a rate equal to the utility's "full-Avoided Costs." FERC adopted PURPA's language in defining "full-Avoided Costs" as incremental costs of alternative electric energy.[30] FERC delegated to state public utility commissions the responsibility to calculate and implement full-Avoided Costs for the utilities that they regulate within each of their states.[31] In doing so, state utility regulatory commissions act pursuant to federal, not state, law and have no power to require that prices diverge from full-Avoided Cost established by FERC as federal law.

To guide state public utility commissions, FERC's regulations list several factors that states should, to the extent practicable, take into account when calculating Avoided Costs, including:[32]

---

28. 16 U.S.C. § 824a-3.

29. Plymouth Rock Energy Assocs. v. Dep't of Pub. Utils., 648 N.E.2d 752, 754 (1995) (quoting 16 U.S.C. § 824a-3(d)).

30. 18 C.F.R. § 292. Avoided costs are defined as the costs to an electric utility of energy or capacity or both that, but for the purchase from a QF, the electric utility would generate or construct itself or purchase from another source. *Id.* at § 292.101(b)(6). Energy costs are the variable costs associated with the production of electric energy (kilowatt-hours), which represent the cost of fuel and some operating and maintenance expenses. *See Plymouth Rock Energy Assocs.*, 648 N.E.2d at 754 n.3. Capacity costs are the costs associated with providing the capability to deliver, consisting primarily of the capital costs of facilities. *Id.*

31. 18 C.F.R. § 292.401 (1983). Under § 210(f)(1) of PURPA, the state public utility commissions are the primary enforcement power: "[E]ach State regulatory authority shall . . . implement such rule (or revised rule) for each electric utility for which it has ratemaking authority." 16 U.S.C. § 824a-3(f)(1) (1982).

32. 18 C.F.R. § 292.304(e) (1983).

- The expected or demonstrated reliability of the QF.
- The duration of the contract.
- The availability of capacity or energy from a QF during the system daily and seasonal peak periods.
- That Avoided Costs may reflect the particular capacity situation faced by each electric utility.
- That Avoided Cost paid can reflect the net power actually delivered to the utility's load center.
- Line losses.

With 64 different state-level legal authorities in the United States (50 states, the District of Columbia, the Commonwealths of Puerto Rico and the Virgin Islands, and 11 U.S. territories located primarily in the Pacific Ocean), various states have determined different methods for determining PURPA Avoided Cost–based rates for QFs' energy and capacity. If used, winning bids are considered equivalent to the utilities' Avoided Cost because they reflect the price at which utilities can procure power.

The Supreme Court unanimously upheld the requirements to pay full-Avoided Cost for QF power and to interconnect with all QFs against challenge by utilities in 1983.[33] Electric utilities also must offer to sell necessary backup,[34] interruptible,[35] maintenance,[36] or supplemental[37] power to QFs at rates that are nondiscriminatory as well as "just and reasonable and in the public interest."[38]

Changes in QF Avoided Cost Rates for Larger Projects

The concept of what rates must be paid to QFs for their power has evolved with congressional amendments and FERC regulatory changes over time.

---

33. Am. Paper Inst. v. Am. Elec. Power Serv. Corp., 461 U.S. 402 (1983).

34. Backup power is electric energy or capacity during an unscheduled outage to supply power and is generally self-generated. 18 C.F.R. § 292.101(b)(9).

35. Interruptible power is power or capacity supplied by an electric utility to a QF subject to interruption under specific conditions. 18 C.F.R. § 292.101(b)(10).

36. Maintenance power is power or capacity supplied by an electric utility to a QF during periods of scheduled outages. 18 C.F.R. § 292.101(b)(11).

37. Supplementary power is power or capacity supplied by an electric utility to a QF to augment self-generated electricity. 18 C.F.R. § 292.101(b)(8).

38. 18 C.F.R. § 292.305(a).

EPAct 2005[39] added section 210(m) to PURPA, which permits the termination of an electric utility's obligation to purchase energy from QFs if FERC finds that the QF has nondiscriminatory access to sell its power through regional wholesale electric markets.[40] If FERC finds that the QF has such nondiscriminatory access, it would eliminate "the QF purchase mandate for utilities operating in the organized markets that have so-called 'Day 2 markets' because they offer transparent spot markets into which all generators can sell" power. FERC regulations provide that for existing Day 2 markets there is a rebuttable presumption that a QF with installed generating capacity of 20 MW or more has nondiscriminatory access to a wholesale market.[41] FERC Order No. 688[42] found that five ISOs and RTOs afforded such nondiscriminatory market access to QFs.[43]

39. Pub. L. No. 109-58, § 1253, 119 Stat. 594 (codified at 16 U.S.C. § 824a-3 (2006)).

40. PURPA section 210(m)(1) sets out the following criteria for nondiscriminatory markets:

> (A)(i) independently administered, auction-based day ahead and real time wholesale markets for the sale of electric energy; and (ii) wholesale markets for long term sales of capacity and electric energy; or
>
> (B)(i) transmission and interconnection services that are provided by a Commission-approved regional transmission entity and administered pursuant to an open access transmission tariff that affords nondiscriminatory treatment to all customers; and (ii) competitive wholesale markets that provide a meaningful opportunity to sell capacity, including long-term and short-term and real-time sales to buyers other than the utility to which the qualifying facility is interconnected. In determining whether a meaningful opportunity to sell exists, the commission shall consider, among other factors, evidence of transactions within the relevant market; or
>
> (C) wholesale markets for the sale of capacity and electric energy that are, at a minimum, of comparable competitive quality as markets described in subparagraphs (A) and (B).

16 U.S.C. § 210(m)(1).

41. 18 U.S.C. § 292.310.

42. PURPA 210(m) Regulations Applicable to Small Power Cogeneration Facilities, 71 Fed. Reg. 64,342 (final rule) (issued Oct. 20, 2006) (to be codified at 18 C.F.R. pt. 292), *aff'd on appeal*, Am. Forest & Paper Ass'n v. Fed. Energy Regul. Comm'n, 550 F.3d 1179 (D.C. Cir. 2008).

43. 18 C.F.R. § 292.309(e) (2009). FERC also found that the California Independent System Operator and the Southwest Power Pool satisfy the criteria for transmission and interconnection services provided by an approved RTO and administered pursuant to open-access transmission tariff affording nondiscriminatory treatment. 18 C.F.R. § 292.309(g) (2009). FERC also found that ERCOT is a market of comparable competitive quality to Midwest ISO, PJM, ISO-NE, and NYISO. 18 C.F.R. § 292.309(f) (2009).

Smaller QFs, of capacity less than 20 MW, which characterizes most solar generators and some other small renewable energy generators, still were entitled to sell power at their election to the utility, even if utilities participate in these ISOs to which larger QF projects were determined by FERC to have wholesale access. No state retail utility is compelled to participate in an integrated ISO interstate market, and many do not. Figure 3.7 illustrates that approximately half of the states have their utilities participating in an interstate ISO or RTO wholesale power market.[44] The amount of power wholesaled before it is sold at retail has shifted from only 8 percent in the 1960s to approximately 44 percent of all capacity today and is progressively climbing each year.

These 2006 PURPA amendments are not retroactive: PURPA section 210(m) and FERC Order No. 688 do not modify the "rights or remedies of any party under any contract or obligation, in effect or pending approval before the appropriate state regulatory authority or nonregulated electric utility on or before August 8, 2005."[45] This is important to know and determine for stakeholders purchasing existing renewable power projects. Having open access to the spot markets in RTOs or ISOs does not necessarily mean that there is access to long-term markets on a nondiscriminatory basis—and some aspect of this resonates through the federal First Circuit Court of Appeals *Allco* decision discussed later.

Eligible QFs have the option under PURPA and FERC rules and are entitled unilaterally to make the choice either to provide their energy to utilities on an "as available" basis or to supply energy and/or capacity pursuant to a legally enforceable obligation/power sale contract. If the QF selects the latter option, it also has the option to have the Avoided Cost rate established at the utility's Avoided Cost calculated either

- at the time of each hourly delivery of the power, or
- at the time the legally enforceable obligation is incurred at the estimated price for the term of a longer-term power purchase agreement with the utility.[46]

---

44. *Regional Transmission Organizations*, Fed. Energy Regul. Comm'n (Nov. 2015), https://www.ferc.gov/industries/electric/indus-act/rto/elec-ovr-rto-map.pdf [https://perma.cc/LSB2-HMVY].

45. 18 C.F.R. § 292.314 (2009).

46. 18 C.F.R. § 292.304(d)(2)(i–ii).

In Massachusetts, in administering the PURPA program and setting the Avoided Cost, the Massachusetts Department of Public Utilities (DPU), by regulation for a standard power purchase agreement, set a rate for all QFs larger than 1 MW capacity at the price the utility paid for power from the "ISO power exchange," ISO-New England. ISO-New England sets that price based on a daily auction rate, which is the Locational Marginal Price (LMP), rather than on the cost for a longer-term dedicated arrangement based on the utility's Avoided Cost estimated by the DPU at the time that the legally enforceable obligation contract for supply was entered. There is a significant difference in the Avoided Cost rate between the actual daily LMP auction rate and the calculated longer-term Avoided Cost estimation for that same purchasing utility established by the state energy regulatory agency.

Solar QF developer Allco filed a complaint arguing that this DPU rate conflicted directly with FERC's rule that QFs are entitled to a long-term rate calculated at the time a legally enforceable obligation is incurred rather than as a short-term "as available" price month after month. A rate determined at daily changing prices at the hour of delivery of power denies QF Allco the federal PURPA-specified option. The First Circuit Court of Appeals upheld that this was illegal, as asserted by Allco.[47] In administering QF rates under PURPA, the states act as delegates of FERC, without any independent state authority to otherwise determine wholesale Avoided Cost rates.

PURPA is still in place and fully operational—constituting the cornerstone foundation for future renewable power generation. Since the Supreme Court upheld the constitutionality of PURPA twice in 1982 and 1983,[48] there has been a proliferation of QFs nationwide. In most years since 1990, more new power capacity has come online from projects developed by QFs and Independent Power Producers than from all new utility-owned power generation facilities combined. Their success spawned deregulation of wholesale and retail electric power in numerous states (see Chapter 13). Next is highlighted the still-in-place constriction of PURPA benefits implemented during the Trump administration, which again changed key QF eligibility factors.

---

47. Allco Renewable Energy Ltd. v. Mass. Elec. Co., 875 F.3d 64 (1st Cir. 2017).

48. FERC v. Mississippi, 456 U.S. 742 (1982); Am. Paper Inst. v. Am. Elec. Power Serv. Corp., 461 U.S. 402 (1983).

FERC Order No. 872 (2020)—Qualification/Value for QF Power Sales

FERC Order No. 872, issued in July 2020, substantially changed how QFs are treated, narrowing the scope of some PURPA benefits for QFs.[49] It changed regulations for QF eligibility and the valuation of power sales by QFs in five significant ways.

Legally Enforceable Obligations

The date and time of a legally enforceable obligation securing PURPA rights and obligations between a utility and a QF establishing their long-term contractual relationship are important: they establish when a QF can lock in the price it will receive for its QF power sale, as well as other PURPA rights. FERC Order No. 872 underscores a QF's necessary demonstration of commercial viability and a financial commitment to developing the QF project. Order No. 872 suggests that a given state could include or require a legally enforceable obligation not to occur until the QF developer has demonstrated project site control, filed and paid the applicable fee to the utility for an interconnection application, and at least applied for (and perhaps received) the required local permitting and zoning compliance necessary for preconstruction approval.

Under Order No. 872, each state would determine its own point in time where the QF obligation occurred and legal rights were established for new projects. This issue of timing has been controversial when interpreted by several state Public Utility Commissions as to how far along in development a QF project needs to be before it is entitled to PURPA QF benefits. This 2020 regulatory change can delay the date of QF entitlements to benefits:

- project security locking in a legally enforceable obligation for each QF
- eligibility for changing capacity value payments[50]
- eligibility for certain limited state RPS RECs in approximately 29 states (see Chapter 8)
- net metering programs available in approximately 40 states (see Chapter 9)

---

49. Qualifying Facility Rates and Requirements Implementation Issues under the Public Utility Regulatory Policies Act of 1978, FERC Order No. 872, Docket Nos. RM19-15-000 & AD16-16-000, 172 FERC ¶ 61,041 (to be codified at 18 C.F.R. pts. 292 & 375) (July 16, 2020).

50. *See* Plymouth Rock Energy Assocs. v. Mass. Dep't of Pub. Utils., 420 Mass. 168, 175 (1995).

Utility Must-Purchase Obligation Opt-Out

One hundred twenty days after promulgation of this FERC Order No. 872 regulatory change, utilities were allowed to opt out of their obligations to purchase power from QFs that have capacity larger than 5 MW, rather than the prior 20 MW threshold that was imposed by EPAct 2005, when the QF is located within an organized wholesale power market. FERC clarified that one factor for rebutting the presumption of access to markets is if there is "a predominant purpose other than selling electricity" that could apply to behind-the-meter distributed energy resources that are greater than 5 MW.[51]

In approximately half of U.S. states in which utilities are members of qualifying federally regulated ISOs or RTOs, this will cause power sales from QFs with capacity larger than 5 MW to be sold into and priced according to a much larger wholesale market with more competitors; FERC created these ISOs and RTOs in order to put competitive downward pressure on daily available wholesale market prices.[52] Neither threshold, nor the fact that it was subsequently lowered to 5 MW by this new rule were not originally part of the PURPA statute or regulations until EPAct 2005 amendments added it, and it was later applied to smaller projects with a capacity greater than 5 MW.

Physical Separation of QF Projects

Traditionally, physical distance alone could separate QF projects to qualify as separate QF Small Power Producers of less than the maximum allowed size or as separate cogenerators satisfying the minimum useful output requirements. FERC Order No. 872 changes the traditional irrebuttable presumption for QF Small Power Producers that projects located more than one mile from another project(s) and under the same or affiliated ownership were to be deemed not part of the same project. That one-mile distance is now changed by Order No. 872 to ten miles in order to qualify for an irrebuttable presumption as separate eligible QF projects. Those that are one to ten miles apart now are afforded a rebuttable presumption of separation. FERC also will now consider shared transformers or generation interconnection

---

51. *Id.*

52. *See In re* Cal. Pub. Utils. Comm'n, S. Cal. Edison Co., Pac. Gas & Elec. Co., San Diego Gas & Elec. Co., FERC Docket Nos. EL10-64-000 & EL10-66-000, 132 FERC ¶ 61,047 (2010), Order on Petitions for Declaratory Order.

facilities, common debt and equity financing, and common permitting and access rights as factors in determining merged versus separate QF projects.

Under the later Order No. 872-A, FERC clarified that if a hydroelectric generating facility is one to ten miles from an affiliated hydro facility yet on the same riven impoundment, a rebuttable presumption applies that they are at separate sites and not combined.[53] The ten-mile distance has an exponential impact on QF eligibility: the common project area within a ten-mile radius is not ten times, but rather one hundred times, greater than the area within a one-mile radius. This could include a large number of solar rooftop installations on separate properties that could conceivably exceed PURPA's Small Power Producer QF limit of 80 MW. Some states, in affording RPS REC or net metering status for subsidies (see Chapters 8 and 9), can incorporate QF status as a requirement to qualify for these state incentives and support.

Challenges to QFs Maintaining Status

FERC now expects material changes in project information regarding QF status, such as ownership after an acquisition, sale, or merger of projects, to be submitted immediately to FERC via a FERC Form No. 556 by the day of the change. FERC stated that "for a small power production facility to qualify as a QF, the owner or operator of the facility must ensure that the Form No. 556 on file with the Commission contains current and accurate information."[54] This could affect eligibility to maintain interconnection queue position. Such a material change would include a change in ownership increasing an equity holder's interest by at least 10 percent from the equity interest previously reported to FERC or entry of a new owner holding 10 percent or more of equity of the project(s) not previously reported.

Under the revised regulations, parties challenging ongoing QF status of generation projects can do so without going to FERC for a declaratory order and paying a substantial associated fee. In Order No. 872, FERC provided interested parties the option to contest or protest any recertifications of an existing QF status if a "substantive change" was proposed to be made. FERC stated in its subsequent Order No. 872-A that such a substantive change

---

53. FERC Order No. 872-A, Order Addressing Arguments Raised on Rehearing and Clarifying Prior Order in Part, Docket Nos. RM19-15-001 & AD16-16-001 (Nov. 19, 2020).

54. Irradiant Partners, LP, 178 FERC ¶ 61,215 (Mar. 24, 2022).

could include "a change in electrical generating equipment that increases power production capacity by the greater of 1 MW or 5 percent of the previously certified capacity of the QF or a change in ownership in which an owner increases its equity interest by at least 10% from the equity interest previously reported."[55]

Avoided Cost Rates

Under the later-clarified final FERC rule, individual states have discretion to require utilities to provide PURPA contracts with a fixed or variable energy rate, or that decision can be left to the interconnecting and purchasing utility.[56] The price a QF receives for selling its power to a utility under the new order is allowed to be constricted as determined by each state, compared to prior FERC orders and rules without fixed Avoided Cost energy rates.[57] These could be set by the "as-available" energy rates for LMP in an ISO.[58] Avoided *capacity* rates are still fixed.

Order No. 872 may call into question a prior holding of FERC that a state Avoided Cost rate *could* be based on a subset of renewable-only resources, as opposed to be determined with reference to the least expensive

---

55. *See* Dalreed Solar, FERC Docket No. QF20-1037-002, 179 FERC ¶ 61,105 (May 13, 2022). Factors that the complainant argued should be included were that the facilities

- are all solar photovoltaic facilities that share a common off-taking utility (which alone is not uncommon)
- are all located on property owned by the same LLC entity
- share a single 200 MW interconnection request to the utility
- share equipment of busses, step-up transformers, relays, and other interconnection facilities
- might also share common easements for operations
- were all developed by Energy of Utah, a single developer
- were all relatively coincident in time in terms of their power purchase agreement (PPA) executions

56. *Id.* FERC clarified in Order No. 872-A that a state may only set Avoided Cost variable rates if the utility has fulfilled its obligations to disclose Avoided Cost data under 18 C.F.R. § 292.302. FERC ruled that if a competitive solicitation is used to set an Avoided Cost rate, it should be "administered and scored" by an independent entity.

57. 18 C.F.R. § 292.304(b)(6). "As available" energy-only sellers of energy are not *required to* be compensated *for any* product but energy. 18 C.F.R. § 292.304(d)(1)(i).

58. In Order No. 872-A, FERC stated that it would "allow states the flexibility to require variable avoided cost energy rates in QF contracts and LEOs [legally enforceable obligations] and thereby reduce the risk to customers."

of all generation resources, if a state so elected.[59] In a later-issued clarification at the end of 2020, FERC affirmed that a state could still elect to take action to tier the Avoided Cost rates applicable to specific renewable energy technologies.[60] A state could set Avoided Costs in a technology-specific range by mandating a procurement for its retail utilities; requiring only certain resources to be relevant; and setting Avoided Cost rates based on the costs of those specific resources that satisfy such technology-, size-, or location-specific mandates. This is consistent with a prior decision of a single U.S. Circuit Court of Appeals.[61]

"As-available" QF power purchase rates are subject to constant change; some utilities during some periods of excess energy have had negative or de minimis "as-available" rates. The LMP in ISOs will change daily and monthly. This new rule would allow prices to be set by competitive auctions; federal courts have found certain states to be not in compliance with their competitive auction processes.[62] Until this rule, QFs were entitled to the PURPA projected long-term rate determined at the time of commitment.[63]

PURPA has remained for more than 45 years as a solid bulwark that determines the rights of power generation, interconnection, and sale for an increasingly large segment of U.S. electric power. What has changed dramatically and substantially is federal tax policy, which provides incentives for certain electric power sector investments and behavior of stakeholders. The next chapter analyzes in detail the hundreds of billions of dollars of federal tax and grant incentives currently available in the Inflation Reduction Act as well as from other sources for the benefit of new electric power. Counsel play an essential role in applying these laws and policy.

---

59. *See In re* Cal. Pub. Utils. Comm'n, S. Cal. Edison Co., Pac. Gas & Elec. Co., San Diego Gas & Elec. Co., FERC Docket Nos. EL10-64-000 & EL10-66-000 (July 15, 2010).

60. FERC Order No. 872-A, *supra* note 53.

61. Californians for Renewable Energy v. Cal. Pub. Utils. Comm'n, 922 F.3d 929, 937 (9th Cir. 2019) (holding that "where a state has [a renewable portfolio standard (RPS)] and the utility is using a QF's energy to meet the RPS, the utility cannot calculate avoided costs based on energy sources that would not also meet the RPS[,]" which "comports with PURPA's goal to put QFs on an equal footing with other energy providers").

62. Winding Creek Solar, LLC v. Peevey, 293 F. Supp. 3d 980, 989–90 (N.D. Cal. 2017), *aff'd sub nom.* Winding Creek Solar, LLC v. Peterman, 932 F.3d 861 (9th Cir. 2019).

63. *See* Allco Renewable Energy Ltd. v. Mass. Elec. Co., 208 F. Supp. 3d 390 (D. Mass. 2016); *aff'd*, 875 F.3d 64 (1st Cir. 2017).

CHAPTER 6

Tax Strategies*

George Harrison and the Beatles sang about taxes and their impacts: Taxes are integral legal considerations regarding power generation and transmission.

Tax Incentives for Power Generation

One unique distinction of the electric power sector is that it is the most capital intensive sector of the U.S. economy by a large margin—much more money is expended annually of a capital nature (greater than one year equipment longevity) than anywhere else in the economy. When that much capital is expended on an ongoing basis annually and locked into for long periods of time to earn revenue, legal skills are required. A high degree of legal counsel involvement is even more necessary when the electric sector remains the most government-regulated sector of the economy and now through new legislation will be heavily subsidized to alter its basic direction.

One cannot operate successfully in the power sector without being very aware of tax consequences related to each decision. Tax impacts are even more prominent now after enactment of President Biden's Inflation Reduction Act (IRA), which contains significantly expanded and extended subsidies and tax incentives for the power sector. The IRA and the bipartisan Infrastructure Investment and Jobs Act (IIJA) together represent historic investments in the nation's energy system, totaling more than $430 billion.[1]

Historically, fossil fuels and nuclear production of electricity received various tax and other subsidies promoting their use when in the second half of the 20th century they constituted approximately 85 percent of the

***None of this chapter or other portions of the book can be used or relied on as tax or legal advice.**

1. U.S. Dep't of Energy, *The Inflation Reduction Act Drives Significant Emissions Reductions and Positions America to Reach Our Climate Goals* 3 (Aug. 2022), https://www.energy.gov/sites/default/files/2022-08/8.18%20InflationReductionAct_Factsheet_Final.pdf.

generation of electric power. In the 21st century, during the administrations of four different U.S. presidents beginning with George W. Bush, more federal subsidy has been devoted not to fossil fuel generation but to renewable power. Data published in the latter half of 2023 by the U.S. Energy Information Administration (EIA) shows that during 2022, all combined federal direct expenditures, tax credits, research and development grants, and Department of Energy (DoE) loan guarantee awards and subsidies[2]

- for solar energy were 302 times larger than those given to nuclear energy;
- for wind energy were 69 times larger than those given to nuclear energy;
- and subsidies and awards for solar and wind energy similarly outpaced those given to oil and gas.

And with the recent proliferation of solar and wind power generation, the prices of each have declined. By 2018, wind projects in the United States had an average levelized cost of $45/MWh for capacity and energy without other subsidies, $58/MWh for solar power.[3] Declining further by 2022, both solar and wind prices were below $30/MWh, with wind power at $29/MWh.[4]

Much, but not all, of the federal subsidies and support is delivered—directly and indirectly—through the federal tax system. The recent success of renewable power is boosted by federal and state tax credits, falling installation prices of renewable technologies,[5] and the proliferation of net metering programs (see Chapter 9).[6] Wind power is forecast by the DoE to be

2. U.S. Energy Info. Admin., Federal Financial Interventions and Subsidies in Energy in Fiscal Years 2016–2022, Figures 4-5, 9-12 (Aug. 2023), https://www.eia.gov/analysis/requests/subsidy/pdf/subsidy.pdf?utm_source=substack&utm_medium=email.

3. Jim Efstathiou Jr. & Brian K. Sullivan, *Smarter Wind Turbines Try to Squeeze More Power on Each Rotation*, Bloomberg Env't Rptr. (May 9, 2018), https://www.bloomberg.com/news/articles/2018-05-09/smarter-wind-turbines-try-to-squeeze-more-power-on-each-rotation.

4. Mark Bolinger et al., *Utility-Scale Solar, 2022 Edition* 33, Lawrence Berkeley Nat'l Lab'y (Sept. 2022), https://perma.cc/L3EV-DBPZ.

5. *See Solar Industry Research Data*, Solar Energy Indus. Ass'n, http://www.seia.org/research-resources/solar-industry-data (last visited Apr. 19, 2024).

6. *See State Net Metering Policies*, Nat'l Conf. of State Legislatures (Nov. 20, 2017), http://www.ncsl.org/research/energy/net-metering-policy-overview-and-state-legislative-updates.aspx; Sean Paul, *The Solar Industry in a Period of Transition*, Geo. Pub. Pol'y Rev. (Nov. 15, 2016), http://gppreview.com/2016/11/15/solar-industry-period-transition/.

cheaper than electricity produced from natural gas by 2025, even without a continuing federal production tax credit incentive for wind power, which is continuing under current law until 2032 and likely longer.[7] The next section examines the federal tax credits that facilitate the next decade's power growth.

The PTC Subsidizing Power Operation; the ITC Subsidizing Construction

The Investment Tax Credit (ITC) and Production Tax Credit (PTC) have motivated a significant amount of renewable energy development in the United States, which has dramatically lowered the cost of solar and wind power.[8] As brief history: the federal PTC was created in 1992 as part of the Energy Policy Act as a mechanism to subsidize wind generation through the federal tax code. The PTC provided a tax credit for the first ten years of operation of renewable energy linked to the amount of units of energy generated, which credit dollar amount escalated for inflation over time and through reauthorizations of the PTC.[9] The credit was initially $0.015/kWh generated. This value inflated automatically through the PTC statute over time to $0.023/kWh generated for a wind turbine for its first ten years of operation.[10] The credit is taken by those who own the facility and is determined based on power produced, which must be sold to a person unrelated to the owner of the facility.

New Federal Tax Treatment for Electricity

There are Biden administration changes in the tax system affecting electric power. The majority of the dramatic potential reductions of GHG emissions to be achieved by 2030 are forecast to be achieved in the electric power sector. The DoE estimates that approximately two-thirds of the carbon sector

---

7. *See* Christopher Martin & Justin Doom, BNA Energy & Climate Report (Mar. 12, 2015).

8. Bolinger, *supra* note 4, at 33.

9. *See* American Recovery and Reinvestment Act of 2009 (H.R. 1, Div. B, §§ 1101 & 1102) (often referred to as ARRA); American Taxpayer Relief Act of 2012 (H.R. 8, § 407); Tax Increase Prevention Act of 2014 (H.R. 5771, § 155); Consolidated Appropriations Act of 2016 (H.R. 2029, § 301); Bipartisan Budget Act of 2018 (H.R. 1892, § 40409).

10. 26 U.S.C. § 45.

reductions incentivized by the 2022 IRA and the 2021 Infrastructure Act will be in the power sector, dwarfing all of the other transportation, building space heating, and industry sectors combined.[11] While the electric power sector is responsible for approximately one-quarter of GHG emissions, federal policy is targeting it to shoulder two-thirds of the reductions in national carbon emissions. Recent forecasts are for power sector CO_2 emissions to decline

- 75–79 percent by 2035[12]
- 80 percent by 2040[13]

The IRA incentives and impacts affecting electric power include the following:

- **Nuclear Electricity**: A nuclear power production tax credit through 2032 to support maintenance of existing nuclear power ($0.015/kWh produced minus 16 percent of the facility's gross receipts in excess of $0.0225/kWh).[14]
- **Building Energy and Power Use**: Extends tax credits for home energy efficiency and clean energy use with $4.3 billion allocated each for states to develop electrification rebate programs and home efficiency rebates.[15]
- **Renewable Electricity**: Extension of existing technology-specific PTCs and ITCs through 2024 with bonus credits for domestic products incorporated, apprentice training, payment of prevailing wages, and siting in "justice" or low-income communities[16]; replaced with technology-neutral Clean Electricity PTCs and ITCs commencing in 2025 with similar bonus credits.[17]

---

11. U.S. Dep't of Energy, *supra* note 1.
12. John Bestine, Elec. Power Rsch. Inst., Presentation at Resources for the Future, IRA Symposium (Feb. 15, 2023).
13. Cara Marcy, Env't Prot. Agency, Presentation at Resources for the Future, IRA Symposium (Feb. 15, 2023).
14. Inflation Reduction Act of 2022 § 13105 (to be codified at 26 U.S.C. § 45U).
15. *Id.* § 50121(a)(1).
16. *Id.* § 13101(d) (to be codified at 26 U.S.C. § 48(a)(5)(C)(ii)).
17. *Id.* §§ 13701, 13702 (to be codified at 26 U.S.C. §§ 45Y, 48E).

- **Offshore Wind Generation**: $100 million for development of inter-regional transmission conduits and optimized integration of electricity generated from offshore wind.[18]
- **Carbon Capture**: Increasing and extending carbon capture tax credits, with the current tax credit for direct air capture (DAC) increased from $50 to $180/ton CO_2 for qualifying DAC projects, created a 30–50 percent subsidy for DAC project costs.[19]
- **Manufacturing Power Sector Components**: A new manufacturing tax credit for the production of clean energy technology components, including solar components, wind turbine and offshore wind components, inverters, and many battery components, as well as the critical minerals needed to produce these components.[20]
- **Industrial Emissions**: Approximately $5.8 billion to invest in projects aimed at reducing emissions from energy-intensive industrial sources.[21]
- **Methane Leak Reduction**: $1.5 billion for methane emission reduction programs, establishing maximum methane emissions rates and penalties applied to different facilities.
- **Greenhouse Gas Reduction Fund**: Environmental Protection Agency (EPA) financial grants to state, local, regional, and tribal programs that provide financial support to low and zero-carbon technologies; green banks that provide financial support for low or zero-emission projects.[22]
- **Hydrogen**: A new ten-year hydrogen production tax credit with four tiers set at a maximum of 4 kilograms of CO_2 equivalent per kilogram of hydrogen,[23] with the Bloomberg forecast growth of green power use

18. *Id.* § 50153.
19. *Id.* § 13104(a) (to be codified at 26 U.S.C. § 45Q(d)).
20. *Id.* § 13501 (to be codified at 26 U.S.C. § 48C).
21. *Id.* § 50161.
22. *Id.* § 60103 (to be codified at 42 U.S.C. § 134).
23. *Id.* § 13204 (to be codified at 26 U.S.C. § 45V). The IRA direct subsidies are $3/kilogram for the cleanest type of hydrogen production. "Renewable hydrogen," also known as zero-carbon hydrogen, is produced using electricity from solar, wind, and other renewable energy sources. The IRA allows combination of tax credits for renewable power generation facilities with the PTCs and ITCs for clean hydrogen production and storage infrastructure, including 30 percent credit for energy storage technology constructed before 2025.

(using renewable energy to operate electrolyzers to separate hydrogen from water and not using natural gas as its hydrogen source).[24] Refining, steel, cement, ammonia, and methanol in the United States consume approximately 10 million tons of hydrogen annually.

Federal Tax Credits for Electric Power

The IRA provides extensions over ten years of the two federal renewable energy tax credits at their then-current 2022 levels:

- A PTC equal to $0.005/kWh as a base amount or a credit for certain technologies of a bit more than half that amount ($0.003/kWh), each applicable for power sold to a third party during the first ten years of operation[25]
- An ITC (at 26 percent of eligible capital costs)[26]
- Extension of other renewable energy tax credits[27]
- Meeting prevailing wage amounts[28] and apprenticeship[29] provisions increases each of the PTCs by up to fivefold[30]
- Also a fivefold potential increase in credit amount for operation of new eligible renewable energy facilities with a net output capacity of less than 1 MW[31]

The IRA in its current form would have the ITC reinstated at a rate that can be up to 30 percent dependent on using local content or materials, hiring apprentices, and paying prevailing wages in the project, with the PTC at $0.015/kWh of electric power produced and sold, as well as for the first time in 15 years make the PTC available for solar facilities. Neither of these two

24. *A Breakneck Growth Pivot Nears for Green Hydrogen*, BLOOMBERGNEF (Nov. 14, 2022), https://about.bnef.com/blog/a-breakneck-growth-pivot-nears-for-green-hydrogen/?utm_source=ActiveCampaign&utm_medium=email&utm_content=Renewable+News+Highlights+November+18+2022&utm_campaign=Renewables+News+Highlights+November+18.

25. Inflation Reduction Act § 13701 (2022) (to be codified at 26 U.S.C. § 45Y(a)).

26. *Id.* § 13702 (to be codified at 26 U.S.C. § 48E(a)).

27. *Id.* § 13101(a).

28. *Id.* § 13101(f) (to be codified at 26 U.S.C. § 45(b)(7)).

29. *Id.* (to be codified at 26 U.S.C. § 45(b)(8)). On apprenticeship, see BENJAMIN COLLINS, CONG. RSCH. SERV., R45171, REGISTERED APPRENTICESHIP: FEDERAL ROLE AND RECENT FEDERAL EFFORTS (2021).

30. Inflation Reduction Act § 13101(f) (2022) (to be codified at 26 U.S.C. § 45(b)(7), (8)).

31. *Id.* (to be codified at 26 U.S.C. § 45(b)(6)(B)).

key electric power credits would phase down for projects placed into service in 2022 or later but would be subject to phase-down once annual GHG emissions fall by at least 75 percent from 2022 levels.[32]

The ITC now includes a 30 percent stand-alone credit for energy storage capacity in excess of 5 kW not in association with a discrete power generation project.[33] There are significant "bonus" credits available to raise the value of each credit depending on where or with what workers, wages, and materials the projects are constructed, which credits also escalate the value of storage tax credits as they do for solar and wind generation credits.[34] Next, we set forth detail about each of these electric tax credits now authorized to remain in place until at least 2032 and likely longer.

The Expanded ITC until 2034 or Longer

Section 48 ITC Extension—First Phase

The IRA extends the ITC at a potential 10 percent or 30 percent (the latter for solar, geothermal, fiber-optic solar, fuel cells, microturbines, small wind projects, offshore wind, combined heat and power, and waste energy projects constructed before January 1, 2025).[35] From the low base credit rate, there is a fivefold multiplier in credit value set forth earlier if a developer satisfies the prevailing wage and apprenticeship requirements or makes penalty payments.[36]

The 30 percent and 10 percent credit bonus amounts require the project taxpayer, contractor, and subcontractors to pay prevailing wages to

32. *Id.* §§ 13701, 13702 (to be codified at 26 U.S.C. §§ 45Y(d)(3), 48E(e)(3)).

33. *Id.* § 13702 (to be codified at 26 U.S.C. § 48E(a)(2)(A)(ii)(III)(bb)).

34. *Id.* § 13102(k) (to be codified at 26 U.S.C. § 48(a)).

35. *Id.* § 13101(d) (to be codified at 26 U.S.C. § 48(a)(5)(C)(ii)).

36. *Id.* § 13102(k) (to be codified at 26 U.S.C. § 48(a)). This is the only tax credit bonus with a "comply or pay" penalty alternative available for the developer to realize the credit. For the additional credit bonuses for domestic content, project location in energy communities that are tied to fossil fuels or located on brownfields, and less than 5 MW solar or wind projects located in low-income communities, there is no penalty payment alternative to the credit if the required conditions are not satisfied. These requirements: for the PTC, which is payable over the ten-year initial period of electric generation, the apprenticeship requirement and prevailing wage requirement in order to realize the ongoing bonus credits over ten years of output would apply for ten years for workers during that period. Wind projects have used the PTC (although they now have a choice of using the ITC going forward under the IRA), and any repairs or alterations during the initial ten years of the project must comply with these requirements to realize the full PTC credit.

laborers and mechanics and use a percentage of apprentice workers during construction and during alteration or repair of a project for its first five years as established by the U.S. Department of Labor (although the U.S. Treasury administers the tax credit provisions of the IRA).[37] The ITC is realized at the time of initial completion of the project. Many states also offer state apprenticeship credits.

Prevailing Wage Bonus Incentive Credit

This prevailing wage includes wages and fringe benefits, so it is a combined wage rate. U.S. prevailing wages vary significantly by region and cost of living and are influenced by whether or not organized labor is active in that region. Good faith effort exceptions only apply to the apprenticeship requirement, which can be satisfied by a good faith request for an apprentice, and no such exceptions are available for not paying prevailing wages. There is a $5,000 penalty paid to the U.S. Treasury for each underpaid laborer on a solar or wind project that seeks to utilize the credit.[38]

Apprenticeship Bonus Incentive Credit

Projects qualifying for these bonus credit amounts will need to engage in using apprentices from apprenticeship programs to gain training and experience in these trades.[39] The required percentage of total labor hours worked by qualified apprentices starts at 10 percent in 2024 and increases in future years to as much as 15 percent.[40] Hiring and mentoring of apprentices generally may be required if four or more individuals are working on a project, and there must be at least one apprentice included in this small group of workers

---

37. *Id.* (to be codified at 26 U.S.C. § 48(a)(10)). Prevailing wages are determined by the U.S. Department of Labor under the Service Contracts Act and apply separately to federally constructed projects covered by the Davis-Bacon Act. See https://sam.gov/content/wage-determinations for the database that shows prevailing wage determinations of particular trades for different laborers by specialty in different states.

38. *Id.* If someone commits an intentional nonpayment of prevailing wages, penalties include making up the deficient wage payment, plus a $10,000 fine paid to the U.S. Treasury per worker not paid at prevailing wages.

39. *Id.* (to be codified at 26 U.S.C. § 48(a)(11)). Project managers will need to make a documented request for apprentices, retain and pay apprentices if they are available, and document all aspects of this. Projects will also need to cause their renewable energy subcontractors to do the same to satisfy the bonus credit requirement.

40. *Id.* § 13101 (to be codified at 26 U.S.C. § 45(b)(8)(A)(ii)).

and more with larger workforces.[41] If one does not comply, one is allowed to make a good faith effort to attempt to find and use apprentices, and if this fails, one can pay a penalty and still realize the bonus tax credits.[42]

There are also significant financial credit bonuses available if strategically planned:

- 10 percent bonus for domestic content requirements for steel, iron, or manufactured components of the project[43]
- 10 percent bonus for projects located in energy communities (these are defined as brownfield sites where there is contamination or fossil fuel–host communities)[44]

Domestic Content Bonus Incentive Credit

The IRA domestic content requirements increase the base rates for tax credits with bonus credits and make the amount available for direct pay in lieu of tax credits for tax-exempt entities under section 501(c)(3) of the Internal Revenue Code and governments for renewable energy, storage, and biogas projects. Such bonus credits are not applicable to hydrogen and carbon capture and storage projects. As part of the IIJA, there was a similar provision only applicable for items procured by and sold to the U.S. government. There is no exception for not meeting domestic content bonus requirements in the IRA for projects of less than 1 MW capacity, as there is for these smaller facilities from the apprenticeship and prevailing wage payment bonus requirements, as well as an exception for projects whose construction commences at least 60 days before promulgation of the relevant regulations for prevailing

---

41. *Id.* (to be codified at 26 U.S.C. § 45(b)(8)(C)). *See* Increased Credit or Deduction Amounts for Satisfying Certain Prevailing Wage and Registered Apprenticeship Requirements, 88 Fed. Reg. 60,018 (proposed Aug. 30, 2023).

42. *Id.* (to be codified at 26 U.S.C. § 45(b)(3)(D)(ii)). On intentional apprenticeship provision violations, the penalty payment is $500/hour for each apprentice deficiency, which for this violation is a cure to receive the higher ITC 30 percent credit. Exceptions to needing to follow prevailing wage and apprenticeship requirements may include:

The 5 percent expenditure "safe harbor" and/or commencement of work

Smaller projects less than 1 MW capacity

43. *Id.* § 13102(l) (to be codified at 26 U.S.C. § 48(a)(12)). For tax preferences for domestic content, see Christopher D. Watson & Molly F. Sherlock, Cong. Rsch. Serv., IN11983, Proposed Tax Preference for Domestic Content in Energy Infrastructure (2022).

44. *Id.* § 13102(o) (to be codified at 26 U.S.C. § 48(a)(14)).

wages and apprenticeship hiring.[45] There is an exception in these bonus credits for not meeting U.S. steel and iron provisions if there is an increase of 25 percent or greater in the cost of construction.[46] Under the IRA:

- 100 percent of steel and iron (not including refinement of steel additives) used in a project must be "produced" in the United States[47] and/or
- 40 percent of all manufactured products for projects and 20 percent for offshore wind projects (with percentages increasing over time) must be produced in the United States for the facility as a whole[48]; suppliers will need to market their products as compliant or not.
  - To increase the value of the PTC, what is covered is the "qualified facility," including the machinery and connections.
  - To increase the value of the ITC, what is covered is the "energy facility" (projects can lock in tax-credit eligibility by "beginning construction").

These bonus incentives of the ITC credit or cash payment from the federal government to the developer/taxpayer increase the amount from 30 percent potentially to 50 percent of power facility cost or as much as 60 percent if serving a low-income community. These credits can cut the net out-of-pocket cost of a new renewable energy development in half. The depreciable basis in property is reduced by one-half of the credit that is taken. Of note, solar and wind projects of less than 1 MW capacity do not need to meet the apprenticeship and prevailing wage provisions to qualify for the 30 percent credit including the bonus,[49] but there is no similar exception for not satisfying the domestic content requirements.

Energy storage facilities are eligible for these credits and bonus credits even if constructed as stand-alone facilities sited apart from and not related to renewable energy projects. Note that energy storage batteries are "manufactured" products, and there is a requirement in the act that manufactured product made in future years must contain a slightly increasing percentage

45. *Id.* § 13102(k) (to be codified at 26 U.S.C. § 48(a)(9), (10)).
46. *Id.* § 13101(g) (to be codified at 26 U.S.C. § 45(b)(10)(D)).
47. *Id.*
48. *Id.* (to be codified at 26 U.S.C. § 45(b)(9)(C)).
49. *Id.* § 13102(k) (to be codified at 26 U.S.C. § 48(a)(9)(B)).

of U.S. content to qualify for bonus credits.[50] This will affect battery storage manufactured products as well as electric power generation manufactured products.

Significance for Stakeholders

The IRA provides a substantial subsidy in the form of an up-front credit or cash payment for a variety of projects beginning construction before 2025:[51] for the first time, the ITC can be paid as cash rather than as a tax credit for certain eligible developers, and under the IRA the ITC becomes more easily transferable without elaborate tax-equity financing.[52] This will allow nontaxable and nonprofit entities to combine with for-profit businesses on these projects. This will incentivize additional renewable power generation in both a centralized and distributed mode, changing the business model (see Chapters 12 and 13). Also eligible for a 30 percent credit are energy storage technologies constructed before January 1, 2025.[53]

It is logical that many of these facilities can be placed either on brownfield sites, where some states already afford greater RPS RECs (see Chapter 8) and/or greater net metering credits (see Chapter 9), or in fossil fuel–host communities. Location in communities where there already are fossil fuel facilities can offer additional advantages: the transmission and distribution infrastructure they utilize may become available as fossil-fuel-fired facilities retire (see Chapter 2).[54]

After 2024, the ITC is replaced by the new technology-neutral Clean Electricity ITC in section 48D of the Tax Act, discussed next.

After 2024: New Clean Electricity ITC under Section 48D

The new IRA-established, technology-neutral ITC (in section 48D) replaces the previous ITC at the end of 2024.[55] Energy-generating taxpayers are allowed to choose between a new PTC (under section 45Y) and this new

---

50. *Id.* § 13101(g) (to be codified at 26 U.S.C. § 45(b)(9)(B)(iii)).

51. *Id.*

52. *Id.* § 13801 (to be codified at 26 U.S.C. § 6417). On tax-equity financing, see MARK P. KEIGHTLEY, DONALD J. MARPLES & MOLLY F. SHERLOCK, CONG. RSCH. SERV., R45693, TAX EQUITY FINANCING: AN INTRODUCTION AND POLICY CONSIDERATIONS (2019).

53. Inflation Reduction Act § 13102(f)(3) (2022) (to be codified at 26 U.S.C. § 48(c)(6)).

54. *Id.* § 13101(g) (to be codified at 26 U.S.C. § 45(b)(11)(B)(i)).

55. *Id.* § 13702 (to be codified at 26 U.S.C. § 48E).

ITC (under section 48D).[56] These credits also can provide cash rather than a tax credit to certain nontaxable entities.[57] There are similar apprenticeship and prevailing wage credit bonus provisions in the new 2025 tax credit provisions as in the IRA provisions discussed earlier for the current tax credit programs.[58] These credits also remain easily transferable without tax-equity financing structures to do so.[59]

As explained later in the PTC discussion, the significant section 186 accelerated depreciation available for renewable energy projects is not transferable to other than the owner(s) of the project, unlike the new federal tax credits and most states' RECs.[60] In addition, in the ITC all the credits are accrued in the year that the project goes into operation and service, unlike the PTC where the credits are spread over ten years of operation, which makes the ITC credit "lumpy" in amount and timing of its realization. The IRS also can later recapture energy credits taken by the transferee, under certain circumstances.

These ITC credits phase out at the later of 2032 or when the electric power sector emits 75 percent less carbon than its 2022 levels.[61] Thereafter, facilities will be able to claim a credit at 100 percent value in the first year, then 75 percent in the second year, 50 percent in the third year, and 0 percent in the fourth year.[62] Reaching this threshold triggers a three-year phase-out with defined annual stepdowns in tax credit value. This new post-2025 phase gets an ITC credit of 30 percent of the investment in the year the facility is placed in service and may qualify for larger bonus credits that can result in the federal government providing tax credits or cash of up to 60 percent of the project cost:[63]

- 10 percent credit bonus for projects located in energy communities (defined as brownfield sites or fossil fuel–host communities)[64]

56. *Id.* §§ 13701, 13702 (to be codified at 26 U.S.C. §§ 45Y, 48E).

57. *Id.* § 13801 (to be codified at 26 U.S.C. § 6417).

58. *Id.* §§ 13701, 13702 (to be codified at 26 U.S.C. §§ 45Y(g)(9), 48E(d)(3)).

59. *Id.* § 13801(b) (to be codified at 26 U.S.C. § 6418). Taxable taxpayers are allowed a one-time transfer of credits, and income received for the transfer is not deemed a taxable amount.

60. *Id.*

61. *Id.* § 13701(a) (to be codified at 26 U.S.C. § 45Y(d)(3)).

62. *Id.* (to be codified at 26 U.S.C. § 45Y(d)(1)).

63. *Id.* § 13702(a) (to be codified at 26 U.S.C. § 48E(a)).

64. *Id.* (to be codified at 26 U.S.C. § 48E(a)(3)(A)).

- 10 percent credit bonus for meeting domestic manufacturing requirements for steel, iron, or manufactured components[65]
- 10 percent bonus for projects located in low-income communities or on tribal land[66]
- 20 percent bonus for projects of less than 5 MW capacity that are located in low-income residential buildings or are part of low-income economic benefit projects—with a cap on total dollar amount of gigawatt-hours of capacity that will benefit from this credit[67]

Significance for Stakeholders

This new credit structure continues the 2022–2024 IRA embellishments of the existing ITC and increases the types of add-on bonus credits. This will steer projects to low-income communities and incentivize use of U.S.-made products. It is still to be determined whether and exactly how foreign equipment manufacturers can assemble/produce foreign-made materials in the United States in order to qualify.

Moreover, projects smaller than 5 MW can include the often expensive costs of interconnection as part of the amount earning this ITC.[68] For the Energy ITC and new Clean Electricity ITC, facilities with maximum net capacity output less than 1 MW are exempt from the prevailing wage, apprenticeship, and content requirements and receive the fivefold credit bonuses automatically.[69] Moreover, section 48C of the act adds a provision for cash payment for certain nonprofits and government agency developers and allows one-time transferability to external parties of the previous credits with no tax consequences for revenue received from such transfer. There is an Advanced Energy Project Credit that extends the 30 percent ITC credit to clean energy projects to strengthen domestic energy manufacturing and support the production and recycling of clean energy products. It also expands to include projects at manufacturing facilities that want to reduce their GHG emissions by at least 20 percent; it is funded at $10 billion for eligible proj-

65. *Id.* (to be codified at 26 U.S.C. § 48E(a)(3)(B)).

66. *Id.* § 13103 (to be codified at 26 U.S.C. § 48(e)).

67. *Id.* (to be codified at 26 U.S.C. § 48(e)(1)(A)(ii)).

68. *Id.* § 13702(a) (to be codified at 26 U.S.C. § 48E(b)(1)(B)(i)(I)) (provides a Clean Investment tax credit for facilities less than 5 MW through 2024).

69. *Id.* § 13102(k) (to be codified at 26 U.S.C. § 48(a)); § 13101(f) (to be codified at 26 U.S.C. § 45(b)(7)).

ects and can be applied to electric storage systems and energy efficiency investments.[70]

Any facility qualifying for either the Clean Energy PTC or ITC would be entitled to five-year modified accelerated cost recovery system (MACRS) depreciation after 2024,[71] as MACRS currently provides for solar and wind generation projects. The depreciable basis in property is reduced by one-half of the credit that is taken.

The Expanded PTC until 2034 or Longer

Section 45 PTC Extension—First Phase

The IRA extends the renewable electricity PTC provided in section 45 of the Tax Act through 2024 when it is replaced by a new technology-neutral Clean Electricity PTC in section 45Y of the Tax Act for projects constructed after 2024.[72] This extension from 2022 to 2024 maintains a PTC credit value of $0.015/kWh generated by eligible facilities.[73] Moreover, it revives the PTC for solar facilities, which eligibility ended in 2006 and now is extended through 2024.[74] It also extends the date of construction for geothermal, wind, closed- and open-loop biomass, landfill gas, municipal solid waste, hydropower, and marine and hydrokinetic facilities for those that commence operation through 2024.[75]

There are significant financial credit bonuses available if strategically planned:

- 10 percent bonus for meeting domestic manufacturing requirements for steel, iron, or manufactured components[76]
- 10 percent bonus for facilities located in energy communities (defined as brownfield sites or fossil fuel–host communities)[77]

---

70. *Id.* § 13501(a) (to be codified at 26 U.S.C. § 48C(e)(2)).
71. *Id.* § 13703(b) (to be codified at 26 U.S.C. § 168(e)(3)(B)).
72. *Id.* § 13101(d) (to be codified at 26 U.S.C. § 168(e)(3)(B)); § 13701 (to be codified at 26 U.S.C. § 45Y).
73. *Id.* § 13101(d) (to be codified at 26 U.S.C. § 45(d)).
74. *Id.* § 13101(c) (to be codified at 26 U.S.C. § 45(d)).
75. *Id.* § 13101(e) (to be codified at 26 U.S.C. § 45(d)).
76. *Id.* § 13101 (to be codified at 26 U.S.C. § 45(b)(9)(B)(ii)).
77. *Id.* (to be codified at 26 U.S.C. § 45(b)(11)(A)).

Significance for Stakeholders

This is a substantial subsidy in the form of payments for each kWh generated by a variety of projects constructed and commencing operation before 2025 whose power output is sold to a third party, including for the first time in 15 years solar generation projects. The act increases the hydropower, municipal solid waste, and marine and hydrokinetic credit to full value (all of which previously qualified only as half-value credits). It also has significance for offshore wind projects, which have had some delays commencing and otherwise could face a credit phase-out for facilities placed in service before 2022. These offshore wind projects are a major component of future power generation capacity (see Chapter 10).

As with the new ITC extension discussed in previous sections, this PTC extension includes cash payment options for certain nonprofit and government owners of projects and makes the credits transferable without elaborate tax-equity financing structures.[78] Only the tax credits are transferable. Solar and wind projects, which have dominated recent U.S. renewable energy projects, enjoy MACRS double-declining-balance accelerated depreciation over five years, which is transferable to other than the owners. Of note, tax-equity financing transfers not only which party enjoys federal tax credits but also the depreciation deductions for the energy project.

Federal loans are available from the DoE, drawn from a $40 billion allocation under section 1703 of the Energy Policy Act of 2005 and a $5 billion fund for activities covered by section 1706 of the act.[79] To realize the renewable electricity PTC, facilities with maximum net output less than 1 MW capacity are exempt from the prevailing wage, apprenticeship, and domestic content requirements and receive these bonus credit values automatically.[80] This will provide an incentive for smaller distributed power projects. This PTC is replaced in 2025 with the new section 45Y credit.

2025 and After: Clean Electricity PTC under Section 45Y

This newly established, technology-neutral PTC supplants the section 45 Renewable Electricity PTC after 2024.[81] Taxpayers will be allowed to choose between a PTC under section 45Y and an ITC under section 48D. The

78. *Id.* § 13801 (to be codified at 26 U.S.C. § 6417).
79. *Id.* § 13101 (to be codified at 26 U.S.C. § 45(b)(6)(B)).
80. *Id.* (to be codified at 26 U.S.C. § 45Y(g)(12)(B)(ii)).
81. *Id.* § 13701(a) (to be codified at 26 U.S.C. § 45Y).

section 45Y credit applies to any zero or negative GHG emissions facility a PTC value of $0.015/kWh of electricity produced and sold to others or stored at energy storage facilities where the facility is placed into service after 2024.[82] Certain developers can realize a cash payment rather than a PTC credit, and these credits are transferable without an elaborate tax-equity financing structure. The credits are set to phase out at the later of 2032 or when the electric power sector emits 75 percent less carbon than 2022 levels.[83] Thereafter, facilities will be able to claim a credit at 100 percent value in the first year, then 75 percent in the second year, 50 percent in the third year, and 0 percent in the fourth year.[84]

Again here, there are bonus credits that can raise the credit to up to an additional 40 percent greater value:

- 10 percent credit bonus for projects located in energy communities (defined as brownfield sites or fossil fuel–host communities) [85]
- 10 percent credit bonus for meeting domestic manufacturing requirements for steel, iron, or manufactured components[86]
- 10 percent bonus for projects located in low-income communities or on tribal land[87]
- 20 percent bonus for projects that are located in low-income residential buildings or are part of low-income economic benefit projects[88]

After 2024 with a technology-neutral credit system for which energy storage is eligible, storage facilities will not need to store only solar and wind electric energy but can store any energy form.

Significance for Stakeholders

This new credit structure continues into 2025 and beyond the 2022–2024 IRA embellishments of the PTC and increases the per-kWh payment with potential add-on bonus credits. This will steer projects to low-income communities and incentivize use of U.S.-made products. It is still to be determined exactly how foreign equipment manufacturers can assemble premade

82. *Id.*
83. *Id.* (to be codified at 26 U.S.C. § 45Y(d)(2)).
84. *Id.*
85. *Id.* (to be codified at 26 U.S.C. § 45Y(g)(7)).
86. *Id.* (to be codified at 26 U.S.C. § 45Y(g)(11)(B)).
87. *Id.* (to be codified at 26 U.S.C. § 45Y(g)(7)(b)(ii)).
88. *Id.* (to be codified at 26 U.S.C. § 45Y(b)(D)).

materials in the United States in order to qualify. Immediately before the IRA and IIJA were enacted, expert estimates were that the levelized cost of wind and solar power would continue to decline in each additional year. The credits are in effect until the later of 2032 or when U.S. electricity sector carbon dioxide emissions are equal to or below 25 percent of 2022 levels. Now with the IRA and IIJA in place until 2032 and beyond, the after-tax costs of these technologies will be substantially less than estimated before.[89]

These tax credits make a significant difference: the National Renewable Energy Laboratory forecast that the nominal value of IRA ITC or PTC credits is $27.50/MWh ($0.0275/kWh) for ten years or $23/MWh over 20 years.[90] This is a significant value almost equal to the final levelized cost of the power. Modelers at the Electric Power Research Institute forecast upcoming cost reductions of existing generation technologies from 2023 to 2035 because of the IRA credits and provisions to be[91]

- for coal generation 60–83 percent by 2035
- for natural gas generation 46–62 percent by 2035, although capacity remains in place

EPA forecasts that by 2040[92]

- U.S. coal capacity will have fallen by 90 percent.
- Coal capacity operation factors will have fallen below 20 percent.
- Natural gas combined cycle plants will not increase.
- Natural gas simple cycle combustion turbines will increase slightly (which can be used for peaking power and backup for intermittent renewable energy).

Of note, there also are new extended residential energy tax credits of 30 percent[93] for do-it-yourself investments in residential clean renewable

---

89. Tyler Stehly & Patrick Duffy, *2021 Cost of Wind Energy Review* 21, Nat'l Renewable Energy Lab'y, https://www.nrel.gov/docs/fy23osti/84774.pdf.

90. Daniel Steinberg, Nat'l Renewable Energy Lab'y, Presentation at Resources for the Future, IRA Symposium (Feb. 15, 2023).

91. John Bestine, Elec. Power Rsch. Inst., Presentation at Resources for the Future, IRA Symposium (Feb. 15, 2023).

92. Cara Marcy, Env't Prot. Agency, Presentation at Resources for the Future, IRA Symposium (Feb. 15, 2023).

93. Inflation Reduction Act of 2022 § 13302 (to be codified at 26 U.S.C. § 25D).

energy[94] and a credit of 30 percent with capped amounts for energy efficiency investments[95] that are installed in residences of low- and moderate-income families, which respectively will decrease demand for centralized power supply. There are even larger 40 percent residential credits for solar and wind projects in low-income communities or on tribal land and 20 percent credits for facilities that are part of low-income residential housing or low-income economic benefit projects.[96]

Methane Incentives and Penalties for the Power Sector

Not as a subsidy, but as an additional charge on certain types of energy sector development and distribution of fossil fuels, the IRA addresses the second most pernicious GHG molecule, methane. It creates an added charge assessed to methane emissions from specific types of facilities that are required to report their GHG emissions to EPA: initially the charge is $900 per metric ton of methane emitted and increases to $1,500 after two years.[97] There is an exemption from the charge if EPA regulations addressing methane emissions are in effect in all states and will "result in equivalent or greater emissions reductions as would be achieved" by the November 2021 proposed EPA rule.[98] The IRA includes the following federal subsidies[99] available for improving methane capture technologies:

- $850 million to provide grants to facilities subject to the methane charge for such technology as improvements "improving and deploying industrial equipment and processes" that reduce methane emission[100]

---

94. *Id.*

95. *Id.* Tax Act, § 25C.

96. *Id.* § 13701 (to be codified at 26 U.S.C. § 45Y(g)(11)(C)(ii)).

97. *Id.* § 60113 (to be codified at 42 U.S.C. § 136(e)(1)). EPA, Standards of Performance for New, Reconstructed, and Modified Sources and Emissions Guidelines for Existing Sources: Oil and Natural Gas Sector Climate Review, 86 Fed. Reg. 63110 (Nov. 15, 2021). For more background on these issues, see Richard K. Lattanzio, Cong. Rsch. Serv., R42986, Methane and Other Air Pollution Issues in Natural Gas Systems (2020), https://sgp.fas.org/crs/misc/R42986.pdf.

98. Inflation Reduction Act § 60113 (2022) (to be codified at 42 U.S.C. § 136(f)(6)(a)(ii)).

99. For more information, see Jonathan L. Ramseur, Cong. Rsch. Serv., R45472, Market-Based Greenhouse Gas Emission Reduction Legislation: 108th through 117th Congresses (2022); Jonathan L. Ramseur, Cong. Rsch. Serv., R47206, Inflation Reduction Act Methane Emissions Charge: In Brief (2022).

100. Inflation Reduction Act § 60113 (2022) (to be codified at 42 U.S.C. § 136(a)).

- $700 million for "marginal conventional wells" for similar purposes as previously, including at oil and natural gas facilities[101]

For more details on the Biden administration policies and tax provisions affecting methane from the energy sector and the agriculture sector, see Chapter 16.

Strategically Selecting among Federal Tax Credits

Wind power projects conventionally used the PTC but have had the alternative of utilizing the federal ITC, which solar power projects traditionally used because they were not allowed to use the PTC.[102] There are two reasons for this. First, the ITC provides a 30 percent of capital investment tax credit upon completion of the renewable energy investment.[103] Because, per kW of generating capacity, the capital cost of solar power generation is greater than that of wind power generation, a flat 30 percent of investment credit applied against the greater amount of investment capital spent to construct a solar project results in a larger tax credit per kW of installed solar capacity than wind capacity. The ITC adds most value for the renewable energy investments with the highest capital cost per unit of generating capacity. As well, until the IRA, the PTC was not available for solar.

Second, wind power generates at a significantly larger capacity factor (the percentage of hours in the year when a power generator actually is able to operate accounting for different output quantity at different times) than does fixed-panel solar power in the United States. Of note, both technologies have a relatively low capacity factor compared to most fossil-fuel-fired generation. Wind and solar power are intermittent in their operations and thus distinct from traditional forms of baseload power deployed in the United States. Both fixed-panel photovoltaic (PV) solar and wind power demonstrate a relatively low availability factor in the 10–50 percent range of hours during a week or month in which they typically have sufficient sunshine or wind to operate, with fixed-panel solar on the lower end of this range.

The record U.S. annual wind capacity factor was 33.9 percent in 2014; the EIA recorded the median wind capacity factor over a recent decade as

101. *Id.* § 60113 (to be codified at 42 U.S.C. § 136(b)).
102. 26 U.S.C. § 45.
103. *Id.* § 48.

31 percent.[104] In the United Kingdom, the wind capacity factor ranged from a low of 21.5 percent in 2010 to a high of 27.9 percent in 2013.[105] The fixed-panel PV solar capacity factor in the United States in many locations is less than 15 percent. Therefore, depending on siting location in the United States (see Chapter 3), wind projects can enjoy a capacity factor more than double that for fixed-panel solar generation.

The stream of credit/payment realized from these two federal tax credits is different: the PTC pays its subsidy per unit of power output actually produced and metered for sale to a third party during its first ten years of operation. Differently, the ITC rebates as an investment tax credit at the time of construction and filing of tax returns a percentage of the initial capital investment in the eligible project regardless of how much the project actually operates, if at all. Wind projects, with typically more hours of operation and power production compared to fixed solar panels, may produce power at a double or triple capacity factor and have an advantage in taking the PTC, which credit compensates the project owner based on its total output of electric power. Based on amount of kWh of production, the PTC is worth more for a higher-capacity project, ceteris paribus.

Opportunity Zones—Power and Storage Location Benefits

Where one locates renewable energy within Opportunity Zones can be doubly remunerative: December 2017 tax law amendments added new Opportunity Zone incentives that offset capital gains, which could be utilized for renewable energy in any of the more than 8,700 designated Opportunity Zones across the United States.[106] Many Opportunity Zones correspond to the less developed land areas where wind power is most available in the United States. For a renewable energy facility, the Opportunity Zone capital gains tax reduction benefit can be realized along with realization of the ITC or PTC federal credits. The benefits of Opportunity Zone incentives

104. Planning Engineer & Rud Istvan, *True Costs of Wind Electricity*, CLIMATE ETC. (May 12, 2015), http://judithcurry.com/2015/05/12/true-costs-of-wind-electricity/.

105. *Id.*

106. Tax Cuts and Jobs Act, Pub. L. No. 115–97, § 1400Z-2, 131 Stat. 2054, 2174 (2017) (codified as amended in I.R.C. § 1400Z-2); *Opportunity Zones Frequently Asked Questions*, INTERNAL REVENUE SERV. (Feb. 27, 2024), https://www.irs.gov/newsroom/opportunity-zones-frequently-asked-questions#designated.

are available to taxpayers when they sell an existing investment and within 180 days thereafter invest the proceeds into a qualified opportunity fund; that fund then invests in Opportunity Zone property, which can be through either direct investment in tangible business property or newly issued equity interests in a partnership or corporation operating a business in an Opportunity Zone.[107]

The Opportunity Zone incentive provides three key capital gain tax benefits to investors.[108] First, for each such investment it allows federal capital gains taxes on the sale, if thereafter invested in qualified opportunity funds in Opportunity Zones, to be deferred until the 2026 tax year.[109] Second, if the taxpayer holds the new qualified opportunity fund for five years, the capital gain ultimately recognized as taxable income when that investment is sold could be reduced by 10 percent.[110] It may be reduced by an additional 5 percent if the taxpayer holds the new investment in the Opportunity Zone for at least seven years.[111] Finally, if the taxpayer holds the investment for at least a decade, capital gains realized from the original sale before rolling that investment into an Opportunity Zone area are free from federal income tax upon disposition of that subsequent investment due to a step-up in basis of the investment to its fair market value at the time of disposition.[112] In other words, all taxes on gain from these investments can be negated.

Operating either power generation or power storage facilities in these zones, those taking advantage of these projects would want to structure their business plan to avoid depreciation recapture on sale or flipping ownership of the asset at a later point. Of note, utilization of these federal tax incentives for an energy generation or storage project, including the location-specific Opportunity Zone credit, can be blocked by any city or town that deploys location-specific zoning prohibitions. See Chapter 10.

107. Tax Cuts and Jobs Act § 1400Z-2(d).
108. *Id.* § 1400Z-2(b).
109. *Id.* § 1400Z-2(b)(1).
110. *Id.* § 1400Z-2(b)(2)(B)(iii).
111. *Id.* § 1400Z-2(b)(2)(B)(iv).
112. *Id.* § 1400Z-2(c).

Tax Law Changes: Not Always Positive for the Electric Sector

The Tax Cuts and Jobs Act enacted at the end of 2017[113] affects investment in the energy sector and other capital-intensive industries.[114] Despite the attention over permanent dramatically lower tax rates for corporations, this tax reform, which helps businesses generally, can have mixed effects for certain projects.[115]

Decrease in Corporate Tax Rate

The Tax Cuts and Jobs Act dramatically lowered the corporate tax rate on a permanent basis, unlike the graduated rate reductions for individual taxpayers, which are temporary and will expire. The corporate tax rate was changed to a flat 21 percent, a reduction of more than 40 percent to the prior top rate. The IRA adds a 15 percent corporate minimum tax, which creates for the first time a significant "floor" beneath the corporate tax rate, also adopted by two-thirds of all world countries to construct a new allocation of taxing rights among nations.[116]

Depreciation Deductions for Power Generation

The Tax Cuts and Jobs Act affects the cash value of depreciation deductions for energy projects. At the new, lower corporate tax rate of 21 percent, down from a prior top rate of 35 percent, the cash value of depreciation and bonus depreciation is reduced. Solar energy projects enjoy an accelerated five-year depreciation period for corporations under section 168 of the code,[117] as well

---

113. Tax Cuts and Jobs Act, Pub. L. No. 115–97, § 11001(a)(j)(1), 131 Stat. 2054, 2054 (2017) (noting that the effective date is "after December 31, 2017").

114. For more information, see Michael H. Levin, *Will the Tax Cuts Act Cut Back AD?*, BioCycle (Feb. 8, 2018), https://www.biocycle.net/2018/02/08/will-tax-cuts-act-cut-back-ad/.

115. Press Release, Ctr. for Am. Progress, As U.S. House Prepares to Vote on Yet More Tax Breaks and Extenders, New CAP Brief Highlights Fiscal Damage Stemming from the Tax Cuts and Jobs Act (Nov. 29, 2018), https://www.americanprogress.org/press/release/2018/11/29/461591/release-u-s-house-prepares-vote-yet-tax-breaks-extenders-new-cap-brief-highlights-fiscal-damage-stemming-tax-cuts-jobs-act/. *See generally* Tax Cuts and Jobs Act, Pub. L. No. 115–97, 131 Stat. 2054, *passim* (2017).

116. *Schumer-Manchin Deal Includes Renewable Energy Provisions, Including ITC, PTC Extensions*, Novogradac (July 28, 2022), https://www.novoco.com/news/schumer-manchin-deal-includes-renewable-energy-provisions-including-itc-ptc-extensions.

117. I.R.C. § 168(e)(3)(B)(vi)(I).

as bonus depreciation.[118] Bonus depreciation earned by corporations in the power industry is estimated to be $10 billion.[119]

Expensing of Power Sector Capital Investments

The Tax Reform Act allows small businesses immediately to expense up to $1 million in qualified expenditures (including costs of modifications to use biogas or of new roofs to support solar panels)—a 33 percent increase from the past allowed amount of $750,000.[120] It also allowed all businesses to claim 100 percent "bonus depreciation" in the first year on equipment purchased after September 27, 2017, and placed in service after January 1, 2018 (subject to a phase-down of 20 percent for equipment placed in service during each year after 2022).[121] The 100 percent amount represented a nominal doubling of the previous bonus depreciation deduction.[122]

Interest Deduction on Debt Financing of Power Projects

The Tax Reform Act capped business interest deductions at 30 percent of an entity's earnings before interest, taxes, depreciation, and amortization.[123] More severe caps are implemented after 2021.[124] Interest deductions previously were not capped, and all interest was deductible.

Net Operating Losses for Electric Power

The Tax Reform Act restricts the value and application of project operating losses.[125] Under past and current tax law, tax losses are not refundable in a given tax year.[126] Therefore they need to be applied to either past or future

---

118. I.R.C. § 168(k)(1)(A)–(B).

119. *See* Paul Carlsen, *"Bonus Depreciation" Boosting Industry Cash Flow about $10 Billion, but More IRS Guidance Awaiting*, ELECTRIC UTIL WK. 25 (Mar. 14, 2011) (asserting that bonus depreciation would provide $10 billion over the next few years).

120. Tax Cuts and Jobs Act, Pub. L. No. 115–97, § 11001(a), 131 Stat. 2054, 2054 (2017); § 13101(a), (f), 131 Stat. at 2101; *see also* Levin, *supra* note 114.

121. Tax Cuts and Jobs Act § 13201(a)(1)–(2), 131 Stat. at 2105.

122. *See id.* (doubling the rate from 50 to 100 percent for equipment "placed in service after September 27, 2017, and before January 1, 2023").

123. *Id.* § 13301(a), 131 Stat. at 2117.

124. *Id.* § 13301(8)(A)(v), 131 Stat. at 2120.

125. *See id.*

126. *See id.*

tax years to offset net operating income. Prior to the 2017 changes, project net operating losses (NOLs) were allowed to be carried back two previous tax years or carried forward 20 future tax years at 100 percent value to offset past or future net taxable income.[127] If applied to one of the prior two years with net income, they would generate immediate refundable tax rebates with an amendment of a prior year tax return. If NOLs were carried forward, the taxpayer would wait for future years to monetize these deductions against future taxable income. The 2017 act also makes use of NOLs unidirectional: it eliminates reverse direction "carryback" of losses; the forward direction is preserved, with 20-year deductibility of NOLs being carried forward.

There also was a change in value of business losses.[128] The 2017 act restricts NOL deductibility to 80 percent of taxable income instead of the prior 100 percent of income deductibility.[129] NOLs were monetized by bringing in new equity owners or partners who had past or future tax year net income against which they could utilize accumulated losses.[130] All owners, whether original or new, are subject to these new restrictions on percentage credit value.[131]

Pass-Through of Electric Power Taxes

The Tax Reform Act affects energy projects that utilize a "pass-through" entity structure, such as an LLC or equivalent structure. The act provides a permanent 20 percent tax deduction for these entities' qualifying business income for income tax calculation.[132] As these tax aspects are passed through to individual energy project owners, if their income is less than $157,500

---

127. *See* Levin, *supra* note 114.

128. *See id.* ("[T]he Act generally restricts NOL deductibility to 80 percent of an acquirer's taxable income.").

129. *Id.*

130. *See* Christopher B. Grady, *Finding the Pearl in the Oyster: Supercharging IPOS through Tax Receivable Agreements*, 111 Nw. U. L. Rev. 483, 506 (2017) ("NOLs occur when a taxpayer has deductions in excess of gross income for a given tax year, resulting in a net loss for the year. Taxpayers are permitted to carry the loss back to apply to the two preceding years, or carry it forward up to twenty years. In either case, the NOL is allowed as a deduction from the taxable income for that year. Monetization occurs through § 381, which permits an acquiring corporation to carry over certain tax attributes, including NOLs, of the acquired corporation.").

131. *See* Levin, *supra* note 114.

132. Tax Cuts and Jobs Act, Pub. L. No. 115–97, § 11011(a), 131 Stat. 2054, 2063 (2017).

for a single taxpayer or $315,000 for a joint taxpayer in the original year of implementation, this tax reduction can be realized.[133]

Alternative Minimum Tax

The Tax Reform Act repealed the corporate Alternative Minimum Tax (AMT) but not the individual AMT.[134] Previously, the AMT raised taxes from energy companies that offset tax by use of energy investment or production tax credits and other "tax preference" items and paid tax under the AMT rather than ordinary tax rates in the tax code.[135] Repeal of the corporate AMT eliminates the risk of AMT recapture during the final six years of eligibility for the ten-year PTC.

State Property Tax Exemptions for Certain Renewable Power Generation

Renewable energy is expected to claim about two-thirds of the spending on new power plants over the next quarter century—dwarfing spending on new fossil fuel electric facilities.[136] Capital-intensive renewable energy generation can incur additional property tax assessments if corporate solar and wind installations are taxable as personal property by local governments. For example, the Massachusetts legislature enacted this tax provision:

> Any solar or wind powered system or device which is being utilized as a primary or auxiliary power system for the purpose of heating or otherwise supplying the energy needs of property [is not] taxable under this chapter; provided, however, that the exemption under this clause shall be allowed only for a period of twenty years from the date of the installation of such system or device.[137]

The Massachusetts Department of Revenue issued an opinion of this provision that would provide an exemption from state property tax only if a corporation had a high enough power demand to use all of the renewable energy it produced, rather than sell the excess power or net meter it by

133. *Id.* § 11011(a), 131 Stat. at 2067.

134. *Id.* § 12001(a)–(b), 131 Stat. at 2092.

135. *See* Levin, *supra* note 114.

136. Ehren Goossens, *Renewables to Beat Fossil Fuels with $3.7 Trillion Solar Boom*, Bloomberg (June 23, 2015), https://www.bloomberg.com/news/articles/2015-06-23/renewables-to-beat-fossil-fuels-with-3-7-trillion-solar-boom.

137. Mass. Gen. Laws ch. 59, § 5 (2018).

transferring its net metering credits to other entities.[138] Corporations challenged this as too restrictive an interpretation.[139] The Massachusetts Appellate Tax Board disagreed with the Massachusetts Department of Revenue. The board held that there was no statutory limitation on the location of the "property taxable under this chapter" and determined that, had the legislature wanted such a limitation, it would have drafted the statute to include one.[140] The Massachusetts Appellate Tax Board held:

> While the [Massachusetts] Department of Revenue . . . interpreted [the exemption] so as to limit its application only to solar property that is located either on the same parcel or a contiguous parcel to the property it is intended to power . . . the Department's limitation . . . [is found] to be an *illusory distinction* which finds *no basis in [the exemption] . . . and* an *incorrect* interpretation of a statute by an administrative agency is entitled to no deference.[141]

This is a favorable court determination for power project developers with multiple locations or that want to sell surplus renewable electric power that they produce. In a subsequent decision of the Massachusetts Appellate Tax Board, applying to a net metered project that earned state net metering credits of which 2 percent were allocated to the residential bills of the taxpayer and 98 percent were credited to the electricity bills of four branches of an unrelated corporation's electricity bills, located in several different towns in Massachusetts, the board interpreted the application of this credit even more flexibly.[142] The recipient corporation agreed to pay the owners 95 percent of the "dollar value for the credited electricity appearing on [their] . . . electricity bill."[143] The renewable energy-producing property was

---

138. Forrestall Enters., Inc. v. Bd. of Assessors, No. F317708, 2014 WL 6863331, at *1, *4 (Mass. App. Tax Bd. Dec. 4, 2014).

139. *Id.* Bruce Forrestall, the sole owner of appellant, Forrestall Enterprises, owned a five-acre property, "the Milk Street property," on which a 240 kW solar PV system containing approximately 856 panels was installed, to be used to power the Forrestall Westborough Properties through a net metering agreement with National Grid. *Id.*.

140. *Id.*

141. *Id.* (emphasis added).

142. KTT, L.L.C. v. Bd. of Assessors of Swansea, No. F322736, 2016 WL 6210310 at 429 (Mass. App. Tax Bd. Oct. 13, 2016).

143. *Id.* The appeal of the town was eventually dropped when a PILOT agreement was negotiated with the town. Michael Holtzman, *16-Year PILOT Agreement Signed for Swansea Solar Farm,*

found to remain untaxable for a period of 20 years from the date of solar project installation, so long as it is producing energy.

Other states also provide property tax exemptions for certain distributed power production. In New Jersey, there is an exemption from local property tax for the value added to a property from corporate renewable energy systems that are used to supply on-site electricity, heating, cooling, or general energy needs.[144] Arizona exempts from property taxes all renewable energy systems used to meet on-site needs.[145] Rhode Island exempts from property taxation a corporate manufacturer's inventory, machinery, and equipment.[146] A person is considered a manufacturer within the state if they use property for the purpose of transforming raw materials into a finished product for trade.[147] In Rhode Island when renewable energy, such as from a wind turbine, is used exclusively for the transformation of natural resources into a finished product, it qualifies as manufacturing equipment and therefore is exempt from property taxation.[148]

A Colorado court held that the state's manufacturing exemption, which encompasses machinery and tools used "directly and predominantly in manufacturing tangible personal property, for sale or profit," did not apply to the corporate taxpayer's machinery used for the generation of electricity.[149] In Arizona, third-party leased solar panels were not deemed as utility property to be taxed by the state, although the court did not resolve, and sent back to the state tax court, questions regarding whether municipalities could assess local property tax on leased solar panels on property.[150]

Herald News (Oct. 12, 2017), https://www.heraldnews.com/story/news/politics/county/2017/10/12/16-year-pilot-agreement-signed/18320462007/.

144. The exemption is the difference between the total assessed value of the property before and after the renewable energy system has been installed. *Abatements and Exemptions: Renewable Energy System Property Tax Exemption*, N.J. Treasury, Div. of Tax'n, https://www.nj.gov/treasury/taxation/lpt/lpt-abatements.shtml#:~:text=Renewable%20Energy%20System%20Property%20Tax%20Exemption,-If%20you%20have&text=The%20exemption%20is%20the%20difference,file%20with%20your%20tax%20assessor (last visited May 10, 2024).

145. Ariz. Rev. Stat. Ann. § 42-11054 (2009).

146. 44 R.I. Gen. Laws § 44–3–3 (2018).

147. *Id.*

148. DePasquale v. Cwiek, 129 A.3d 72, 74 (R.I. 2016).

149. *See* Dep't of Revenue v. Pub. Serv. Co. of Colo., 330 P.3d 385, 387 (Colo. 2014).

150. SolarCity Corp. v. Ariz. Dep't of Revenue, 413 P.3d 678, 680, 683 (Ariz. 2018).

Prerequisite Compliance for Certain Energy Projects Needing Federal Permits or with Federal Financing

Power generation and transmission projects often trigger a preconstruction federal review that can require a great amount of time and resources prior to obtaining necessary siting, construction, and operating permits. Environmental review and environmental impact statements (EISs) have been embedded in both federal and many state laws since the early 1970s.[151] Section 102(c) in the federal National Environmental Protection Act (NEPA) requires preconstruction environmental impact studies "where a major federal action significantly affects the quality of the human environment."[152] Federal agencies must comply with NEPA before there are "any irreversible and irretrievable commitments of resources which would be involved in the proposed action should it be implemented."[153]

While an EIS need not include all of the underlying data on which it is based,[154] it must disclose and discuss responsible opposing views,[155] taking a "hard look" at the environmental consequences of the decision to go forward with a project.[156] The considered effects include "ecological (such as the effects on natural resources and on the components, structures, and functioning of affected ecosystems), aesthetic, historic, cultural, economic, social, or health, whether direct, indirect, or cumulative," effects.[157] Under NEPA regulations, agencies must consider all reasonable alternatives, including those not specifically under their authority to implement.[158]

The Government Accountability Office estimated that approximately 94 percent of agency actions requiring possible environmental review escape such review based on Categorical Exclusions, while approximately 5 percent proceed only to much more abbreviated Environmental Assessments

---

151. National Environmental Policy Act of 1969 § 102, 42 U.S.C. § 4332.

152. *Id.* § 102(2)(C), 42 U.S.C. § 4332(C).

153. 42 U.S.C. § 4332(C)(v); *see also* 40 C.F.R. §§ 1501.2, 1502.5(a).

154. *See* Sierra Club v. Kimbell, 595 F. Supp. 2d 1021, 1039 (D. Minn. 2009) ("There is no requirement that an EIS include all of the underlying data on which it is based.").

155. Pac. Coast Fed'n of Fishermen's Ass'ns v. Nat'l Marine Fisheries Serv., 482 F.2d 1248, 1253 (W.D. Wash. 2007).

156. Wilderness Soc'y v. Salazar, 603 F. Supp. 2d 52, 59 (D.D.C. 2009).

157. 40 C.F.R. § 1508.8.

158. *See* 40 C.F.R. § 1502.14; NRDC v. Morton, 458 F.2d 827 (D.C. Cir. 1972).

(EAs), leaving less than 1 percent of all reviewed projects that are required to proceed to a full EIS.[159] Full EISs now typically number less than 190 filed each year by all federal government agencies; federal court cases challenging agency compliance with NEPA are now filed on less than 100 of these decisions annually, with approximately half challenging the adequacy or completeness of the EIS that is prepared.[160] Cost and time for completion are another significant factor for power projects: a NEPA task force report "estimated that an EIS typically cost[s] from $250,000 to $2 million," whereas "an EA typically costs from $5,000 to $200,000."[161] From 2000 to 2012, the average preparation time for an EIS was 4.6 years, having increased on average at a rate of 34 days per year.[162]

NEPA (non)compliance is seeding new battles regarding power supply options and the regulatory approval process—even pitting one new renewable energy technology against another. In 2022, a multistate solar PV power developer legally challenged the first tranche of multiple separate offshore wind power projects in the Northeast on NEPA noncompliance grounds.[163] At the end of 2023, the DoE proposed rules to categorically exclude either EISs or EAs for solar projects on already developed land of any size instead of the previous limit of ten acres, energy storage projects on or adjacent to already disturbed land, or any upgrading of transmission lines of any length rather than the previous limit of no more than 20 miles in length. Such a change avoiding significant time previously devoted to NEPA review for renewable projects and their need for transmission upgrades and

---

159. *See* U.S. Gov't Accountability Off., National Environmental Policy Act: Little Information Exists on NEPA Analyses 8–9, 13–14, 16 (2014) [hereinafter GAO], https://www.gao.gov/assets/670/662546.pdf (implying that environmental impact assessments are rare, contrary to general expectations).

160. Letter from Robert H. Abrams et al. to Chairman Bishop et al. (Apr. 24, 2018), https://web.archive.org/web/20211216215230/https://cpr-assets.s3.amazonaws.com/documents/Law_Professor_Letter_House_NEPA_Hearing_042418.pdf.

161. GAO, *supra* note 159, at 13–14.

162. *See* Annual NEPA Report 2012 of the National Environmental Policy Act (NEPA) Practice 11 (Judith Charles et al. eds., 2013), https://ceq.doe.gov/docs/get-involved/NAEP_2012_NEPA_Annual_Report.pdf (noting that the average completion time for an EIS was about 4.6 years in 2012). The average completion time for an EA issued by DoE was 13 months. GAO, *supra* note 159, at 14–15.

163. Allco Renewable Energy Ltd. v. Haaland, No. 1:21-cv-11171, 2022 WL 18033002 (D. Mass. Jan. 7, 2022), first amended complaint (Feb. 23, 2022).

improvements addresses one issue; still remaining can be bottlenecks for some distributed renewable energy supply related to city zoning (see Chapter 10) or state permits (see Chapter 11).

After the analysis of these revenue and credit incentives embedded in federal tax regulations for new power infrastructure projects, the next chapter pivots to focus on the analysis of costs affecting the environment, mandated by the Supreme Court.

CHAPTER 7

Environmental Cost-Benefit Analysis for Power

Supreme Court: U.S. Electricity Regulation Must Consider Costs

The flip side of the prior chapter's examination of incentives and revenue embedded in new statutory laws affecting electric power is cost. Cost now becomes a major required consideration when regulating electricity and its environmental impacts according to the U.S. Supreme Court, which for the first time recently required consideration of cost in its 5–4 decision in *Michigan v. EPA*.[1] This new cost consideration now moves to the center of what the National Academy of Engineers considers the most significant engineering achievement of all time—the U.S. electric system and grid.[2] Electric power has gravitas: the World Bank determined that electricity is one of the most powerful economic development enablers/multipliers.[3]

How did cost become a consideration imposed by the country's highest court? It began in the executive branch: both the Obama administration[4] and the Trump administration[5] used unilateral federal executive orders, without

---

1. Michigan v. Env't Prot. Agency, 135 S. Ct. 2699 (2015).

2. George Constable & Bob Somerville, A Century of Innovation: Twenty Engineering Achievements That Transformed Our Lives (2003).

3. World Bank Indep. Eval. Grp., The Welfare Impact of Rural Electrification: A Reassessment of the Costs and Benefits (2008).

4. *See* Steven Ferrey, *Presidential Executive Action: Unilaterally Changing the World's Critical Technology and Infrastructure*, 64 Drake L.R. 43 (2016).

5. Jacqueline Alemany, *Trump Signs Executive Order Dismantling Obama Environmental Regulations*, CBS News (Mar. 28, 2017), http://www.cbsnews.com/news/trump-signs-executive-order-dismantling-obama-environmental-regulations/; Dan Boyce, *Trump Targets EPA and Obama Climate Change Regulations*, Inside Energy (Mar. 29, 2017), http://insideenergy.org/2017/03/29/trump-targets-epa-and-obama-climate-change-regulations/.

involving the Congress, to make policy affecting electric power. A study conducted by EPA over more than 20 years concluded that the nation's power plants using coal as their fuel are the largest source of nonnatural mercury deposition into the environment.[6] Coal-fired power-generation units produce more hazardous emissions, such as mercury, compared to other fossil-fuel power generation technologies.[7] Mercury (Hg) is a naturally occurring element,[8] released to the environment in significant quantities through burning coal.[9] Mercury is a pollutant that is regulated as a hazardous chemical by the Clean Air Act.[10]

The Obama administration Environmental Protection Agency (EPA) promulgated its Mercury and Air Toxics Standard (MATS) rule to rein in and discourage coal use for electricity generation and thereby to reduce its climate-changing emissions.[11] The cost and benefit of reducing coal-power plants' hazardous mercury air pollution under the rule:

- Costs imposed on the U.S. electric industry—approximately $9.6 billion annually
- *Direct* public mercury reduction benefits—$4–$5 million annually[12]
- These costs were approximately 2,000 times greater than estimated *direct* benefits

---

6. *Fact Sheet: Final Consideration of Cost in the Appropriate and Necessary Finding for the Mercury and Air Toxics Standards for Power Plants*, U.S. Env't Prot. Agency (Apr. 4, 2016), https://www.epa.gov/sites/production/files/2016-05/documents/20160414_mats_ff_fr_fs.pdf; *see Pollution*, Nat'l Wildlife Fed., https://www.nwf.org/Educational-Resources/Wildlife-Guide/Threats-to-Wildlife/Pollution (last visited May 10, 2024) ("Coal-fired power plants are the single largest source of mercury contamination in the United States, responsible for approximately 50 percent of human-caused mercury emissions. Other sources include waste incinerators that burn mercury-containing products and chlorine manufacturers. However, unlike these sources, power plants haven't had to limit their mercury pollution.").

7. Env't Prot. Agency, Reducing Toxic Pollution from Power Plants: EPA's Proposed Mercury Standards 2 (2011), https://www.epa.gov/mats/cleaner-power-plants#controls; James E. McCarthy & Claudia Copeland, Cong. Rsch. Serv., R41914, EPA's Regulation of Coal-Fired Power: Is a "Train Wreck" Coming? (2011), https://www.fas.org/sgp/crs/misc/R41914.pdf.

8. *Basic Information about Mercury and Air Toxics Standards*, U.S. Env't Prot. Agency (Jan. 8, 2024), https://www.epa.gov/mats/basic-information-about-mercury-and-air-toxics-standards.

9. *Id.*

10. 42 U.S.C. § 7412.

11. Michigan v. Env't Prot. Agency, 135 S. Ct. 2699, 2705–06 (2015) (citing 77 Fed. Reg. 9326).

12. *Id.*

- Does not include indirect cobenefits unrelated to mercury emissions (discussed more later)

The Supreme Court held this unilateral executive branch federal MATS rule to be illegal unless it first considered costs. Efforts of the Obama administration to regulate electric power generation and its climate impacts were bracketed before and after by three other Supreme Court decisions:

- First was an executive branch attempt to regulate interstate migration of power plant criteria air pollutants, eventually upheld by the Supreme Court in *EME Homer City Generation LP v. EPA*.[13]
- A year later, the executive branch attempted to restrict coal plant hazardous mercury emissions, which was overturned and remanded by the Supreme Court in the *Michigan v. EPA* challenge.[14]
- A year after the *Michigan* decision, the Clean Power Plan (CPP) executive branch attempt to restrict CO_2 global warming emissions focusing on coal-fired electric power plants was preliminarily enjoined indefinitely by the Supreme Court in the *West Virginia v. EPA* case in 2016.[15]
- In 2022, again in *West Virginia v. EPA*, the CPP executive branch rule affecting power plants was held to be illegal pursuant to the Major Questions Doctrine.[16] See Chapter 4 for more on this case.

The MATS Costs and Benefits Focused on Power Generation

The key cost aspect of the MATS Supreme Court opinion focused on power generation facilities: the final rule set standards for all hazardous air pollutants emitted by coal and oil-fired electric generating units with a generation capacity of 25 megawatts or greater.[17] MATS was specifically aimed at reducing power plants' emissions of hazardous air pollutants, including arsenic, chromium, nickel, hydrochloric acid, and hydrofluoric acid, in addition

13. EME Homer City Generation LP v. EPA, 696 F.3d 7 (D.C. Cir. 2012), *rev'd*, E.P.A. v. EME Homer City Generation, L.P., 134 S. Ct. 1584 (2014).

14. *Michigan*, 135 S. Ct. at 2711.

15. West Virginia v. EPA, Order 15-A773 (Feb. 9, 2016) (stay by Court).

16. West Virginia v. EPA, 597 U.S. 697 (2022).

17. *Basic Information about Mercury and Air Toxics Standards*, U.S. Env't Prot. Agency (Jan. 8, 2024), https://www.epa.gov/mats/basic-information-about-mercury-and-air-toxics-standards; 77 Fed. Reg. 9304 (Feb. 16, 2012) (to be codified at 40 C.F.R. pts. 60 & 63). *See* 77 Fed. Reg. at 9309.

to mercury.[18] The rule provided existing electricity generators four years to come into compliance, with an additional year available to the power plants that the Federal Energy Regulatory Commission (FERC) had deemed reliability-critical, that is, essential to maintaining adequate reliable power supply, voltage, and ancillary support for the nation's bulk power system or restarting the electrical network in case of a blackout.[19]

EPA's MATS regulation was challenged by Michigan and 22 other states along with some industry stakeholders, arguing that the EPA in promulgating the rule did not consider cost.[20] The MATS rule was estimated by EPA to "avert up to 11,000 premature deaths, 4,700 heart attacks, and 130,000 asthma attacks every year" as benefits.[21] Challengers argued that the EPA's MATS rule to control emission of mercury was unreasonable, as the rule, according to EPA's calculations, would require coal-fired power plants to spend about $9.6 billion annually while realizing *direct* benefits of only $4–$6 million from the reduction of directly targeted mercury emissions.[22] This created a 1:2,000 direct benefit–cost ratio showing cost greatly exceeding direct benefits.

EPA countered that cost was irrelevant in making its Clean Air Act rule.[23] EPA argued that it did not do an analysis of regulation-related cost because the language of the Clean Air Act does not explicitly require EPA to consider cost for such regulations. Whenever the statute is ambiguous, EPA's argument was that it could interpret and resolve the ambiguity reasonably within its discretion. More states challenged the MATS rule than supported it.[24] The Supreme Court overturned the EPA MATS regulation of mercury and other hazardous pollutants because

---

18. *Fact Sheet: Mercury and Air Toxics Standards for Power Plants*, U.S. Env't Prot. Agency (Dec. 21, 2011), https://www.epa.gov/mats/epa-announces-mercury-and-air-toxics-standards-mats-power-plants-rules-and-fact-sheets.

19. *Id.* at 2.

20. Michigan v. Env't Prot. Agency, 135 S. Ct. 2699, 2704 (2015).

21. *Healthier Americans*, U.S. Env't Prot. Agency (Jan. 25, 2024), https://www.epa.gov/mats/healthier-americans.

22. *Michigan*, 135 S. Ct. at 2705–06 (citing 77 Fed. Reg. 9326).

23. *Id.* at 2706.

24. *Id.* at 2705–06. Fifteen states supported the EPA's MATS regulation before the Court. *See generally* Brief in Opposition, *Michigan*, 135 S. Ct. 2699 (2014) (Nos. 14-46, 14-47, 14-49).

> [o]ne would not say that it is even rational, never mind "appropriate," to impose billions of dollars in economic costs in return for a few dollars in health or environmental benefits.[25]

The Supreme Court did not require EPA to perform a formal benefit-cost analysis. Rather, the decision required the EPA to consider cost, without restricting how it would do so regarding power plants to be regulated.

Double-Counting Benefits of Electric Power Technologies?

So-called cobenefits changed the cost-benefit calculation: EPA stated the cost of the MATS program to the electric industry to be about $9.6 billion a year and calculated the total direct *and* indirect and ancillary cobenefits (the latter from reduction of sulfur dioxide, nitrogen oxides, and particulate matter that were criteria emissions, not hazardous emissions, which are the subject of the MATS regulation) to be approximately $37–$90 billion per year.[26] Almost all of the EPA-calculated total benefits are from indirect cobenefits unrelated to the MATS rule, which only regulates mercury and hazardous emissions.[27] Opponents claimed that EPA's consideration of any such indirect cobenefit double-counts benefits not regulated by this rule.[28]

Particulate matter is not a hazardous chemical and is identified by the statute as a criteria pollutant already otherwise controlled to an "adequate margin of safety"[29] under a different section of the Clean Air Act's National Ambient Air Quality Standards (NAAQS).[30] The NAAQS for criteria pollutants emitted by electric generation facilities, like NO_x, already are set by EPA at safe levels, based on the science. EPA admitted that the overwhelming majority of its total estimated MATS rule benefits—99.9 percent—are due

25. *Michigan*, 135 S. Ct. at 2707 (relying on Motor Vehicle Mfrs. Ass'n of U.S., Inc. v. State Farm Mut. Auto. Ins. Co., 463 U.S. 29 (1983)).

26. U.S. Env't Prot. Agency, Regulatory Impact Analysis for the Final Mercury and Air Toxic Standards ES-1 (2011).

27. *See Michigan v. EPA: Costs and Benefits Matter*, U.S. Senate (July 9, 2015), https://www.rpc.senate.gov/policy-papers/michigan-v-epa-costs-and-benefits-matter.

28. *IER President Releases Statement on New EPA Regs*, Inst. for Energy Rsch. (Dec. 21, 2011), http://instituteforenergyresearch.org/press/ier-president-statement-on-new-epa-regs/.

29. The EPA must establish NAAQS for pollutants; pursuant to section 109(b) of the Clean Air Act, those standards must be "requisite to protect public health" with "an adequate margin of safety." 42 U.S.C. §§ 7408(a), 7409(b)(1).

30. *See* 42 U.S.C. §§ 7408(a), 7409(b)(1).

to reduction of particulate matter and sulfur dioxide, which, as criteria pollutants, were not regulated by or required to be reduced by the challenged MATS rule.[31] Under the MATS regulation, these indirect cobenefits are *not* incidental in quantitative amount—they are totally responsible, alone as 99.9 percent of the calculated reduced mortality benefits, for changing the cost-benefit calculation to make total benefits exceed cost.

One question raised in *Michigan* was whether it is legitimate in comparing costs and benefits of a particular regulation to count cobenefits from reduction of pollutants that are not regulated by the particular federal agency rule: several members of the Supreme Court hearing the *Michigan* case "were critical that the EPA's cost-benefit analysis for the MATS rule attributed billions in annual public health benefits to the standards, even though the agency could only quantify between $4–$6 million in benefits to reduction of hazardous air pollutants."[32] While the cost consideration is now mandated by this Supreme Court decision, the states, stakeholders, and the scientific community are split on the inclusion or noninclusion of incidental cobenefits in any analysis assessing costs and benefits of federal environmental regulations. The Supreme Court has yet to determine this key question.

As highlighted in the bullets earlier, following the *Michigan* decision were two related Supreme Court decisions involving regulation of the electric power sector also involving cobenefit consideration necessary for benefits to exceed costs. The Obama administration's CPP, stricken by the Supreme Court in 2022 (see Chapter 4), also counted a very large amount of cobenefits from reduction of other than its expressly and solely targeted CO_2 and counted many international climate benefits in proportion to relatively limited domestic climate benefits, again with costs imposed on the domestic U.S. electric power industry.[33] Including the cobenefits changed the results from CPP costs that far exceed the direct benefits to all incidental cobenefits exceeding costs. The Congressional Research Service analysis concluded that

> [t]here are recurring questions regarding . . . . whether to count both direct benefits and cobenefits (i.e., benefits achieved that were

31. *Id.*

32. Patrick Ambrosio, *Supreme Court Remands EPA Mercury Rule for Failing to Consider Cost to Power Plants*, BNA Daily Env't Rep. (June 30, 2015), http://www.bna.com/supreme-court-remands-n17179928911/.

33. *See* Andrew M. Grossman, *Michigan v. EPA: A Mandate for Agencies to Consider Costs*, 2015 Cato Sup. Ct. Rev. 281, 306–07 (2015).

not the purpose of the regulation); how to account for benefits for which there is no accepted measurement or valuation methodology; whether to include reductions in the "social cost of carbon" as a benefit and, if so, how to measure those benefits; and whether certain benefits or costs are double-counted when simultaneous proposals address the same pollutant.[34]

Going forward, climate-change emission issues from the generation of electric power are the meta-variable prompting government regulation of electric power in the United States. Global energy-related emissions of carbon are expected to increase 57 percent from 2005 to 2030.[35] At current rates of energy development worldwide, energy-related CO_2 emissions in 2050 would be 150 percent of their current levels under business-as-usual development, primarily due to increased global energy use,[36] as forecast by the Organization for Economic Cooperation and Development. The Intergovernmental Panel on Climate Change in 2014 concluded that in order to maintain global warming below 2°C, there must be a 40–70 percent reduction of GHG emissions from 2010 levels by 2050.[37]

U.S. Presidential Policy and Actions regarding Electric Energy

In 2013, without concurrence of the Congress and using executive branch regulations, President Obama announced his Climate Action Plan and directed EPA to work expeditiously to promulgate CO_2 emission standards (leading to restrictions) for all existing fossil-fuel-fired electric power plants.[38] EPA estimated the benefits of its four Clean Air Act unilateral

34. Cong. Rsch. Serv., R41561, EPA Regulations: Too Much, Too Little, or On Track? 4 n.16 (2016).

35. U.S. Gov't Accountability Off., GAO-09-151, International Climate Change Programs: Lessons Learned from the European Union's Emissions Trading Scheme and the Kyoto Protocol's Clean Development Mechanism (2008), http://www.gao.gov/assets/290/283397.pdf.

36. Org. for Econ. Coop. & Dev., *The OECD Environmental Outlook to 2050: Key Findings on Climate Change* (Nov. 2012), https://web-archive.oecd.org/2012-11-12/90022-Outlook%20to%202050_Climate%20Change%20Chapter_HIGLIGHTS-FINA-8pager-UPDATED%20NOV2012.pdf.

37. Intergovernmental Panel on Climate Change, *Climate Change 2014 Synthesis Report Summary for Policymakers*, https://www.ipcc.ch/pdf/assessment-report/ar5/syr/AR5_SYR_FINAL_SPM.pdf.

38. Exec. Off. of the President, The President's Climate Action Plan (June 2013), https://obamawhitehouse.archives.gov/sites/default/files/image/president27sclimateactionplan.pdf.

executive branch regulations would accrue a combined annual economic value of approximately $500 billion, amounting to $2 trillion in 2020 and after:[39]

- The Cross-State Air Pollution Rule, promulgated in July 2011, required 27 eastern states to reduce the amount of emissions from cross-border power plants.[40] EPA estimated that this rule accrues total economic benefits between $120 and $280 billion annually.[41]
- The MATS rule, promulgated in December 2011, regulated mercury and other hazardous air pollution emitted from both new and old power plants to deliver between $37 and $90 billion of benefits annually.[42]
- The Industrial Boiler Rule, promulgated in April 2012, lowered the amount of air pollution that is released from commercial, industrial, and institutional boilers to generate between $27 and $67 billion annually in health benefits.[43]
- The Cement Kiln Rule, promulgated in August 2010, reduced mercury and other air pollutants from cement plants across the country to generate an estimated $7–$19 billion annually in benefits.[44]

EPA estimated the economic benefits of the four preceding rules based on saved lives, averted emergency and hospital visits, prevented nonfatal heart attacks, and cost savings from avoiding missed work and school days.[45]

39. Nicholas Z. Muller & Robert Mendelson, *Efficient Pollution Regulations: Getting the Prices Right*, 99 Am. Econ. Rev. 1714 (2009).

40. *See Overview of the Cross-State Air Pollution Rule (CSAPR)*, U.S. Env't Prot. Agency (Oct. 20, 2023), https://www.epa.gov/csapr/overview-cross-state-air-pollution-rule-csapr.

41. *Cross-State Air Pollution Rule: Reducing Air Pollution, Protecting Public Health*, U.S. Env't Prot. Agency (Sept. 2016), https://www.epa.gov/sites/production/files/2016-09/documents/csapr presentation.pdf.

42. *Basic Information about Mercury and Air Toxics Standards*, U.S. Env't Prot. Agency (Jan. 8, 2024), https://www.epa.gov/mats/basic-information-about-mercury-and-air-toxics-standards.

43. Vol. 78, No. 21 Federal Register 7139 (Jan. 31, 2013), https://www.gpo.gov/fdsys/pkg/FhoR-2013-01-31/pdf/2012-31646.pdf.

44. Env't Prot. Agency, *Final Amendments to National Air Toxics Emission Standards and New Source Performance Standards for Portland Cement Manufacturing*, https://www.epa.gov/sites/production/files/2016-04/documents/080910_neshap_factsheet.pdf.

45. James Bradbury, *Bills That Would Limit the U.S. EPA's Clean Air Act Authorities*, World Res. Inst. (Apr. 19, 2011), http://www.wri.org/stories/2011/04/bills-would-limit-us-epas-clean-air-act

The EPA calculation of indirect and direct costs and benefits related to climate-related Clean Air Act regulations is displayed in Table 7.1.

Table 7.1 Costs and Benefits of Clean Air Act Climate-Related EPA Regulations[46]

Statute	Type	Year	EPA Regulation	Annual Costs	Benefits
CAA	Report	2009	Greenhouse Gas Reporting Rule	$867 per facility	
CAA 111	NSPS	2015	Clean Power Plan	$5.1-$8.4 billion	$32-$54 billion
CAA 111	NSPS	2016	Methane Emission for Oil & Gas Industries	$530 million	$690 million
CAA 112	MACT	1970	Power Plant MATS Mercury & Air Toxics	$9.6 billion	Hg alone is $4-$6 million; cobenefits $37-$90 billion
CAA 111	NSPS	2012	Fracking Wells & Gas Distribution		$11-$19 million
Along with 112	HAPs	2012			Part of cell above

With the promulgation of Executive Order 12,291 in 1981, President Ronald Reagan introduced the requirement that any major proposed federal regulation require a benefit-cost analysis and that "[r]egulatory action shall not be undertaken unless the potential benefits to society for the regulation outweigh the potential costs to society."[47] This requires a positive net benefit to be shown in the analysis when the regulatory actions are going to cause an economic impact on a scale of more than $100 million per year, unless applicable statutes explicitly order otherwise.[48] President Bill Clinton's 1993 Executive Order 12,866 provided:

> In deciding whether and how to regulate, agencies should assess all costs and benefits of available regulatory alternatives, including the alternative of not regulating. . . . Further, in choosing among

-authorities; FRANK ACKERMAN & LISA HEINZERLING, PRICELESS: ON KNOWING THE PRICE OF EVERYTHING AND THE VALUE OF NOTHING 59-61 (2004).

46. The author, using U.S. Congressional Research Service information. *See* TOO MUCH, TOO LITTLE, OR ON TRACK? *infra* at 8, 13, 14, 19 (provides information that author uses to construct table).

47. 46 Fed. Reg. 13,193, 3 C.F.R. 127 (1981).

48. The Unfunded Mandates Reform Acts of 1995, Pub. L. No. 104-4, 109 Stat. 48 (1995) (codified at 2 U.S.C. § 32); Exec. Order No. 12,866, 58 Fed. Reg. 51,735 (1993).

> alternative regulatory approaches, agencies should select those approaches that maximize net benefits (including potential economic, environmental, public health and safety, and other advantages; distributive impacts; and equity), unless a statute requires another regulatory approach.

The federal Office of Management and Budget instructed agencies to conduct benefit-cost analysis to improve transparency in the regulatory process unless the same is prohibited by law. While all the prior executive orders of prior presidents remain in effect, President Obama issued Executive Order 13,563 reaffirming that benefit-cost analysis is a mandatory part of the regulatory rulemaking process. The Biden administration in 2023 altered the discount rates of 3 percent and 7 percent (the latter for the rate of return to capital) applied for the prior two decades to federal government analyses[49] to an even lower 2 percent, effective for regulations issued in 2025 and after.[50] This will substantially increase the benefit-cost ratio because net benefits are clean air continuing indefinitely through the term modeled, while costs are for implementation up front and therefore are not affected by future values being discounted. Lowering the discount rate increases the values of future benefits while implicitly ignoring initial costs of implementation. The 2023 changes also direct assessing the impacts of regulations on specific populations of different incomes and exposures to pollution.

In contrast, in the 2015 Supreme Court case *Michigan v. EPA*, EPA asserted that cost did not play any role during its MATS rulemaking, causing the Supreme Court to overrule the agency.

Scientific Context: Coal-Fired Electric Power Plant Operation

There is now a federal focus on coal both before and after the Supreme Court *Michigan* decision in terms of its cost and its polluting emissions when burned to produce power. The Congressional Research Service noted that

---

49. Hiroshi Matsushima & Max Sarinsky, *Analytical Clarity: How Updated Climate-Damage Values and Discount Rates Will Affect Regulatory Analysis* 1, Inst. for Pol'y Integrity (Dec. 2023), policyintegrity.org/files/publications/How_Updated_Climate-Damage_Values_and_Discount_Rates_Will_Affect_Regulatory_Analysis_Policy_Brief_v2.pdf.

50. OMB Circular No. A-4: Explanation and Response to Public Input (Nov. 2023), https://www.whitehouse.gov/wp-content/uploads/2023/11/CircularA-4Explanation.pdf.

"[c]oal is an inherently 'dirty' fuel" that emits "sulfur dioxide (SO_2), nitrogen oxides (NO_x), particulates, mercury, acid gases, and other pollutants, in greater abundance than other fossil fuels."[51] When burned to produce electricity, coal is the most pollutant-emitting fossil fuel in wide use.[52] Coal releases approximately 29 percent more carbon per unit of energy produced than does oil and 80 percent more carbon per energy unit than does natural gas. Coal-fired power plants emit significantly more sulfur dioxide (SO_2), nitrogen oxides (NO_x), and particulate matter, three of the six Clean Air Act–regulated criteria pollutants, per megawatt-hour of electric power generated compared to natural-gas and oil-fired plants.

As of 2015, in 19 U.S. states, coal was the dominant source of electricity generation, and in 13 states, it supplied a majority of power generation.[53] Though power plants were not mandated by other EPA regulation to reduce mercury emissions per se, power plants indirectly are capturing about 27 tons of mercury per year through the emission controls installed directly to reduce other criteria pollutants: NO_x, SO_2, and particulate matter.[54] Coal-fired steam boiler cycle plants waste approximately two-thirds of their energy as by-product heat expelled to the environment while converting only approximately one-third of coal carbon energy into mechanical power to turn generation turbines if not part of a cogeneration system.[55]

Due to the cost of federal regulation–mandated controls and the decreasing price of competitive fuels, the deployment and use of coal for electricity in the United States have been rapidly decreasing since 2010, so that coal now supplies a significantly smaller and decreasing share of U.S. power.[56] Natural gas generation and renewable energy power-generating capacity have

---

51. McCarthy & Copeland, *supra* note 7.

52. *Id.*

53. John Muyskens, Dan Keating & Samuel Granados, *Mapping How the United States Generates Its Electricity*, Wash. Post (Mar. 28, 2017), http://www.washingtonpost.com/graphics/national/power-plants/.

54. *Id.*

55. Karin Kirk, *The Little-Known, Massive Advantage That Renewables Hold over Coal*, Yale Climate Connections (May 30, 2023), https://yaleclimateconnections.org/2023/05/the-little-known-massive-advantage-that-renewables-hold-over-coal/.

56. *See* Wendy Koch, *EPA Seeks 30% Cut in Power Plant Carbon Emissions by 2030*, USA Today (June 3, 2014), http://www.usatoday.com/story/money/business/2014/06/02/epa-proposes-sharp-cuts-power-plant-emissions/9859913/.

been rapidly supplanting coal generation in the last ten years.[57] Sixty gigawatts of existing coal-fired power generation capacity were closed between 2015 and 2020.[58] U.S. coal-fired generating capacity is projected to decrease to 262 gigawatts in 2040, according to the U.S. Energy Information Agency, which would result in another 15 percent decrease.[59]

Changes in Carbon Costs and Benefits

The key to cost consideration—yet to be more defined by the Supreme Court after its *Michigan* decision—is affected by how reduced emissions' benefits are modeled when power plant operation is not dispatched. Raising the value of benefits changes the cost-benefit ratio to the same extent as changing the value of costs. The Obama, Trump, and Biden administration valuations are fundamentally different.

The Biden administration increased by more than 400 percent the federal valuation of carbon emissions utilized by the Trump administration, to $51/ton from the Trump administration's $10/ton, without going through a rulemaking process or allowing public comment.[60] The federal circuit court of appeals reversed the trial court stay, and thereafter the U.S. Supreme Court concurred in 2022 in a brief opinion upholding no injunction of the president's action unilaterally to set the value of carbon emissions in determining costs and benefits of environmental regulation.[61] And there is a second boost of this value: proposed by the Biden administration and proceeding through public and scientific comment is an almost 300 percent increase in value to $190/ton of carbon saved from being emitted.

---

57. *See Natural Gas, Renewables Projected to Provide Larger Shares of Electricity Generation*, U.S. Energy Info. Admin. (May 4, 2015), http://www.eia.gov/todayinenergy/detail.cfm?id=21072.

58. Michael Bastasch, *Report: EPA Regulations to Accelerate Coal Plant Shutdowns*, The Daily Caller (Feb. 14, 2014), http://dailycaller.com/2014/02/14/report-epa-regulations-to-accelerate-coal-plant-shutdowns/.

59. *Id.*

60. Executive Order on Protecting Public Health and the Environment and Restoring Science to Tackle the Climate Crisis (Jan. 20, 2020), https://www.whitehouse.gov/briefing-room/presidential-actions/2021/01/20/executive-order-protecting-public-health-and-environment-and-restoring-science-to-tackle-climate-crisis/.

61. Louisiana v. Biden, 596 U.S. __ (May 26, 2022).

A federal appellate court in 2022 upheld that FERC must consider foreseeable indirect upstream and downstream GHG impacts of projects seeking FERC approval if the impacts are known.[62] The "social cost of greenhouse gases" estimate is used in rulemaking processes and environmental permitting decisions to approximate economic damages associated with burning fossil fuels in electric power generation.

Congressional testimony in 2014 by FERC Commissioner Clark characterized the unresolved conflict between proposed environmental regulation to assist climate goals and the countervailing pressure to protect power system reliability and resiliency as a looming "jurisdictional train wreck."[63] The narrow majority in *Michigan* stated that "no regulation is 'appropriate' if it does significantly more harm than good."[64] Quoting Justice Breyer's concurring opinion in *Riverkeeper*, the majority further reasoned that

> [a]gencies have long treated cost as a centrally relevant factor when deciding whether to regulate. Consideration of cost reflects the understanding that reasonable regulation ordinarily requires paying attention to the advantages *and* the disadvantages of agency decisions. It also reflects the reality that "too much wasteful expenditure devoted to one problem may well mean considerably fewer resources available to deal effectively with other (perhaps more serious) problems."[65]

Going forward, this cost factor will play a starring role: long-term resiliency values of certain types of power generation may be factored in. As detailed in Chapter 4, the 2022 Supreme Court decision in *West Virginia v. EPA* blocked federal executive branch regulations or rules that affect the order of electric power dispatch in the United States. This rule violated the Major Questions Doctrine where the Congress has not legislatively allocated such unilateral regulatory power to the president to make decisions. This

---

62. Food & Water Watch & Berkshire Env't Action Team v. Fed. Energy Regul. Comm'n, 28 F.4th 277 (D.C. Cir. 2022).

63. Lynn Garner, *FERC Comm'rs Split on Party Lines over EPA's Carbon Rule for Power Plants*, Bloomberg BNA Energy & Climate Rep. (July 29, 2014), http://info.bna.com/climate/summary_news.aspx?ID=274977.

64. *Id.*

65. *Id.*

restriction of executive branch authority over changing power sector operation regarding various generation facilities, along with the *Michigan* requirement now to consider costs of such actions, changes the legal terrain. The precise details of these restrictions are still awaiting definition.

The Supreme Court has made cost a new requirement for federal rulemaking in the electric power sector when the Clean Air Act is involved, as it often is. See also Chapter 15 on how this could affect elements of the proposed Green New Deal.

Next, we shift from these *federal* changed requirements on cost affecting the power industry to key legal changes, incentives, and regulatory subsidies provided at the *state* level that now are greatly elevated in legal importance as the United States rapidly moves to incorporate sustainable electricity into power infrastructure.

CHAPTER 8

Renewable Portfolio Standards

In the U.S. federalist legal system, states retain independent legal authority. Not only do states regulate retail power supply (see Chapter 4), but they also retain Tenth Amendment reserved power regarding the electric sector. We switch from analyzing federal rules for the power sector to in this chapter comparing how the 50 states provide incentives as the electric system makes a rapid pivot to fundamentally change its technology and direction.

In this chapter, we analyze the U.S. subsidy for future operation of certain electric generation sources available in 60 percent of states: Renewable Portfolio Standard (RPS) Renewable Energy Credit (REC) programs. In Chapter 9, we analyze a second state subsidy for electric generation sources in 80 percent of U.S. states. RPS REC programs are the most consistent subsidy program reshaping the technology, nature, and shape of the U.S. electric sector. RPS REC programs have existed for four decades in the United States.

There also are significant federal renewable energy subsidies embodied in new federal renewable energy tax credits and accelerated depreciation (see Chapter 6). Federal tax incentives have been volatile and inconsistent: federal renewable ITC and PTC tax credits have changed in amount, in stages and degree of development progress to vest their eligibility, and in their refundability to taxpayers and phased out and resuscitated in different presidential administrations (see Chapter 6).

Renewable Portfolio Standards

Twenty-nine states, the District of Columbia, and Puerto Rico have enacted state RPSs.[1] A state resource portfolio standard requires utilities and certain retail sellers of electric power to the public to provide state-created evidence of a state-mandated amount of renewable energy credits obtained as a percentage of their electricity sources sold to retail consumers. An RPS requires

---

1. *See Renewable & Clean Energy Standards*, DATABASE OF STATE INCENTIVES FOR RENEWABLES & EFFICIENCY (Sept. 2020), https://perma.cc/GZ89-PSB6.

that electric utilities—and in some states other competitive retailers of power—purchase evidence that they have acquired the "green attributes" of a regulatorily set percentage of the electricity that they supply to consumers from generation of state-defined renewable energy. If this requirement is not satisfied, any such covered retail electric supplier in an RPS state pays alternative compliance penalty (ACP) amounts to the state government for its shortfall of RECs.

The number of RPS states has remained constant recently at 29 states. These state RPS programs were initiated between 1983 and 2022 and have been amended periodically, as shown in Figure 8.1.[2] Beginning in 2017, 15 of these states also have enacted Clean Energy Standards (CES) requiring certain percentages of power generation to be supplied with "clean" technologies which include renewables and other zero-carbon generation technologies including nuclear power, as shown in Figure 8.1. More than half of the states have raised the RPS percentages of total retail power sales that must be achieved by their state retail energy suppliers, and 18 have added so-called carve-out categories to focus state incentives on specified renewable energy technologies (typically solar).[3]

Figure 8.1[4] States with RPS Programs and Revisions over Time

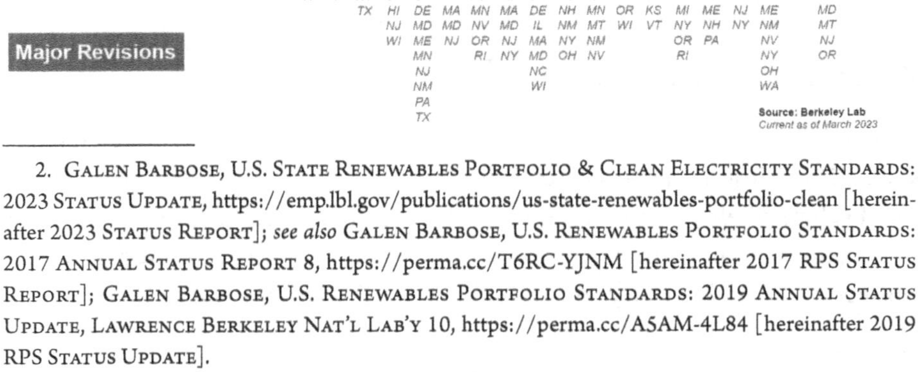

---

2. Galen Barbose, U.S. State Renewables Portfolio & Clean Electricity Standards: 2023 Status Update, https://emp.lbl.gov/publications/us-state-renewables-portfolio-clean [hereinafter 2023 Status Report]; *see also* Galen Barbose, U.S. Renewables Portfolio Standards: 2017 Annual Status Report 8, https://perma.cc/T6RC-YJNM [hereinafter 2017 RPS Status Report]; Galen Barbose, U.S. Renewables Portfolio Standards: 2019 Annual Status Update, Lawrence Berkeley Nat'l Lab'y 10, https://perma.cc/A5AM-4L84 [hereinafter 2019 RPS Status Update].

3. 2019 RPS Status Update, *supra* note 2, at 7.

4. 2017 RPS Status Report, *supra* note 2.

The 29 U.S. states maintaining RPS programs and their percentage requirements are illustrated in Figure 8.2. The required state percentage of retail energy delivered from renewable energy generation resources ranges from 2 to 50 percent of annual retail electric power sales in different state RPS programs.[5] Many states routinely increase their RPS required annual percentages as their renewable energy goals increase in successive years.[6]

RECs are virtual state-created credits reflecting renewable energy generation that can be traded and transferred as permitted by state law.[7] In RPS programs, electric utilities (and, in some deregulated states, other nonutility retail suppliers allowed to compete in the supply of electricity) purchase RECs from eligible renewable or zero-carbon generation projects, which earn RECs by generating megawatts (MW) of eligible renewable energy. In terms of eligible technologies, all states accept solar photovoltaic (PV), solar thermal, and wind technologies.[8] States vary as to what additional technologies qualify.

Renewable power generators receive state RECs linked to their actual metered power output and can sell those RECs to retail power sellers in the state, which are required to acquire different, typically increasing annually, percentages of those RECs each year.[9] Ten regional electronic REC tracking systems assign a unique serial number to each megawatt-hour (MWh) of renewable electricity generation created, manage, and retire RECs to ensure

---

5. *See generally Find Policies & Incentives by State*, Database of State Incentives for Renewables & Efficiency, https://perma.cc/A8WD-63BE (last visited Apr. 24, 2024).

6. *See* Figure 8.2. California periodically strengthened its RPS from 20 percent renewable energy by 2010 and in 2015 required 50 percent renewable energy to be used by 2030. *See California Renewables Portfolio Standard*, Database of State Incentives for Renewables & Efficiency (Sept. 24, 2018), https://perma.cc/24P4-CJSS. At a similar time in June 2015, Hawaii established a law requiring 100 percent of electricity to be renewable before 2045. H.B. 623, 28th Leg., Reg. Sess. (Haw. 2015).

7. *See Renewable Energy Certificates (RECs)*, U.S. Env't Prot. Agency, https://perma.cc/3b2f-nth8 (last visited Apr. 24, 2024).

8. *Local Renewable Energy Benefits and Resources*, U.S. Env't Prot. Agency, https://perma.cc/X66V-AQ27 (last visited Apr. 24, 2024).

9. *Renewable Energy Credits (RECs)*, EnergySage (Dec. 23, 2020), https://perma.cc/LX5Y-L9YL.

that each REC is counted only once.[10] These legally required RPS programs cover approximately half of nationwide retail electricity sales.[11]

Figure 8.2[12] RPS Policies in 29 States and DC

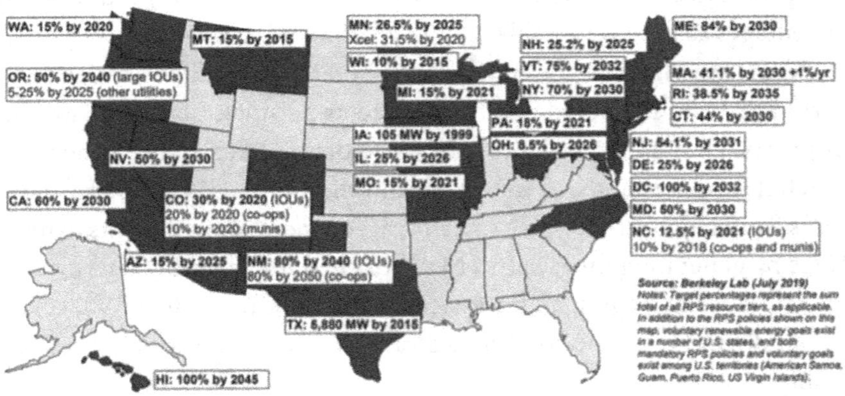

Analyzing the 29 states plus DC with an RPS program, 16 of these 29 have future RPS targets requiring at least 50 percent of retail sales to be from what their state laws differently define as renewable energy, while 17 states have a 100 percent Clean Electricity Standard (CES) or RPS future target.[13] Particularly in northeastern and mid-Atlantic states, RPS policies have played a key role in successfully incentivizing renewable energy adoptions in their electric sectors. RPS and CES policies now require approximately 300 TWh of additional clean electricity supply by 2030 and 800 TWh by 2050, requiring total U.S. nonhydro renewable energy generation to reach 28 percent of electricity sales by 2050 (compared to approximately 17 percent today).[14] This is in addition to federal policy where the Biden-Harris administration seeks to make virtually all electric generation clean by 2035.

Nine of the 29 RPS states and DC increased their RPS targets in a recent five-year period:[15]

---

10. *Renewable Electricity: How Do You Know You Are Using It?*, Nat'l Renewable Energy Lab'y, https://perma.cc/C2QS-C4E2 (last visited Apr. 24, 2024).

11. Ryan Wiser & Galen Barbose, *Renewable Portfolio Standards in the United States*, 154E Lawrence Berkeley Nat'l Lab'y 1 (2008).

12. 2019 RPS Status Update, *supra* note 2.

13. 2023 Status Report, *supra* note 2.

14. *Id.*

15. *Id.* at 12.

- California: 60 percent by 2030 (and 100 percent zero-carbon by 2045)
- Connecticut: 40 percent Class I by 2030
- DC: 100 percent by 2032, with 10 percent solar by 2041
- Massachusetts: Annual increase of 2 percent of sales/year from 2020 to 2029
- Maryland: 50 percent Tier 1 by 2030, including 14.5 percent solar and about 9.5 percent offshore wind
- Maine: 50 percent Class I by 2030
- New Jersey: 50 percent Tier 1 by 2030
- New Mexico: 80 percent by 2040 (and 100 percent zero-carbon by 2045)
- Nevada: 50 percent by 2030
- New York: 70 percent by 2030 (and 100 percent zero-carbon by 2040)

In the future, there is expected to be more reliance on RPS RECs to achieve renewable energy penetration goals. The renewable electric energy RPS targets of the six New England states over the next two decades range from 20 to 90 percent renewable energy in place and operating by 2040.[16] The majority of U.S. states that have adopted a 100 percent clean energy goal do not exercise state control over power sector siting.[17] See Chapters 10 and 11.

Numerous states in the Northeast and Mid-Atlantic regions have established procurement targets for offshore wind; New England state requirements for renewable energy are planned to be achieved by solar PV incentives and by large amounts of offshore wind. For example, Massachusetts plans 3,000 MW of additional solar power through the Solar Massachusetts Renewable Target (SMART) program and 4,000 MW of offshore wind. This 7,000 MW of power supply is approximately the demand for electricity on a typical day in Massachusetts. Massachusetts, Rhode Island, and Connecticut have awarded contracts to procure 3.1 GW of offshore wind and are planning to procure an additional 5.8 GW of offshore wind by 2030 to meet their targets (wind is an intermittent supplier of electricity).

16. *See* Todd Schatzki et al., ISO New Eng. & Analysis Grp., Pathways Study: Evaluation of Pathways to a Future Grid, fig. II-1 (2022), https://www.iso-ne.com/static-assets/documents/2022/04/schatzki-et-al-pathways-final.pdf.

17. *See Table of 100% Clean Energy States*, Clean Energy State Alliance, https://www.cesa.org/projects/100-clean-energy-collaborative/table-of-100-clean-energy-states/ (last visited Apr. 24, 2024). Fifteen of the 17 states that are members of the Clean Energy State Alliance do not effectively preempt local aesthetic zoning, which can frustrate wind project infrastructure in their states.

Solar Carve-Out SRECs: States with SREC Programs

A few of the RPS states also have created additional legal programs creating Solar Renewable Energy Credits (SRECs) through which solar projects can earn additional SREC credits that state utilities and retail electricity suppliers must purchase from the solar generators on an annual basis pursuant to state law. Seven of the 29 RPS states plus DC have created state solar carve-out RECs: Delaware, DC, Illinois, Maryland, Massachusetts,[18] New Jersey, Pennsylvania, and Ohio. Four other states that do not have an in-state SREC program—Indiana, Kentucky, Michigan, and West Virginia—instead have areas of the state where SRECs can be generated eligible for compliance sales satisfying those seven other RPS states' active SREC programs.

These are all states located in the northeastern quadrant of the United States. These SREC programs significantly motivate new in-state generation. These RPS carve-out programs in the Northeast and Midwest provide RECs only to certain eligible solar project generation as set forth in each state's law or regulations. Typically, these SRECs are traded at prices greater than the standard REC prices (typically $10–$50/MWh). Those higher SREC carve-out prices as of 2020 in six states plus the District of Columbia are shown in Table 8.1.

Table 8.1[19] SREC Prices and ACP Prices in U.S. REC Market

State	Price/MWh (2020)	ACP/MWh (2021)
Washington, D.C.	$440	$500
Massachusetts	$315	$448
New Jersey	$225	$248
Maryland	$77	$80
Pennsylvania	$40	
Ohio	$7.50	$45
Delaware		$150

18. Note that Massachusetts stopped accepting new system owners into its SREC program in late 2018, transitioning to its SMART program to replace SRECs.

19. *SREC Prices: Explaining How to Sell Your RECs in the U.S.*, EnergySage, https://perma.cc/VHA8-GALF (last visited Apr. 24, 2024).

Related U.S. Solar Capacity

SRECs and RECs influence the power technology market in states with SREC programs. Twenty-one percent of all wind project development and 59 percent of all solar energy development in the United States occurred in states with RPS programs.[20] Many of the states with the best wind power regimes do not have RPS programs. As part of solar development in states with RPS programs, more than 25 percent of total solar generation development was in seven of the 29 states with solar carve-out SREC programs and the remainder in states with generic RPS programs.[21] Since 2000, state RPS programs have been linked to the majority of new solar projects added annually; likewise, ordinary multitechnology RPS programs were linked to the majority of new wind power projects built between 2006 and 2012.[22]

The incentives in solar carve-out programs have led to a significant increase in solar projects nationwide, with a recent large increase in nonresidential projects. In the last few years, the most significant increase is in so-called community solar, accompanied by certain legal issues regarding whether some of these state community solar provisions might or might not be constitutionally preempted as establishing wholesale power rates not consistent with Avoided Cost (see discussion later and in Chapter 5) and not allowed to be set by states pursuant to the Federal Power Act (see Chapter 4).

The SMART Program

Massachusetts illustrates a new mechanism for RPS REC programs utilizing a tariff, rather than a credit. Massachusetts entered a different dimension when it created wholesale power sale rates for solar power, which was a new requirement imposed on Massachusetts utilities to replace the state's REC program after it and net metering in the state had reached the maximum capacity allowed by the legislature. The Massachusetts Department of Energy Resources (DOER) launched its RPS SREC programs in 2010 with Massachusetts SREC-I, a Massachusetts-specific solar carve-out carrying a capacity limit cap of 400 MW, which limit was met and exceeded quickly

20. 2017 RPS STATUS REPORT, *supra* note 2 at 18.
21. *Id.*
22. *Id.*

in the spring of 2013.[23] In 2014, the DOER launched its SREC-II program, which allowed Massachusetts projects to install 1,600 MW of solar capacity by 2020.[24]

The SREC-II program terminated two years earlier than expected in November 2018 when SREC-II surpassed its established goal and cap of 1,600 MW of solar capacity eligible and participating.[25] The RPS solar Carve-Out I program, which targeted solar deployment between 2010 and 2014, sought to achieve 1.6 percent solar power deployment in the state by 2020. The subsequent RPS solar Carve-Out II program, which targeted solar deployment from 2014 to 2020, sought to achieve 3.8 percent solar power in the state by 2020.

The SMART program was launched to replace SREC with a tariff system.[26] The SMART program, which began in 2018, seeks to incentivize the deployment of 3,200 MW of solar power. The SMART system tariffs awarded different tariff amounts based on social equity values rather than based only on the value of the solar energy produced for the distribution grid.[27] SMART land-use and off-taker "adders" are added to the tariff received by solar.

The maximum size for eligible individual solar projects in the SMART program is 5 MW AC (alternating current), and after each 200 MW block of the target total 3,200 MW is subscribed by projects, the tariff received by future solar projects for each successive 200 MW block of solar power decreases by 4 percent.[28] At the beginning of 2020, Massachusetts SRECs were trading in the vicinity of $300/SREC,[29] maintaining their position as the most remunerative large SREC in any state program in the nation, as shown in Table 8.2.[30]

---

23. Renewable Energy Portfolio Standard—Class I, 225 Mass. Code Regs. § 14.00 (2021).

24. *Massachusetts*, SRECTrade, https://www.srectrade.com/markets/rps/srec/massachusetts#:~:text=On%20April%2025%2C%202014%2C%20the,1%2C600%20MW%20prior%20to%202020 (last visited May 10, 2024).

25. *Id.*

26. Solar Massachusetts Renewable Target (SMART) Program, 225 Mass. Code Regs. § 20.00 (2020).

27. *Id.* § 20.07–.08.

28. *Id.* § 20.05–.07.

29. *SRECs in Massachusetts: Prices and Program Status*, EnergySage, https://perma.cc/LRP3-DD8W (last visited Apr. 24, 2024).

30. *Id.* The District of Columbia had SRECs trading at a higher value; however, there is not much land available in DC for larger field-mounted solar projects.

The SMART program operates through a complex set of calculations. It differentiates the amount of subsidy received by a solar project by the utility that serves the project; the applicable residential, commercial, or industrial retail electric rate structure; and a complex set of "adders" and "subtractors" affecting the final received SMART tariff value for various unrelated land-use and power off-taker characteristics that are favored or disfavored by state policy.[31] There are certain preferred locations where no tariff "subtractors" apply to agricultural land uses for solar and to nonagricultural building- or canopy-mounted solar panels, as well as for solar projects sited at a brownfield or a current or former landfill or for certain smaller solar projects.[32]

Table 8.2[33] SMART Program

Under the SMART program, each project builds up its SMART incentive based on the type of solar project being built.

Base Compensation Rate Multipliers: Projects up to 1 MW	
Generation Unit Capacity	**Base Compensation Rate Factor (% of Clearing Price)**
Low Income Solar Tariff Generation Unit less than or equal to 25 kW AC	230%
Less than or equal to 25 kW AC	200%
Greater than 25 kW to 250 kW	150%
Greater than 250 kW to 500 kW	125%
Greater than 500 kW to 1,000 kW	110%

The size of a project also affects its ability to earn size-sensitive multipliers in addition to the base SMART tariff it receives for selling its power wholesale to the grid; multipliers can range from 110 to 230 percent as shown in Table 8.2.[34] As well, size determines whether a solar project receives the SMART tariff for ten years or 20 years. Each of these, as well as whether the off-taker of the solar power is a low-income customer, determines the ultimate tariff and subsidy amount that the solar generation developer receives and whether that subsidy lasts for ten years or 20 years before ceasing.[35]

31. 225 Mass. Code Regs. § 20.08.
32. *Id.*
33. *Id.* § 14.07.
34. *Id.* § 20.07(b).
35. *See Solar Massachusetts Renewable Target (SMART) Solar Incentive Calculator*, Mass.gov, https://perma.cc/QVL8-LTQU (last visited Apr. 24, 2024).

Lawrence Berkeley Laboratory studies in 2024 analyzing 2010–2022 data nationwide document that higher-income households and predominately owner-occupied housing, rather than rental housing, and predominately in states with RPS REC programs, are adopting rooftop solar projects in disproportionately larger amounts than their percentages in the population.[36] Higher-income households installed an average 24 percent larger PV system on their residential roofs than did lower-income households.[37] Nonwhite minority households had installed a disproportionately larger percentage of rooftop solar systems than their percentage in the population.[38] Ninety-four percent of all PV rooftop solar systems were installed in single-family housing rather than multifamily housing.[39]

Therefore, the tariff that the solar project receives as a subsidy is influenced by multiple factors not directly related to the cost, value, or benefit of solar power and is instead based in part on its location and land use, former use of the property, size of the project, and who utilizes the electric power produced. The SMART program could be a preview of the next advanced iteration of SREC programs. Its intricacy involves details of tariff subsidy differentiation by off-taker and locational factors that do not pertain to the commodity value of the solar electricity produced.

The States and RPS REC Prices

Demand and supply factors determine REC and SREC trading prices when solar generators sell RECs earned to utilities and retail power suppliers. The effective price cap for REC or SREC trades is established by the market and capped by each state's ACP price, which is the penalty retailers of power pay to the state if they do not obtain and surrender to the state an adequate percentage of RECs in each period. The New England Power Pool (NEPOOL) Class I RECs were sold for roughly $40/MWh in 2023, resting just underneath the Alternative Compliance Payment (ACP) caps; the PJM ISO Tier I REC prices were approximately $30/MWh in 2023, although REC prices fluctuate during each year.[40]

---

36. Sydney Forrester et al., Residential Solar Adopter Income Demographic Trends: 2023 Update, Lawrence Berkeley Lab'y (2024).

37. *Id.*

38. *Id.*

39. *Id.*

40. 2023 Status Report, *supra* note 2.

The ACPs effectively have acted as a ceiling price, with bid and accepted REC sale prices hovering a bit below the ACP. The ACP in many states declines over time, as the price of solar PV panels has declined. The ACPs in some SREC states and DC are shown in Table 8.1. State to state, there is a 3:1 difference in ACP prices.

The Cost to Ratepaying Consumers of REC and SREC Programs

Where a solar project receives an SREC in those states with programs, this amount of subsidy represents a fivefold to 13-fold added revenue gain for the SREC seller in addition to the average approximately (in the United States since the 2008 recession) $0.035/kWh wholesale value of the electricity produced and sold from the solar project.[41] RPS compliance costs were $4.7 billion in 2018, which when spread over retail rates was an increase of 2.6 percent of average retail electricity bills in those RPS states; these values were $4.0 billion and 1.7 percent of retail bills in 2017.[42] Figure 8.3 shows the RPS rate impact in certain restructured retail choice states where there is retail competition, such as Massachusetts showing a 12 percent impact on electricity bills passed on to customers, as well as the right side of Figure 8.3 tracking the percentage rate impacts of RPS policies on retail rates in conventionally regulated RPS states.

These added costs of RPS programs are most pronounced in the 13 deregulated retail states and much less so in the nine traditionally monopolized states in Figure 8.3. For example, in the five deregulated New England states plus Vermont, which is not deregulated, shown on the left side of Figure 8.3, costs to all electricity consumers have risen from 2 to 12 percent, with two of those states, Massachusetts and Rhode Island, bearing increases of 12 percent and 6 percent, respectively. This can be primarily due to the solar carve-out RPS programs in certain states. On the other hand, conventionally regulated Vermont in New England, shown on the right side of Figure 8.3, saw the cost of its RPS program increase retail rates less than 1 percent.

41. *See* Indep. Sys. Operator New Eng., https://perma.cc/T6MN-YF94 (last visited Apr. 24, 2024).

42. 2019 RPS Status Update, *supra* note 2, at 37, 40.

Figure 8.3[43] Total RPS Compliance Costs in Regulated and Not Regulated States

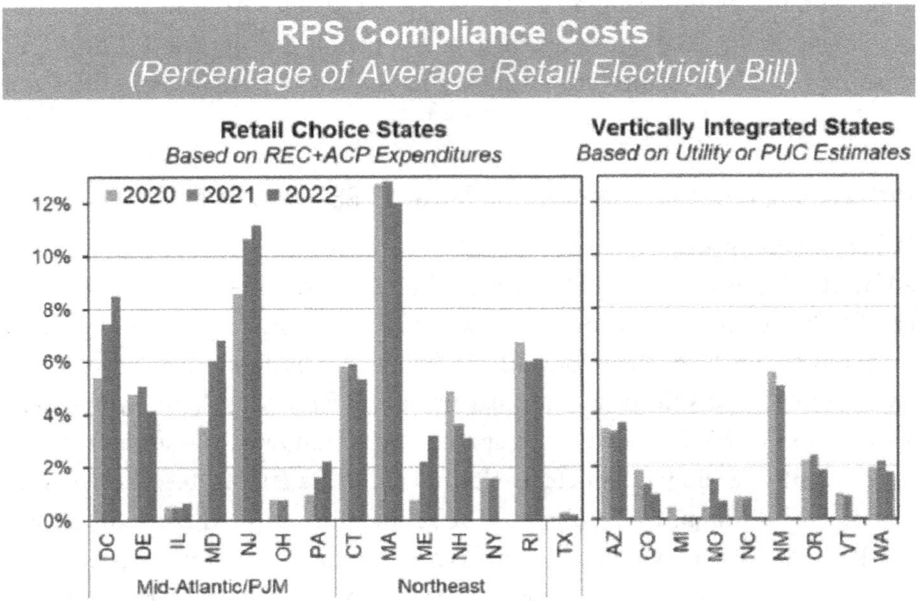

The cost of RECs is passed through the distribution charge on retail bills, although the cost of solar or other renewable energy supply is an electricity commodity component charge, rather than a power distribution charge. The utilities do not bear these costs; their customers bear these costs for each kWh distributed to them by the utility. For example, in Massachusetts, a retail choice state, whose RPS system raises consumer rates by 12 percent as shown in Figure 8.3, the distribution cost line item comprises approximately 32.3 percent of the total of a residential consumer Eversource utility bill, meaning that the distribution cost component actually has been increased by approximately 37 percent since it absorbs 100 percent of the RPS cost.

Figure 8.4 forecasts the cost impact of RPS policies in 2030 increasing the retail electric prices in leading solar states such as California and Massachusetts potentially by as much as 20 percent. The distribution charge is increased by an even larger percentage, as it also is increased to absorb and pass on to consumers the additional substantial cost of net metering

43. 2023 Status Report, *supra* note 2.

subsidies for excess solar energy sent back to the utility grid, as discussed in more detail in Chapter 9.

Figure 8.4[44]

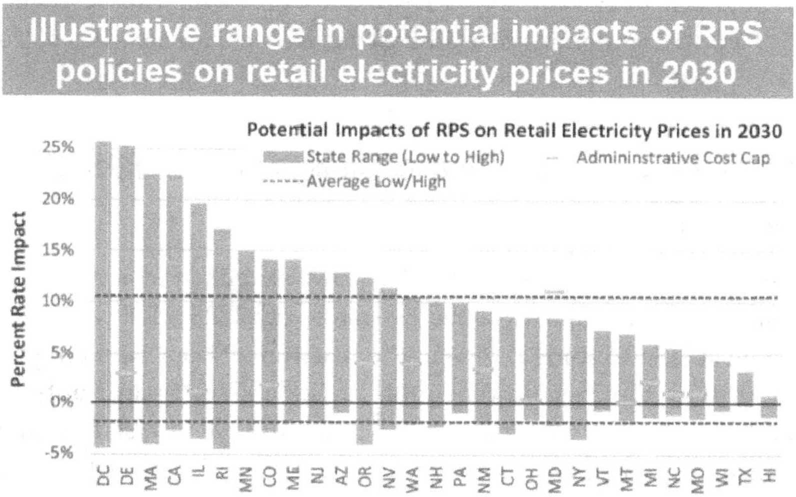

Source: Lawrence Berkeley National Laboratory, Putting the Rate Impacts of Distributed Solar into Context, January 2017. https://emp.lbl.gov/publications/putting-potential-rate-impacts

REC prices in Massachusetts are the highest in the nation, followed by REC prices in Maryland and DC. This makes the cost to Massachusetts consumers of the REC program the highest in the nation and the subsidy transfers to solar projects in Massachusetts the most lucrative in the nation. However, this RPS program in Massachusetts was found to have resulted in the second most solar energy generation per capita in the United States (second only to Hawaii), due to its RPS program with its community solar program. Massachusetts law created a price floor under vintage REC prices by employing a unique clearinghouse system that provides a state-sponsored mechanism to sell to utilities and retail power suppliers unsold RECs, extending those REC utilization dates so that they do not expire or become stranded or sacrificed without compensating the renewable project.

---

44. Galen Barbose, Lawrence Berkeley Nat'l Lab'y, Putting the Potential Rate Impacts of Distributed Solar into Context 21 (fig. 15) (2017).

By contrast, Maryland REC prices are restrained by ACP ceiling prices capped at a lower $60/MWh, while Delaware and Pennsylvania are oversupplied with renewable electricity output, in part due to those states allowing out-of-state projects to earn Delaware or Pennsylvania RECs.[45] By doing so, Delaware and Pennsylvania avoid Dormant Commerce Clause challenges to their RPS REC programs that other states have experienced, as discussed next.

The Dormant Commerce Clause, Discrimination, RPS RECs

State Renewable Energy Discrimination

The issue of discrimination in state REC laws examined in a 2012 law article[46] found that the majority of the 29 states with RPS REC programs discriminated at least to some degree in the structure of their RPS programs in favor of in-state or in-region renewable power and/or against out-of-state renewable energy that instantaneously flowed through interstate commerce into their states and was consumed. Eleven states also feature solar carve-out incentives as a matter of state law, as well as the seven states with in-state geographically determined REC multipliers as of 2019, that potentially could be susceptible to constitutional challenge.[47]

Judge Richard Posner made this 2012 article noting Dormant Commerce Clause applications to state RPS programs the foundation for one finding regarding the balance between state and federal authority over power transmission and renewable energy. Writing for a unanimous Seventh Circuit Court of Appeals, Judge Posner declared that Michigan and other Midwest states could not provide RPS REC subsidies only to in-state-produced renewable energy; to deny them to out-of-state renewable energy transmitted into their states would violate the Dormant Commerce Clause of the Constitution.[48] The article also was cited by the Massachusetts Supreme Judicial

45. 2023 Status Report, *supra* note 2.

46. Steven Ferrey, *Threading the Constitutional Needle with Care*, 7 U. Tex. J. Oil, Gas & Energy L. 59 (2012).

47. Galen Barbose, U.S. Renewables Portfolio Standards 2021 Status Update: Early Release, Lawrence Berkeley Nat'l Lab'y 10, https://perma.cc/29GF-ZG87. Arizona, Minnesota, Missouri, Illinois, North Carolina, Pennsylvania, Maryland, New Jersey, Massachusetts, Vermont, and New Hampshire have solar carve-out RECs, and Oregon, New Mexico, and Colorado combine solar carve-out RECs with REC credit multipliers.

48. Ill. Com. Comm'n v. Fed. Regul. Comm'n, 721 F.3d 764 (7th Cir. 2013).

Court in 2020 as its authority to uphold a new $1 billion Massachusetts program for renewable energy.[49]

The exact same 29 states have maintained their RPS REC programs without any new states adopting RPS programs, and none of the 29 has terminated an RPS program during more than a decade. These programs have remained as important renewable incentives in the United States during the 21st century, as federal tax incentives have fluctuated (see Chapter 6).

Commerce Clause Geographic RPS REC Discrimination

Adding detail on types of discrimination: as of 2012, 29 states had enacted state RPS programs.[50] At that time, a majority of these programs discriminated in some way in favor of renewable energy generated in the state or immediate geographic region and against renewable energy generated in other states.[51] Some prohibited their REC credits for out-of-state or out-of-region generation facilities.[52] A number of the 29 states with RPS programs in 2012 credit multipliers, geographic restrictions, or preferences to promote in-state/in-region generation of renewable energy, to the disadvantage of external power, in the following magnitudes:

- **In-state REC multipliers in 27.5 percent of RPS states.** Eight of the 29 RPS states, or 27.5 percent, had REC multipliers for in-state generation:
  - Arizona[53]
  - Colorado[54]
  - Delaware[55]
  - Maine[56]
  - Michigan[57]

---

49. Nextera Energy Res., LLC v. Mass. Dep't of Pub. Utils., 485 Mass. 595 (2020).

50. Ferrey, *supra* note 46.

51. *Id.*

52. K.S. Corey & B.J. Sweazey, U.S. Nat'l Renewable Energy Lab'y, NREL/TP Report No. 670-41409, Renewable Portfolio Standards in the States: Balancing Goals and Implementation Standards, tbl. 2 (2007).

53. Ariz. Admin. Code § R14-2-1806(D)–(E) (2009).

54. Colo. Rev. Stat. § 40-2-124(c)(V)(A)–(D), (c)(IX), (d) (2013).

55. Del. Code Ann. tit. 26, § 356(a)(1), (d)–(e) (2012).

56. Me. Rev. Stat. tit. 35-A, § 3605 (2010).

57. Mich. Comp. Laws Serv. § 460.1039(1) (LexisNexis 2010).

  - Missouri[58]
  - Nevada[59]
  - Washington[60]
- **In-state generation REC requirement in 14 percent of RPS states.** Four of the 29 RPS states, or 14 percent, including two states that also provide for a geographically discriminatory REC multiplier (later), had either a requirement or preference for in-state generation:
  - California[61]
  - Colorado[62]
  - North Carolina[63]
  - Ohio[64]
- **In-state product or labor preferences in 14 percent of RPS states.** Four of the 29 RPS states, or 14 percent, provided program preferences for the use of in-state manufactured products or in-state labor forces:
  - Arizona[65]
  - Delaware[66]
  - Michigan[67]
  - Montana[68]
- **In-region generation REC requirement in 38 percent of RPS states.** Eleven of the 29 RPS states, or 38 percent, had a requirement for in-region (rather than in-state) geographic location of renewable

---

58. Mo. Ann. Stat. § 393.1030(1) (West 2013).

59. Nev. Rev. Stat. Ann. § 704.7822 (LexisNexis 2011).

60. Wash. Admin. Code § 194-37-110 (2008).

61. Cal. Pub. Utils. Code § 399.11 *et seq.* (2011). California Renewable Portfolio Standard, *See*, Database of State Incentives for Renewables & Efficiency, https://perma.cc/H3SX-P32V (explaining that a maximum of 25 percent of RPS compliance can be achieved through the use of tradable RECs; therefore, the remainder of the RPS compliance must be attained through in-state balancing authority power sales).

62. Colo. Rev. Stat. Ann. § 40-2-124(e)(II)–(III) (West 2013).

63. N.C. Gen. Stat. Ann. § 133.8(b)(2)(e) (West 2012).

64. Ohio Rev. Code Ann. § 4928.64(B)(3) (LexisNexis 2012).

65. Ariz. Admin. Code § R13-2-1806(D)–(E) (2007).

66. Del. Code. Ann. tit. 26, § 351(b)–(c) (2009).

67. Mich. Comp. Laws Serv. § 460.1001(2)(a)–(d) (LexisNexis 2010).

68. Mont. Code Ann. § 69-3-2005(3)(a) (2013).

electric generation to be awarded RECs, including one that also had in-state multipliers and one with an in-state preference:

- Connecticut[69]
- Illinois[70]
- Maine[71]
- Maryland[72]
- Massachusetts[73]
- New Hampshire[74]
- North Carolina[75]
- Ohio[76]
- Oregon[77]
- Pennsylvania[78]
- Rhode Island[79]

- **In-state distributed power requirement in 38 percent of RPS states.** Eleven of the 29 states, or 38 percent, had an in-state requirement for certain distributed power.[80]
- **In-state capital or labor benefit in 15 percent of RPS states.** Four of the 29 states, or 14 percent, had a benefit for an in-state capital component or labor.
- **Multiple of the prior preferences.** Some states had multiple multipliers and preferences.
- **No geographic preferences in 24 percent of RPS states.** Seven of the 29 RPS states, or 24 percent, had no geographic preferences in their laws.

---

69. Conn. Gen. Stat. Ann. § 16-245a(b) (West 2013).
70. 20 Ill. Comp. Stat. Ann. 3855/1-56(b) (West 2012).
71. 65-407-311 Me. Code R. § 6 (LexisNexis 2011).
72. Md. Code Regs. 20.61.03(D) (2011).
73. Mass. Ann. Laws ch. 25A, § 11F(a) (LexisNexis 2011).
74. N.H. Rev. Stat. Ann. § 362-F:6(I) (LexisNexis 2011).
75. N.C. Gen. Stat. Ann. § 133.8(b)(2) (2011).
76. Ohio Rev. Code Ann. § 4928.64(C)(5) (LexisNexis 2012).
77. Or. Rev. Stat. § 469A.135(1)(a), (2) (2011).
78. 73 Pa. Stat. & Cons. Stat. § 1648.4 (West 2007).
79. 39 R.I. Gen. Laws § 39-26-4(d) (2016).
80. Ferrey, *supra* note 46, at 75–77.

Evolving RPS Structure of States

This section documents how these same RPS REC states have changed their policies regarding in-state and external renewable power generation transmitted into their states for consumers.

In-State REC Multipliers

Of the eight states that maintained RPS REC multipliers only for in-state-sited electric generation in 2011, five continued to offer RPS REC multipliers in 2020. This is a decrease of more than one-third of the eight states that were discriminating in 2011. Three states—Arizona, Delaware, and Nevada—ceased offering RPS REC multipliers for in-state-sited electric generation. Therefore, 37.5 percent of the eight states that in 2011 expressly provided such in-state-only REC multiplier incentives ended their past geographic discrimination.

Five states—Kansas, Maryland, Ohio, Oregon, and Texas—as of 2011–2012 had issues of timing of the project for RPS RECs that favored in-state projects. Of these five states, only Maryland continues to offer constitutionally questionable RPS REC multipliers. Kansas, Ohio, Oregon, and Texas have allowed their time windows for eligible new renewable energy projects to lapse, effectively ending certain geographic in-state RPS discrimination in these states. Therefore, 80 percent of these five states no longer have such in-state discrimination in their REC programs.

Of the 13 states with some form of in-state REC multipliers embodied in state law, seven states, or more than 50 percent, today have ceased at least one or more elements of their statutory geographic discrimination regarding where the renewable power was generated that was present in 2011. These 13 states represent 59 percent of the 22 states that had some form of geographic discrimination in their REC statutes in 2011. This alone constitutes a substantial legal change.

Indirect Requirements for In-State RPS REC Generation

Massachusetts as noted earlier transitioned to a new indirect SMART wholesale power transfer rate subsidy for in-state solar projects that excludes external solar projects. California provides an indirect in-state preference for renewable energy that in operation decreases demand for and disadvantages externally produced energy. Despite previously not having an

SREC program, in March 2010, the California Public Utilities Commission approved the use of tradable renewable energy credits (TRECs) in the California Renewable Portfolio Standard program.[81]

Under this revised California framework, parties are allowed to meet the RPS by purchasing RECs "unbundled" or separated from purchasing the associated renewable energy that creates the REC. Initially, the use of TRECs for RPS compliance was limited to no more than 25 percent of a given investor-owned utility's (IOU's) or electric service provider's annual REC obligation. This limit decreased to 10 percent of the utility's RPS requirement by 2017.[82] Effectively, a limit on purchase or use of TRECs restricts the remaining amount of RECs that utilities must obtain to be "bundled" with power generated from renewable energy facilities located in California or connected to a balancing authority in the California utility grid, which predominately serve in-state generation sources.

California required a majority of its awarded RECs to be bundled with the sale of electricity produced by renewable resources in or connected to in-state transmission, thus disadvantaging renewable generation sited out of state.[83] This requires the significant majority of usable RECs to be created by in-state renewable energy generation. In Chapter 9, there is discussion of more restrictive 2023 changes in California's net metering program, which also supports renewable energy generation.

In-Region RPS REC Requirements

Eleven states in 2021 maintained RPS REC requirements for in-*region* geographic location of renewable generation. This was the same number and involved the same states doing so in 2011. A state discriminating against another state's commerce is the most common form of discrimination

81. *See Overview of the California Renewable Portfolio Standard Program*, SRECTrade, https://perma.cc/5QFA-TBCL (last visited Apr. 24, 2024).

82. *Id.* SBX1-2 (April 2011) capped the use of TRECs at 25 percent for the compliance period ending December 31, 2013, decreased to 10 percent of the utility's RPS requirement by 2017; *see also* Cal. Pub. Utils. Comm'n, 2019 California Renewables Portfolio Standard: Annual Report 60 , https://perma.cc/M3SD-W8N6 (noting that these 2020 percentages remain in place indefinitely).

83. The California Public Utilities Commission staff recognized that this could invoke constitutional problems. *See Renewable Energy Certificates and the California Renewables Portfolio Standard Program* 90–91, Cal. Pub. Utils. Comm'n, Div. of Strategic Planning (Apr. 20, 2006).

enacted or enabled at the state level and therefore makes up the majority of cases brought before courts constituting energy sector Dormant Commerce Clause precedent. However, in-state discrimination is not the only form of constitutionally impermissible Dormant Commerce Clause discrimination. The Dormant Commerce Clause prohibits any geographic discrimination based on the generation of commerce, whether or not such discrimination is based on being "in" or "out" of state political boundaries.[84] And electricity generation is commerce, articulated by the Supreme Court four decades ago.[85]

Placing this in context, the 11 states that had regional discrimination in their RPS statutes in 2011 still maintain that geographic discrimination. In most cases, this requires that renewable power generation eligible to earn RPS RECs in a given state must originate from the regional ISO states in which the states' retail utilities, which must purchase the RECs created, participate in wholesale market transactions. For example, five of these 11 states are the five RPS states of the six states in ISO New England (NE) that have RPS programs (excluding Vermont) and recognize RECs from renewable power generation in the other New England states participating in ISO NE.[86]

RPS REC Benefits for In-State Components and Labor

Three states in 2021 maintained RPS RECs awarded to in-state workers or in-state manufactured components employed for the creation of additional state RPS RECs. A decade before, in 2011, there were four such states. However, Arizona has not extended its state statute indicating a preference or requirement for "In-State Power Plant Installation, Manufacturing, and Installation Content Extra Credit Multipliers."[87] So this is a decrease of 25 percent of states awarding this in-state REC preference over a decade.

Of note, the federal Inflation Reduction Act also subsidizes disproportionately in-country domestic content/materials incorporated in future renewable energy projects earning PTC and ITC federal tax credits (see Chapter 6). The Dormant Commerce Clause of the federal Constitution that

84. Ne. Bancorp, Inc. v. Bd. of Governors of Fed. Rsrv. Sys., 472 U.S. 159, 174 (1985) (citing Lewis v. BT Inv. Mgrs., Inc., 447 U.S. 27, 39–44 (1980); Sporhase v. Nebraska *ex rel.* Douglas, 458 U.S. 941 (1982)).

85. FERC v. Mississippi, 456 U.S. 742, 757 (1982).

86. *See* Indep. Sys. Operator New Eng., *supra* note 41.

87. Ariz. Admin. Code § 14-2-1806(D)–(E) (2017).

makes in-state REC preferences and multipliers for electricity legally suspect allows the federal government to subsidize and tax commerce in a differential manner.

How States Structure Their RPS Geographic Preferences

Seven of the 22 states that provided geographic preferences in their RPS programs in 2011 have ended geographic preferences and no longer offer REC multipliers to new projects. It is significant that one-third of the 22 states with some form of geographic discrimination in 2011 have allowed such elements to lapse, now raising to 14 the number of the 29 RPS states that no longer have state laws that discriminate in their treatment of renewable energy.

State regulation of interstate commerce in electricity is particularly susceptible to being stricken for geographic Commerce Clause discrimination in three aspects. First, the technical, scientific reality is that electricity moves instantaneously in interstate commerce: the Supreme Court noted that it is now "possible for a customer in Vermont [to] purchase electricity from an environmentally friendly power producer in California or a cogeneration facility in Oklahoma."[88] Second, the Supreme Court resolved any dispute or vagueness as to whether electric power wherever created is a uniform article in interstate U.S. commerce:[89]

> [I]t is difficult to conceive of a more basic element of interstate commerce than electric energy, a product used in virtually every home and every commercial or manufacturing facility. No State relies solely on its own resources in this respect.[90]

Third, FERC exclusively regulates ISO and RTO operations and requires them to discourage in-state and regional discrimination and to encourage open multistate competition. FERC orders require each ISO wholesale power and transmission market to operate competitively in a

---

88. New York v. FERC, 535 U.S. 1, 8 (2002) (citing Transmission Access Pol'y Study Grp. v. FERC, 225 F.3d 667, 681 (D.C. Cir. 2000)).

89. *See also id.* at 16 (transmissions on the interconnected national grids constitute transmissions in interstate commerce).

90. FERC v. Mississippi, 456 U.S. 742, 757 (1982).

nondiscriminatory manner. FERC orders on this are set forth in more detail in Chapter 4 and noted concisely here:

- FERC Order No. 888 created open-access nondiscriminatory transmission access for all electricity produced by independent power producers, whether renewable or nuclear.[91]
- FERC Order No. 2003 extended interconnection to the grid on a nondiscriminatory basis, prohibiting transmission facility owners from discriminating.[92]
- FERC Order No. 1000 required ISOs to eliminate discrimination regarding transmission tariffs.[93]
- FERC Order No. 2222 allowed small renewable projects to be aggregated to participate nondiscriminatorily, if they wish, in all ISO markets.[94]

Feed-In Tariffs Not Legally Imposed on Regulated IOUs

A feed-in tariff (FiT) is a regulatory requirement imposed by utility regulators on regulated IOUs to purchase on a wholesale basis certain designated types of independent power generation, typically from renewable resources or combined heat and power units, at prices well in excess of the market value of wholesale power and/or in excess of the PURPA Avoided Cost (see Chapter 5). Costs of FiTs are passed on to consumers by utilities. Advocates for renewable power are still urging U.S. states to adopt FiTs, although they have been held by FERC and courts as unconstitutional when ordered by regulators for private IOUs in the United States.

The federal courts and FERC separately struck FiTs in California in the 1990s and in 2010, respectively.[95] FERC rejected all of California's arguments

---

91. Order No. 888, 18 C.F.R. pts. 35 & 385 (1996); *see also* Steven Ferrey, The New Rules 41–42 (Pennwell 2000).

92. Nat'l Ass'n of Regul. Util. Comm'rs v. FERC, 475 F.3d 1277 (D.C. Cir. 2007).

93. Transmission Planning and Cost Allocation by Transmission Owning and Operating Public Utilities, 136 FERC ¶ 61,051 (2011).

94. Participation of Distributed Energy Resource Aggregations in Markets Operated by Regional Transmission Organizations and Independent System Operators, 172 FERC ¶ 61,247 (2020).

95. Indep. Energy Producers Ass'n v. Cal. Pub. Utils. Comm'n, 36 F.3d 848, 853 (9th Cir. 1994); S. Cal. Edison Co., 70 FERC ¶ 61,215 (1995); *In re* Cal. Pub. Utils. Comm'n, S. Cal. Edison Co., Pac. Gas & Elec. Co., San Diego Gas & Elec. Co., FERC Docket Nos. EL10-64-000 & EL10-66-000, 132 FERC ¶ 61,047 (2010), Order on Petitions for Declaratory Order.

regarding its generic environmental rationales for above-market wholesale rates in excess of limits under federal law or as set by FERC.[96] Renewable wholesale generators could receive tariffs no more than fair wholesale market prices under federal law.[97] FERC reiterated that only the federal government can regulate commerce between the states, and California cannot attempt to regulate commerce outside its borders.[98] This ban on state regulators imposing FiTs does not pertain to municipal utilities or co-ops that are not state regulated, and several of these have utilized FiTs to include more renewable energy in their supplied generation mix.

In the next chapter, we move from coverage of RPS REC subsidies for power generation in approximately 60 percent of the states to net metering, which is the most prevalent state incentive and subsidy for new power in the United States. Net metering as a power subsidy is distinct from the legal prohibitions of retail "submetering" of electric power. Net metering can be utilized strategically.

96. *Id.* ¶¶ 17–18. FERC rejected all of California's arguments regarding generic environmental rationales for wholesale rates in excess of limits under federal law or set by FERC.

97. *In re* Cal. Pub. Utils. Comm'n et al., 133 FERC ¶ 61,059 (2010), Order Granting Clarification and Dismissing Rehearing.

98. *Id.*

CHAPTER 9

Net Metering

Net Metering: Back-Door New Power Support

This chapter analyzes a second substantial state subsidy for future operation of certain energy sources that also is "grandfathered" for existing projects in approximately 80 percent of U.S. states. This chapter also analyzes the critical distinction between legal net metering and often not legal submetering in different states. While constitutional challenges have resulted in some recent restrictions in use of prior RPS REC in-state incentives (see the sections of Chapter 8 under "The Dormant Commerce Clause, Discrimination, RPS RECs"), net metering has been and remains the most widely provided state incentive and subsidy for renewable energy in the United States:

- Net metering can compensate renewable energy at up to 500 percent more than the actual market value of the electric power transacted.
- Net metering subsidizes each behind-the-retail-meter kilowatt-hour (kWh) generated during the operational life of renewable energy projects that is sent back to the grid, unlike the federal Investment Tax Credit, which provides a year-one tax subsidy (see Chapter 6).
- The electric sector is responsible for more than one-quarter of global warming emissions and is projected to bear approximately two-thirds of the reduction of U.S. carbon emissions (see Chapter 2),[1] which is subsidized by net metered renewable credits.

Net metering allows consumers with individual state-designated renewable power generation facilities to earn a credit at above-market retail rates

1. Bloomberg Philanthropies, Fulfilling America's Pledge 5–6, 19 (2018), https://www.bbhub.io/dotorg/sites/28/2018/09/Fulfilling-Americas-Pledge-2018.pdf; Sources of Greenhouse Gas Emissions, U.S. Env't Prot. Agency (Apr. 11, 2024), https://www.epa.gov/ghgemissions/sources-greenhouse-gas-emissions.

for wholesale power transferred to their utilities. Net metering operates as a state-created legal utility bill subsidy provided in approximately 80 percent of U.S. states and the District of Columbia to promote renewable power generation. As examined later in this chapter, two federal regulatory decisions, in *MidAmerican*[2] and *SunEdison,*[3] raised and left unanswered issues about whether some states' net metering programs may violate federal law and the Constitution's Supremacy Clause.

Separately, new regulations promulgated a regulatory restriction on federal renewable energy law that limited federal incentives for small renewable energy projects by[4]

- Making less certain the date and time that a small renewable energy project can obtain a legally enforceable obligation from a utility to purchase its power output
- Permitting utilities in certain markets to opt out of their obligations to purchase power from small renewable power projects larger than 5 MW
- Making it easier and less expensive to challenge a small renewable power project's federally established rights and benefits
- Reducing the potential level of Avoided Cost prices that small renewable energy projects receive for the power they produce and allowing the price to include monthly varying prices,[5] which makes it difficult to obtain financing

How a Meter Shifts Electric Sector Cash Flows

When a customer uses electricity from the utility, the meter runs forward—but when the amount of electricity produced on-site by the consumer exceeds the amount used, the excess generation flowing back to the utility causes the consumer's retail meter to run in reverse. If net metering is allowed by a state for a particular generator of power, this allows consumers to receive financial credits from the utility that state rate-making orders

2. MidAmerican Energy Co., 94 FERC ¶ 61,340 (2001).
3. Sun Edison LLC, 129 FERC ¶¶ 61,146, 61,620 (2009).
4. FERC Order No. 872 (July 2020).
5. This is contrary to the ruling in *Winding Creek Solar, LLC v. Peevey*, 293 F. Supp. 3d 980, 989–90 (N.D. Cal. 2017), *aff'd sub nom*. Winding Creek Solar, LLC v. Peterman, 932 F.3d 861 (9th Cir. 2019).

ultimately pass on as costs to other utility customers as costs of distribution service.[6] Net metering provides monetary benefits to net metering customers and, since the measuring meter is located on the customer's property, does not cause the customer to incur distributed losses that instead are absorbed by the utility's customers.[7]

Customers are given credit by the utility for every kWh of electricity exported to the utility, turning the meter in reverse during such energy export from customers. Since only a single rate applies to the net amount of electric use registered as it passes in both directions through a single retail customer meter, net metering effectively credits and compensates the generator at, or near, the full retail rate associated with that meter.[8] The retail or near-retail value typically credited and received for that net metered power by the customer is an amount in excess of

- The utility's federally specified Avoided Cost price pursuant to federal law[9] (see Chapter 5)
- The wholesale rate established by the Federal Energy Regulatory Commission (FERC) or by federally regulated independent system operators (ISOs), which manage the utility grids and wholesale power transactions for more than half of U.S. electricity (see Chapter 4)

Depending on state policies, net metering credits may be turned into cash for the net metering customer at the end of the month or billing period, carried as credits for the customer into the next utility billing period, or forfeited to the utility to apply toward unpaid bills of other customers. Net metering prevents surplus solar power produced midday during maximum insolation from being curtailed and losing its value. It has been estimated that future curtailment for daily solar and wind power in New England could be

---

6. *See* Steven Ferrey, *Torquing the Levers of International Power*, 15 WASH. U. GLOBAL STUD. L. REV. 255, 287–88 (2016) (costs are passed through to customers' energy bills). *See also Glossary*, DATABASE OF STATE INCENTIVES FOR RENEWABLES & EFFICIENCY, https://perma.cc/E32X-8GX6 (last visited May 1, 2024) (credits at the utility's full retail rate).

7. *Id.* at 287 (transmission and distribution losses of 4–8 percent are not realized with distributed generation used on-site).

8. *See Glossary*, *supra* note 6 ("In effect, the customer uses excess generation to offset electricity that the customer otherwise would have to purchase at the utility's full retail rate."). Whether electricity is a good or a service and how it should be treated under the law are looked at differently in different states.

9. *See* Steven Ferrey, *The Medium Is the Message*, 35 VA. ENV'T L.J. 231, 257 (2017).

as much as 2 terawatt-hours. In a three-month period, CAISO in California already was required to curtail 485 MW of wind power and 657 MW of solar generation in four instances for six hours to balance supply and demand on the system.[10]

Evolution of Net Metering

Net metering's popularity has ebbed and flowed. Net metering enjoyed federal encouragement through section 1251(a)(11) of the Energy Policy Act of 2005, which provides that "each electric utility shall make available upon request net metering service to any electric consumer that the electric utility services."[11] State regulatory agencies were required to "consider" the implementation of net metering at the state level.[12] Net metering's high-water mark came in 2015, when 44 states, the District of Columbia, Guam, Puerto Rico, American Samoa, and the U.S. Virgin Islands had adopted some form of mandatory net metering policies for their regulated utilities.[13] Utilities in three additional states—Idaho, South Carolina, and Texas—have implemented voluntary individual net metering programs for one utility.[14]

There are 35 states, the District of Columbia, and four U.S. territories with mandatory net metering rules.[15] In addition, there are five states[16] in transition to statewide distributed generation compensation rules other than

10. David Howarth & Bill Monsen, *Renewables Face Daytime Curtailments in California*, Project Fin. Newswire 12–13 (2014), https://www.projectfinance.law/media/1584/pfn_1114.pdf.

11. Energy Policy Act of 2005 § 1251(a)(11).

12. *SCC 21 Sponsored Standards: 1547 Series of Standards*, IEEE Standards Ass'n, https://sagroups.ieee.org/scc21/ (last visited June 24, 2024).

13. *Net Metering*, Database of State Incentives for Renewables & Efficiency (Mar. 2015), http://ncsolarcen-prod.s3.amazonaws.com/wp-content/uploads/2015/04/Net-Metering-Policies.pdf.

14. Benjamin Inskeep, *Net Metering Updates*, Database of State Incentives for Renewables & Efficiency (2020), htttps://www.slideserve.com/gmichelle/net-metering-updates-powerpoint-ppt-presentation.

15. Cherrelle Eid, Javier Reneses Guillén, Pablo Frías Marín & Rudy Hakvoort, *The Economic Effect of Electricity Net-Metering with Solar PV: Consequences for Network Cost Recovery, Cross Subsidies and Policy Objectives*, 75 Energy Pol'y 244 (2014); Angela Picciariello, Claudio Vergara, Javier Reneses, Pablo Frías & Lennart Söder, *Electricity Distribution Tariffs and Distributed Generation: Quantifying Cross-Subsidies from Consumers to Prosumers*, 37 Utils. Pol'y 23 (2015).

16. *Net Metering*, Database of State Incentives for Renewables & Efficiency (Oct. 2019), https://s3.amazonaws.com/ncsolarcen-prod/wp-content/uploads/2019/10/DSIRE_Net_Metering_Oct2019.pdf. The states transitioning to policies other than net metering are Illinois, Indiana, Kentucky, Michigan, and New York. *Id.*

net metering, as well as five states[17] having changed from their prior state net metering programs to distributed generation compensation rules other than net metering. California in 2023 changed significantly its compensation for new net metering as discussed more later.

Of the states in transition to statewide generation compensation rules other than net metering, Illinois will be replacing retail net metering with a localized value-of-solar rate as soon as distributed solar capacity reaches 5 percent of a utility's total peak demand.[18] Indiana will be phasing out net metering, and the program replacing it will lower the retail rate compensation for residents who install devices to use solar or wind power.[19] Kentucky's bill, which went into effect January 1, 2020, increased the maximum net metering facility size to 45 kW and also required the Public Service Commission to set crediting structures specific for each utility, which are based on the dollar value of the credit, as opposed to the previous kWh netting.[20] Such utilities are now authorized to set up rates to incorporate all costs incurred to serve customers.[21]

Netting Size Limitations and Credits

Some states have capacity limits on the size of net metered systems expressed as either total kW capacity of a net metered generation unit or a percentage limit as a function of an individual customer's retail capacity demand.[22] Most states allow unused net metering credit carryover to the next monthly billing period. The longevity of such carried-over credits varies by state, with some states causing credits to expire in 12 months or at the end of the year, while other states allow perpetual carryover of credits to future bills.

---

17. *Id.* The states with statewide distributed generation compensation rules other than net metering are Arizona, Georgia, Hawaii, Louisiana, Mississippi, and Utah. *Id.*

18. *Illinois Net Metering*, Database of State Incentives for Renewables & Efficiency (Mar. 7, 2024), https://programs.dsireusa.org/system/program/detail/2700.

19. *Indiana Net Metering*, Database of State Incentives for Renewables & Efficiency (Mar. 7, 2024), https://programs.dsireusa.org/system/program/detail/342.

20. *Kentucky Net Metering*, Database of State Incentives for Renewables & Efficiency (Mar. 7, 2024), https://programs.dsireusa.org/system/program/detail/1081.

21. *Id.*

22. *See State Net Metering Policies*, Nat'l Conf. of State Legislatures (Nov. 20, 2017), https://www.ncsl.org/energy/state-net-metering-policies. In terms of limits, Arizona has a limit of 125 percent of a customer's total connected load. South Carolina, Virginia, and Wisconsin allow up to 20 kW. New Jersey and Ohio have no capacity limit, Massachusetts allows system facilities for public off-takers up to 10 MW, and New Mexico allows up to 80 MW per facility.

The net metered customer enjoys a free virtual energy "banking" service even though the utility, in reality, cannot "bank" electricity.[23] A net metering customer does not financially compensate the utility for moving its power on the grid to effectuate this energy "banking" or in most states for any share of cost recovery for distribution system investments made by the utility to service the client. Though the net metering customers use the distribution grid twice, exporting and receiving "banked" power back for use, they never pay for either use of these grid services.

The utilities credit (or pay) the net metering customer for the kWh of electricity sent on a wholesale basis to the grid, although their value is credited at or near a much higher bundled retail rate value. The utility and its *non*–net metering customers who ultimately incur the cost pass-through of all revenue lost by the utility through net metering are paying more—often triple or quadruple the price—for the net metered power than the utility would pay for other wholesale power available in the market. In the 40 net metered states, the utility must accept and credit or pay for this power whenever an eligible distributed renewable generation unit produces it, rather than when the utility needs more power to distribute to its customers. There is no advance notice required from the net metered customer to the utility for the amount or timing of power being net metered back to the utility.[24]

State Second Thoughts on Net Metering

The solar energy industry in the United States has experienced rapid expansion in recent years, with a compound annual growth rate of more than 60 percent between 2007 and 2016.[25] One factor behind the rise of the solar energy industry in the United States is the proliferation of state net metering

23. *See Electricity and Energy Storage*, World Nuclear Ass'n (May 18, 2023), https://www.world-nuclear.org/information-library/current-and-future-generation/electricity-and-energy-storage.aspx ("Electricity cannot itself be stored on any scale . . . .").

24. ISOs in the nation accept 100 percent of all solar and wind net metered power whenever it is able to be produced into their wholesale power markets, so there is always a market. *See Market Rule 1*, ISO New Eng., https://www.iso-ne.com/participate/rules-procedures/tariff/market-rule-1 (last visited June 24, 2024).

25. *See* Press Release, Solar Energy Indus. Ass'n, U.S. Solar Market Has Record-Breaking Year, Total Market Poised to Triple in Next Five Years (Mar. 8, 2017), http://www.seia.org/news/us-solar-market-has-record-breaking-year-total-market-poised-triple-next-five-years.

programs.[26] Utilities express concerns about the system cost shifting that occurs from those engaged in net metering to those who are not; some ratepayers express the same concern regarding cost being shifted to them.[27] In 2016, 28 of the (then) 44 states with net metering programs considered curtailing them.[28]

In 2016, the Arizona Corporation Commission issued a decision to eliminate net metering for new solar customers and replace it with a net-feed-in tariff. In 2019 Connecticut extended net metering through 2021 and succeeded it with a net metering–equivalent value. In December 2020, the Utah Public Service Commission established a new compensation rate at roughly 45 percent below the average retail rate to quantify the value of power exported from behind-the-meter solar energy systems. Five states abandoned net metering and implemented alternative compensation schemes in its place: Arizona, Hawaii, Indiana, Maine, and Nevada.[29]

Net metering in 2017 at 0.4 percent penetration of all electricity consumers was estimated to have raised average national electricity rates by +/– 0.2 percent.[30] At projected penetration rates of ~3 percent in 2030, net metering is forecast to raise average national electric rates by +/– 1.6 percent.[31]

---

26. *See State Net Metering Policies*, *supra* note 22; Sean Paul, *The Solar Industry in a Period of Transition*, GEO. PUB. POL'Y REV. (Nov. 15, 2016), http://gppreview.com/2016/11/15/solar-industry-period-transition/.

27. *See* Stephen Lacey, *As Net Metering Battles Move to Small Markets, Solar Advocates Claim Early Victories*, GREENTECH MEDIA (Mar. 20, 2014); *The Fight to Put a Value on Rooftop Solar Power*, CLIMATENEXUS (Apr. 20, 2017), https://climatenexus.org/climate-issues/energy/the-net-metering-fight/; Mark Muro & Devashree Saha, *Rooftop Solar: Net Metering Is a Net Benefit*, BROOKINGS INST. (May 23, 2016), https://www.brookings.edu/research/rooftop-solar-net-metering-is-a-net-benefit/.

28. *See* Autumn Proudlove et al., *50 States of Solar: Q4 2016 Quarterly Report & Annual Review Executive Summary*, N.C. CLEAN ENERGY TECH. CTR. (Jan. 2017), http://ncsolarcen-prod.s3.amazonaws.com/wp-content/uploads/2017/02/Q42016_ExecSummary.pdf; Benjamin Inskeep & Kathryn Wright, *50 States of Solar: A Quarterly Look at America's Fast-Evolving Distributed Solar Policy Conversation*, N.C. CLEAN ENERGY TECH. CTR. (Apr. 2015), https://psc.ky.gov/pscecf/2020-00350/dspenard%40strobobarkley.com/04012021044154/2021.04.01_kyseia_response_ku_lge_16_b_attachment_2.pdf; Diane Cardwell, *Solar Power Battle Puts Hawaii at Forefront of Worldwide Changes*, N.Y. TIMES (Apr. 18, 2015), https://www.nytimes.com/2015/04/19/business/energy-environment/solar-power-battle-puts-hawaii-at-forefront-of-worldwide-changes.html?_r=0.

29. *State Net Metering Policies*, *supra* note 22.

30. Ryan Wiser, Galen Barbose & Mark Bolinger, *Retail Rate Impacts of Renewable Electricity: Some First Thoughts* 26, LBL 1007261 (2017), https://eta-publications.lbl.gov/sites/default/files/lbnl-1007261.pdf.

31. *Id.*

Each 2 percent penetration of net metering adoption raises rates for all other non–net metered customers (which still represent approximately 99 percent of all U.S. electric consumers) by half of that amount of penetration—so a 2 percent increase in net metered benefits for an additional 1 percent of consumers raises rates for the other 99 percent of consumers by approximately 1 percent.

In May 2022, more than 200 environmental organizations and rooftop solar companies petitioned the U.S. Federal Trade Commission (FTC) to exercise its authority under section 6(b) of the Federal Trade Commission Act to study U.S. electric utility industry practices that they claimed impede renewable energy competition, which the FTC polices, and harm consumers.[32] The petition characterizes that it is "unfair competitive behavior" for any of the approximately 40 net metering states to reduce their net metering rates or compensate net metering customers at "below-retail tariff rates." One observer noted, "It appears that they did so to stave off actions by certain states to reduce compensation for energy produced under net energy metering laws and policies":[33]

> [T]he customer producing energy from rooftop solar . . . gets paid a rate equal to the utility's cost of energy plus the utility's costs of transmission, distribution, back-up power, and much more. This compensation is many times higher than the amount paid for energy and capacity sold by solar and wind power developers selling to the market or bilaterally . . . . This over payment to NEM [net energy metering] participants results in the costs of the utilities' transmission and distribution system (as well as many other costs) being shifted from the NEM participants to other customers . . . .[34]

The state of California operates the largest net metering program in the nation. California's 2016 NEM 2.0 continued to compensate the net metered

32. Press Release, Ctr. for Biological Diversity, Legal Petition Seeks Federal Trade Commission Investigation of Energy Utility Abuses (May 18, 2022), https://biologicaldiversity.org/w/news/press-releases/egal-petition-seeks-federal-trade-commission-investigation-of-energy-utility-abuses-2022-05-18/.

33. Jennifer L. Key & Richard L. Roberts, *The FTC Petition—A Thinly-Veiled Attempt to Protect Full Net Energy Metering for DERs*, STEPTOE (May 26, 2022), https://www.steptoe.com/en/news-publications/purpa-and-distributed-energy-resources-blog/the-ftc-petition-a-thinly-veiled-attempt-to-protect-full-net-energy-metering-for-ders.html.

34. *Id.*

customers near the retail rate with customers charged based on time-of-use rates. The California Public Utilities Commission (CPUC) five years later conducted a study that demonstrated that NEM 2.0 had negatively impacted nonparticipant ratepayers and harmed low-income customers:

> Prior to the installation of the NEM-eligible generator, residential NEM 2.0 customers pay approximately $112.5 million higher bills relative to the costs for the utility to provide them service. Following the installation of the NEM generator, these same customers are estimated to pay approximately $618.6 million less on their bills relative to the utilities' cost to provide service.[35]

The CPUC reported that by 2020, net metering could cost non–solar electricity customers between $370 million and $1.1 billion per year,[36] with revenue loss and the costs of the accounting and distribution of these net metered credits passed on to the utility's general ratepayers. In December 2022, the CPUC unanimously approved a revised NEM 3.0 for new net metering customers, decreasing by as much as approximately 75 percent the net metering credit value for the excess electricity, in the future to be credited at an Avoided Cost (PURPA-compliant) rate for unused credits.[37] This successor tariff also replaces retail rate compensation for net exported energy with Avoided Cost that will vary according to grid needs, rather than a rate near the retail rate, with high differentials between winter off-peak and summer on-peak rates, which structure will promote the installation of storage with solar systems to control when net metering power is exported.[38] Under NEM 3.0, there no longer is a near 1:1 credit value ratio for the value of excess consumer power sent to the grid due to the now lower value of power

35. Verdant, Net-Energy Metering 2 0 Lookback Study (2021), https://www.cpuc.ca.gov/-/media/cpuc-website/divisions/energy-division/documents/net-energy-metering-nem/nemrevisit/nem-2_lookback_study.pdf.

36. Ker Than, *As Solar Power Grows, Dispute Flares over U.S. Utility Bills*, Nat'l Geo. (Dec. 24, 2013), https://www.nationalgeographic.com/science/article/131226-utilities-dispute-net-metering-for-solar; *see also* Tom Tanton, *A Critique of Brookings Institution's Mark Muro and Devashree Saha:* Rooftop Solar: Net Metering Is a Net Benefit, EE Legal (July 5, 2016), https://eelegal.org/tanton-a-critique-of-brookings-institututions-mark-muro-and-devashree-saha-rooftop-solar-net-metering-is-a-net-benefit/.

37. Cal. Pub. Utils. Comm'n, Order Instituting Rulemaking to Revisit Net Energy Metering Tariffs Pursuant to Decision 16-01-044, and to Address Other Issues Related to Net Energy Metering, Rulemaking 20-08-020 (Dec. 19, 2022).

38. *Id.*

credited to the consumer. Net metering agreements in place before mid-April 2023 are not affected for 20 years as long as the size of the solar system does not increase.

Federal Net Meter Orders and Rulings

As a base principle, the Federal Power Act grants FERC the ability to regulate "the sale of electric energy at wholesale in interstate commerce."[39] The same statutory section, however, does not permit FERC to regulate several other types of electricity transactions grouped in what the Supreme Court has termed the "retail sale of electricity."[40] See Chapter 4. The question of whether net metering constitutes a wholesale or retail transaction of electricity determines whether it is legal for a state to determine a rate under the Federal Power Act. Traditional net metering escapes federal electric wholesale price regulation, according to the case law, in three cases where the facts underlying the decision were limited, leaving key issues not fully resolved.[41]

The First Decision: *MidAmerican*—2001

In 2001, FERC held in its *MidAmerican* decision,[42] the first of three cases adjudicating the legality of net metering, that no sale occurs when net metering accounts for less power export from the renewable power generator than the amount of power sold back by the utility to the distributed generator in a given billing period (usually one month)—put differently, net metering is not a wholesale transaction if the customer consumes more energy from the utility than they transmit back to the utility.[43] If there is zero net transfer of power back to the utility, there is no net wholesale sale of power, which is the threshold for FERC jurisdiction.

Subsequently, the Iowa Supreme Court held, in the case of *Windway Technologies*,[44] that state laws requiring rate-regulated utilities to use net metering are not inconsistent with PURPA.[45] See Chapter 5 regarding

39. 16 U.S.C. § 824(b)(1).
40. *Id.*; Hughes v. Talen Energy Mktg., LLC, 136 S. Ct. 1288, 1292 (2016).
41. *See Glossary*, *supra* note 6.
42. MidAmerican Energy Co., 94 FERC ¶ 61,340 (2001).
43. *Id.* ¶¶ 62,261, 62,263.
44. Windway Techs., Inc. v. Midland Power Co-op., 696 N.W.2d 303, 307 (Iowa 2005).
45. *Id.*; *MidAmerican*, 94 FERC ¶¶ 62,263–64.

PURPA. However, the Iowa court found no federal case or regulatory decision holding that net metering is required by PURPA.[46] Conversely in the matter of *Gregory Swecker*, FERC determined that the utility must provide net metering.[47]

The Second Decision: *SunEdison*—2009

In *Sun Edison LLC*, in 2009, FERC reiterated that net metering practices under state regulations are not wholesale power sale transactions but merely meter reading conventions:[48]

> We agree that, where the net metering participant (i.e., the end-use customer that is the purchaser of the solar-generated electric energy from SunEdison) does not, in turn, make a net sale to a utility, the sale of electric energy by SunEdison to the end-use customer is not a sale for resale, and our jurisdiction under the FPA is not implicated. That is, under the holding of *MidAmerican*, where there is no net sale over the applicable billing period to the local load-serving utility, there is no sale.

Note that the "net" flow of net metered power again in this case was in the traditional direction from the utility supplier to the user or project owner. In *SunEdison*, FERC noted that the retail customer's net consumption of electricity from the grid is critical: "A participant in a net metering program must be a net consumer of electricity—but for portions of the day or portions of the billing cycle, it may produce more electricity than it can use itself."[49] Such state net metering decisions were not federally preempted by the Federal Power Act and the Supremacy Clause of the Constitution.[50] Limited strictly to the applicant's warranties of the net direction of power flow, FERC found that these transactions are not wholesale sales in interstate commerce under the Federal Power Act and therefore concluded they do not involve FERC jurisdictional wholesale sales at impermissible prices under the act:

46. *Windway Techs., Inc.*, 696 N.W.2d at 307–09.
47. Swecker, 111 FERC ¶¶ 61,365, 62,585 (2005).
48. Sun Edison LLC, 129 FERC ¶¶ 61,146, 61,621 (2009).
49. *Id.* ¶ 61,620.
50. *Id.* ¶¶ 62,261, 62,263.

> *Because* we have found that, where the end-use customer makes no net sale *to* the local load-serving utility with which it has a net metering arrangement, the sale of electric energy by SunEdison to the end-use customer in such circumstances does not constitute a sale for resale (and also would not involve transmission in interstate commerce), and in such circumstances the sales are not subject to the Commission's jurisdiction under Part II of the FPA. . . .[51]

The parties stipulated that the SunEdison power project size required the end-use customer to purchase 100 percent of its power output, which was only about 30 percent of the total electric requirements of the customer, from the third-party solar rooftop owner SunEdison, with the remaining 70 percent provided by the utility—that is, the net flow of electricity was from the utility to the end user.[52] This was pivotal in FERC's legal determination:

> *Only if* the end-use customer participating in the net metering program produces more energy than it needs over the applicable billing period, and thus is considered to have made a net sale of energy *to* a utility over the applicable billing period, has the Commission asserted jurisdiction. If the entity making a net sale is a QF [Qualifying Facility] that has been exempted from section 205 of the FPA by section 292.601 of our regulations, no filing under the FPA is necessary to permit the net sale; however, if the entity is either not a QF or is a QF that is not exempted from section 205 of the FPA by section 292.601 of our regulations, a filing under the FPA is necessary. . . .[53]

The Third Decision: *NERA*—2020

There is a third FERC decision. In an April 2020 petition to FERC, the New England Ratepayers Association (NERA) asserted that net metering caused inequitable cost shifts among customer categories and was a wholesale power sale subject to FERC's, rather than to the state's, jurisdiction.[54] This petition sought a declaratory order of exclusive federal jurisdiction over energy

51. *Id.* ¶ 61,621 (emphasis added).

52. *Id.* ¶ 61,619.

53. *Id.* (footnotes omitted, emphasis added).

54. FERC Docket EL20-42, Petition at 1; *see also* Jasmine Melvin, *FERC Rejects Anti-Net Metering Petition but Issues Raised Could Resurface*, S&P Glob. Mkt. Intel. (July 16, 2020), https://www.spglobal.com/marketintelligence/en/news-insights/latest-news-headlines/ferc-rejects-anti-net-metering-petition-but-issues-raised-could-resurface-59467688.

sales from distributed generation where the output exceeds the customer's demand and is required to be valued and priced at Avoided Cost as a section 210 PURPA sale or as a wholesale power sale pursuant to sections 205 and 206 of the Federal Power Act.[55]

This was a generic petition, without raising facts regarding a certain state net metering program or an affected project, which hamstrung it procedurally. FERC determined that the issues presented in the petition "do not warrant a generic statement from the Commission at this time . . . [because they did not] identify a specific controversy or harm that the Commission should address in a declaratory order," according to FERC's July 2020 open meeting record.[56] Two FERC commissioners suggested that certain basic federal and state jurisdictional issues raised in the petition may warrant further attention if specific state facts were raised:

> [T]oday's Order does not address any of the important, substantive issues underlying the Petition. To that end, the Commission's Order is not a decision on whether the Commission lacks jurisdiction over the energy sales made through net metering; nor is it a decision on the merits of the issues raised by and contained in the Petition.[57]

FERC has not yet had a specific case before it in which to address the legal question of what happens when substantial amounts of net excess generation under net metering are credited or purchased by the utility, the flip side of the coin presented in the *MidAmerican* and *SunEdison* cases.

Net Metering Differences Incorporated in State Laws

This section outlines and compares each state's net metering program, noting any key changes in the decade from 2012 to 2022 and the result found in today's net metering regulations.

---

55. FERC Docket EL20-42, Petition at 1; *see also* Paul Ciampoli, *FERC Dismisses Net Metering Jurisdiction Petition on Procedural Grounds*, AM. PUB. POWER ASS'N (July 16, 2020), https://www.publicpower.org/periodical/article/ferc-dismisses-net-metering-jurisdiction-petition-procedural-grounds.

56. Ciampoli, *supra* note 55.

57. New Eng. Ratepayers Ass'n, 172 FERC ¶ 61,042 (July 16, 2020) (McNamee, Commissioner, concurring opinion). Commissioner Danly expressed concern that there was a need going forward to address the substantive issue to avoid inconsistent federal court treatment of wholesale power transfers in a "patchwork quilt of conflicting decisions. . . Confusion, delay and inconsistent rules—some of which will apply to individual states or parts of states—will be the inevitable result." *Id.* at 4 (Danly, Commissioner, concurring).

The buy/credit price relationship for retail power moving across an interconnection is one key mechanism to control net cash compensation, as are limits on system oversizing or changes to transmission and distribution charges to be significantly based on peak demand charges or per-meter charges, rather than based on conventional linear energy volumetric charges. Each previous iteration and current changes affect the legality of net metering in the U.S. system by whether the net metering "cash-out" at the end of the billing period, if any, is at the federally allowed Avoided Cost rate under PURPA or at a higher retail net metering rate. The latter is not allowed for a wholesale market transaction where power is purchased by a utility and is not subject to state determination since it is entirely within federal jurisdiction under the Federal Power Act.

Categories of Utility Payments for Excess Power Export

Net metering programs fall into three different categories in terms of how they treat excess net metering credits earned but not quickly utilized:

- Surrender excess net metering credits to the utility.
- Sell excess credits from the generator to the utility at the Avoided Cost rate.
- Sell excess credits to the utility at another rate typically higher than Avoided Cost.

The following table shows how each state handles this key issue of how state net metering programs handle surplus net metering quantities to the utility.

Surrender to the Utility	Alaska, American Samoa, Kentucky, North Carolina, Montana, U.S. Virgin Islands, Utah, Vermont, Washington
Sell at Avoided Cost	Arizona, Arkansas, Connecticut, Delaware, Florida, Georgia, Iowa, Louisiana, Minnesota, Missouri, Nebraska, New Hampshire, New Jersey, New Mexico, New York, North Dakota, Oklahoma, Oregon, South Carolina, Virginia, Wyoming
Sell at Another Rate	California, Colorado, District of Columbia, Guam, Illinois, Indiana, Kansas, Maryland, Massachusetts, Michigan, Ohio, Pennsylvania, Puerto Rico, Rhode Island, West Virginia, Wisconsin

In 2012, a dozen of the then-43 net metering states would confiscate from the renewable energy generator all unused credits with no compensation at the end of one year:

- Arkansas[58]
- Hawaii[59]
- Illinois[60]
- Kansas[61]
- Maine[62]
- Missouri[63]
- Montana[64]
- North Carolina[65]
- Oregon[66]
- Utah[67]
- Vermont[68]
- Washington[69]

Now, forfeiture of excess net metering credits after one year, shown as "surrender to the utility" in the preceding table, still occurs in nine of the 40 states and several territories that maintain net metering programs; however, those states are different than the list of states in 2012, with some no longer doing this, others having dropped state net metering entirely, and other states commencing this practice. Now the nine states and territories are

- American Samoa[70]
- Montana[71]
- North Carolina[72]

---

58. Ark. Code Ann. § 23-18-604 (LexisNexis 2012).

59. Haw. Pub. Util. Comm'n Order, Docket 2006-0084. Hawaii's evolving metering program is described at https://programs.dsireusa.org/system/program/detail/596/smart-renewable-energy-tariffs.

60. 220 Ill. Comp. Stat. 5/16-107.5 (2012).

61. Kan. Stat. Ann. § 66-1264 (2011).

62. Me. Stat. tit. 35-A, § 3209-A (2012).

63. Miss. Code Ann. § 386.890 (2011).

64. Mont. Code Ann. § 69-8-603 (2011).

65. N.C. Util. Comm'n, Docket No. E-100, Sub 83 (2009).

66. Or. Rev. Stat. Ann. § 757.300(3)(c)–(d) (West 2011).

67. Utah Code Ann. § 54-15-104(1), (3)(a)(ii) (West 2011).

68. Vt. Stat. Ann. tit. 30, § 219(e)(3)(B)–(C) (West 2011).

69. Wash. Rev. Code Ann. § 80.60 (2012).

70. *American Samoa—Net Metering*, Database of State Incentives for Renewables & Efficiency (Mar. 24, 2023), http://programs.dsireusa.org/system/program/detail/3218.

71. Mont. Code Ann. § 69-8-603 (2011).

72. N.C. Util. Comm'n, Docket No. E-100, Sub 83 (2009).

- Oregon[73]
- Pennsylvania[74]
- U.S. Virgin Islands[75]
- Utah[76]
- Vermont[77]
- Washington[78]

Georgia and Hawaii terminated their net metering programs. Hawaii had 12 percent of rooftops with solar panels installed, the highest percentage in the United States.[79] With this large number of net metering solar participants, more surplus power was being produced than was being used.[80] Consequently, "the energy [could] flow back to the substation . . . which [could] lead to reliability problems and possibly surges. And if crews are working in the area, there's a potential danger."[81] In response, Hawaii eliminated its net metering program entirely in 2015, replacing it with two options: self-supply and grid supply.[82] Self-supply "does not allow customers to export any rooftop PV energy back to the grid, except very limited amounts for a short duration,[83] and its receipt is not compensated by the utility."[84] Grid supply allows customer export of energy to the grid, for which they receive a lower-value credit than under net metering.[85]

---

73. Or. Rev. Stat. Ann. § 757.300(3)(c) (West 2011).

74. 73 Pa. Stat. Ann. § 1648.2 (West 2011).

75. 12-23 V.I. Code R. § 1141-47 (2007).

76. Utah Code Ann. § 54-15-104(1) (West 2011).

77. Vt. Stat. Ann. tit. 30, § 219(e)(3)(C) (West 2011).

78. Wash. Rev. Code Ann. § 80.60 (2012).

79. *See* Christian Roselund, *Hawaii Shuts Down Net Metering to New Customers*, PV Mag. (Oct. 14, 2015), https://www.pv-magazine.com/2015/10/14/hawaii-shuts-down-net-metering-to-new-customers_100021550/.

80. *See generally* Emily Walker, *What to Know about Hawaii's Transition to Clean Energy*, EnergySage (May 6, 2022), https://www.energysage.com/blog/hawaiis-clean-energy-transition/.

81. Anne C. Mulkern, *A Solar Boom So Successful, It's Been Halted*, Sci. Am. (Dec. 20, 2013), https://www.scientificamerican.com/article/a-solar-boom-so-successfull-its-been-halted/.

82. *See State Net Metering Policies*, *supra* note 22; Phil Cross, *Net Metering Skirmishes in Hawaii, California, Mississippi, Nevada*, Pub. Utils. Fort., Feb. 2016, at 56.

83. *Id.*

84. Mark Dyson & Jesse Morris, *Hawaii Just Ended Net Metering for Solar. Now What?*, RMI Outlet (Oct. 16, 2015), https://rmi.org/hawaii-just-ended-net-metering-solar-now/.

85. Cross, *supra* note 82; *see* Krysti Shallenberger, *Hawaii Regulators Nix Bid to Raise Caps on Grid-Supply Rooftop Solar Incentive*, Util. Dive (Dec. 15, 2016). Compensation is based on "the 12-month average on-peak avoided cost ending in June 2015" and is lower than the retail rate.

A "surrender to the utility" of excess credits without compensation as shown in the preceding table faces no legal issues under the *MidAmerican* and *SunEdison* decisions because no wholesale sale of electricity to the utility occurs. The sale to the utility of net metered power at the federal PURPA wholesale Avoided Cost rate in the second row of the table is allowable under the Iowa Supreme Court's analysis in its *Windway Technologies* decision and under PURPA, because solar QFs under PURPA are allowed to sell as much of their output as they wish at Avoided Cost rates. See Chapter 5.

The legality of transfer to the utility through net metering (the "sell at another rate" category shown in the bottom row of the table) could depend on the amount of electricity sold: if the net metering users/customers transfer or sell enough electricity back to the utilities that the utilities experience a net negative transfer of electricity to customers at the end of the billing period, then under the key FERC decisions on net metering this could qualify as a wholesale transaction and thus could be preempted by the Federal Power Act and the Supremacy Clause. This is a particular issue for state programs with net metering programs where unlimited net metering credits can be sold to any other customer of the utility at whatever price can be negotiated.

Fixed charges proposed in California or other states to be imposed on some net metering customers in state retail power distribution rates can mitigate or eliminate the negative impacts of net metering not otherwise contributing to distribution system costs to handle net metered power. In 2021, two of four FERC commissioners at that time, including its chairperson, issued a letter stating there was a "strong case" such fixed charges in Alabama "may be violating the Commission's PURPA regulations, undermining the statute's purpose of encouraging Qualifying Facilities."[86]

The Technique of Aggregated Community Systems

Meter aggregation and community net metering allow net metering credits from a single generation facility at a single site to be shared among multiple customers at different addresses. Shared or community solar net metering shares power net metering credits among multiple consumers, none of whom

86. *See ZEO: S-1/A General Form of Registration Statement for All Companies Including Face-Amount Certificate Companies*, Sec. & Exch. Comm'n (May 23, 2024), https://finance.yahoo.com/sec-filing/ZEO/0001213900-24-046320_1865506/.

pays any delivery charges to move energy from remote solar projects to them at multiple physically unrelated dispersed locations. Whether or not sharing credits involves something approaching or similar to a wholesale transaction has not been determined in a case presented to FERC or the courts.

Figure 9.1[87]

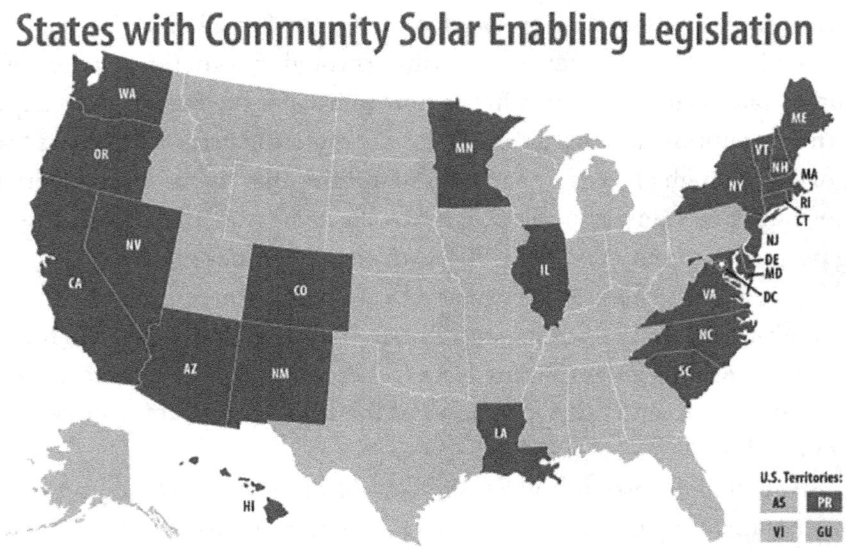

As shown in Figure 9.1, 22 states have adopted and now utilize community solar net metering regulations.[88] These states deem as shared renewable energy generation through programs for customers living far from the eligible physical renewable energy facility or in multifamily dwellings or condominiums with separate electric utility accounts not physically hosting the

87. *Shared Renewables*, U.S. Env'T Prot. Agency (Jan. 23, 2024), https://www.epa.gov/green-power-markets/shared-renewables.

88. *See Community Energy Projects*, Shared Renewables, http://www.sharedrenewables.org/community-energy-projects (last visited May 2, 2024). These states are California, Colorado, Connecticut, Delaware, Hawaii, Illinois, Maine, Maryland, Massachusetts, Minnesota, New Hampshire, Nevada, New Jersey, New Mexico, New York, North Carolina, Oregon, Rhode Island, South Carolina, Vermont, Virginia, and Washington. The District of Columbia has also adopted community solar net metering. About the Massachusetts virtual net metering program that allows sale and transfer of net metering credits, see https://www.mass.gov/info-details/net-metering-guide.

renewable generation.[89] Total net metered credits earned are allocated to others' accounts on a percentage basis at the request of the net metered customer or "host." Most shared renewable energy projects employ solar energy, while at least ten states also allow by regulation wind, biomass, or geothermal renewable energy projects to be community net metering projects.[90]

How and Where Things Legally Have Evolved

There is a substantial list of approximately one-third of the net metering states and territories that provide cash compensation when customers permanently transfer title to unused net metering credits and power at a rate other than at the federally allowed Avoided Cost rate prescribed under the PURPA amendments to the Federal Power Act. See Chapter 5. This category included until it changed its program at the end of 2022 (see earlier "State Second Thoughts on Net Metering" subsection) the state with the largest population, California, where any state's net metering credit buyback rates in excess of Avoided Cost raise still-unresolved questions about legality should they be challenged under the Federal Power Act as wholesale transactions of power with the utility.

Since 2012, there has been a retraction in 75 percent of those states that in 2012 set rates for excess net metered power credits above the federal maximum PURPA Avoided Cost rate and at or closer to the state retail power rate.[91] Moreover, some additional equilibrium has been induced in state net metering practices: where in 2012, 28 percent of the then-43 net metering states confiscated from the renewable energy generators all unused net energy generation credits at the end of each year without any

89. *See State Net Metering Policies*, *supra* note 22.

90. *Community Energy Projects*, *supra* note 88.

91. Three states that had compensated net energy generation through net metering at the retail rate, Minnesota, Georgia, and Wisconsin, have ceased that practice now, reducing the amount to no more than the federally allowed Avoided Cost or, in Georgia's case, discontinuing net metering. This leaves only Pennsylvania at the retail rate. For historical reference, see Steven Ferrey, *Nothing but Net: Renewable Energy and the Environment, MidAmerican Legal Fictions, and Supremacy Doctrine*, 14 Duke Env't L. & Pol'y F. 1, 15 (2003); Steven Ferrey, *Virtual "Nets" and Law: Power Navigates the Supremacy Clause*, 24 Geo. Int'l Env't L. Rev. 267, 270 (2013).

compensation,[92] that number is now reduced by 16.7 percent.[93] The *MidAmerican* and *SunEdison* opinions raise but do not resolve two key legal questions that state net metering programs will need to be cognizant of:

- The legality of some states' compensating wholesale surplus net metered power at a rate above the Federal Power Act's PURPA stipulated maximum full Avoided Cost rate.
- Where a state allows a renewable power generator's sale of earned net metering credits to other parties, whether such state is authorizing a wholesale power transaction that is not within state authority pursuant to the Federal Power Act's exclusive federal jurisdiction over all terms and approvals of wholesale sales of power and associated elements.

FERC Order No. 2222

In 2020, FERC issued regulatory Order No. 2222, which offered a way to monetize surplus self-generated power as an alternative to state retail net metering. Order No. 2222 allows distributed energy resources (DERs) to operate on a level playing field in the organized capacity, energy, and ancillary services markets operated by regional grid operators.[94] While regulating wholesale electricity transactions, the order leaves state net metering untouched as a retail transaction in the 40 states that have state net metering laws.[95]

The rule also directs power grid operators to allow DERs that participate in one or more retail programs to participate in its wholesale markets and to provide multiple wholesale services but also to include any appropriate,

---

92. The 12 of the 43 net metering states doing so since 2012 were Arkansas, Hawaii, Illinois, Kansas, Maine, Missouri, Montana, North Carolina, Oregon, Utah, Vermont, and Washington.

93. The ten states still recently confiscating net energy generation credits without compensation after one year were Illinois, Kansas, Missouri, Montana, North Carolina, Oregon, Pennsylvania, Utah, Vermont, and Washington. Hawaii terminated its net metering program.

94. FERC Order No. 2222, RM18-9-00 (Sept. 17, 2020). Each transmission tariff must set a size requirement for resource aggregations that may not exceed 100 kW and address technical considerations of locational requirements for DER aggregations; distribution factors and bidding parameters; information and data requirements; metering and telemetry requirements; and coordination among the regional grid operator, the DER aggregator, the distribution utility, and the relevant retail regulatory authority. See FERC Order No. 841, in which the court affirmed the commission's exclusive jurisdiction over the regional wholesale power markets and the criteria for participation in those markets.

95. FERC Order No. 2222, *supra* note 94.

narrowly designed restrictions necessary to avoid double-counting of retail and wholesale market financial benefits.[96] The rule does not allow retail regulatory authorities to broadly prohibit DERs from participating in the regional markets, but it does allow them to continue preventing these aggregated sources from bidding.

In revised Order No. 2222-A, FERC backed away from exercising jurisdiction over interconnection of distributed QFs selling wholesale power to DER aggregators. The rule explains that state and local authorities remain responsible for the interconnection of individual DERs for the purpose of participating in wholesale markets through a DER aggregation. Order No. 2222 has a size limitation: a DER must be of an individual or aggregated size of at least 100 kW to participate directly in FERC-regulated wholesale markets.[97]

A key difference in eligibility between state net metering and Order No. 2222 wholesale market participation is that while FERC has a minimum size limitation, some state net metering programs have maximum size limitations.[98] The "sweet spot" created by Order No. 2222 may be to create a market to aggregate individual projects of sizes less than 100 kW each that cannot otherwise participate due to the size restrictions. Some states set limits on the total percentage of a utility's customers or maximum sale capacity that can adopt net metering; several states already have hit their net metering caps and cannot include any additional projects. Such projects might therefore resort to Order No. 2222 wholesale power participation with their surplus power.

Order No. 2222 has the potential to fundamentally transform net metering by allowing distributed energy resources to aggregate and sell at wholesale their output to the grid, instead of net metering their power to earn a

---

96. *Id.* FERC Order No. 2222 proposed 11 directives to break down barriers to smaller distributed participants from participating in an aggregate collective format. Aggregation could make it easier to comply with various FERC requirements to go on- and offline under certain grid management protocols. Data requirements and data acquisition costs to comply with grid requirements could be more than small unaggregated entities could shoulder individually. A single aggregator managing a larger portfolio of assets is in a better position to represent issues that arise with regard to the ISO or RTO (regional transmission organization) grid operators and respective responsibilities.

97. *Id. See also* FERC Order No. 841.

98. Some states limit net metering size to that of a two- to four-unit house typical consumption of 10–20 kW, although a significant segment of the net metering states allow large projects up to 1–2 MW or have no limit at all.

net metering credit for future use. An obvious aggregator could be the utility, which has access to all information on its utility customers and could optimize monetization of the excess power produced and transferred through net metering that net metering law requires utilities to accept and credit in 40 states.[99] This order provides another alternative that allows states to work around the *MidAmerican* and *SunEdison* decisions.

While net metering programs, unlike RPS programs, have been quite volatile in terms of which states maintain them and their provisions over time, they remain the most widely employed state incentive for renewable power generation. They also offer the advantage that net metering credits accrue over time coincident with the generation of power from eligible generation facilities. Therefore, depending on state program details, state net metering subsidies can and do in some states last as long as the renewable generation technology generates power.

Submetering of Power Not Permitted in Several States

The opposite of virtual aggregate metering of individual accounts, discussed earlier, is disaggregating a single retail meter. A key consideration in the business model on the retail end of transactions is the option to meter and bill customers for their usage and collect payment. For retail sales of power, such sales and assessments are regulated by the states, U.S. commonwealths, U.S. territories, and the District of Columbia rather than through any exercise of federal authority. Submetering, also known as "check metering," is where the owner of a multiunit residential or commercial property is served by a single utility master meter and that owner or landlord thereafter privately submeters to monitor individual electric power usage and pass on the charge to the ultimate user/tenant. It typically may apply to particular situations:

- With at least one-third of residential units occupied by tenants who are not the owner of the unit.
- With a large amount of commercial office space and industrial space not owner-occupied.
- With partial retail deregulation and the ability of tenants to purchase power from alternative deregulated suppliers in a significant number of states.

99. FERC Order No. 2222, *supra* note 94, ¶ 42.

- With the increase in modular scale distributed power generation that allows buildings to self-generate and distribute power apart from utility power

Technically, it is possible to submeter retail power, although it is not legally allowed in several states or only allowed with restrictions. At the time of the most recent survey, submetering was barred or controlled by statutes, regulations, or rulings in 22 states, three counties, and the District of Columbia.[100] These 22 states may or may not prohibit the owner/landlord from levying additional fees and service charges on the user of the electricity. In several states, state common law court decisions, rather than specific statutes or regulations, have provided prohibitions of submetering. Submetering retail power can constitute a violation of the exclusive franchise of utilities to sell all retail power in the majority of states that still are conventionally regulating monopoly utilities. With evolving business models (see Chapters 12 and 13), stakeholders in the power sector need to be aware of rules and relevant legal decisions regarding submetering, as well as conditions imposed on submetering in some of the approximately half of the states that allow it.

There is another side to the state incentive/subsidy coin presented in Chapter 8 and this chapter. The next two chapters highlight how many local (Chapter 10) and state (Chapter 11) governments recently have begun using their authority and jurisdiction over power facilities: to block eligible renewable electric power technologies and infrastructure that would otherwise directly benefit from the state incentives analyzed in Chapter 8 and this chapter. These next two chapters proceed from the work of the REPEAT modeling research team at Princeton University that the Biden administration used to support its Inflation Reduction Act only enacted with the tiebreaking vote of Vice President Kamala Harris—the REPEAT team subsequently determined that as much as 80 percent of the Inflation Reduction Act plan objectives could be frustrated by the exercise of state and local government power and other requirements delaying necessary renewable power infrastructure improvements, undercutting these new federal laws. These ongoing legal conflicts will be a constant factor in legal work to navigate in new directions between now and 2035 to realize policy goals.

100. *See Submetering Survey*, Nat'l Conf. of State Legislatures (2015).

CHAPTER 10

Local Siting Limitations and Legal Strategies

Managing Local Control over Power Generation Siting

The prior two chapters examined key state incentives and subsidies for power generation. We now switch to the significant power exercised by cities and states to block federal laws on electric power alterations to address climate change policies. In terms of control, there is local municipal control over siting of electric power generation. This chapter highlights the exclusive local and state regulatory legal control over critical electric power generation infrastructure siting and strategic options for counsel and stakeholders managing these matters to possibly work around certain local barriers. The next chapter, Chapter 11, examines the exclusive state authority over construction or upgrading of necessary transmission and distribution infrastructure to deliver power to consumers.

Biden Administration Changes to the Electric Sector

The Biden administration in 2021 and again in 2022 successfully enacted unprecedented landmark infrastructure legislation investing hundreds of billions of dollars for sustainable energy infrastructure development to address global warming.[1] However, this historic federal electric infrastructure spending is eclipsed already by some municipal governments legally "zoning out"

1. Section 40105 of the Infrastructure Investment and Jobs Act adds additional criteria for the federal designation of national interest electric transmission corridors; it amends section 216 of the Federal Power Act requirements to allow the federal government to intervene with state transmission siting authority when a state commission fails to act within one year or denies certain transmission applications under applicable law. *See Massive Bipartisan Infrastructure Bill Includes Billions in Funding and Process Improvements for Energy and Infrastructure*, Kirkland & Ellis (Nov. 7, 2021), https://www.kirkland.com/publications/blog-post/2021/08/bipartisan-infrastructure-bill.

sustainable infrastructure. Supreme Court decisions support lower-level local control over national sustainable electric power infrastructure: tens of thousands of municipal governments in the United States now exercise a legal veto, if they choose to use it, on critical new electric infrastructure.

There are critical-path legal bottlenecks that can be created at the discretion of 35,000 separate cities and towns in the United States. Pursuant to the Tenth Amendment to the Constitution, enforced by recent Supreme Court decisions, each town substantially controls what type of electric infrastructure can or cannot be sited on its land. Numerous cities and towns now are deploying "aesthetic" local zoning to deny otherwise cost-effective energy generation a place on their land. With renewable energy electric technologies now the least expensive energy options, the financial incentives, grants, and tax subsidies in the Biden-Harris administration laws do not sufficiently address or solve the legal bottlenecks now in place at lower town, county, and state levels. Distant neighbors, even when they do not experience any conventional legal nuisances, now can and do prevent renewable wind turbines being sited that alter their existing distant scenic views over property that they do not own. Municipal "aesthetic" zoning exercised by any of the more than 35,000 local governments counted in the U.S. census[2] unilaterally can frustrate sustainable electric infrastructure.

The Biden administration pledged to replace all electric power generation by 2035 using fossil fuels with renewable energy.[3] Electric power infrastructure has enjoyed exceptions to traditional local zoning through the exercise of eminent domain power for certain essential infrastructure.[4] Notwithstanding this, hundreds of communities in the United States now "aesthetically" zone out wind power turbines,[5] which are the most significant

2. *Cities 101—Number of Local Governments*, NAT'L LEAGUE OF CITIES, https://www.nlc.org/resource/cities-101-number-of-local-governments/#:~:text=The%20most%20recent%20data%20from,governments%2C%20and%203%2C031%20county%20governments (last visited May 2, 2024). The most recent data from the U.S. Census Bureau (2012) counted 35,879 general-purpose local governments (which includes 19,519 municipal governments and 16,360 town and township governments) and 3,031 county governments. *Id.*

3. *See* Patrick Whittle & Cathy Bussewitz, *Biden Faces Steep Challenges to Reach Renewable Energy Goals*, ABC NEWS (Mar. 3, 2021), https://perma.cc/D7YY-VXK6.

4. Steven Ferrey, *Eminent Domain and Serrated Power*, 39 HAW. L. REV. 173, 204 (2016).

5. Julia Pyper, *7 Charts That Show Wind Power Is Surging in the US and Abroad*, GREEN TECH MEDIA (Aug. 14, 2016), https://www.greentechmedia.com/articles/read/7-charts-that-show-wind-power-is-surging-in-the-us-and-abroad#gs.thjU7Ls [https://perma.cc/8TFQ-4XAW].

new source of renewable electric power generation in the United States, and other communities are blocking large solar photovoltaic installations.[6]

Technology Change and Siting Additional Generation

Ascending Wind Power Generation

Wind generation is the most deployed new renewable power source during the 21st century.

Wind, as well as solar and natural gas generation, has dominated new sources of electric energy deployed in the United States recently.[7] In 2015, more than half of new generating capacity was wind energy.[8] U.S. total annual electricity generation from wind increased from about 6 billion kilowatt-hours (kWh) in 2000 to approximately 300 billion kWh in 2019, then constituting about 7.3 percent of total U.S. utility-scale electricity generation.[9] In 2019, electricity generation from wind surpassed renewable hydro power, previously the dominant renewable power resource in the United States, and is now the most-used source of renewable energy for electricity generation on an annual basis in the United States.[10]

Renewable energy sources are forecast to overtake natural gas as the dominant source of electricity generation in the United States in 2031, even without continuation of current federal tax subsidies (which now in fact do

6. *Wind Explained*, U.S. ENERGY INFO. ADMIN. (Dec. 27, 2023), https://www.eia.gov/energyexplained/wind/electricity-generation-from-wind.php#:~:text=U.S.%20total%20annual%20Electricity%20generation,U.S.%20utility%2Dscale%20electricity%20generation [https://perma.cc/9DJF-4423].

7. *Id.*; *Energy Dept. Reports: U.S. Wind Energy Production and Manufacturing Reaches Record Highs*, ENERGY.GOV (Aug. 6, 2013), https://perma.cc/RJ76-727U; *see also New Electric Generating Capacity in 2020 Will Come Primarily from Wind and Solar*, U.S. ENERGY INFO. ADMIN. (Jan. 14, 2020), https://www.eia.gov/todayinenergy/detail.php?id=42495#:~:text=New%20electric%20generating%20capacity%20in%202020%20will%20come%20primarily%20from%20wind%20and%20solar,-Source%3A%20U.S.%20Energy&text=According%20to%20the%20U.S.%20Energy,start%20commercial%20operation%20in%202020.

8. *Wind Explained*, *supra* note 6.

9. U.S. ENERGY INFO. ADMIN., https://www.eia.gov/energyexplained/wind/electricity-generation-fromwind.php#:~:text=U.S.%20total%20annual%20Electricity%20generation,U.S.%20utility%2Dscale%20electricity%20generation.

10. *U.S. Renewable Energy Consumption Surpasses Coal for the First Time in Over 130 Years*, U.S. ENERGY INFO. ADMIN. (May 28, 2020), https://www.eia.gov/todayinenergy/detail.php?id=43895 [https://perma.cc/9V29-JWD9].

continue), as wind and solar generation costs plunge.[11] See Chapter 6. Wind power additions mean the United States now has the second most installed wind generation capacity in the world.[12]

More-Efficient Wind Technology Increases Local Resistance

Cost matters: the capital cost of new wind power projects has decreased to be competitive with the cost of more traditional new fossil fuel resources for electricity generation.[13] In 2017, wind projects in the United States generated electricity at a cost, on average, of $45 per megawatt-hour (MWh) for capacity and energy without other subsidies,[14] and some large wind power projects can now produce power at the relatively low cost of $10–$20/MWh.[15] In a recent study, unsubsidized wind power and utility-scale solar projects came in at lower price ranges than any other analyzed resource, including gas, coal, and nuclear power.[16] Unsubsidized wind power ranges from $28 to $54/MWh; factoring in subsidies, wind prices plunge to $11–$45/MWh. See Chapter 3. Wind power is forecast by the U.S. Department of Energy to be cheaper than electricity produced from natural gas by 2025, even without a

11. Naureen S. Malik, *Renewables Will Top Gas in 2031 as Largest Energy Source*, 47 Env't Rep. 1839, 1845 (2017).

12. *Onshore Wind Net Capacity Additions by Country or Region, 2015–2022*, Int'l Energy Agency (Nov. 10, 2020), https://www.iea.org/data-and-statistics/charts/onshore-wind-net-capacity-additions-by-country-or-region-2015-2022 [https://perma.cc/C59A-BMLQ].

13. Tara Patel, *Fossil Fuels Losing Cost Advantage over Solar, Wind, IEA Says*, Bloomberg (Aug. 31, 2015), http://www.bloomberg.com/news/articles/2015-08-31/solar-wind-power-costs-drop-as-fossil-fuels-increase-iea-says [https://perma.cc/5UX4-RWRS]; *see also Advantages and Challenges of Wind Energy*, Off. of Energy Efficiency & Renewable Energy, https://www.energy.gov/eere/wind/advantages-and-challenges-wind-energy [https://perma.cc/X5AJ-4YBU] (last visited May 2, 2024).

14. Jim Efstathiou Jr. & Brian K. Sullivan, *Smarter Wind Turbines Try to Squeeze More Power on Each Rotation*, Bloomberg Env't Rptr. (May 9, 2018), https://www.bloomberg.com/news/articles/2018-05-09/smarter-wind-turbines-try-to-squeeze-more-power-on-each-rotation.

15. *Advantages and Challenges of Wind Energy*, *supra* note 13.

16. Lazard projects that unsubsidized wind power and utility-scale solar come in at lower price ranges than any other analyzed resource including gas, coal, and nuclear. Silvio Marcacci, *Renewable Energy Prices Hit Record Lows: How Can Utilities Benefit from Unstoppable Solar and Wind?*, Forbes (Jan. 21, 2020), https://www.forbes.com/sites/energyinnovation/2020/01/21/renewable-energy-prices-hit-record-lows-how-can-utilities-benefit-from-unstoppable-solar-and-wind/?sh=577034ff2c84 [https://perma.cc/NE96-UHL3].

continuing federal production tax credit incentive, which continues in fact.[17] See Chapter 6 analyzing the federal tax credits.

However, there is another complicating side of this issue: some of this continuing decrease in the cost per unit of wind power generated results from exponentially increased kinetic wind power capture with increasing turbine height, which permits a larger diameter turbine rotor blade to be used. For example, the typical turbine's generating capacity, blade length, and elevation of the mast have increased rapidly over time, making wind speeds at higher elevations more accessible and improving wind generation capacity factors, thus reducing generating costs.[18] As the blade lengthens, the swept area of the turbine blade creates added power generation by the square of that change in the length of the blade. Taller wind turbines capture stronger winds with speed not impaired by trees on the land or offshore in open water; the amount of power produced increases at the rate of the cube of the wind speed hitting the blades.

Therefore, a modest increase of 10 percent for a 100-foot blade to 110 feet achieves a squared 100 percent increase in power. Similarly, location higher on a ridge line capturing only a 10 percent greater wind speed at that greater height, such as capturing a wind speed averaging 16.5 mph instead of 15 mph, cubes the power output to 1,000 percent. Together, a taller turbine mast that captures a 10 percent increase in wind speed at greater height and a 10 percent longer blade result in a massive increase in effective electric power generation.

Thus, larger, more visible wind turbines that are more cost-efficient can create substantially more sustainable power generation, although the added height and blade span also have more scenic visual impact. And here lies the confrontation with local "aesthetic" overlay zoning.

---

17. *See* Christopher Martin & Justin Doom, BNA Energy & Climate Report (2015); *see also U.S. Wind Energy Production Tax Credit Extended through 2021*, U.S. Energy Info. Admin. (Jan. 28, 2021), https://www.eia.gov/todayinenergy/detail.php?id=46576 [https://perma.cc/82AH-THH8].

18. Paul L. Joskow, *Facilitating Transmission Expansion to Support Efficient Decarbonization of the Electricity Sector* 6 (MIT Ctr. for Energy & Env't Pol'y Rsch., CEEPR WP 2021-009, 2021), https://ceepr.mit.edu/workingpaper/facilitating-transmission-expansion-to-support-efficient-decarbonization-of-the-electricity-sector/.

Comparative Footprints: Renewable Power and Fossil Power

Wind power requires lots of land. Wind power is a much less dense form of electric power generation compared to fossil-fuel or nuclear sources of energy.[19] To site wind turbines requires four times as much land area than for a gas-fired power plant that would generate similar amounts of power.[20] The United States, based on current wind power operating experience and technology, would require approximately 460,000 onshore wind turbines—seven times the current installed wind turbine base—to produce 50 percent of the U.S. electricity supply.[21]

Wind power requires more land in the United States, because wind generation capacity factors range from 0.26 to 0.52, with a fleetwide average capacity factor of 0.35.[22] This compares to a wind capacity factor from 0.21 to 0.279 in the United Kingdom.[23] Intermittent wind power generation with such low average capacity factors of 0.21 to 0.52 needs additional land to produce energy and capacity that are equivalent to fossil-fueled or nuclear power with much higher capacity factors. Such intermittent capacity at uncontrollable times does not contribute as significantly to power system reliability.

---

19. Uma Outka, *The Renewable Energy Footprint*, 30 Stan. Env't L. Rev. 241, 243nn.7 & 9 (quoting Robert I. McDonald et al., *Energy Sprawl or Energy Efficiency: Climate Policy Impacts on Natural Habitat for the United States of America*, 4(8) PLoS ONE (2009), doi:10.1371/journal.pone.0006802); *see also* Christopher Joyce, *Renewable Energy Needs Land, Lots of Land*, fig. 3, NPR (Aug. 28, 2009), https://www.npr.org/2009/08/28/112323643/Renewable-Energy-Needs-Land-Lots-Of-Land.

20. Dustin Solberg, *Wind's Big Footprint: Clean Energy Still Needs Safeguards for Nature*, Nature Conservancy: Cool Green Sci. (Nov. 29, 2017), https://blog.nature.org/science/2017/11/29/winds-big-footprint-clean-energy-still-needs-safeguards-for-nature/ [https://perma.cc/5PVD-ARPJ] ("For the energy they produce, wind turbines have a disproportionately large footprint on the land. At 72.1 square kilometers per terawatt, wind's footprint is bigger than natural gas, or coal or petroleum (at 18.6, 9.7 and 44.7, respectively)."). *See also* Samantha Gross, *Renewables, Land Use, and Local Opposition in the United States*, Brookings Inst. (Jan. 2020), https://www.brookings.edu/articles/renewables-land-use-and-local-opposition-in-the-united-states/.

21. Gabriel Collins & Michelle Michot Foss, Baker Inst., The Global Energy Transition's Looming Valley of Death (2022).

22. *Wind Energy Factsheet*, Pub. No. CSS07-09, Univ. of Mich. Ctr. for Sustainable Sys. (2020), http://css.umich.edu/factsheets/wind-energy-factsheet [https://perma.cc/Z83S-EALW]; *2020 Could Be a Record Year for U.S. Wind Turbine Installations*, U.S. Energy Info. Admin. (Nov. 12, 2020), https://www.eia.gov/todayinenergy/detail.php?id=45856 [https://perma.cc/KQ3H-Z8T3].

23. *Wind Energy Factsheet*, Pub. No. CSS07-09, Univ. of Mich. Ctr. for Sustainable Sys. (2020), http://css.umich.edu/factsheets/wind-energy-factsheet [https://perma.cc/Z83S-EALW].

Local Implementation of "Aesthetic" Zoning Barring Sustainable Power

Environmental Overlay Zoning

Overlay districts are superimposed and overlaid on existing zoned areas. Overlay zones impose protective limitations and restrictions on a land area notwithstanding that area's basic physical zoning district, in order to protect environmentally sensitive areas.

One feature of modern wind turbines is their height. Sited on mountain ridgelines to harness the strongest winds, wind power turbines can obstruct viewsheds.[24] There is a well-established line of precedents allowing local zoning ordinances to block tall structures.[25] A town could use, and towns have used, overlay districts to attempt to prohibit wind power turbines: a town may define overlay districts for aesthetic character or scenic vistas, designed to protect the aesthetics and character of hilltops and ridgeline open-space views. It is these higher hills and ridgelines where taller wind power turbines capturing stronger winds are most productive in many eastern U.S. land regions. Such an overlay zone may restrict or prohibit siting wind power turbines, either by expressly prohibiting wind towers in the overlay districts or by limiting height.

Municipal "Aesthetic" Zoning Out of Sustainable Generation

A number of cities and towns in the United States have enacted Ridgeline and Hilltop Overlay Districts to protect hills and other elevated land areas

---

24. *Wind Explained: Where Wind Power Is Harnessed*, U.S. Energy Info. Admin. (Apr. 20, 2023), https://www.eia.gov/energyexplained/wind/where-wind-power-is-harnessed.php. Favorable places for wind turbines are where the annual average wind speed is at least 9 miles per hour (mph) for small wind turbines and 13 mph for utility-scale turbines. Wind speeds are slower close to the Earth's surface and faster at higher altitudes, with the average hub height of modern wind turbines at 88 meters. *Wind Power Fundamentals*, Mass. Inst. of Tech. (2010), https://web.mit.edu/windenergy/windweek/Presentations/Wind%20Energy%20101.pdf; U.S. Dep't of Energy, EERE 2018 Wind Technologies Market Report (2019); *Wind Energy Factsheet*, *supra* note 22. Wind speed typically increases with altitude and increases over open areas without windbreaks such as trees or buildings. Favorable sites for wind turbines include the tops of smooth, rounded hills; open plains and water; and mountain gaps that funnel and intensify wind. *Wind Turbine Heights and Capacities Have Increased over the Past Decade*, U.S. Energy Info. Admin. (Nov. 29, 2017), https://www.eia.gov/todayinenergy/detail.php?id=33912.

25. Dowdell v. Bloomquist, 847 A.2d 827 (R.I. 2004); MJD Props., LLC v. Haley, 189 Wash. App. 963, 358 P.3d 476 (2015); Tranfield v. Arcuni-Eng., 2019 ME 135, 215 A.3d 222.

from any aesthetic impacts of wind turbine projects.[26] The Mountain Ridge Protection Act of 1983 prohibits in North Carolina any ridgetop placement of wind turbines that have a total capacity of 3 MW or greater.[27] Watauga County, North Carolina, was the first local government to adopt a restrictive wind energy system ordinance.[28] County boards of commissioners in Kansas can enact ordinances restricting or banning the development of large-scale wind facilities on their aesthetic impacts.[29] Controversy erupted in communities along the Connecticut River Valley where developers proposed wind turbines placed on hilltops and ridgelines traversing local communities.[30] Towns enacted ridgeline and hilltop overlay districts to prohibit wind towers and turbines and to address concerns that commercial wind turbines would degrade viewsheds of uplands around the town.[31] The Vermont Public Service Board denied a certificate of public good for the 6 MW East Haven Wind Farm proposed to be sited on an abandoned Air Force radar base, because it would obstruct aesthetic views.[32] Various federal district courts hold that a town can enact a temporary ban or moratorium for aesthetic reasons to block additional wind generation facilities.[33]

---

26. For example, Hampden and Wilbraham, Massachusetts, which are located along ridgelines of central Massachusetts, have enacted Ridgeline and Hilltop Overlay Districts.

27. *See* N.C. Gen. Stat. §§ 113A-205 to -214 (1983), https://www.ncleg.net/EnactedLegislation/Statutes/HTML/ByArticle/Chapter_113A/Article_14.html.

28. Monte Mitchell, *Watauga to Allow Windmills—Commissioners Adopt Rules for Single Systems; Process Stricter for Commercial Use*, Winston-Salem (NC) J. (Aug. 8, 2006), https://perma.cc/86BT-9NKH.

29. Zimmerman v. Bd. of Cnty., 722 N.W.2d 240, 247 (Wis. 2009); Housley Carr, *Kansas Supreme Court Backs County Ban on Wind Farms Based on Esthetic Reasons*, Elec. Util. Week, Nov. 9, 2009, at 23.

30. Frank Juliano, *State's Energy Answer Not Blowing in the Wind*, News Times (Dec. 12, 2010), https://www.newstimes.com/local/article/State-s-energy-answer-not-blowing-in-the-wind-877284.php.

31. *Id.*

32. *Vermont Wind Project Shot Down over Impact on Landscape after Five Years of Planning*, BNA, Elec. Util. Week, Mar. 20, 2006, at 12.

33. Ecogen, LLC v. Town of Italy, 461 F. Supp. 2d 149, 157 (W.D.N.Y. 2006) (citing Greene v. Town of Blooming Grove, 879 F.2d 1061, 1063 (2d Cir. 1989); City of Cleburne v. Cleburne Living Ctr., 473 U.S. 432, 440 (1985)). In applying those principles here, defendants' subjective motivation in enacting the moratorium is irrelevant. United States v. Carlton, 512 U.S. 26, 36–37 (1994) (O'Connor, J., concurring); Tri Cnty. Paving, Inc. v. Ashe Cnty., 281 F.3d 430, 439 (4th Cir. 2002); Homar v. Gilbert, 89 F.3d 1009, 1029–30 (3d Cir. 1996) (Alito, J., concurring in part and dissenting in part), *rev'd on other grounds*, 520 U.S. 924 (1997).

Deference to Local Aesthetic Zoning

Any zoning amendment, even if restrictive of wind projects, benefits from a presumption of its legal validity for the lower-level local agency, if it is later challenged in court: municipal land-use decisions are entitled to court deference because a "local board of appeals brings to the matter an intimate understanding of the immediate circumstances, of local conditions, and of the background and purposes of the entire by-law."[34]

Zoning amendments are categorized as local legislative actions, passed in many cases by a supermajority of the local zoning authority.[35] Thus, a community not supportive of wind turbines can enact a highly restrictive amendment to its zoning ordinance that makes the community unattractive or cost prohibitive to wind or other renewable power generation projects based on size, configuration, or aesthetic or other qualities. Should a prospective wind developer challenge a restrictive zoning amendment, the legal burden is placed on the wind developer, as plaintiff, to prove by a preponderance of the evidence that the zoning amendment is arbitrary, capricious, an abuse of local discretion, and unreasonable or substantially unrelated to the public's health and safety.[36] This is a difficult standard for any affected developer of a tall, moving wind project to satisfy to overturn a restrictive zoning law.

A municipality has discretion to adopt a variety of physical lot sizes, structures, and allowed use requirements to restrict development within its borders. In the category of lot physical characteristics are significant lot line setbacks, maximum restrictions on the percentage of the lot's area that can be built on or used, a limit on the number of separate structures and/or buildings allowed on each parcel, and height restrictions—all of which directly affect and restrict modern wind turbines.

Broad local and state zoning ordinances regulating or preserving aesthetic characteristics now are deemed constitutionally permissible provided they "have any reasonable tendency to promote the public morals, health, or

---

34. Fitzsimonds v. Bd. of Appeals of Chatham, 484 N.E.2d 113, 116 (Mass. 1985). *See also* Manning v. Bos. Redev. Auth., 509 N.E.2d 1173, 1179 (Mass. 1987) (holding "substantial deference" granted to local administrative agency's interpretation of local zoning law).

35. *See* Mass. Gen. Laws ch. 40A, § 5 (passing an amendment to a local bylaw in Massachusetts requires a two-thirds supermajority).

36. Bartram v. Zoning Comm'n of City of Bridgeport, 136 Conn. 89, 68 A.2d 308 (1949).

safety or the public comfort, welfare, or prosperity."[37] A court can uphold a local zoning board's ruling that a wind power project would interfere with municipal viewsheds and is prohibited, assuming that the challenged bylaw reasonably relates to protection of the public safety. This zoning discretion of the local municipality dominates the host states' subsidy of wind power through renewable portfolio standard subsidies that exist as state law in 29 U.S. states, as well as net metering options in 40 states. See Chapters 8 and 9.

A federal court in New York found that aesthetic considerations are a rational basis for zoning regulation.[38] There is precedent also to deny state siting permits for wind projects when they would obstruct aesthetic views.[39] Neighbors successfully challenged on aesthetic grounds a proposed single 100-foot-tall wind turbine approximately 450 feet from the owner neighbor's property line intruding on the neighbor's distant view.[40]

No Federal Role and Limited State Role to Preempt Local Zoning

Local governments exclusively retain under the Tenth Amendment and exercise their police power over all electric facility land use and siting.[41] Distribution of power, as opposed to the transmission of power, is regulated by the states exclusively.[42] A state could expressly or impliedly preempt local discretion over wind power siting infrastructure; this would cause some

37. Carter v. Harper, 196 N.W. 451, 454 (Wis. 1923) (aesthetic zoning must be reasonably related to public health and safety).

38. Ecogen, LLC v. Town of Italy, 461 F. Supp. 2d 149, 158 (W.D.N.Y. 2006) (citing Sprint Spectrum L.P. v. Willoth, 176 F.3d 630, 645 (2d Cir. 1999) ("Aesthetics is generally a valid subject of municipal regulation and concern[.]"); distinguishing Cellular Tel. Co. v. Town of Oyster Bay, 166 F.3d 490, 495 (2nd Cir. 1999) ("In New York, aesthetics can be a valid ground for local zoning decisions[.]")); Martin v. Corp. of Presiding Bishop of Church of Jesus Christ of Latter-Day Saints, 434 Mass. 141, 146, 747 N.E.2d 131, 136 (2001).

39. *Vermont Wind Project Shot Down over Impact on Landscape after Five Years of Planning*, *supra* note 32.

40. *In re* Halnon, 174 Vt. 514 (2002).

41. *What FERC Does*, Fed. Regul. Energy Comm'n (Feb. 12, 2024), https://www.ferc.gov/about/what-ferc/what-ferc-does [https://perma.cc/AT58-VTRX].

42. Pub. Util. Dist. No. 1 v. FERC, 471 F.3d 1053, 1058 (9th Cir. 2006); Transmission Planning and Cost Allocation by Transmission Owning and Operating Public Utilities (Order 1000), 76 Fed. Reg. 49,842 (Aug. 11, 2011), 136 FERC Stats. & Regs. ¶ 61,051 (2011).

cities to argue that this would impermissibly interfere with the residual local police power over land use. Approximately half of the states also add state regulation over certain power facility siting, which may or may not preempt additional local permitting. However, such state siting authority often is not applicable to typical smaller wind power projects.

Recent Supreme Court Decision

In a limited subset of locations, there also can be federal preemption of local land-use permitting decisions. The federal government controls permitting for development on federal lands.[43] Federal preemption may serve to overrule state and local control over certain statutory-provided types of development proposals, including telecommunications towers providing personal wireless services to local areas.[44]

There is no area of energy that is more thoroughly regulated at the national level than civilian use of nuclear energy for power production. In *Virginia Uranium v. Warren*,[45] the Supreme Court considered whether the Atomic Energy Act (AEA) preempts Virginia's outright ban on the mining of uranium on land and its land use within the commonwealth. The Court affirmed state and local control over nuclear-related land use, notwithstanding federal regulation of nuclear health and safety, explaining that while the AEA "gives the Nuclear Regulatory Commission significant authority over the milling, transfer, use, and disposal of uranium, as well as the construction and operation of nuclear power plants," the federal statute "leave[s] untouched the States' historic authority over the regulation of mining activities on private lands within their borders."[46] Underscoring deference to local zoning, in the most recent decision construing local zoning laws, the Supreme Court in *Murr v. Wisconsin* deferred to local zoning bylaws regulating construction permits on land.[47]

---

43. U.S. Const., art. IV, § 3, cl. 2. The Property Clause gives Congress authority over federal property generally, and the Supreme Court has described Congress's power to legislate under this clause as "without limitation."

44. *See* Telecommunications Act of 1996, 47 U.S.C. § 332(c)(7) (2000) (disallowing states and local government from prohibiting provisioning of wireless services).

45. Va. Uranium v. Warren, 139 S. Ct. 1894 (2019).

46. *Id.* at 1900.

47. Murr v. Wisconsin, 137 S. Ct. 1933 (2017).

Illusive State Preemptive Power over Their Cities

The Supreme Court has articulated that states exercise "traditional and primary power over land and water use."[48] Although there is precedent finding state preemption of local land-use and zoning law in realms other than power project siting, it has been employed somewhat sparingly. The state–local relationships legally vary. Most states follow Dillon's Rule, which does not grant local governments any authority that is not expressly delegated to them by state legislative statute. Fewer states follow Home Rule, which vests in the localities all powers not expressly reserved by state statute. The former type of state legal system is preemptive at the state level of government, while the latter vests localities with extensive reserved power unless the state conscripts such powers by legislation.

State governments create local power, and each state should be able to preempt its local governments' exercises of zoning power to frustrate renewable energy and address climate change. States can exercise a similar indirect power by not approving changes to local zoning law. Energy facility siting of both electric transmission lines and generation infrastructure remains jurisdictionally vested in local and state governments rather than the federal government. See Chapter 4.

States with State Electric Power Siting Authority

Some states also preempt siting of certain electric generation facilities.[49] An analysis of the level at which each of the 50 states allocates electric energy generation facility siting authority illustrates several models balancing local land-use control and state preemption:

- In 23 of the 50 states, there is no state electric energy generation siting authority exercised as a matter of law for new power generation facilities to be sited and constructed. In this group, siting electric power

48. Solid Waste Agency of N. Cook Cnty. v. U.S. Army Corps of Eng'rs, 531 U.S. 159, 174 (2001), Stevens, J., dissenting ("Hess v. Port Authority TransHudson Corporation, 513 U. S. 30, 44 (1994) ('[R]egulation of land use [is] a function traditionally performed by local governments'). Rather than expressing a desire to readjust the federal-state balance in this manner, Congress chose to 'recognize, preserve, and protect the primary responsibilities and rights of States . . . to plan the development and use . . . of land and water resources . . . .' 33 U. S. C. § 1251(b))."). This dissenting opinion has now become the Supreme Court majority opinion in 2024 in *Sackett v. EPA*.

49. *See* Mass. Gen. Laws ch. 164, § 69 H; 980 CMR, Energy Facilities Siting Board, §§ 1–12.

facilities is exclusively a local determination operating in the void of state siting authority.[50]

- The remaining 27 states plus the District of Columbia exercise state authority over power facility siting, with some having divested some of their energy infrastructure siting authority to localities as noted later.

Utilities Compared to IPPs as Energy Developers

Figure 10.1[51] Cumulative U.S. Wind Power Capacity by Owner

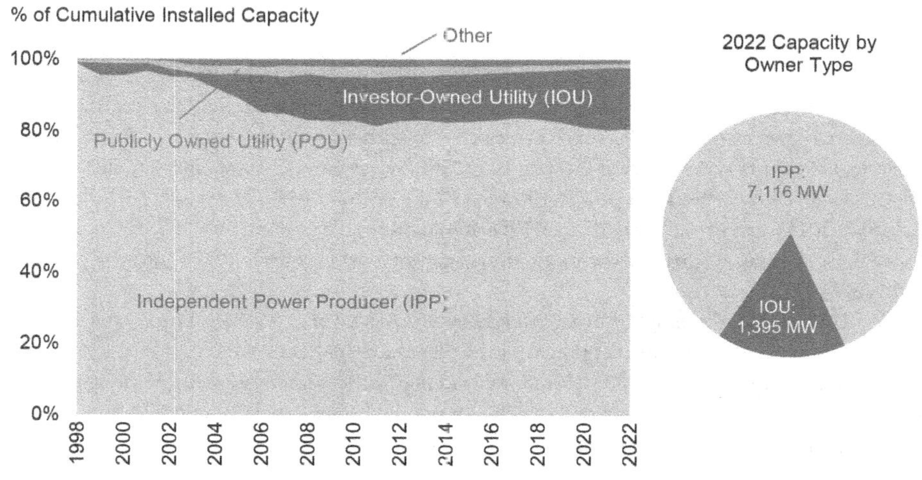

Source: Berkeley Lab estimates based on ACP

In addition to which level of state or local government exercises energy facility siting authority, there is a key differentiation as to the type of wind energy project developer. Eighty percent of new generation facilities each year are constructed by unregulated nonutility independent power producers (IPPs), rather than by regulated utilities.[52] See Figure 10.1. This dominant IPP role

50. These states are Alabama, Alaska, Arkansas, Colorado, Delaware, Georgia, Hawaii, Idaho, Illinois, Indiana, Kansas, Louisiana, Michigan, Mississippi, Missouri, Oklahoma, Pennsylvania, South Carolina, Tennessee, Texas, Utah, West Virginia, and Wisconsin.

51. *Land-Based Wind Market Report*, Energy Mkts. & Pol'y, Berkeley Lab, https://emp.lbl.gov/wind-technologies-market-report (last visited May 3, 2024).

52. *Id.* "In the 1970s, vertically integrated utility companies (investor-owned, municipal, or cooperative utilities) controlled over 95 *percent* of the electric generation in the United States. . . . [B]y 2004 electric utilities owned less than 60 percent of electric generating capacity. Increasingly, decisions affecting retail customers and

is forecast to continue.[53] Of note, 12 states exempt from state authority any nonutility IPP electric infrastructure, which now dominates U.S. wind power development: Alabama,[54] Arkansas,[55] Colorado,[56] Delaware,[57] Indiana,[58] Idaho,[59] Kansas,[60] Michigan,[61] Mississippi,[62] Missouri,[63] Texas,[64] and Wyoming, with Wyoming being a state that regulates utility power siting at the state level.[65] In these 12 states, independent nonutility companies must only satisfy local land-use/zoning authorities for basic construction permission.

Five additional states require the applicant project developer of a wind facility *separately* to obtain all local land-use approvals from the local municipalities: New Jersey,[66] Nevada,[67] North Carolina,[68] Wisconsin,[69] and

---

electricity rates are split among federal, state, and new private, regional entities." ELECTRIC ENERGY MARKET COMPETITION TASK FORCE, REPORT TO CONGRESS ON WHOLESALE AND RETAIL COMPETITION MARKETS FOR ELECTRIC ENERGY 10 (2006); Steven Ferrey, *Sale of Electricity, in* THE LAW OF CLEAN ENERGY: EFFICIENCY AND RENEWABLES 217–18 (Michael B. Gerrard ed., ABA 2011); *see Scheduled 2015 Capacity Additions Mostly Wind and Natural Gas; Retirements Mostly Coal*, U.S. ENERGY INFO. ADMIN. (Mar. 10, 2015),www.eia.gov/todayinenergy/detail.cfm?id=20292 [https://perma.cc/9FWB-TV7W].

53. *U.S. Solar Market Insight*, SOLAR ENERGY INDUS. ASS'N (Mar. 6, 2024), http://www.seia.org/research-resources/us-solar-market-insight [https://perma.cc/PA7B-LVXM].

54. ALA. CODE § 37-4-2 (2020). The Alabama Public Service Commission has no siting jurisdiction over "wind generation or generation facilities proposed by non-regulated utilities." REPORT FOR THE MINN. PUB. UTILS. COMM'N, WIND ENERGY AND WIND PARK SITING AND ZONING BEST PRACTICES AND GUIDANCE FOR STATES, NARUC (2012).

55. ARK. CODE ANN. § 23-3-201. *See Electric Section*, ARK. PUB. SERV. COMM'N (Apr. 18, 2015), http://www.apscservices.info/electric.asp.

56. *See* COLO. REV. STAT. ANN. § 40-5-101.

57. *See* DEL. CODE ANN. tit. 26, § 201(a); *but see id.* § 203A(a)(2).

58. IND. CODE ANN. § 8-1-8.5-2.

59. IDAHO CODE ANN. §§ 61-526 to -528.

60. EDISON ELEC. INST., SURVEY OF TRANSMISSION SITING PRACTICES IN THE MIDWEST 47 (2004) [hereinafter EEI].

61. *See* MICH. COMP. LAWS ANN. § 460.502.

62. MISS. CODE ANN. § 77-3-14(6).

63. *See* MO. ANN. STAT. §§ 386.020(15), 393.170.

64. TEX. CODE ANN. § 37.051; *see also* EEI, *supra* note 60, at 117.

65. WYO. STAT. ANN. § 37-2-205.

66. *See* Eric Garofano, Note, *Losing Power: Siting Power Plants in New York State*, 4 ALB. GOV'T L. REV. 728, 745 (2011).

67. NEV. REV. STAT. ANN. § 704.890.

68. 4 N.C. ADMIN. CODE 11.R8-63.

69. EEI, *supra* note 60, at 3; WIS. DEP'T OF NAT. RES., ELECTRIC UTILITY PRE-CPCN APPROVALS AND APPLICATIONS (2004), https://perma.cc/963U-CNEP.

Virginia.[70] Three of these five states allow local regulations to be preempted only under specified limited special circumstances: New Jersey,[71] Nevada,[72] and Wisconsin.[73]

These factors effectively leave 22 states plus the District of Columbia exercising state-level energy facility siting jurisdiction: Arizona,[74] California,[75] Connecticut,[76] the District of Columbia,[77] Florida,[78] Iowa,[79] Kentucky,[80] Maine,[81] Maryland,[82] Massachusetts,[83] Minnesota,[84] Montana,[85] Nebraska,[86] New Hampshire,[87] New Mexico,[88] New York,[89] North Dakota,[90] Ohio,[91] Oregon,[92] Rhode Island,[93] South Dakota,[94] Vermont,[95] and Washington.[96] Two other jurisdictions are uniquely positioned: the District of Columbia has no state-level authority with its nonstate political structure and status; Nebraska, because no power plants are investor-owned or regulated,

70. *See* Va. Code Ann. § 56-234.3.

71. N.J. Stat. Ann. § 40:55D-19.

72. Nev. Rev. Stat. Ann. § 704.890.

73. EEI, *supra* note 60, at 3.

74. Ariz. Rev. Stat. Ann. § 40-360.05(2).

75. *See* Garofano, *supra* note 66, at 744; *see also* Cal. Pub. Res. Code § 25500 (2020).

76. *See* Conn. Stat. Ann. §§ 16-50X, 16-243

77. D.C. Code § 34-302.

78. Fla. Stat. Ann. § 403.502, .506, .508(f).

79. Iowa Code Ann. § 476A.5.

80. *See* Ky. Rev. Stat. Ann. § 278.704(1), (3).

81. *See* Me. Rev. Stat. Ann. tit. 12, § 685.

82. Md. Pub. Serv. Comm. § 20.79.01.04.

83. *See* Mass. Gen. Laws ch. 164, § 69K.

84. Minn. Stat. Ann. § 216E.03(1), .05(1), .10.

85. Mont. Code Ann. § 75-20-103, -401.

86. Neb. Rev. Stat. Ann. § 70-1012 (LexisNexis).

87. N.H. Rev. Stat. Ann. § 162-H:1.

88. *See* N.M. Stat. Ann. § 62-9-3(G).

89. N.Y. Powers of Mun. & State Agencies Law § 168(e).

90. N.D. Cent. Code § 49-22-07(1).

91. Ohio Rev. Code Ann. § 4906.13(B); *see also* Garofano, *supra* note 66, at 745.

92. *See Energy Facility Siting*, Oregon.gov, http://www.oregon.gov/energy/Siting/Pages/process.aspx [https://perma.cc/G84Z-6MR3] (last visited May 3, 2024); *see also* Or. Rev. Stat. § 469.401(3) (2020).

93. R.I. Gen. Laws Ann. § 42-98-9(a).

94. S.D. Codified Laws § 49-41B-7.

95. City of South Burlington v. Vt. Elec. Power Co., 344 A.2d 19 (1975) (Public Service Commission preempted the city's orders).

96. *See* Wash. Rev. Code § 80.50.030.

does not have a public utility commission to regulate these nonexistent entities.[97] This leaves 20 of the original 28 state-level regulations in plenary application to various power generation projects.

Exceptions for Small and Distributed Electric Projects

However, in the diminishing number of states that regulate power siting to totally preempt local regulation of energy facilities even if they also regulate IPP developers in addition to utilities, that state siting authority does not cover many smaller wind or solar projects because there are minimum size thresholds for the state to exercise jurisdiction. These thresholds are set too high to include modest-sized onshore wind turbine or solar projects in 15 of the remaining 20 states among the original 28 states (Arizona, California, Florida, Maryland, Massachusetts, Minnesota, Montana, New Hampshire, New Mexico, New York, Ohio, Oregon, Rhode Island, South Dakota, and Washington):[98]

- Iowa,[99] New York,[100] Oregon,[101] and Washington[102] mandate commission approval and certification for electric generation plants with a capacity of 25 MW or more.
- New Hampshire exercises jurisdiction over facilities of at least 30 MW.[103]
- Rhode Island may exercise siting jurisdiction over facilities of 40 MW or more.[104]

---

97. Neb. Power Rev. Bd., Nebraska Power Review Board Orientation Manual, ch. 2 (2024), http://www.powerreviewboard.nebraska.gov/prbmanual/2.html [https://perma.cc/EUA3-F38V].

98. The 28 states are Arizona, California, Connecticut, the District of Columbia, Florida, Iowa, Kentucky, Maine, Maryland, Massachusetts, Minnesota, Montana, Nebraska, Nevada, New Hampshire, New Jersey, New York, New Mexico, North Carolina, North Dakota, Ohio, Oregon, Rhode Island, South Dakota, Vermont, Virginia, Wisconsin, and Washington.

99. Iowa Code Ann. § 476A.

100. *See* N.Y. Powers of Mun. & State Agencies Law § 172; Patricia E. Salkin, 2 New York Zoning Law and Practice § 11:23.10 (2014).

101. *See* Or. Rev. Stat. § 460.300.

102. *See Energy Facility Siting*, *supra* note 92.

103. N.H. Rev. Stat. Ann. § 162-H:2.

104. R.I. Gen. Laws Ann. § 42-93-3.

- Minnesota,[105] Montana,[106] North Dakota,[107] and Ohio[108] exercise jurisdiction over new plants of 50 MW or more.
- Maryland[109] and Nevada[110] regulate new facilities of 70 MW or more.
- Florida[111] regulates new electric generation facilities of 75 MW or more.
- Arizona,[112] California,[113] Massachusetts,[114] South Dakota,[115] and Wisconsin[116] exercise siting authority over facilities of 100 MW or more.
- New Mexico[117] and North Carolina[118] set jurisdiction over new facilities at 300 MW or more.

Many land-based wind projects, as well as most solar projects, do not exceed 25, 50, or 100 MW in capacity such that state law would not trigger relevant preemptive state jurisdiction over siting the project in 15 of these remaining 20 states (including the District of Columbia). This size limit leaves only local land-use control.

Less State Control Than Meets the Eye

Thus, analyzing the 28 states with any state-level electric generation facility siting authority that could preempt local "aesthetic" zoning or other land-use laws that might bar a project:

---

105. Minn. Stat. Ann. § 21B.2421.

106. *See Energy Facility Siting, supra* note 92.

107. N.D. Cent. Code § 49-22-03(5)(b).

108. Ohio Rev. Code Ann. § 4906.04.

109. Md. Code Ann., Construction of On-Site Generation Stations § 7-207.1; Md. Code Regs. 20.79.01.03 (2020).

110. Nev. Rev. Stat. Ann. § 704.860.

111. *See* Fla. Stat. Ann. § 403.506.

112. Ariz. Rev. Stat. Ann. § 40-360(9).

113. *See* Garofano, *supra* note 66; *see also* Cal. Pub. Res. Code § 25541.

114. *See* Mass. Gen. Laws ch. 164, § 69J.

115. S.D. Codified Laws § 49-41B-2.

116. *See* Wis. Code Ann. § 196.491.

117. *See* N.M. Stat. Ann. § 62-9-3(G), -3(a).

118. N.C. Gen. Stat. Ann. § 62-110; 4 N.C. Admin. Code 8-61.

- Four of these states require that the project also separately obtain local zoning and land-use approvals, which provides the local government an effective veto.
- Fifteen of these states can exercise jurisdiction only over larger projects that do not include many smaller or medium-sized wind, solar, or cogeneration projects.
- One of these states does not regulation nonutility independent power.
- Therefore, only five states are able to exercise significant state authority over typically sized new projects: Connecticut, Iowa, Kentucky, Maine, and Vermont.

While it initially appears that 28 states are legally structured to preempt their municipalities' local power infrastructure siting authority, that number is significantly narrowed when that authority is scaled against the ownership and size reality of many new electricity projects. Screened out also from state preemption are those states that still require a local permit: only five states have effective preemptive state-level authority for sustainable new power generation siting. Thus, exclusive local jurisdiction over typical wind power electric generation project siting remains the U.S. norm in 90 percent of the states. This failure to exercise state control over power sector siting includes the majority of U.S. states that have adopted a 100 percent clean energy goal.[119]

Strategic Exceptions to Municipal Zoning Out of Generation

How might this change over time? For the 15 states that do not extend state jurisdiction to smaller-size energy projects, the size designation in the statute could be amended to include smaller-size project siting. While local governments control local land use for the electric sector, there are a few places where this does not apply. The first opportunity to avoid local zoning restrictions is to locate electric generation on U.S. land that is not subject to any lower-level local, county, or municipal control. More than 600 million acres

---

119. *See Table of 100% Clean Energy States*, Clean Energy State Alliance, https://www.cesa.org/projects/100-clean-energy-collaborative/table-of-100-clean-energy-states/ (last visited May 3, 2024). Fifteen of the 17 states that are members of the Clean Energy State Alliance do not effectively preempt local "aesthetic" zoning, which can frustrate wind project infrastructure in their states.

primarily in the western one-third of the United States, constituting 30 percent of U.S. land, is owned by the federal government and under its exclusively federal public management or trusteeship:[120] 58 percent of this federal land is restricted in terms of usage but can be adapted for multiple uses.[121] The federal executive branch exercises control as to what multiple uses are permitted.Two percent of this federal land is held in trust for sovereign Native American tribes.

Second, the federal government exercises exclusive authority over offshore water-based wind generation projects located three miles or more from a state's land boundary,[122] which covers shore in the oceans along U.S. coasts and in the Great Lakes. The Bureau of Ocean Energy Management (BOEM) in the Department of the Interior (DoI) regulates the permit process for offshore wind,[123] whereas the Federal Energy Regulatory Commission regulates the permit process for ocean oil and gas under the Department of Energy. And the federal EPA, rather than state environmental agencies, exclusively determines and enforces any environmental requirements. Figure 10.2 shows the DoI BOEM Atlantic Ocean wind power federal lease areas now in various stages of development.

---

120. *Federal Lands of the United States Map*, GISGEOGRAPHY (June 4, 2022), https://perma.cc/NF9X-88YH.

121. John D. Leshy, *Still Made for You and Me?*, AM. SCHOLAR (Sept. 14, 2020), https://theamericanscholar.org/still-made-for-you-and-me/ (Twenty-five percent is congressionally protected in manners that make it more difficult to develop but allow multiple uses. A remaining 33 percent is protected by prior executive branch decisions that can be reversed by future presidents, unless subsequently prohibited by Congress.).

122. CONG. RSCH. SERV., R40175, OFFSHORE WIND ENERGY DEVELOPMENT: LEGAL FRAMEWORK (2023), https://fas.org/sgp/crs/misc/R40175.pdf. BUREAU OF OCEAN ENERGY MGMT., INFORMATION GUIDELINES FOR A RENEWABLE ENERGY CONSTRUCTION AND OPERATIONS PLAN (COP) v. 4.0 (2020), https://www.boem.gov/sites/default/files/documents/about-boem/COP%20Guidelines.pdf. BOEM has a four-step process for its permitting of offshore wind development on the outer continental shelf, incorporating planning and analysis, lease issuance, site assessment, and construction and operations requirements.

123. 30 C.F.R. § 585.

Figure 10.2[124] BOEM Offshore Wind Lease Map

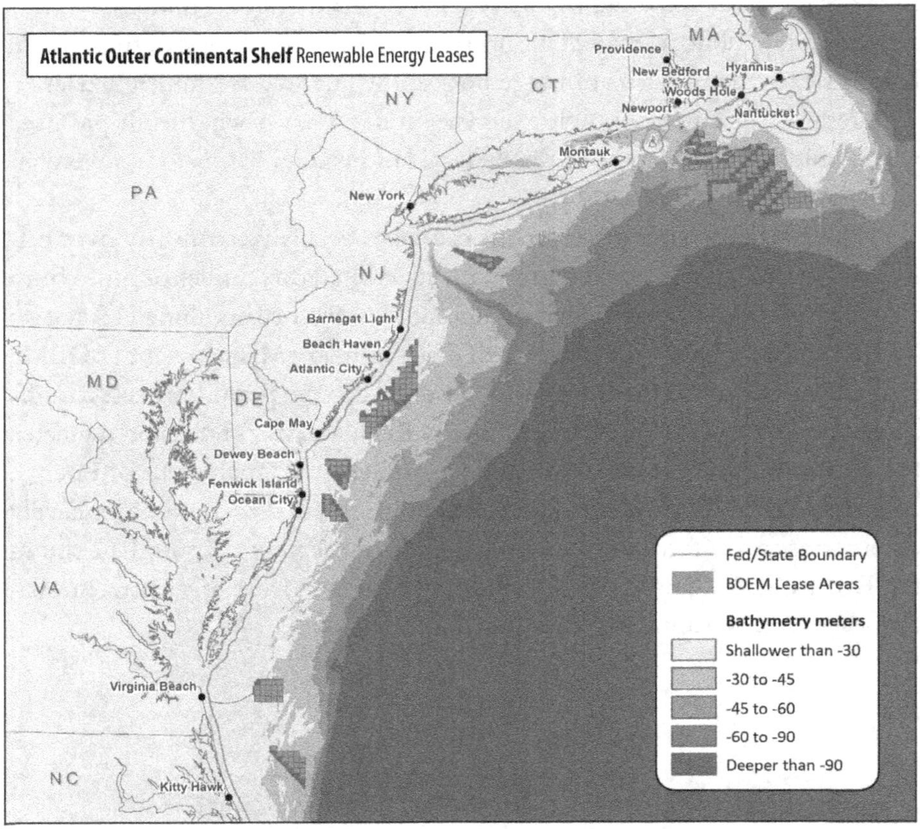

There is exclusive federal control over 30 percent of U.S. land and over all ocean areas more than three miles off state coasts or in the U.S.'s southern half of the five Great Lakes bordering Canada, all of which waters exhibit some of the best wind velocities in the United States, this identifies a substantial area of water and land on which to site electric power resources. Total installed wind power capacity in each of the states varies substantially.[125]

124. Bureau of Ocean Energy Mgmt., Outer Continental Shelf Renewable Energy Leases Map Book 2 (2019), https://www.boem.gov/sites/default/files/renewable-energy-program/Mapping-and-Data/Renewable_Energy_Leases_Map_Book_March_2019.pdf.

125. *U.S. Installed and Potential Wind Power Capacity and Generation*, Off. of Energy Efficiency & Renewable Energy, https://windexchange.energy.gov/maps-data/321 (last visited May 3, 2024).

The next chapter examines the extensive exclusive state power to site or now totally block any new transmission and distribution lines necessary to deliver sustainable electric power from more dispersed/distributed locations to consumers. The much-underappreciated state and local powers analyzed in this chapter and in the next chapter are exercised to control and block new power generation in several states and hundreds of cities and towns. The Princeton University team, whose work the Biden administration used to enact its Inflation Reduction Act, observed that a signficant percentage of new sustainable infrastructure could be frustrated by state or other resistance.[126] This creates a substantial critical path obstacle for siting interstate transmission to move electricity to where it is needed if the U.S. economy is to operate efficiently and compete in the global economy. These ongoing legal state/federal/local conflicts will be a constant element of legal advice as the plan to electrify the entire economy by 2035 proceeds.

---

126. Jesse D. Jenkins et al., *Electricity Transmission Is Key to Unlock the Full Potential of the Inflation Reduction Act*, Rapid Energy Pol'y Eval. & Analysis Toolkit (Sept. 2022), https://repeatproject.org/docs/REPEAT_IRA_Transmission_2022-09-22.pdf.

CHAPTER 11

State Siting Limitations and Legal Strategies

State Legal Control and Veto over Necessary New Electric Infrastructure

The Princeton University team whose work the Biden administration used to win support for its Inflation Reduction Act (IRA) in order to pass in the U.S. Senate, with Vice President Kamala Harris casting the clinching vote, warns that 80 percent or more of its objectives for sustainability power supply could be frustrated by state or other resistance:

> Constraining transmission growth severely limits the expansion of wind and solar power. If electricity transmission cannot be expanded fast enough, power sector emissions and associated pollution and public health impacts could increase significantly as gas and coal-fired power plants produce more to meet growing demand from electric vehicles and other electrification spurred by IRA. If transmission cannot be expanded faster than recent historical rates (~1%/year), growing demand from electric vehicles and other electrification spurred by IRA results in [800 million tons per year of additional greenhouse gas emissions by 2030].[1]

An extra 800 million tons per year of CO_2 emissions released under the current and ongoing transmission buildout is more than a 20 percent difference in annual power sector CO_2 emissions sacrificed due to greater transmission infrastructure construction not being accelerated beyond its current

---

1. Jesse D. Jenkins et al., *Electricity Transmission Is Key to Unlock the Full Potential of the Inflation Reduction Act*, Rapid Energy Pol'y Eval. & Analysis Toolkit (Sept. 2022), https://repeatproject.org/docs/REPEAT_IRA_Transmission_2022-09-22.pdf.

pace. This chapter analyzes how state government is able seamlessly to create such a legal obstacle, unsuccessful past attempts to federally preempt state jurisdiction over transmission siting, and the omission in the Biden administration's IRA that appears could fail to remedy this critical path obstacle.

Effective Subnational Local Control

As set forth in detail in the prior chapter, local governments in the United States have almost unfettered legal discretion and control under Supreme Court precedent construing the Tenth Amendment of the Constitution concerning land-use decisions of what electric power generation is sited on their land. That "local veto" occurs notwithstanding the 2022 IRA and the 2021 Biden Infrastructure Investment and Jobs Act (IIJA) (see Chapter 6) establishing national policy to implement 100 percent zero-carbon electric generation by 2035. Maneuvering state and local control over their land to reject federally promoted sustainable power infrastructure is not a rare hypothetical; it already is everywhere manifest: a significant number of U.S. municipalities have exercised their authority to reject wind power and large solar generation projects:

- More than 500 recent decisions from California to Vermont block wind and solar projects.[2]
- A 2022 Columbia University study of every state identified[3]
  - 121 local policies restricting new wind and solar projects in 31 different states and
  - 204 renewable energy projects that were contested in 49 of the 50 states.

The Columbia study concluded: "These include moratoria on wind or solar energy development; outright bans on wind or solar energy development; regulations that are so restrictive that they can act as de facto bans on wind or solar energy development; and zoning amendments that are designed to block a specific proposed project. While local governments at times enact legislation in response to a specific project proposal, . . . some

2. Robert Bryce, *Renewable Rejection Database* (2023), https://perma.cc/2ATY-Y6GJ (used with permission).

3. Hillary Aidun et al., Opposition to Renewable Energy Facilities in the United States 2 (Sabin Ctr. for Climate Change Law 2022), https://scholarship.law.columbia.edu/cgi/viewcontent.cgi?article=1186&context=sabin_climate_change.

municipalities have banned, placed moratoria on, or significantly restricted wind and solar energy development even absent a proposed project."[4]

Sustainable electric power infrastructure will require a much larger use of land than conventional electric power generation. Under U.S. law, land is controlled by state and local government, notwithstanding federal policy. Land and its use become key critical path metrics in a shift to sustainable energy infrastructure. There is a substantial variation in land use for sustainable energy: wind power and solar power are much less dense energy sources than traditional fossil fuel or nuclear sources of electric power production.[5] Wind power requires land—lots of land—in some cases 500 to 1,000 percent more land than traditional fossil fuel and nuclear technologies per megawatt-hour (MWh) of electric power.

Despite numerous vigorous federal and state incentives for developing wind energy projects (see Chapters 6, 8, and 9, respectively), even before the IIJA, the exclusive legal authority of local governments to regulate use of land presented a formidable barrier to wind project siting in the United States.[6] Local and state exclusive legal control over land use allows local "aesthetic zoning" restricting or banning wind power development. A recent article in *Forbes* magazine documents numerous examples:[7]

- Vermont's only then-pending wind project, which had proposed only a single wind turbine, was withdrawn after facing fierce local opposition.
- In a 2015 vote in Irasburg, Vermont, citizens rejected 274–9 a 5 MW wind project that was proposed to be built near their town.

---

4. *Id.* at 1.

5. Uma Outka, *The Renewable Energy Footprint*, 30 STAN. ENV'T L. REV. 241, 241 n.7 (2011) (quoting Robert I. McDonald et al., *Energy Sprawl or Energy Efficiency: Climate Policy Impacts on Natural Habitat for the United States of America*, 4(8) PLoS ONE (2009), doi:10.1371/journal.pone.0006802); *see also* Christopher Joyce, *Renewable Energy Needs Land, Lots of Land*, fig. 3, NPR (Aug. 28, 2009), https://www.npr.org/2009/08/28/112323643/Renewable-Energy-Needs-Land-Lots-Of-Land.

6. *See* Jim Green & Mick Sagrillo, *Zoning for Distributed Wind Power—Breaking Down Barriers*, Conference Paper, NREL/CP-500-38157, NAT'L RENEWABLE ENERGY LAB'Y (2005), http://www.nrel.gov/docs/fy05osti/38167.pdf.

7. Robert Bryce, *Here's the List of 317 Wind Energy Rejections the Sierra Club Doesn't Want You to See*, FORBES (Sept. 26, 2021), https://www.forbes.com/sites/robertbryce/2021/09/26/heres-the-list-of-317-wind-energy-rejections-the-sierra-club-doesnt-want-you-to-see/?sh=1841189e5bad (list of 317 local communities or government entities from Maine to Hawaii that have entirely rejected or restricted wind projects in the United States since 2015).

- In 2016, residents in the town of Swanton, Vermont, rejected by a vote of 731 to 160 a seven-turbine wind project proposed to be built on a ridgeline.
- In June 2021, the Shasta County, California, Planning Commission unanimously rejected the proposed 216 MW Fountain Wind project with up to 71 turbines standing 679 feet high near the town of Burney, California.
- In March 2021, the Select Board in Scituate, Massachusetts, ordered an already-built wind turbine to be shut down at night from mid-May to mid-October because its operation was disturbing residents' sleep.
- In April 2021, the Planning Board in Foster, Rhode Island, voted 5–1 to ban wind turbines in the town.
- In April 2021, Worth County, Iowa, enacted a temporary moratorium on new wind projects.

Local government rejections or withdrawal of permit applications for proposed large solar projects in 2021 occurred in Pennsylvania,[8] Montana,[9] Nevada,[10] Wisconsin,[11] and Virginia.[12]

Wind, for the first two decades of the 21st century, was the dominant choice for new renewable power in the United States: total annual wind electricity generation increased from about 6 billion kilowatt-hours (kWh) in 2000 to about 300 billion kWh in 2019—a 5,000 percent increase in two decades.[13] The amount of wind power added each year in the last two decades is substantial.[14]

---

8. *Id.* Mount Joy Township supervisors rejected a plan for a 1,000-acre solar project proposed by Florida-based NextEra Energy Resources that would have been Pennsylvania's largest solar project.

9. *Id.* A permit for a 1,600-acre solar project was denied by the Butte-Silver Bow Zoning Board by a vote of 5–0.

10. *Id.* A proposed 850 MW project that aimed to cover 14 square miles north of Las Vegas with solar panels was withdrawn.

11. *Id.* Residents in Dane County are fighting the proposed 300 MW Koshkonong Solar Center.

12. *Id.* This would have affected thousands of acres near the town of Culpeper, Virginia.

13. *See Wind Explained*, U.S. Energy Info. Admin. (Dec. 27, 2023), https://www.eia.gov/energyexplained/wind/electricity-generation-from-wind.php#:~:text=U.S.%20total%20annual%20Electricity%20generation,U.S.%20utility%2Dscale%20electricity%20generation.

14. Off. of Energy Efficiency & Renewable Energy, Land-Based Wind Market Report: 2022 Edition 3 (fig. 2), perma.cc/45V5-F7D7. The nearly 136 GW of cumulative capacity includes the 30 MW Block Island offshore wind plant and the 12 MW Coastal Virginia Offshore Wind pilot project.

Going forward, wind power will continue to be a significant choice for new electric generation based on cost advantages: it is forecast by the U.S. Department of Energy to be cheaper than electricity produced from natural gas by 2025, even without a continuing federal production tax credit incentive for wind; the levelized cost of wind energy during the first two decades of the 21st century decreased from $0.094/kWh ($94/MWh) to $0.035/ kWh ($35/MWh).[15] See Chapter 6 detailing the continuation of generous federal law tax credits. However, even if less expensive, wind and certain large solar power projects require legal rights over thousands of miles of additional land for transmission infrastructure to move renewable power to consumers—local and state governments traditionally control whether that land will or will not be made available.

Renewable Wind Power and Consumers Do Not Coincide Geographically and Require Extensive Additional Transmission

Chapter 3 illustrates how and where renewable energy resources are distributed across the United States. The transmission grid is called "'the world's largest machine,' with its more than 500,000 miles of high-voltage transmission lines, 5 million miles of distribution lines, and thousands of power plants."[16] That high-voltage transmission network is recognized as the most important engineering feat of the 20th century.[17] The U.S. transmission grid at first glance may appear at night seamlessly interconnected by lines of light across the United States.

However, the grid is more nuanced and complex. In the United States there is an eastern interconnection, a western interconnection, and a separate largely disconnected area (most but not all of Texas), as displayed in

15. *See* Christopher Martin & Justin Doom, BNA Energy & Climate Report (2015).

16. Brian Potter, *How to Save America's Transmission System*, IFP (Feb. 22, 2024), https://ifp.org/how-to-save-americas-transmission-system/; *see also* Theodore U. Marston, *The US Electric Power System Infrastructure and Its Vulnerabilities*, Nat'l Acad. of Eng'g (June 15, 2018), https://www.nae.edu/19579/19582/21020/183082/183133/The-US-Electric-Power-System-Infrastructure-and-Its-Vulnerabilities#:~:text=The%20US%20electricity%20supply%20system%20has%20more%20than,at%20high%20voltages%20%28i.e.%2C%20>230%20kilovolts%2C%20kV%29.%20 ("The US electricity supply system has more than 600,000 circuit miles of alternating current (AC) transmission lines, of which 240,000 operate at high voltages (i.e., >230 kilovolts, kV).").

17. Mason Willrich, *Electricity Transmission Policy for America: Enabling a Smart Grid, End to End*, Elec. J. 77 (Dec. 2009).

Figure 4.1 (see page 83). Because of its deliberate decision not to substantially interconnect with the rest of the country, Texas's wholesale electric power and transmission sector is not jurisdictionally regulated by the Federal Energy Regulatory Commission (FERC). It is regulated by the Electric Reliability Council of Texas and has repeatedly fought against its deemed interconnection to the national grid.[18] See Chapter 4 for legal details about the unique Texas grid.

For the other 47 continental U.S. states, FERC exercises jurisdiction to regulate unbundled transmission terms, prices, and conditions to move the fast-increasing amount and percentage of wholesale power transmitted through the U.S. grid, including from the majority of new merchant generation projects constructed each year this century. When states set final retail power rates, they are required by the Filed Rate Doctrine to incorporate filed FERC rates, unless there are imprudency factors to include in setting rates.[19] There is minimal interconnection between these three U.S. continental transmission grids.[20] The U.S. Department of Energy recently explained the scale of the central electric grid in the United States: today, the U.S. transmission and distribution system is a vast physical complex of

> interlocked machines and wires, with a correspondingly complex set of institutions overseeing and guiding it through policies, statutes, and regulations. The U.S. grid delivers approximately 3,857 terawatt-hours [or trillion watt-hours] of electrical energy from electric power generators to 159 million residential, commercial, and industrial customers. This is accomplished via 19,000 individual generators at about 7,000 operational power plants in the United States with a nameplate generation capacity of at least one megawatt (MW). These generators send electricity over 642,000 miles of high-voltage transmission lines and 6.3 million miles of distribution lines. Together with its electric generation component, the grid is sometimes referred to as the world's largest machine; in 2000, the

18. Jared M. Fleisher, *ERCOT's Jurisdictional Status: A Legal History and Contemporary Appraisal*, 3 Tex. J. Oil Gas & Energy L. 5, 8 (2007).

19. *See* Nantahala Power & Light Co. v. Thornburg, 476 U.S. 953 (1986); Miss. Power & Light Co. v. Mississippi *ex rel.* Moore, 487 U.S. 354 (1988); Entergy La., Inc. v. La. Pub. Serv. Comm'n, 539 U.S. 39 (2003).

20. *See U.S. Electric System Is Made Up of Interconnections and Balancing Authorities*, U.S. Energy Info. Admin. (July 20, 2016), https://www.eia.gov/todayinenergy/detail.php?id=27152.

National Academy of Engineering named electrification as the greatest engineering achievement of the 20th century.[21]

The U.S. transmission system is at capacity along the relatively weak seams between its three separate parts shown in Figure 4.1 (see page 83). Some regional transmission organizations (RTOs) (such as the Midcontinent Independent System Operator, MISO) have now started to move away from age-based retirements for existing fossil fuel generators. Of note, unlike some of the independent system operators (ISOs), nothing in the MISO tariff affects existing exclusive state jurisdiction over the construction of additional capacity or traditional state authority to set and enforce compliance with standards for adequacy under its jurisdiction. Wind, solar, hybrid, and battery predominate what is waiting in various transmission queues.

Moving Renewable Power Contrasted with Moving Fossil Fuel

Conventionally, the technical and legal task of permitting projects for fossil fuel is moved to the place of the prime mover power generation technology in relative proximity to where customers consume. A fossil fuel energy source, such as natural gas, oil, or coal, is transported to where society chooses to site a fossil-fuel-fired power plant:[22] "Natural gas can be transported by pipelines, coal by railroads and barges, and oil by pipelines, barges, and tankers."[23] Fundamentally different: wind follows its own course and cannot be moved much by human intervention. Wind turbines must come to the best high-velocity wind areas, as shown in Figure 11.1.

The best wind resources located in the center of the United States are not near urban electric load centers, as shown in Figure 11.1. Therefore, new electric transmission infrastructure must now gain rights to use thousands of miles of land to move that power from its point of generation to U.S. consumers and businesses in cities that were established long before modern wind turbines and solar panels were in use.

---

21. U.S. Dep't of Energy, Quadrennial Energy Rev. Rep., ch. III, at 3–4 (2015), http://energy.gov/sites/prod/files/2015/04/f22/QER_Ch3.pdf.

22. Paul L. Joskow, *Facilitating Transmission Expansion to Support Efficient Decarbonization of the Electricity Sector* 2 (MIT Ctr. for Energy & Env't Pol'y Rsch., CEEPR WP 2021-009, 2021), https://ceepr.mit.edu/workingpaper/facilitating-transmission-expansion-to-support-efficient-decarbonization-of-the-electricity-sector/.

23. *Id.*

Figure 11.1[24] Wind Speeds

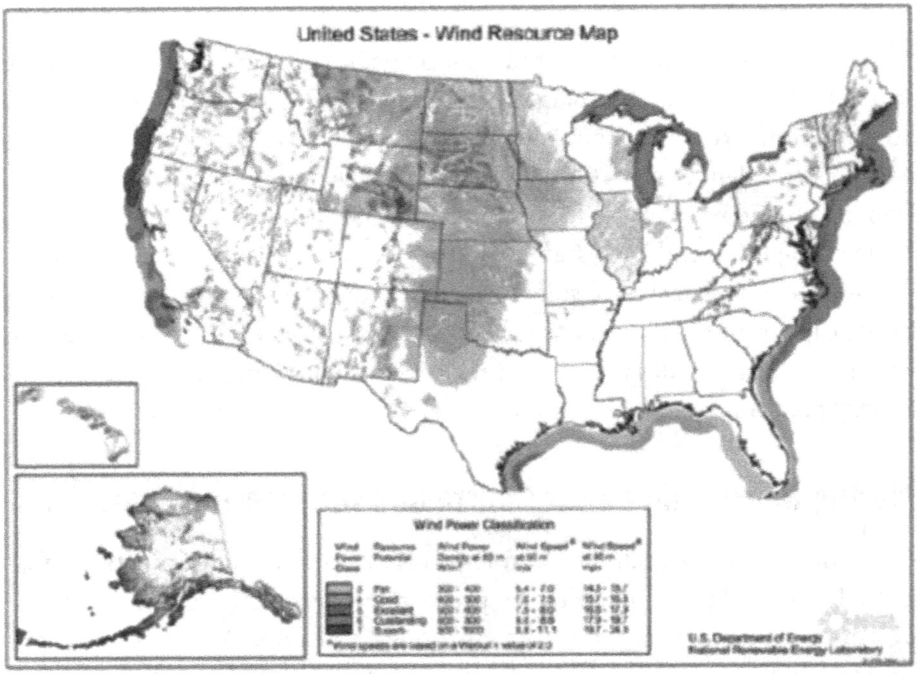

Wind power in the high-wind areas of the U.S. Great Plains needs to be transported to major cities located further east; wind in the Rocky Mountain states needs to be transported as electric power to California.[25] These best wind locations generally are not near major U.S. population centers where power is demanded; the locations of higher-speed wind power resources are shown in Figure 11.1.[26]

With the IRA and IIJA now in place, electricity use is forecast to increase rapidly until 2030 and 2035 as the economy transitions to electric power, almost tripling from currently approximately 17.5 percent of primary energy use to 40–50 percent of all primary energy use.[27] The IRA and IIJA subsidize new electric energy facility development not from ratepayer funds paid by

24. *DOE Provides Detailed Onshore Wind Resource Map,* U.S. ENERGY INFO. ADMIN. (Jan. 19, 2012), https://www.eia.gov/todayinenergy/detail.php?id=4630.

25. *See Wind Explained, supra* note 13.

26. *Id.; Wind Resource Maps and Data,* NAT'L RENEWABLE ENERGY LAB'Y, https://www.nrel.gov/gis/wind-resource-maps.html (last visited May 6, 2024).

27. Resources for the Future, IRA Symposium (Feb. 15, 2023).

those who use delivered electricity but from taxpayer credits decreasing federal tax revenues.

The Joint Coordinated System Plan, on behalf of several power pools and ISOs, predicted that a 5 percent wind generation component achieved by 2024 could require the construction of roughly 10,000 miles of additional high-voltage transmission lines at an estimated cost of $50 billion to deliver that power. A more aggressive 20 percent wind penetration target could require the construction of 15,000 miles of additional high-voltage transmission lines at a cost of approximately $80 billion in order to deliver the power from more remote locations to consumers.[28] Without first legally siting these transmission facilities, a transition to renewable energy and its impact on the U.S. and world environment could be constrained by 80 percent from expectations, according to Princeton analysis.[29]

State Legal Authority to Block New Transmission Lines

Historically, FERC does not exercise jurisdiction over the siting and construction of those same interstate transmission facilities not on federal land. The Federal Power Act provides FERC exclusive federal authority only over transactions, contractual terms, and prices of power sales over the physical electric transmission system lines.[30] The lines, poles, transformers, and protective equipment—the physical hardware assets—are not included within the grant of federal jurisdiction under the Federal Power Act.[31]

Note that Alaska and Hawaii, geographically isolated from the other 48 states, are not engaging in any interstate transactions and therefore are not subject to FERC's authority. As covered in more detail in Chapter 4, the Federal Power Act is the statute that provides federal jurisdiction over "the transmission of electric energy in interstate commerce and . . . the sale of electric energy at wholesale in interstate commerce" with the exception of "facilities used for the generation of electric energy or . . . facilities used in local distribution or only for the transmission of electric energy in intrastate

---

28. Matthew L. Wald, Richard Perez-Pena & Neela Banerjee, *The Blackout: What Went Wrong; Experts Asking Why Problems Spread So Far*, N.Y. Times, Aug. 16, 2003, at A1.

29. *See* Jenkins et al., *supra* note 1.

30. 16 U.S.C. §§ 824 *et seq.*

31. *Id.*

commerce."[32] The Federal Power Act clarified that if the electric energy is "transmitted from a state and consumed at any point outside" that state, then the electric energy is transmitted in interstate commerce.[33]

Therefore, states through which electric transmission lines are placed retain and exercise traditional exclusive land-use control over the siting or upgrading of power transmission facilities, notwithstanding that the purpose of new transmission infrastructure is to serve other states' interstate power transmission needs. This hardware and its siting remain within state and/or local authority pursuant to the federalist state/federal split of jurisdiction embodied in the Federal Power Act. This split of authority was upheld by the Supreme Court 40 years ago.[34] The U.S. multilevel federalist form of government now is copied and duplicated by a limited number of world nations—although they include all of the North American nations as well as the most significant and economically successful democratic (non-Communist) countries on five continents.[35]

In addition to local power analyzed in the prior chapter, this chapter next analyzes largely unrestrained state power to permit or block siting the hundreds of thousands of miles of new transmission lines and infrastructure to deliver new renewable power to consumers. For example, a large power-line project connecting Kansas wind power and solar resources to Missouri, Illinois, and Indiana, known as the Grain Belt Express, since originally planned in 2010 still has not been able to obtain approval from every local and state jurisdiction its transmission lines would pass through.[36] Without state cooperation to site these new lines, recent estimates forecast that 50–80 percent

---

32. *Id.* § 824(b)(1)–(2).

33. *Id.* § 824(c).

34. FERC v. Mississippi, 456 U.S. 742 (1982); Am. Paper Inst. v. Am. Elec. Power Serv. Corp., 461 U.S. 402 (1983).

35. *See List of Countries by System of Government*, WIKIPEDIA, https://perma.cc/MER7-N55R (last visited May 6, 2024). The significant nations with federalist forms of government include

United States (50 states, 2 commonwealths, and 12 territories or districts)
Canada (10 provinces and 2 territories)
Mexico (31 states)
Brazil (26 states)
Germany (16 states)
Switzerland (26 cantons)
Argentina (23 provinces)
Australia (6 states and 2 territories)
India (28 states and 7 territories)

36. German Lopez, *Permission to Build*, N.Y. TIMES, June 12, 2023.

of the Biden climate plan will be frustrated.[37] And multiple states are blocking these necessary new transmission lines. The next sections below address recent efforts to create an exception for certain limited federal preemption of state transmission siting discretion.

Unsuccessful 2005 Federal Efforts to Preempt State Control

Reserved Tenth Amendment legal authority permits a state to block siting or upgrading a transmission line in or through its state needed to transmit renewable or other power to adjacent states. To attempt to preempt state resistance, Congress in the Energy Policy Act of 2005 (EPAct 2005) attempted to expand the powers of the federal Department of Energy and FERC to intercede to exercise certain siting authority over interstate electric power transmission line projects:

- Mandating that the U.S. Department of Energy undertake a transmission congestion study every three years[38]
- Allowing the Department of Energy to designate congested transmission corridors called National Interest Electric Transmission Corridors (NIETCs) in "any geographic area experiencing electric energy transmission capacity constraints or congestion that adversely affects consumers"[39]
- Establishing an expedited FERC "backstop authority" to issue construction permits for transmission facility projects in NIETCs if states withhold approval for more than a year and establishing less than comprehensive federal eminent domain rights for these NIETC projects whose rights otherwise are within state authority[40]

Although there is new 2021 authority for federal exercise of transmission authority discussed later, it also contains limitations to effectively preempting all state authority via the exercise of eminent domain. To exercise

---

37. *Id.; see* Nathanael Greene & Jacqueline Ennis, *Now We All Have to Be Wind, Solar, and Transmission Builders*, Nat. Res. Def. Council (Dec 26, 2022), https://www.nrdc.org/bio/nathanael-greene/now-we-all-have-be-wind-solar-and-transmission-builders (showing that "over 80% of the potential carbon emissions reductions of the Inflation Reduction Act by 2030 will be lost if transmission growth is limited to its recent growth rate").

38. *See* Cal. Wilderness Coal. v. U.S. Dep't of Energy, 631 F.3d 1072 (9th Cir. 2011).

39. Energy Policy Act of 2005, 16 U.S.C. §§ 824P *et seq.*

40. FERC issued Order No. 689 in 2006, creating a multiyear process for obtaining a federal permit to construct transmission within an NIETC. 71 Fed. Reg. 69,440 (Dec. 1, 2006).

such eminent domain legal authority for electric transmission siting projects under section 1221 of EPAct 2005, the Department of Energy would (1) first complete a transmission congestion study to identify a transmission-congested area, (2) designate an NIETC covering the site, and (3) obtain an expedited construction permit from FERC after a state withholds a decision on new transmission facilities for more than one year. Thereafter, federal legal eminent domain power to take or use land for transmission facilities and lines could be obtained by the project developer in federal district court or state court. Only two NIETCs have been designated by the U.S. Department of Energy since EPAct 2005 enactment almost two decades ago; both of those federal actions to site high-priority electric power transmission infrastructure to benefit transmission-congested areas were overturned and vacated by separate federal courts.[41]

First, after suit by two state public utility commissions (PUCs), a federal appellate court in 2009 blocked FERC from acting to "backstop" and grant a federal permit for electric power infrastructure under section 216 of the Federal Power Act for a new power transmission line that would carry additional power to New York and other congested eastern cities, when the state across which new transmission lines would traverse had denied the permit pursuant to conventional state PUC authority over such facilities.[42] The court determined that under the plain language of EPAct 2005, as long as the state took some action on the application, FERC's section 216 authority to intercede in the siting process for electric infrastructure was not empowered. Here, the affected state had taken action in one year denying the permit for that proposed new transmission infrastructure; there had been no delay in the state making a final decision on the application.

Two years later, in 2011, on a second attempt to exercise intercession of federal siting authority, the Ninth Circuit ruled that the U.S. Department of Energy failed to properly consult with affected states in preparing a congestion study regarding transmission corridors in mid-Atlantic and southwestern states required by section 216 of EPAct 2005 and further ruled that it failed to consider the environmental effects of designating NIETCs pursuant to the National Environmental Policy Act (NEPA).[43] Despite a statute granting preemptive authority to FERC, these two circuit court opinions

41. *Cal. Wilderness Coal.*, 631 F.3d 1072.

42. Piedmont Env't Council v. FERC, 558 F.3d 304 (4th Cir. 2009).

43. *Cal. Wilderness Coal.*, 631 F.3d 1072.

eliminated any exercise of federal authority to site electric transmission infrastructure in the United States under the Federal Power Act until more recent amendment of the Federal Power Act in the IIJA. Siting for wind and other renewable power infrastructure remained within exclusive state and local, rather than federal, legal jurisdiction.

The Remaining Critical Barrier: No Legal Eminent Domain over State Public Land to Install Infrastructure

The federal government traditionally is not able preemptively to exercise land-use decisions, except on federal land. And to arrive at population centers, a fair proportion of new power generation located on federal land must exit it to traverse state and/or private land. While the IIJA provides new, still unused and legally untested power to the federal government to preempt state power transmission facility permitting in limited designated priority areas, that law includes new federal eminent domain power over private land but *not* over state land.

And state land can matter critically along the many miles of interstate transmission lines. State land includes most of the land under interstate highways, all state park land, land in many conservation easements, and non-private land under rivers and creeks. Given that more than 90 percent of continental U.S. states have rivers or streams as part of their state boundaries, the right of way to cross those rivers with a transmission line to move additional power into the adjacent state remains subject to state jurisdiction and discretion. Notwithstanding any of the Biden-era amendments of federal laws, a variety of eastern and western states refused new interstate transmission lines running through their states to serve other states.[44]

The Biden debt ceiling increase legislation in 2023 somewhat weakened NEPA in order to, in theory, reduce NEPA review of new transmission infrastructure, as was done in amending the IIJA and the IRA. However, legislators again missed addressing the critical path impediment—not NEPA but state legal authority to deny eminent domain for any new transmission infrastructure crossing state public land. These omissions allow several key states, if they so choose, legally to block certain new interstate renewable energy infrastructure or upgrades necessary to serve new power generation technologies to address climate.

44. *See supra* at n. 45–50.

In addition, recent holdings of the Supreme Court have deferred to local zoning authority regarding land-use matters.[45] Electric transmission in North America transcends being only a U.S. issue; within the Americas, it is a multicontinental international issue. Transmission capacity also is necessary to move renewable Canadian hydropower to New England.[46] In 2018, from among four dozen applicants in a competitive procurement, Massachusetts chose the Northern Pass project to transmit 1,090 MW of hydroelectric power produced by Quebec Hydro in Canada to Massachusetts distribution utilities through New Hampshire.[47] Alone, this project's baseload renewable energy capacity would have constituted an increase of approximately 15 percent of the renewable hydroelectric capacity serving New England and an increase of approximately 20 percent of all renewable energy serving all of the six New England states.

The high-voltage direct current (HVDC) portion of the transmission project would have been located entirely in New Hampshire; the costs of the transmission facilities were to be paid for by consumers in Massachusetts and Connecticut, with no cost imposed on New Hampshire customers.[48] A permit for the HVDC portion of the Northern Pass project subsequently was rejected by the energy regulatory agency in New Hampshire, and that rejection was upheld by the New Hampshire Supreme Court in 2019 when challenged.[49] Without the state permit to site interstate transmission infrastructure in New Hampshire, even though all New England interstate transmission facilities are managed by ISO-NE, which is FERC-regulated, the project was never approved and was abandoned.

---

45. *See* Murr v. Wisconsin, 137 S. Ct. 1933 (2017); Va. Uranium v. Warren, 139 S. Ct. 1894 (2019).

46. Tim Faulkner, *Massachusetts Set to Import Hydropower from Canada*, ecoRI (Jan. 30, 2018), https://www.ecori.org/renewable-energy/2018/1/29/7xk446y6yai0d979hr8m8seoyui2ok.

47. *Id.*; Bob Salzburg, *Mass. Taps Eversource's Northern Pass for Hydropower Project*, WBUR (Jan. 25, 2018), https://www.wbur.org/bostonomix/2018/01/25/hydropower-massachusetts-eversource [https://perma.cc/M3HB-JVPG].

48. Annie Ropeik, *Site Evaluation Committee Casts Unanimous Vote against Northern Pass Project*, N.H. Pub. Radio (Feb. 1, 2018), https://www.nhpr.org/nh-news/2018-02-01/site-evaluation-committee-casts-unanimous-vote-against-northern-pass-project.

49. Annie Ropeik, *In Unanimous Vote, N.H. Supreme Court Upholds Northern Pass Denial*, WBUR (July 19, 2019), https://www.wbur.org/news/2019/07/19/northern-pass-rejected-eversource-new-hampshire.

The Supreme Court most recently deferred to local zoning bylaws to interpret what can and cannot be developed on local property.[50] Zoning for land use is among the "police powers" that municipalities retain under constitutional Tenth Amendment authority, unless state statutes retain that authority at the state level, preempting their towns' authorities. There is no traditional federal authority over land and land use unless that land is federally owned or the land's use is instrumental in activities in interstate commerce.[51] The Supreme Court recently considered whether the federal Atomic Energy Act preempted Virginia's outright ban on the mining of uranium on its land and held there was no federal preemption of local land use even for extensively federally regulated nuclear power fuel matters.[52]

Despite national and international climate exigencies that focus on a rapid electric sector reduction of carbon emissions (see Chapter 2), the federal government has few tools to site expeditiously or effectively new power generation or interstate electric transmission facilities. More assertive provisions in the Biden legislation still may face multiyear NEPA Environmental Impact Statement (EIS) requirements, with possible NEPA EIS litigation further delaying NEPA compliance. In addition, some states may challenge any federal usurpation of their traditional transmission facility siting authority.

New Transmission and Distribution Needs

The federal debt ceiling bill signed by President Biden in June 2023 requires added federal effort on transmission infrastructure planning, requiring the North American Electric Reliability Corporation (NERC) to report to FERC within 18 months and report to Congress within 12 months of the public comment period with any recommendations for statutory changes. FERC also issued regulation for NERC and grid operators to plan for severe weather events' grid impact.[53] In most years from 2014 to 2024, additions of

---

50. Murr v. Wisconsin, 137 S. Ct. 1933 (2017).

51. Hodel v. Va. Surface Mining & Reclamation Ass'n, Inc., 452 U.S. 264 (1981); *cf.* New York v. United States, 505 U.S. 144 (1992).

52. Va. Uranium v. Warren, 139 S. Ct. 1894 (2019).

53. FERC Order No. 896 (June 23, 2023).

renewable wind and solar power constituted the majority of total additions to power generation in the United States.[54]

Massive new transmission lines are required as soon as possible to transmit new wind power at high voltage from the mountain states to southern California, from the Midwest rural plains to Chicago and Detroit, and from the Texas rural panhandle to Dallas and Houston. Despite numerous federal and state incentives for developing wind energy projects (see Chapters 6, 8, and 9) and the efforts of the Biden-Harris administration to override or preempt traditional state legal authority regarding new transmission lines, the authority of state and local governments to restrict electric infrastructure remains a formidable barrier to certain locations for wind projects across the United States.[55] Siting of wind power turbines and the electric transmission lines to reach those turbines is jurisdictionally vested in local and state law rather than in the federal government, with only limited still-untested possible exceptions.

Lower-level municipal governments legally control land-use law and regulation pursuant to the Tenth Amendment. While renewable energy generation by wind requires lots of land—as much as 1,000 percent more land than traditional fossil fuel power generation—the critical path issue is not the scarcity of land in the United States. One estimate is that seven to ten acres per installed MW are necessary for large solar projects.[56] Current and proposed solar land uses would need a fairly minimal percentage of total county land—typically less than 0.5 percent of most counties' land footprint across the United States.[57]

The critical legal path is legal jurisdiction to permit electric infrastructure, not insufficient physical land: state governments exercise legal authority over siting the electric utility infrastructure technology that is required to transmit power from new generation units to consumers. States and localities retain jurisdiction over the legal authority to permit physical construction. Municipalities and states control traditional siting of power infrastructure

54. Mark Bolinger, *Utility-Scale Wind and Solar in the U.S.: Comparative Trends in Deployment, Cost, Performance, Pricing, and Market Value* 5, Lawrence Berkeley Nat'l Lab'y (2020), https://perma.cc/QRU2-NAMV.

55. *See* Green & Sagrillo, *supra* note 6.

56. Sean Ong et al., Nat'l Renewable Energy Lab'y, NREL/TP-6A20-56290, Land-Use Requirements for Solar Power Plants in the United States 8 (2013), https://www.nrel.gov/docs/fy13osti/56290.pdf.

57. Jessi Wyatt & Maggie Kristian, *The True Land Footprint of Solar Energy*, Great Plains Inst. (Sept. 14, 2021), https://betterenergy.org/blog/the-true-land-footprint-of-solar-energy/.

technology, and there is no court precedent yet supporting any federal preemption.

State Transmission Discrimination

The Constitution's Dormant Commerce Clause (see Chapter 8) does not permit states legally to subsidize or favor particular in-state generation companies or technologies at the expense of externally sited power generation companies supplying transmission. The different federal circuit courts of appeals do not agree on what constitutes impermissible/unconstitutional state geographic discrimination in terms of siting electric transmission infrastructure. The Fifth Circuit Court of Appeals found it possible to challenge a Texas law regulating transmission line siting[58] as a violation of the Dormant Commerce Clause.[59] A transmission developer designated by an RTO to construct a new line argued that because the law blocks companies without a physical presence in Texas from building transmission facilities, reserving development opportunities in Texas only for in-state utilities, the law violates the Dormant Commerce Clause.[60] The court concluded after "wad[ing] through the thicket of electricity regulation" that Texas's law does impermissibly discriminate against interstate commerce.

In contrast, the Eighth Circuit Court of Appeals upheld a similar law enacted by Minnesota against a challenge in part because the law benefited incumbent transmission providers who were headquartered outside of the state of Minnesota, and thus the "law applies evenhandedly to all entities, regardless of whether they are Minnesota-based entities or based elsewhere."[61] The project developer, LSP, argued that the law "discriminates against interstate commerce three times over":

- On its face by "securing lucrative business opportunities . . . for favored local operators"
- In effect by "granting entities with an in-state presence a preference at the direct expense of out-of-state entities that lack such a presence"
- With a legislative discriminatory purpose of insulating in-state companies from competition

58. S.B. 1938 (Tex. 2019), 2019 Tex. Sess. Law Serv. ch. 44 (S.B. 1983) (West); Tex. Util. Code Ann. § 37.051–.157 (West 2019).

59. NextEra Energy Cap. Holdings, Inc. v. Lake, 48 F.4th 306 (5th Cir. 2022).

60. *Id.* at 310.

61. LSP Transmission, LLC, v. Sieben, 954 F.3d 1018, 1028 (8th Cir. 2022).

The Eighth Circuit panel found none of these facial, "effect," or "purposed" claims persuasive. The court noted that the state's legally enacted Right-of-First-Refusal (ROFR) restrictions actually serve the state's goal of delivering reliable and cost-effective electric power and the "law is not primarily aimed at protecting in-state interests but at maintaining a regulatory system that has worked."[62] The panel found that preserving the status quo in transmission development is "within the purview of a State's legitimate interest in regulating the intrastate transmission of electric energy."[63] FERC Order No. 1000 regarding state ROFRs and transmission nondiscrimination tries to prevent discrimination (see Chapter 4).

Biden Administration Statutory Change; Legal Inadequacies

Going forward, President Biden called his enacted IIJA the "most significant long-term investment in our infrastructure and competitiveness in nearly a century."[64] Electric transmission line capacity would have to be tripled by 2050 to connect the needed amount of new wind and solar power to the grid.[65] This new law attempts to create limited federal preemption to site new transmission infrastructure in some congested U.S. areas. On average, $35 billion annually is spent on transmission.[66]

The IIJA authorizes $65 billion for energy projects that could include certain electricity transmission projects, although these expenditures are also divided so as to be devoted to preventing outages, research and development of grid reliability and resilience, development of technologies to enhance grid flexibility, and funds for state energy programs.[67] Even $10 billion is a small portion of the estimated costs to connect the country to use all renewable energy, as President Biden pledged. Princeton University researchers found that it would require a 60 percent expansion of the U.S. high-voltage

62. *Id.* at 1029.

63. *Id.* at 1030.

64. *What the Infrastructure Deal Means for Energy*, E&E NEWS ENERGYWIRE (July 30, 2021), https://www.eenews.net/articles/what-the-infrastructure-deal-means-for-energy/.

65. *Id.*

66. *Utilities Continue to Increase Spending on the Electric Transmission System*, U.S. ENERGY INFO. ADMIN. (Mar. 26, 2021), https://www.eia.gov/todayinenergy/detail.php?id=47316.

67. *What the Infrastructure Deal Means for Energy*, *supra* note 64; *see also UPDATED FACT SHEET: Bipartisan Infrastructure Investment and Jobs Act*, THE WHITE HOUSE (Aug. 2, 2021), https://www.whitehouse.gov/briefing-room/statements-releases/2021/08/02/updated-fact-sheet-bipartisan-infrastructure-investment-and-jobs-act/.

transmission network by 2030, with capacity tripled by 2050, to connect the needed additional wind and solar power to the grid.[68] The capital cost of these new power lines is estimated by the Princeton study at $360 billion by 2030 and $2.4 trillion by 2050.[69]

The IIJA attempts to reinvigorate elements of the previously stricken EPAct 2005 federal authority, discussed earlier in this chapter, to compel high-priority transmission facility siting through federal preemption of traditional state legal authority.[70] It would do so by allowing FERC to issue permits if state agencies reject certain transmission proposals or fail to act on them within a year.[71] However, before interceding, FERC would need to consider whether the applicant for a transmission project had "engaged states and non-federal entities in good faith consultations and in a timely manner."[72] The U.S. Department of Energy issued a new transmission congestion study.

Environmental groups and activists have opposed major transmission projects because of their presumed negative environmental impacts.[73] More court challenges by resistant states and groups can be anticipated going forward as FERC attempts to preempt and alter the exclusive exercise of state and local transmission siting authority that has existed for the entire 80 years of the Federal Power Act. Should such superseding FERC authority be upheld by the courts, rapid progress on new transmission lines would be subject to several other legal requirements:

- NEPA can require EISs, which typically require multiple years and millions of dollars, to be completed in final form.[74]
- Such FERC decisions must accommodate other permitting decisions by state PUCs.[75]

---

68. Eric Larson et al., *Net-Zero America: Potential Pathways, Infrastructure, and Impacts*, PRINCETON UNIV. (Oct. 29, 2021), https://netzeroamerica.princeton.edu/img/Princeton%20NZA%20FINAL%20REPORT%20SUMMARY%20(29Oct2021).pdf.

69. *Id.* at 6.

70. *What the Infrastructure Deal Means for Energy*, *supra* note 64; *UPDATED FACT SHEET*, *supra* note 67.

71. *Id.*

72. *Id.*

73. *Id.*

74. 42 U.S.C. § 4332(2)(C). President Biden proposed new regulations categorically exempting from NEPA requirements new transmission lines if they occupy existing rights-of-way.

75. Jonathan Brightbill et al., *What Infrastructure Act Means for Transmission Line Projects*, LAW360 (Jan. 13, 2022), https://www.law360.com/articles/1455049/what-infrastructure-act-means-for-transmission-line-projects.

- Most significantly as a critical path absolute barrier, even if FERC can grant eminent domain transmission rights of way over private lands, there is no such federal legal preemptive authority over state-owned public lands, which include the bottom of all rivers and many roads, over which states exercise plenary land-use jurisdiction.[76]

Moreover, as examined in Chapter 12, even if transmission projects are approved, the United States suffers a significant current incapacity to manufacture domestically the needed transformers for electric power grid upgrades and expansions.[77] Not only are those transformers foreign-made and delivery backlogged, but their price has also inflated at double the rate of the cost of other commodities during recent inflation.[78] According to Tony Clark, a former chair of FERC, "I think members of Congress are overestimating the federal government's ability to approve transmission lines in a speedy manner while underestimating the controversy this will foment amongst constituents" and place FERC "in a difficult position."[79]

Work-Arounds and Exceptions That May or May Not Suffice

There are two areas where the federal government under an exception does exercise siting power. First, 30 percent of U.S. land, predominately in the western states, is federally owned land subject to federal control rather than local control.[80] However, this addresses only part of the challenge: while the federal government controls transmission facility siting on its land, concentrated U.S. population centers generally are not located on federal land. Once transmission lines exit federal land, the federal government has no traditional Federal Power Act authority over the power transmission or distribution

---

76. Federal Power Act § 216(e); 40 C.F.R. § 1508.18; John Decker et al., *The Federal Government's High-Wire Act: Setting FERC Up to Employ Its Transmission Siting Backstop Authority*, Vinson & Elkins (June 6, 2023), https://www.velaw.com/insights/the-federal-governments-high-wire-act-setting-ferc-up-to-employ-its-transmission-siting-backstop-authority/.

77. Robert Bryce, *Untransformed* (Mar. 31, 2023), https://robertbryce.substack.com/p/untransformed.

78. *Id.*

79. Molly Christian, *Infrastructure Bill Aims to Solve Piece of US Transmission Puzzle*, S&P Global (Oct. 7, 2021), https://www.spglobal.com/marketintelligence/en/news-insights/latest-news-headlines/infrastructure-bill-aims-to-solve-piece-of-us-transmission-puzzle-66748368.

80. U.S. Const. art. IV, § 3, cl. 2.

facility technologies that need to be upgraded or extended to transmit power to distant population centers.

Second, the federal government controls siting on large areas under water. In the oceans (and the Great Lakes), the federal government exercises exclusive authority over wind power technology siting in water commencing three miles from shore.[81] More wind power could and will be placed in U.S. ocean or Great Lake waters. Figure 10.2 shows the progress to date of the Department of Interior Bureau of Ocean Energy Management Atlantic Ocean federal wind power leased areas to private developers now under various stages of development.[82]

Again, as with the previous alternative location option, these locations create a substantial, but not wholly sufficient, condition to avoid local legal barriers that could challenge transmission siting. Offshore wind turbine interconnections to transmission lines need to emerge from the ocean or Great Lakes onto land to connect to the existing land-based electric transmission grid system to deliver power and capacity. States remain in control of such transmission technology siting on their land, unless the new Biden administration acts are successful in changing that.

Ultimately, land requirements do not present a quantity issue in the United States. The issue is which level of government exercises the legal control to permit that land for infrastructure siting. As detailed in Chapter 10, 45 of the 50 states have left that authority to site new moderately sized renewable power generation predominately at the local level rather than preempting it at the state level. Moreover, state governments control legal permissions to cross public land under rivers, streams, and interstate highways with newly sited transmission and distribution infrastructure to move new power within or outside of the state.

None of this will even be adequately tested or litigated during President Biden's first term. Consequently, much remains to be legally determined. To avoid these delays, uncertainties, and critical path blockages, creative siting of new generation and its transmission infrastructure becomes a meta variable to address for new renewable energy developers and their clients.

---

81. 30 C.F.R. § 585.

82. Bureau of Ocean Energy Mgmt., Outer Continental Shelf Renewable Energy Leases Map Book 2 (2019), https://www.boem.gov/sites/default/files/renewable-energy-program/Mapping-and-Data/Renewable_Energy_Leases_Map_Book_March_2019.pdf.

Part III of the book devotes two chapters to outlining in detail the changing business model that needs to be employed by energy companies and stakeholders working closely with legal counsel on these next steps. Chapter 12 examines changes in technology and their relevant legal context; Chapter 13 analyzes regulatory changes contorting the fabric of the legal business model going forward.

PART III

A New Business Model for Power

"A man hears what he wants to hear and disregards the rest . . ."

—*The Boxer,* Paul Simon, 1969

Part III of this book features two detailed chapters tracking how, when law and regulation affecting electric power and climate change are significantly altered, a different and new business model becomes necessary to navigate through these changing legal waters. Stakeholders and clients will need to find and gravitate to this new route for doing business successfully in the 21st century as world, national, and state governments mandate that the power sector bear the most significant burden to rapidly reduce greenhouse gas emissions.

Part III provides what counsel and their clients should absorb regarding ongoing changes and not disregard. In Chapter 12, the now-changing power technology mandated by new law is examined to extract how that changes successful business ventures from now on. Chapter 13 focuses on changing regulations at state (PUC) and federal (FERC) levels that now will affect how business must react to them in this new environment.

For attorneys, the next two chapters might be shared with clients active in energy, environment, and any business affected by the move to electrify the U.S. economy.

CHAPTER 12

Changing Electric Technology Repowers Law

"Energy is the golden thread that connects economic growth, increased social equity, and an environment that allows the world to thrive."

Ban Ki-moon, U.N. Secretary General[1]

The electricity business is changing, and that change is accelerating at "Moore's Law" pace. This chapter examines how alterations in technology for electric power now modify a successful business strategy. The next chapter, Chapter 13, turns the page to analyze the recent federal and state legal orders and regulatory changes that modify the best strategies within the new business model. In this part, read Chapter 13 after this chapter.

Despite all the regulatory and technology changes described in this and the next chapters, in terms of physics, electricity functions as a constant that has not altered. It remains the same force delivered as 60 Hz, 120 volt, AC oscillating electrons inhabiting the outer orbit of copper wires. Notwithstanding this constant, the economics and business are changing beneath the wires.

Even Water or Its Absence Now Changes Power Technology

The fossil fuel base that currently generates the significant majority of U.S. electric power typically can require significant water for facility cooling, affected by growing water scarcity in several areas of the United States. Hydropower generation, in use since the first harnessing of electric power and until recently the largest source of U.S. and world renewable power, also is affected by changing water availability. The United Nations Environment

1. The Sec'y-Gen.'s High-Level Grp. on Sustainable Energy for All, Sustainable Energy for All: A Framework for Action 4 (2012).

Program warned in late 2022 that if drought conditions persist, the two largest hydroelectric reservoirs in the United States—Lake Mead and Lake Powell—could eventually reach "dead pool" status, where water levels fall too low to flow downstream.[2]

New Power Stakeholders

Enabling expanding retail participation in wholesale electricity markets and a national effort effectively to tackle climate change by enabling renewable power, new stakeholders pursuing distributed power generation are altering the business model. Demand response as a growing component of supply and more distributed power generation change the entry points, participants, and options for successful participants in the electric power industry. Shifting demand to nonpeak periods and storing prodigiously more electric power than in past eras are now on the business horizon. Several key states are remolding regulatory rules governing their electric sectors that fundamentally change the role of, and financial incentives for, utilities, consumers, competitors, and distributed power generators. All industry stakeholders will need to adapt to a changing electric sector business model.

Changing Power Demand

For the last 40 years, U.S. electricity prices have remained relatively constant in real dollar terms.[3] This is because there has been slowing electric load growth with zero growth in electricity sales since 2008 (or earlier) in most regions of the United States. Although the size and influence of electric power are much larger: the United States spent $1.3 trillion on energy in 2018, with U.S. energy consumption currently projected to grow more than twice as fast as any other end-use sector from 2021 to 2050 as population and economic growth outweighs efficiency gains.[4] With the Biden-Harris

---

2. Elise Hammond et al., *The Latest on the Colorado River and Lake Mead Report*, CNN (Aug. 16, 2022), https://www.cnn.com/us/live-news/lake-mead-colorado-river-report/index.html.

3. Ryan Wiser, Galen Barbose & Mark Bolinger, *Retail Rate Impacts of Renewable Electricity: Some First Thoughts* 5, LBL 1007261 (2017), https://eta-publications.lbl.gov/sites/default/files/lbnl-1007261.pdf.

4. *See In 2018, U.S. Energy Expenditures Increased for the Second Consecutive Year*, U.S. Energy Info. Admin. (Sept. 10, 2020), https://www.eia.gov/todayinenergy/detail.php?id=45076.

administration push to substitute electricity for fossil fuels in heating, transportation, and other applications, along with rapidly expanding power demands for artificial intelligence (AI) and crypto curreny mining uses, this zero or negative load growth is about to reverse significantly for the foreseeable future.

How the Electric Business Model Adapts

"The things we call technologies are ways of building order in our world."[5]

The electric power industry has undergone different trends than other large U.S. industries. Key industries in the United States for other commodities and services have become more consolidated through mergers, acquisitions, brand, and capital or regulatory barriers to entry, as noted by Jonathan Tepper:[6]

- Two corporations control 90 percent of the U.S. beer market.
- Five banks control approximately half of the nation's banking assets.
- Many states' health insurance markets have two insurers with an 80 percent market share.
- Four companies control 85 percent of the U.S. beef market.
- Three companies control 70 percent of the world's pesticide market.

The same structural reality is *not* true regarding the electric utility industry: instead, the Federal Energy Regulatory Commission (FERC) has encouraged greater competition rather than consolidation. In the last half century, the power sector has through regulatory and other legal changes

- Encouraged new renewable and waste technologies owned by nonutility entities since PURPA enactment in 1978—see Chapter 5
- Undergone state partial deregulation of retail power increasing nonutility ownership of power generation, which now encompasses more than 40 percent of all power generation

---

5. Langdon Winner, The Whale and the Reactor: A Search for Limits in an Age of High Technology 28 (Univ. of Chi. Press 1986).

6. Jonathan Tepper, The Myth of Capitalism (2018); *see also* Press Release, The Myth of Capitalism: Monopolies and the Death of Competition (Oct. 24, 2018), https://newsroom.wiley.com/press-releases/press-release-details/2018/The-Myth-of-Capitalism-Monopolies-and-the-Death-of-Competition/default.aspx.

- Operated under different state-specific subsidies of distributed renewable power through state RPS REC and net metering incentives—see Chapters 8 and 9
- Imposed externality CO_2 charges on fossil fuel power generation in 20 percent of U.S. states through the east coast RGGI since 2009 and through California regulation since 2012
- Caused multiparty wholesale power transactions to climb from 8 percent of all power sales before 2000 to now more than 40 percent of all power sales and still climbing each year

For electric power, regulation matters. FERC, the federal power regulator, facilitated and implemented key electric sector changes:

- Allowed nonutility sponsorship and payment for new transmission capacity since FERC Order No. 1000 in 2011 (see Chapter 4)
- Required open access to monopoly utility power transmission system services via FERC Order No. 888 (see Chapter 4)
- Introduced entrepreneurs into the power generation business, spawning development of new business models for the industry
- Encouraged demand response to compete with new generation since 2008 via FERC Order No. 719 and took additional steps in FERC Order No. 745 in 2011 and FERC Order No. 2222 in 2020 (see Chapter 4 and Chapter 8)
- Began accommodating and integrating energy storage in 2018 via FERC Order No. 841

Even though the public may think of renewable solar and wind power as everywhere available, business planners must think strategically regarding electric power. Location matters in terms of both the construction costs at different sites and the availability of necessary transmission infrastructure. Some sites are better than others, and there is a significant advantage to early entry for new power. And time matters: as an example, later entrants of offshore wind projects can expect to incur higher costs as the best shallow offshore sites are already taken and as more expensive added upgrades of transmission infrastructure are required to serve these projects.

The next sections analyze the key technology changes and regulatory responses and how the business model must adapt to several now-shifting factors.

Critical Technology Changes

Transitioning from Baseload Fossil Fuel and Nuclear Electric Power to Intermittent Renewable Power

Nuclear Power

Power technology is changing. In the most recent three decades, only four conventional nuclear power plants were under construction in the United States:

- Two plants in South Carolina under construction were canceled in 2017 after a $9 billion expenditure, which drove Westinghouse, its builder, into bankruptcy under its construction contract.
- Two plants in Georgia constituting the first new nuclear units to be built in the United States in more than three decades are at least seven years behind schedule, and their original $14 billion price tag has at least doubled to date. Georgia Power announced in the fourth quarter of 2022 that the fuel load into the Vogtle Unit 3 reactor core had begun near Waynesboro, Georgia.

Smaller modular nuclear reactors are under development for future centralized as well as smaller distributed application. The recent Inflation Reduction Act and the Infrastructure Investment and Jobs Act (IIJA) provide

- Department of Energy loans authorized for $40 billion for clean energy projects that include nuclear energy[7]
- A zero-emission nuclear power Production Tax Credit (PTC) for *existing* nuclear power facilities worth approximately $15/MWh ($0.015/kWh) available through 2032[8]
- A technology-neutral PTC of $25/MWh ($0.025/kWh) for ten years of plant operation

---

7. *Inflation Reduction Act Guidebook*, THE WHITE HOUSE (Sept. 21, 2023), https://www.whitehouse.gov/cleanenergy/inflation-reduction-act-guidebook/.

8. 26 U.S.C. § 45U.

- A 30 percent Investment Tax Credit (ITC) for new plants placed in operation in 2025 or after[9]
- For the PTC and ITC for new plants after 2025, a 10 percent bonus for new facilities sited in certain energy communities, including those with retiring coal plants converting to nuclear power generation
- For the PTC and ITC for new plants after 2025, a 10 percent bonus for facilities meeting domestic U.S. content requirements for steel and other components
- For existing nuclear plants facing closure, $6 billion authorized in the Civil Nuclear Credit Program in the IIJA, with $1.1 billion already allocated by the Department of Energy to the PG&E Diablo Canyon Power Plant in California[10]

The operating costs of U.S. nuclear power plants are estimated to average $29.13/kWh, of which the $15/MWh zero-emission nuclear power PTC would cover half for ten years for existing plants.[11] The remaining costs could be covered by revenue from selling the power produced. A Department of Energy report found that siting a new nuclear facility at the site of a retired coal plant would realize a 15–35 percent cost savings versus siting on a greenfield site and determined that of 237 retired coal facility sites, "80% (125 sites) are amenable to siting an advanced nuclear reactor, and 22% (35 sites) are amenable to siting a large LWR [light-water reactor]."[12] These closed large coal facility sites also may offer the benefit of an existing now-unused transmission corridor from the coal plant, which solves one of the major transmission obstacles facing new zero-carbon facilities. See Chapter 11.

A significant number of states have followed California and banned by law the siting of new civilian nuclear power plants until there is a federal

9. *Inflation Reduction Act Keeps Momentum Building for Nuclear Power*, Off. of Nuclear Energy (Sept. 8, 2022), https://www.energy.gov/ne/articles/inflation-reduction-act-keeps-momentum-building-nuclear-power.

10. *Civil Nuclear Credit Program*, Energy.gov, https://www.energy.gov/gdo/civil-nuclear-credit-program (last visited May 8, 2024).

11. *Electricity Production Costs for Nuclear Power Plants in the United States from 2002 to 2022*, Statista (Dec. 2023), https://www.statista.com/statistics/184754/cost-of-nuclear-electricity-production-in-the-us-since-2000/.

12. J. Hansen et al., Investigating Benefits and Challenges of Converting Retiring Coal Plants into Nuclear Plants, INL/RPT-22-67964, U.S. Dep't of Energy (Sept. 13, 2022), https://fuelcycleoptions.inl.gov/SiteAssets/SitePages/Home/C2N2022Report.pdf.

approved high-level civilian nuclear waste disposal site. The Yucca Mountain site was canceled during the Obama administration and at any time resumed has a decade or more to revitalize a federal storage facility.

Oil, Coal, and Natural Gas

Coal supplies 27 percent of global primary energy, although in the United States this number has already quickly shrunk from half of U.S. electricity generated in 2005 to about 16 percent now and is still declining. The Environmental Protection Agency (EPA) recently issued a rule requiring coal plants across 23 states further to reduce criteria air pollutants, which was enjoind by the Supreme Court in its final decision of its 2024 term.[13] Another EPA rule proposed stronger limits on facilities' emissions of mercury and other toxic metals, and yet another would reduce over half a billion pounds of wastewater pollution.[14]

Oil and natural gas combined still supplied nearly 60 percent of global primary energy in 2020—a roughly similar proportional share as in 1965, although serving an energy system that is more than 3.5 times larger now. The International Energy Agency projected that global oil demand will climb by approximately 2 percent in 2023, despite a soft international economy, and increase by 1 percent in 2024.[15] Jet fuel sales are expected to increase dramatically from $352 million in 2022 to about $656 million by 2029.[16] For natural gas, "domestic gas use in 2022 jumped by a whopping 5.4% . . . . [T]he Energy Information Administration reported that gas consumption set monthly records in 9 of 12 months in 2022."[17]

Figure 12.1 shows that two-thirds of U.S. primary energy consumption is from oil and natural gas and more than three-quarters of it from fossil fuels.[18]

---

13. Ohio, et al v. EPA, Applications For Stay No. 23A349 (Supreme Court, June 27, 2024).

14. Press Release, U.S. Env't Prot. Agency, Biden-Harris Administration Finalizes Suite of Standards to Reduce Pollution from Fossil Fuel-Fired Power Plants (Apr. 25, 2024), https://www.epa.gov/newsreleases/biden-harris-administration-finalizes-suite-standards-reduce-pollution-fossil-fuel.

15. *Oil Market Report—July 2023*, Int'l Energy Agency, https://www.iea.org/reports/oil-market-report-july-2023?utm_source=substack&utm_medium=email (last visited May 8, 2024).

16. Fortune Business Insights, *Aviation Fuel Market Size Expected to Rise $654.79 Billion at CAGR 9.3% by 2029*, GlobeNewswire (July 10, 2023), https://www.globenewswire.com/news-release/2023/07/10/2701479/0/en/Aviation-Fuel-Market-Size-Expected-to-Rise-654-79-billion-at-CAGR-9-3-by-2029.html?utm_source=substack&utm_medium=email.

17. Robert Bryce, *The Energy Transition Isn't* (July 1, 2023), https://robertbryce.substack.com/p/the-energy-transition-isnt?utm_source=substack&utm_medium=email.

18. https://www.eia.gov/tools/faqs/faq.php?id=427&t=3.

Figure 12.1[19]

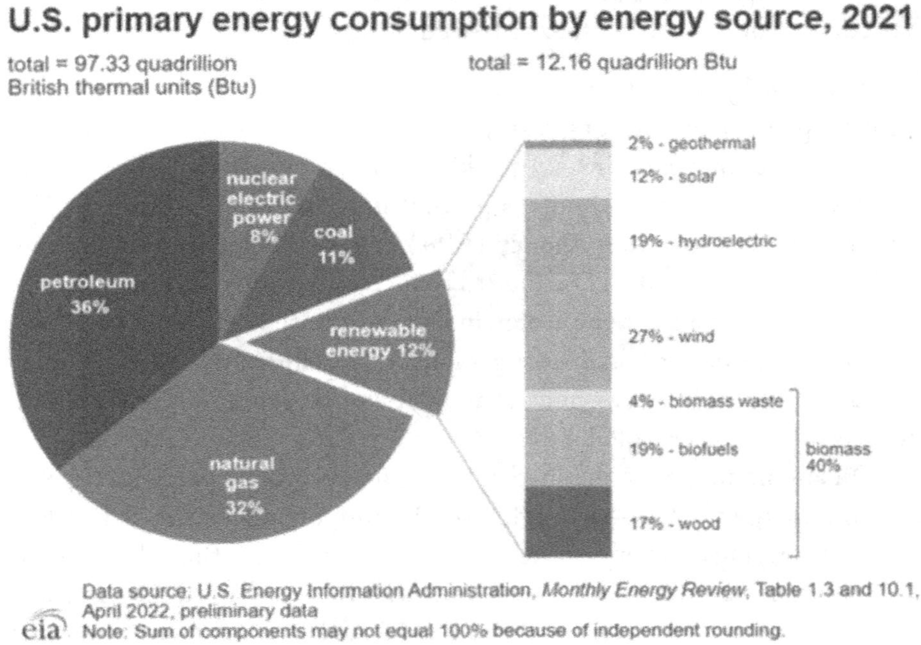

While U.S. policy proceeds to subsidize renewable energy (see Chapter 6), telescoping analysis to world demand for energy in a recent year of data from the Statistical Review of World Energy shows wind and solar power increasing less than fossil fuel use globally and in the United States. Between 2004 and 2022, while the global use of wind and solar power increased by 5 percent, hydrocarbon consumption grew by 110 exajoules (EJ), 3.4 times faster than wind and solar, which grew by 32 EJ.[20] In 2022, global wind, solar, hydro, biomass, and geothermal power surpassed coal-fired generation in the electric power sector for the first time; global wind output grew by 13 percent and solar increased by 24 percent, with U.S. percentage increases comparable.[21] However, because the United States increased use of fossil fuel hydrocarbon energy several times more than its use of solar and wind energy, in 2022 the United States had the world's

19. *U.S. Energy Facts Explained*, U.S. Energy Info. Admin. (Aug. 16, 2023), https://www.eia.gov/energyexplained/us-energy-facts/#:~:text=Download%20image%20U.S.%20primary%20energy,natural%20gas%2032%25%20petroleum%2036%25.

20. Bryce, *supra* note 16.

21. *Id.*

third-largest annual increase in CO_2 emissions.[22] For context, wind and solar power produce renewable electricity, while fossil fuels produce electricity and also are used abundantly for transportation, aviation, and industrial processes. Even with massive global spending during a recent 18-year period on wind and solar power, use of hydrocarbon fuels increased more than three times faster.[23]

For equilibrating supply and maintaining demand in the next half century:

- The world has proven gas reserves equivalent to 52.3 times its annual consumption.
- The world has proven oil reserves equivalent to 47 times its annual consumption.
- Fossil fuel from known reserves equals current consumption levels for a half century.
- Some additional fossil fuel reserves will be discovered.

The U.S.'s energy future depends on by whom and from where energy will be supplied. OPEC's and the rest of the world's production of oil has been relatively flat for the last two decades, with increased oil and gas production in recent decades coming from the United States (production more than doubled in the last ten years) and Russia. One indicator of anticipated future demand for oil and natural gas: ExxonMobil in late 2023 announced its largest acquisition this century, paying $64.5 billion for Pioneer Natural Resources to more than double ExxonMobil's U.S. Permian Basin oil and natural gas production volume.[24] The United States will continue as a major producer and world exporter of fossil fuels, even if U.S. use of fossil fuels declines dramatically. As proven reserves of fossil fuels decrease, they will become more expensive.[25]

---

22. *Id.* U.S. emissions in 2022 totaled 4,826 gigatons.

23. *Id.*

24. Bill McColl, *ExxonMobil Completes Nearly $60B Pioneer Deal—Here's What You Need to Know*, INVESTOPEDIA (May 3, 2024), https://www.msn.com/en-us/money/companies/exxonmobil-completes-nearly-60b-pioneer-deal-heres-what-you-need-to-know/ar-AA1o6gx1#:~:text=The%20acquisition%20is%20expected%20to%20more%20than%20double,%2460%20billion%20after%20getting%20approval%20from%20U.S.%20regulators.

25. *See Petroleum & Other Liquids: U.S. Crude Oil First Purchase Price*, U.S. ENERGY INFO. ADMIN. (Jan. 3, 2023), https://perma.cc/3XYE-J5UG. *See* John Mauldin, *Turning Bullish on Energy*, MAULDIN ECON. (Oct. 28, 2022), https://perma.cc/5UVV-ZHKC (graphing world oil prices from 1974 to 2022).

Because of enactment of the Biden administration Inflation Reduction Act, EPA forecasts that by 2040[26]

- U.S. coal capacity will have fallen by 90 percent
- U.S. coal operating capacity factors will have fallen below 20 percent
- Natural gas combined cycle plants will not increase
- Natural gas simple cycle combustion turbines (which can be used for peaking power and backup for intermittent renewable energy) will increase slightly

Renewable Power

Globally, energy production from renewable sources in 2024 had reached a point where "[a]pproximately one-seventh of the world's primary energy is now sourced from renewable technologies."[27] Future vehicles will use electricity and constitute a significant additional demand as well as a mobile form of power storage thanks to their battery operations. Electric vehicles (EVs) in use presently comprise less than 1 percent of the global light-duty fleet, and in most places, the electricity to charge their batteries still is derived predominantly from carbon-based fossil fuels. In terms of the demand for EVs creating a commensurately large increase in demand for electricity, the rate of change could be limited not by the U.S. supply of electricity but by the availability at competitive prices of rare earth minerals for the batteries that store the electricity to power EVs. Here are the numbers: in the world today, there are more than 1.45 billion cars and trucks. This is a large number of vehicles to transition to electric power. North America has by a large factor the most vehicles per capita with 710 vehicles per 1,000 people or 0.71 vehicles per capita, with other landmasses having significantly fewer vehicles per capita, as follows:[28]

North America:	0.71
Europe:	0.52
South America:	0.22
Middle East:	0.18

26. Cara Marcy, Env't Prot. Agency, Presentation at Resources for the Future, IRA Symposium (Feb. 15, 2023).

27. Hannah Ritchie et al., *Renewable Energy*, Our World in Data (Jan. 2024), https://ourworldindata.org/renewable-energy.

28. David Bonnici & Mike Stevens, *It's 2024, How Many Cars Are There in the World?*, Which Car? (Feb. 9, 2024), https://www.whichcar.com.au/news/how-many-cars-are-there-in-the-world.

Asia/Pacific:	0.14
Africa:	0.05
Antarctica:	0.05

On electric power supplied from batteries, entropy of usable energy is incurred, losing potential energy with each charge and discharge converting power. EVs require including almost ten times the amount of key minerals and metals as for conventional gasoline- and diesel-powered vehicles.[29] These rare earth minerals include significant amounts of copper, lithium, nickel, zinc, graphite, and cobalt—many of which are sourced from a limited number of foreign countries with whom the United States has experienced often volatile relations, adding an additional supply dimension to the future of EV power demand.

The Space Occupied by New Wind Power in the Business Model

The United States had 150,427 MW of wind power capacity at the beginning of 2023, when approximately "10 percent of electricity in the U.S. was produced by wind. A decade earlier in 2014, wind accounted for 4% of the total electricity generated. The EIA forecasts that electricity generation from wind will grow by 6% in 2024, while coal and natural gas will continue to decline."[30] Timing is everything now. Wind project performance has increased over time: the average capacity factor of recently built wind projects was over 40 percent, considerably higher than projects built earlier.[31] Levelized energy prices of large wind projects remain low, around $20/MWh, with the average levelized cost of wind energy (LCOE) at $33/MWh as shown in Figure 12.2. Experts expect future onshore and offshore wind costs to decline 37–49 percent by 2050.[32]

---

29. *See Minerals Used in Electric Cars Compared to Conventional Cars*, INT'L ENERGY AGENCY (Oct. 26, 2022), https://perma.cc/7W9B-PK43 (graphing the comparison of minerals used in electric cars to those used in conventional cars). *See also* THE ROLE OF CRITICAL MINERALS IN CLEAN ENERGY TRANSITIONS: WORLD ENERGY OUTLOOK SPECIAL REPORT 26, INT'L ENERGY AGENCY (2022), https://perma.cc/7TCG-GYUH; Mauldin, *supra* note 24.

30. *U.S. Installed and Potential Wind Power Capacity and Generation*, WINDEXCHANGE, https://windexchange.energy.gov/maps-data/321 (last visited June 25, 2024); CLIMATE CENTRAL, A DECADE OF GROWTH IN SOLAR AND WIND POWER: TRENDS ACROSS THE U.S., box 6 (2024), https://www.climatecentral.org/report/solar-and-wind-power-2024.

31. *Land-Based Wind Market Report*, ENERGY TECHS. AREA, BERKELEY LAB, https://emp.lbl.gov/wind-technologies-market-report (last visited May 14, 2024).

32. Ryan Wiser et al., *Expert Elicitation Survey Predicts 37% to 49% Declines in Wind Energy Costs by 2050*, 6 NATURE ENERGY 555 (2021), https://www.nature.com/articles/s41560-021-00810-z.

Figure 12.2[33] Recent and Future Levelized Cost of Wind Energy

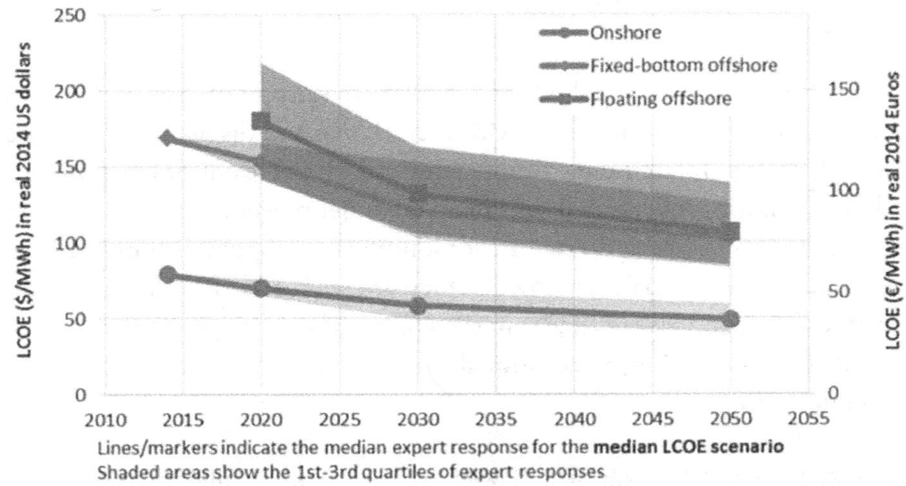

In the changing business model for renewable energy generation, there are now more options regarding to whom power producers sell power output as well as how ownership of a project is structured: "U.S. investor-owned electric companies accounted for 1,470,748 GWh, or 34.7 percent, of total U.S. electricity generation in 2022. Electricity generation at independent power producer-owned plants totaled 1,990,850 GWh, accounting for 46.9 percent of the total electricity generation in the United States in 2022."[34] This is a 400 percent increase from two decades before.[35] Wind project ownership has been dominated by IPPs during the last two decades; IPPs now own the largest share of power generation, which has also rapidly changed

33. *Wind Power Costs Reduced Dramatically*, Energy Techs. Area, Berkeley Lab (Sept. 20, 2016), https://eta.lbl.gov/news/wind-power-costs-reduced-dramatically.

34. *Resources & Media: Industry Data*, Edison Elec. Inst., https://www.eei.org/resources-and-media/industry-data (last visited June 25, 2024).

35. *See Industry Data*, Edison Elec. Inst. (Jan. 21, 2023), https://perma.cc/7M5G-LF7M). *See also* U.S. Energy Info. Admin., Electric Power Monthly with Data for Aug. 2015, tbls. 1.2, 1.3, 1.4, 1.5, 1.6a (2015), http://www.eia.gov/electricity/monthly/archive/October2015.pdf [https://perma.cc/U5UZ-YLT6]; Promoting Wholesale Competition through Open Access Non-Discriminatory Transmission Services by Public Utilities, 61 Fed. Reg. 21,540, 21,545, 21,549 (May 10, 1996) (to be codified at 18 C.F.R. pts. 35, 385).

the business model and introduced new stakeholders to be served with legal counsel.[36]

And to whom producers sell power output has new expanding options since some states partially deregulated retail power provision and as more stakeholders enter the sector, rendering the business model more multidimensional. Figure 12.3 illustrates the distribution of sales of wind power output to investor-owned utilities (IOUs), public power providers, and power marketers, as well as an increasing number of merchant IPP stakeholders and direct retail sales bypassing utilities in recent years.[37]

Figure 12.3[38] Purchasers of Wind Power 1998–2020

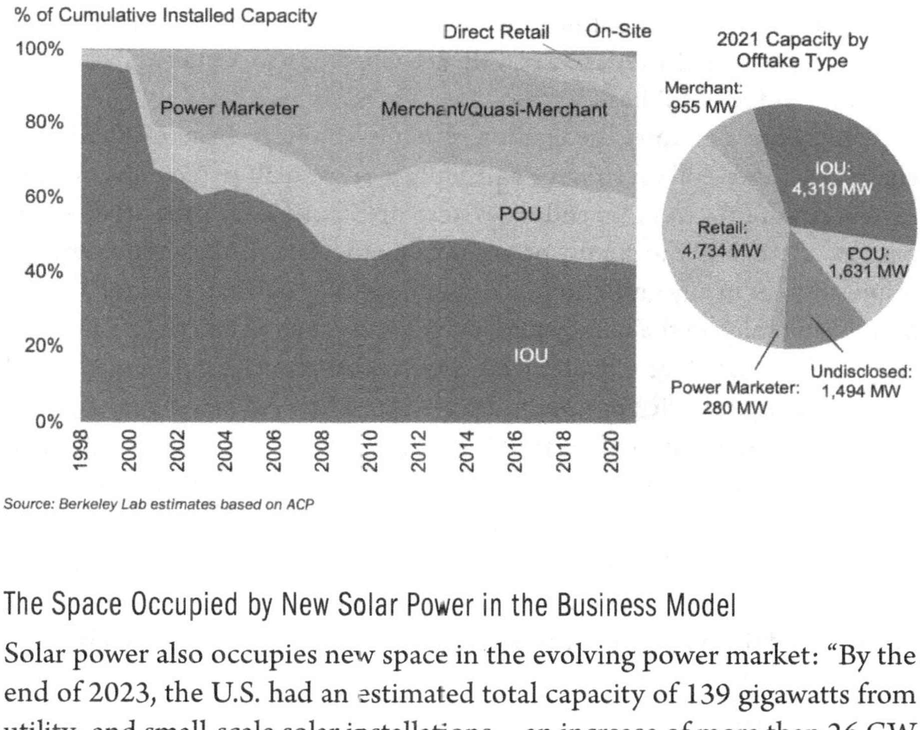

Source: Berkeley Lab estimates based on ACP

The Space Occupied by New Solar Power in the Business Model

Solar power also occupies new space in the evolving power market: "By the end of 2023, the U.S. had an estimated total capacity of 139 gigawatts from utility- and small-scale solar installations—an increase of more than 26 GW

36. U.S. Dep't of Energy Off. of Energy Efficiency & Renewable Energy, Land-Based Wind Market Report: 2022 Edition 22, fig. 22, https://perma.cc/LPT2-XPCD (graphing cumulative and 2021 wind power capacity categorized by owner type).

37. *Id.*

38. *Id.* at 23, fig. 23 (graphing cumulative and 2021 wind power capacity categorized by power offtake arrangement).

or 23% from 2022. During 2023, the U.S. produced an estimated 238,121 GWh of electricity from utility- and small-scale solar installations combined. This is an increase of 33,042 GWh or 16% compared to 2022."[39]

Solar power now is a cost-effective option. Photovoltaic (PV) solar panel cost has fallen dramatically from ~$1.90/W in 2009 to $0.70/W now.[40] Inverter prices, for the equipment necessary to convert PV direct current to alternating current, also declined by more than 60 percent from $0.60–$1.00+/W in 2005 to under $0.20/W in 2013[41] and have continued declining. This has allowed the solar PV markets to grow at an average of more than 40 percent each year since 2000.[42] The LCOE of new solar and wind power in 2020 was competitive with the operating LCOE of existing coal, nuclear, and combined cycle gas plant operation, according to Lazard.[43] New renewable energy LCOE has continued to decline, and the Inflation Reduction Act has since substantially reduced LCOE. See Chapter 6 for detailed discussion of the act and its subsidies.

The sources of power generation revenue within the business model are changing. Renewable resources earn only a very small percentage of their revenue cash flow in independent system operator (ISO) capacity markets because their ability to supply power reliably to meet capacity requirements is intermittent in any given hour. Renewable energy currently earns its greatest revenue value in the energy market for kWh supplied and from REC subsidies in 29 states (see Chapter 8). Capacity market prices in the ISOs and states offering capacity payments are expected to yield lower prices in the future as the proportion of renewable energy penetration increases, although this also may advantage solar and wind power, which earn the smallest proportion of business model revenue from capacity markets.

Lazard models the capacity factor that determine capacity market revenue for wind power onshore as 38–55 percent, wind offshore as 48–52 percent, and fixed panel solar power as 13–23 percent.[44] Locational latitude

39. Climate Central, *supra* note 29.

40. Wilson Rickerson et al., Int'l Energy Agency–Renewable Energy Tech. Deployment, Residential Prosumers: Drivers and Policy Options (Re-Prosumers) 9 (2014).

41. *Id.*

42. *Id.* at 10.

43. *Lazard's Levelized Cost of Energy Analysis—Version 14.0* (Oct. 2020), https://www.lazard.com/media/kwrjairh/lazards-levelized-cost-of-energy-version-140.pdf.

44. *Id.*

influences solar capacity factors, with proximity to the equator yielding progressively higher capacity factors, which favors the southern portion of the United States over the northern portion. Summer ISO market capacity value of solar can be as high as 40 percent for tracking/tilt solar panels that follow the sun across the sky daily and seasonally and can be less for new wind projects, with each declining as its technology penetration increases.[45] Fixed-panel solar offers de minimis winter capacity value because it is not available at U.S. latitudes during late afternoon and early evening peak demand hours.

Battery Storage

Storage is a new variable in the business model. Battery storage added to renewable energy projects can alter generation capacity value. However, the returns on business investment in battery storage are heavily dependent on reliability and duration earning capacity market revenues. There is greater market value in longer-duration eight-hour storage.[46] Long-duration storage between now and 2030 will begin to implement technologies that can move beyond lithium-ion technologies to manage longer-duration storage of power supply without declining economies of scale as duration increases. The value of shorter-duration storage declines rapidly as the penetration of storage resources increases.

Operation and Maintenance/Degradation

A key business issue related to cost and scale in the electric sector is maintenance and replacement expenses associated with the current stock of generation facilities as technology changes and equipment degrades. Solar PV units in the electric system degrade in panel output over time but at different rates depending on the scale of generation capacity. Looking at data from one state regarding more than 90,000 solar PV facilities in operation between 2010 and 2019 reveals the following solar PV degradation rates[47] for different sizes/scales of PV units:

---

45. Erin Smith, Raghu Palavadi Naga, Eric Pinsker-Smith & John Keene, Capacity Accreditation, Part 2: Relevance of Capacity Revenues and Updates from the Northeast, fig. 2, SUSTAINABLE ENERGY ADVANTAGE (June 22, 2022), https://www.seadvantage.com/blog-post/capacity-accreditation-part-2/.

46. *Id.* at fig. 3.

47. Sustainable Energy Advantage, *Where Did the Sun Go? A Quick Look at Solar Panel Degradation in Massachusetts* (May 2022), https://www.seadvantage.com/blog-post/where-did-the-sun-go/. This uses Massachusetts's Department of Energy Resources data; production in years that had 10 percent

Solar Unit Size	Average Annual Degradation
Small (< 25 kW)	-1.51%
Medium (25 kW-1 MW)	-1.08%
Large (> 1 MW)	-0.56%

Scale matters, even with modular and/or distributed generation. As shown in the preceding table, small PV rooftop units experienced power output degradation rates of more than 1.5 percent per year, approximately triple that of larger field-mounted PV projects greater than 1 MW. Annual mean degradation estimates that in the past have been stated to be a uniform 0.5 percent/year appear to underestimate real-world PV degradation rates for small and intermediate-size PV systems. This data would indicate that after 25 years of operation,

- Small-sized projects with a generating capacity of less than 25 kW would be at only 62 percent of their original generating capacity.
- Medium-sized projects with a generating capacity between 25 kW and 1 MW would be at 75 percent of their original generating capacity.
- Large-sized projects with a generating capacity exceeding 1 MW would be at 86 percent of their original generating capacity.

Accurate modeling of capital degradation and replacement matters particularly for capital-intensive renewable power facilities. This data demonstrates that for life cycle cost replacement modeling, larger PV solar projects would not require as rapid a replacement schedule for solar panels, the most expensive component in a PV project, as would smaller rooftop projects. In addition to operation & maintenance (O&M) expenses, various federal incentives such as the PTC credit (see Chapter 6) and incentives in 29 states for RECs (see Chapter 8) and in 39 states for net metering (see Chapter 9) are directly a function of amount of power generated. There is a substantial difference in output, and thus revenue earned, between 62 percent and 86 percent, for example. This slower rate of generation output degradation also indicates why large field-mounted solar PV projects will remain more cost-effective than smaller PV projects into the future.

---

less sunshine (i.e., irradiance) versus the 20-year average were given a 10 percent upward adjustment to their production to ensure that the analysis was "weather neutral" and was not biased by especially sunny or cloudy years.

This becomes important with valuation for future revenue generation and maintenance expense outlays associated with sale and purchase of existing PV projects. These different degradation values need to be accounted for differentially in business model yearly revenue and operating expense projections over time; also, degradation rates will directly affect the revenue realized from state RPS REC subsidies (see Chapter 8), net metering subsidies (see Chapter 9), and federal PTC credits over their current 10-year payout (see Chapter 6). These need to be accurately factored into long-term business models.[48]

Distributed Generation Changes the Model

Different-size projects impose different demands and costs on the transmission system that do not necessarily favor large PV projects.

At the beginning: Thomas Edison, upon harnessing electric energy to power the filament in an incandescent light bulb, had an original vision of a decentralized, direct current–based electric power industry composed of small individual businesses operating in close proximity to each other.[49] Under such a model, the majority of electric power generation would be distributed on the site of the primary consumer of that power and/or to adjoining sites where it was not necessary to cross roads or nonusers' properties (crossing any public ways raises separate complex right-of-way and eminent domain issues and also may violate the monopoly distribution franchise of utilities in a given state). Edison's model did not prevail over centralized electric power supply in the 20th century in the United States.

Technology trends during the late industrial age favored centralization of utility supply. In the early years of electric power, generating stations were less reliable than the transmission and distribution (T&D) grid. Therefore, to reinforce the weakest link in the network by having many generating stations, it made sense to connect many generation facilities as part of a single centralized common T&D network. This also made it possible to connect the many diverse load profiles and power demands of various customers, thus smoothing cumulative total system demand and allowing centralized

48. *Id.* These estimates align with the results of earlier studies by the U.S. government's Natural Renewable Energy Laboratory and its Lawrence Berkeley Laboratory.

49. *The War of the Currents: AC vs. DC Power*, U.S. Dep't of Energy (Nov. 18, 2014), https://www.energy.gov/articles/war-currents-ac-vs-dc-power.

lowest-cost generation equipment to run more efficiently at higher load factors.[50]

Refocusing All to Present Time

Now, distributed renewable energy is proving to be the fastest-growing source of new U.S. power. The California and Hawaii Public Utilities Commissions require the activation of some advanced inverter functionality to head off presumed grid reliability issues, which may require more expensive equipment and more oversight of the operation of distributed solar energy systems over time.[51]

A renewable decentralized energy system has also proven to be as reliable in terms of equipment operative availability as is centralized power supply, if one discounts that the sunlight or strong wind power for renewable technology is not available for most of the hours during the typical day. As a vivid example of distributed power resiliency, at the end of March 2022 as part of the Russian invasion of Ukraine, a missile damaged 416 PV panels as well as four inverters at a 3.9 MW solar facility in Ukraine's Kharkiv region; one week later, staff had disconnected the damaged PV strings to keep operational 1.8 MW of power generation.[52] There currently are regulatory U.S., federal, and state incentives for distributed power generation. Lazard has noted that solar is distributed and, although intermittent, can be dispatched for peaking power or load-following.[53]

Energy Cost Changes in the U.S. Market

Much of the innovation responsible for the solar industry's explosive growth relates to financial and regulatory changes rather than technology. Third-party ownership of residential PV systems has been a dominant variable factor in the renewable business model, with third-party ownership comprising more than 80 percent of PV systems in certain high-solar-use states, such as Arizona and California. The change in technology has implications beyond a

50. *See generally Electricity Explained: How Electricity Is Delivered to Consumers*, U.S. Energy Info. Admin. (Apr. 16, 2024), https://www.eia.gov/energyexplained/electricity/delivery-to-consumers.php.

51. *See* IEEE 1547-2018/UL-1741 SB standard inverters.

52. *Ukrainian Solar Plant Partly Resumes Operations after Bombing*, PV Mag. (June 2, 2022), https://www.pv-magazine.com/2022/06/02/ukrainian-solar-plant-partly-resumes-operations-after-bombing/.

53. *Lazard's Levelized Cost of Energy Analysis*, *supra* note 42.

utility service territory, affecting international cash flow and national balance of payments. Today, the United States can supply the natural gas, oil, and coal necessary for fossil fuel generation, which takes advantage of domestic supply chains and internalizes U.S. cash flows.

Assessing cash flows related to renewable energy capital investments: China-based firms control approximately 60 percent of wind turbine production, 70 percent of solar PV panel output, and 70–100 percent of EV battery production (depending upon particular battery chemistry). Approximately 80 percent of the solar panels installed in the United States in recent years were constructed internationally and came from Asian countries Cambodia, Malaysia, Thailand, Vietnam, and China.[54]

Rare Earth Materials Necessary for New Power

Key minerals are required in greater amounts for renewable energy technologies and for power storage than for conventional power generation. Wind power and solar power require much more copper, zinc, manganese, cobalt, and rare earth minerals than conventional fossil fuel and nuclear generation facilities.[55] It is becoming more challenging to find new deposits of copper, nickel, cobalt, and rare earth minerals of any real size in the United States and, even where they are found in U.S. earth, it is very difficult to get their mining expeditiously permitted. This access to and permitted extraction of minerals may exert constraints on a U.S. transition to renewable energy.

Adding enough wind capacity to supply 1 percent of the primary energy used by the world today could require 100,000 or more tons of various rare earth metals, most of which are sourced from China, along with more than

---

54. Int'l Energy Agency, Special Report on Solar PV Global Supply Chains (2022), https://iea.blob.core.windows.net/assets/4eedd256-b3db-4bc6-b5aa-2711ddfc1f90/SpecialReportonSolarPVGlobalSupplyChains.pdf ("Today, China's share in all the manufacturing stages of solar panels (such as polysilicon, ingots, wafers, cells and modules) exceeds 80% . . . . Chinese investments in Malaysia and Viet Nam also made these countries major exporters of PV products, accounting for around 10% and 5% respectively of their trade surpluses since 2017."); *see also* Eric Wesoff, *Major US Solar Manufacturers Call for Strict New Solar-Panel Tariffs*, Canary Media (Apr. 24, 2024), https://www.canarymedia.com/articles/solar/major-us-solar-manufacturers-call-for-strict-new-solar-panel-tariffs#:~:text=And%20shipments%20from%20Southeast%20Asia,analysis%20firm%20S%26P%20Global ("[S]hipments from Southeast Asia are not slowing: Cambodia, Malaysia, Thailand, and Vietnam accounted for 84 percent of U.S. solar panel imports in the fourth quarter of 2023. That's up from 78 percent in the third quarter.").

55. The Role of Critical Minerals in Clean Energy Transitions, *supra* note 28, at 26.

4.5 million tons of copper, primarily sourced from South America.[56] China dominates supply, processing, and refining of strategic metals such as rare earth elements, copper, aluminum, nickel, vanadium, and more.[57]

An International Energy Agency (IEA) study determined that the demand for critical minerals necessary for both expanded renewable power generation technologies and for expansion of transmission lines to move it will require almost 3,000 percent more critical minerals by 2040, while supplies of lithium and nickel must increase by 2040 by 4,000 percent.[58] "A typical electric car requires six times the mineral inputs of a conventional car, and an onshore wind plant requires nine times more mineral resources than a gas-fired power plant" as of 2022, according to the IEA.[59] And the availability of rare earth minerals is separate from significant supply chain problems to obtain and pay for necessary expansion of the transmission grid:

> Buddy Hasten [CEO of the Arkansas Electric Cooperative Corporation, which owns ERMCO Distribution Transformers, one of America's biggest manufacturers of electric transformers] said the supply shortages go beyond distribution transformers and include power transformers, the big machines that you see in substations. "None of those are made in America," said Hasten. Adding more high-voltage transmission, he said, will require "more big transformers. The lead time on those is now two to three years. But we depend on foreign companies for all of those."[60]

---

56. *Id.* at 121 (showing the geographical concentration: analysis of project pipelines indicates that, in most cases, the geographical concentration of production is unlikely to change in the near term).

57. Gabriel Collins & Michelle Michot Foss, *The Global Energy Transition's Looming Valley of Death*, Rice Univ. Baker Inst. (Jan. 27, 2022), https://www.bakerinstitute.org/research/global-energy-transitions-looming-valley-death; *see also* INT'L ENERGY AGENCY, CLEAN ENERGY SUPPLY CHAINS VULNERABILITIES (2023), https://www.iea.org/reports/energy-technology-perspectives-2023/clean-energy-supply-chains-vulnerabilities ("The Democratic Republic of Congo supplies 70% of cobalt today; the People's Republic of China (hereafter 'China') 60% of rare earth elements (REEs); and Indonesia 40% of nickel. Australia accounts for 55% of lithium mining and Chile for 25%. Processing of these minerals is also highly concentrated, with China being responsible for the refining of 90% of REEs and 60–70% of lithium and cobalt.").

58. *See* THE ROLE OF CRITICAL MINERALS IN CLEAN ENERGY TRANSITIONS, *supra* note 28, at 198.

59. *See* Caitlin Purdy & Rodrigo Castillo, *The Future of Mining in Latin America: Critical Minerals and the Global Energy Transition*, BROOKINGS INST. (July 2022), https://perma.cc/779C-HUSB.

60. Robert Bryce, *Untransformed* (Mar. 31, 2023), https://robertbryce.substack.com/p/untransformed.

And in addition to significant supply chain delays amid no U.S. in-country manufacture,

> prices for the hardware needed to deliver electricity to homes and businesses are increasing faster than the price of the juice itself. . . . Transformer manufacturers can't keep up with booming demand and lead times for some transformers are being measured in years. . . . While overall inflation in the U.S. economy was 8% last year, the cost of utility products—a host of items ranging from pole-mounted transformers and copper wire to anchor bolts and wood poles—soared by 18%. And that inflation came on top of the 2021 increase of 14%. Thus, utility product costs have risen by 32%, or more than twice the inflation rate across the U.S. over the past two years.[61]

The business model must factor in U.S. tariff policy, which in the past and currently has imposed added tariff penalties on certain foreign PV panels and other equipment imported into the United States where the exporting country was considered to have engaged in unfair commercial practices in trying to gain and maintain market dominance. In operating under a new business model, it matters whether energy infrastructure investments

- Are front-loaded, as are many renewable energy and energy storage projects
- Are or are not offset by federal incentives or subsidies:
  - Investment Tax Credits
  - Accelerated depreciation
  - Protection from carbon emission surcharges
- Are or are not offset by state incentives:
  - Renewable Portfolio Standard Renewable Energy Credits in 29 states
  - Net metering credits in 39 states
- If imported, occur in a time of inflation or deflation of world currencies and exchange rates of the U.S. dollar against foreign currencies

All of this is analyzed next.

61. *Id.*

Understanding Inflation and Cost of Capital Affecting the Changing Electricity Future

Domestic Energy Inflation Affecting the Business Model Retail Impact on Choice of Technology

The U.S. and world economies recently experienced volatile inflation as well as stagflation. In the United States just in 2022, the sectors of the economy with significant retail price inflation were all energy-related:[62]

Oil (41.5 percent)
Natural gas (19.3 percent)
Electricity (14.3 percent)

It is notable that electricity prices inflated less than fossil fuel prices.[63] To look more deeply into how this affects the electricity business, we can disaggregate energy and electricity inflation. The energy component of the Consumer Price Index (CPI) reflects the retail purchase by consumers of energy (for direct electric needs, space conditioning, transportation, etc.). Often overlooked, the largest component of Core CPI for goods and services *indirectly* includes a significant amount of electricity and other energy inputs—the two largest components of Core CPI are housing, for which construction and construction materials are energy intensive, and healthcare, which now is electricity intensive in the United States. Core CPI increases reflect such volatile energy and commodity price inflation indirectly as an inflationary input to higher goods and services prices.

In the United States from 2019 (prepandemic) to 2022, the commodity and service Core CPI, along with energy and food CPI, show that energy price increases have worked their way indirectly into commodity and service Core CPI inflation beginning in 2021. Energy had a deflationary impact on U.S. CPI in 2019–2020 during the early stages of the COVID pandemic (in 2019, before COVID, crude oil was priced in the $50–$60/barrel range),

---

62. Press Release, U.S. Bureau of Labor Stats., Consumer Price Index—December 2022 (Jan. 12, 2023), https://www.bls.gov/news.release/archives/cpi_01122023.pdf ("The fuel oil index rose 41.5 percent over the last 12 months, the index for electricity rose 14.3 percent, and the index for natural gas increased 19.3 percent over the same period.").

63. *See TED: The Economics Daily—Consumer Price Index: 2022 in Review*, U.S. Bureau of Labor Stat. (Jan. 17, 2023), https://perma.cc/S63M-RPL8.

plunged lower in 2020, recovered, and then moved higher in 2021, exerting a dramatic direct and indirect inflationary impact on CPI in 2021–2022.[64]

Inflation, Interest Rates, Cost of Capital for Power

Cost of capital is a key consideration, and inflation and Federal Reserve policy affecting interest rates matter because they raise the cost of capital. Wind and conventional fixed nontilt solar, while capital cost–intensive, are now generally comparable in capital cost per unit of output to residential rooftop and larger field-mounted solar and less than geothermal, coal, and nuclear power, according to Lazard's capital cost comparison.[65] A low cost of capital helps renewable wind, solar, hydro, and geothermal power technologies, which have a high cost of capital and zero fuel operating costs.

International Energy Inflation Impact

Understanding energy markets and price impacts requires some international context: a Chicago Federal Reserve report compared the *change* in inflation in the 26 most developed OECD countries with which the United States competes. The report breaks down energy, food, and "core" inflation (i.e., everything except food and energy) between May 2019 (pre-pandemic) and three years later, May 2022, when the pandemic had ebbed but inflation was at four-decade highs.[66]

Unlike many European countries, the United States is notable in that core inflation items are responsible for more than half of its acceleration of inflation, while food and energy play a comparatively less significant role in the United States than in other countries. Commodities in world markets, such as food and oil, frequently are priced in U.S. dollars, and those countries importing significant energy supplies priced in U.S. dollars from any other country even if not the United States confront greater perceived energy inflation than do U.S. consumers.[67] The tendency of changing energy prices to

64. *Id.*

65. *Lazard's Levelized Cost of Energy Analysis*, *supra* note 42.

66. *See* Bart Hobijn et al., *Chicago Fed Letter, No. 470: What Is Driving U.S. Inflation amid a Global Inflation Surge?*, Fed. Reserve Bank of Chi. (Aug. 2022), https://perma.cc/4FFU-HQNU.

67. Note that if the dollar weakens, that will incrementally raise prices of any imported energy to the United States, making the task of fighting U.S. inflation more difficult. *Id.* See TradingView, *Currency Strength over the Last Year* (Sept. 28, 2022), https://perma.cc/DG2Q-W78S (tweeting the graph

accelerate or decelerate inflation varies due to differences among countries in intensity of energy consumption. A country that consumes more energy as a share of its total household spending will experience a greater total inflationary impact due to energy price increases.

All goods associated with energy and international trade are a huge segment of the world economy. Significant exogenous factors can and will influence price and costs in the U.S. energy sector. For example, in 2022 after the Ukraine invasion, the price of Russian gas underwent an average inflationary increase of approximately fourfold in Europe and at extreme times as much as eightfold. While Europe is experiencing a significant shortage of natural gas, the United States will not experience this due to its fracking of natural gas increasing domestic supply, even given the significant demand in the United States for natural gas for electric power production.

Here is one illustration of a U.S. impact related to supply balance changes exacerbated by regulatory factors: New England became more dependent on natural gas for electricity generation, and demand in winter months strained the region's decades-old pipeline network. U.S. regions cannot buy liquefied natural gas (LNG) from other parts of the United States because the Jones Act requires that it be transported on U.S.-flagged tankers, which do not exist. When the United States in past years needed to import LNG, it only could be from overseas, for which there is no U.S.-flagging ship requirement under U.S. law. With the fuel shortage in Europe due to limited Russian natural gas imports, the United States and New England would pay rising LNG import prices because of the Jones Act. There now is natural gas pipeline supply to New England from Canada, as well as more domestic fracked natural gas available.

U.S. LNG import facilities are now applying and being repermitted as LNG export facilities to meet recently unsatisfied LNG demand from Europe, Japan, and other parts of the world. The United States is forecast as the country to most increase LNG export between 2021 and 2030 (for

---

with caption). *See also* George Kaloudis, *Sorry, Ether: Sound Money Doesn't Exist and Neither Does "Ultra" Sound Money*, CoinDesk (Oct. 2, 2022), https://perma.cc/49KL-3L4C (arguing that the graph of currency strength throughout 2022 reflects the Dollar Milkshake Theory that "[a]ll debt-based fiat currencies will fall in value over time, but the U.S. dollar—as the world's reserve currency and base of most financial debt—will fall slower than all the others, and all value will accrue to the dollar"). The dollar is "like the straw in the other country's currency milkshake, sucking up capital investment because of its reserve status." *Id.*

more on the influence of natural gas markets, see Chapter 13).[68] This could cause U.S. natural gas prices to increase from trading more in world markets at higher prices. Those higher gas market prices confer a competitive price advantage on certain U.S. renewable electric technologies (see Chapter 2) benefiting from Biden administration tax credits (see Chapter 6) and state renewable electric incentives (see Chapters 8 and 9).

Energy used at the retail level (including purchases of electricity) plays a lesser role in total retail consumer expenditures in the United States than in many of the major OECD countries Energy costs play the absolute smallest role in the relatively low acceleration in Mexico's rate of inflation. The energy supplies of U.S. neighbor countries Mexico and Canada are connected to the United States by pipelines and electric transmission lines, which conduits can be increased in capacity.

Mexico has a stable supply of lower-cost fossil fuel energy and remains one of the largest natural gas and oil producers in the world. It offers less expensive and more abundant fossil fuel energy supply than China.[69] Mexico now boasts the second-cheapest labor costs in the world (behind India and lower than China) and in 2023 surpassed China and Canada to become the top U.S. trading partner, a special position in an evolving business model serving critical energy-intensive manufacturing.[70]

---

68. Int'l Energy Agency, Gas 2020, at 53, https://perma.cc/5LT6-2A5U (graphing LNG imports and exports).

69. The U.S. Energy Information Administration notes that most of China's oil production comes from legacy oil fields that are expensive to maintain. Natural gas can cost 50 percent to 170 percent more in China (https://www.eia.gov/international/analysis/country/CHN) than in Mexico (https://www.eia.gov/international/overview/country/MEX), which is close to the United States and has more stable supply chains to the United States.

70. *See* Luis Torres, *Mexico Seeks to Solidify Rank as Top U.S. Trade Partner, Push Further Past China*, Fed. Reserve Bank of Dall. (July 11, 2023), https://www.dallasfed.org/research/economics/2023/0711; *Comparing Mexico's Industrial Manufacturing Costs to China's: A Shift in Global Production*, NovaLink (May 17, 2024), https://novalinkmx.com/2024/05/17/mexicos-industrial-manufacturing-costs/#:~:text=While%20China%27s%20labor%20costs%20have%20increased%20significantly%20over,savings%20for%20companies%2C%20especially%20those%20in%20labor-intensive%20industries ("While China's labor costs have increased significantly over the years, Mexico's labor costs have remained relatively low. According to a recent study, Mexico's average labor cost per hour is around $4.50, compared to China's $6.50. This cost difference can result in substantial savings for companies, especially those in labor-intensive industries."). *See also Mexico vs. China Manufacturing*, Ivemsa, https://www.ivemsa.com/manufacturing-in-mexico/mexico-vs-china-manufacturing/#:~:text=Labor%20Costs,more%20easily%20predict%20labor%20costs (last visited June 25, 2024) ("For years, wages in China were much lower than Mexico's. Now, Mexico's manufacturing labor costs are 20% lower than in China.").

In terms of supply-chain security, during the COVID pandemic when China shut down major manufacturing centers and entire cities for extended periods, causing world supply chain bottlenecks, Mexico stayed open for business. Moreover, Mexico (and Canada) will be considered as supplying domestic content, necessary to earn higher federal tax credits for energy projects under the Inflation Reduction Act. See Chapter 6.

This could relocate more manufacturing to the American continent, with Mexico offering these advantages and the United States and Canada being the two G7 countries with the most stable electric and fossil fuel energy supplies. The United States has enough oil and gas production to keep energy prices significantly lower, creating an incentive to relocate energy-intensive and electricity-intensive manufacturing to this side of the Atlantic and Pacific Oceans rather than to Europe or China, along with avoiding recent supply-chain bottlenecks. For more on manufacturing options and greater electric power use in the Americas, see Chapter 13.

Business Model Inputs and Impacts

State renewable generation mandates and federal tax credits (see Chapter 6) have added into wholesale power markets renewable generating assets at the lowest cost segment of the wholesale power supply curve—at zero variable cost in terms of daily wholesale power supply bids—making them the winning low bidder and dispatched whenever they generate power when the sun is shining or wind is blowing. This substantially affects modeling future cash flow and operations.

In ISOs, generating unit dispatch occurs in order of lowest price. The simultaneous loss of output and the erosion of prices cause the payments in ISO markets for capacity costs to traditional generation technologies to decline. The recent falling share of conventional fossil-fuel-fired generation is attributable to the rapidly rising output of new renewable power generation facilities being dispatched as an early priority. Modelers at the Electric Power Research Institute forecast these reductions of generation technologies from 2023 forward:[71]

71. John Bestine, Elec. Power Rsch. Inst., Presentation at Resources for the Future, IRA Symposium (Feb. 15, 2023).

- For coal generation, a 60–83 percent decline by 2035
- For natural gas generation, a 46–62 percent decline by 2035, although natural gas capacity remains in place but operates less

This change in power technologies, their rapidly declining prices, and the speed with which modular renewable energy generation can be sited and constructed have changed the electric business model. Similarly, the regulatory environment at the federal level has evolved, and the retail regulatory environment in some states has changed, as discussed later. Stakeholders, distributed generation, and structural composition of the grid have changed. All of this occurs within larger international pressures on climate warming. See Chapter 2.

Capacity Markets and Intermittent New Power

A key characteristic of many renewable energy technologies must be factored into the business model. Wind and fixed panel/nontilt solar power demonstrate a relatively low availability factor of range of hours and capacity during a week or month in which they operate. And those hours of wind and solar power availability are dependent on weather and cannot be adjusted to match the times that the system most needs power to meet consumer demand.

The capacity factor of a generation technology documents what percentage of maximum power generation equipment nameplate rating is realized in operation. Gas-fire combined cycle units are projected to decline in capacity value as they are operated in the future more for load-following and peak-period performance rather than for baseload operation; as more renewable energy is online, its generation profile over the day and season is followed by combined cycle units.[72]

In 40 percent of the U.S. states, capacity is separately compensated through ISO forward capacity market payments apart from actual power generation energy payments. U.S. electricity capacity markets were established to enhance the reliability of the power grid by compensating generators to be available to supply power when needed to meet peak power demand.

72. Todd Schatzki et al., *Pathways Study: Evaluation of Pathways to a Future Grid*, fig. II-1, Analysis Grp. (2022), https://www.iso-ne.com/static-assets/documents/2022/04/schatzki-et-al-pathways-final.pdf.

Capacity markets evolved into complex billion-dollar institutions that provide a substantial revenue stream to qualified electric generation. There is a lack of shared empirical data regarding wind turbine reliability in particular locations during peak hours to earn revenue in capacity markets because wind generation data from existing turbines is considered proprietary and/or business secrets that are not in the public domain. The degree to which new solar or wind power generation projects can earn capacity market payments from PJM, ISO-NE, and other ISOs that provide capacity payments constitutes an increasingly significant revenue stream to be factored into the evolving business model.

With more intermittent power generation serving the grid, markets will need to respond to changes in demand, energy sources, and technologies, resulting in new power dispatch protocols. As distributed solar generation has increased, the magnitude and frequency of voltage fluctuations are more of a problem, increasing maintenance costs and causing earlier replacement of certain equipment.[73] When solar PV output into a distribution line exceeds the instantaneous load on that line, power backflows between the low-voltage and medium-voltage lines can occur, causing reliability problems.[74] There can be stability issues caused by technology changes when PV inverters trip off because of grid voltage or frequency fluctuations.[75]

Grid modifications, upgraded circuits and transformers, and expansion of the transmission and distribution infrastructure will be necessary to accommodate the influx of intermittent renewable generation. These technology and operational changes create both different costs and changing revenues. In that one-third of the U.S. electric market not featuring traditional exclusive supply by regulated utilities operating pursuant to traditional state regulatory recovery of all reasonable expenses, these changing costs are borne by IPP and Qualifying Facility independent generation entities.

Changes to Accommodate Electricity Storage Technology

Amid all these changes, what has *not* changed is electricity itself: electric circuits are the physical means for conveying power to different places served by transmission and distribution lines.[76] Electricity is identical in every

73. Rickerson et al., *supra* note 39, at 52.
74. *Id.* at 53–54.
75. *Id.* at 54.
76. Hugh D. Young & Roger A. Freedman, University Physics 799 (9th ed. 1996).

state at every moment: an energy field transmitted as alternating current at 60 hertz or cycles per second.

However, unlike all other forms of energy including natural gas, coal, oil, and wood, the moving electrons cannot be efficiently stored as electricity for more than a few seconds before they are lost as waste heat. Therefore, the supply of electricity must match the demand for it over the centralized utility grid on an instantaneous, constant, real-time, and ongoing basis, or else the electric system shuts down or expensive equipment is damaged. See Chapter 14. Either too much or too little power causes system instability and can damage equipment on a second-by-second basis.

Storage of electricity has been the missing link in the traditional electric sector business model. Surplus solar electricity generated during midday hours when demand is not at peak can be stored in batteries not as electricity but instead converted to chemical energy, or electricity can be converted to compressed air or other forms. The storage system then discharges the stored power during peak demand times, earning higher locational marginal prices.[77]

Surplus electric power storage creates a double benefit. First, it arbitrages the provision of storable power to higher-demand times of day at more remunerative prices. Second, storage avoids another significant potential loss. During periods when consumer power loads are low, without storage the surplus solar power will be curtailed by the grid operator or balancing authority. Simply stated: curtailment is an order to not supply to the grid surplus intermittent solar PV or wind power; there is no compensation for any power supplied during such a period.

In practice this results in solar and wind power experiencing a negative price for their output when generators must pay other systems to take their power or disconnect from the grid so that distributed power remains off the grid. It is forecast that curtailment for New England with the projected amounts of solar and wind to satisfy New England states' clean energy laws between 2027 and 2031 could be as much as 2 TWh of solar power on a given day. This means that without storage, this 2 TWh will not be purchased and may have negative value, causing the renewable generator to pay for putting power into the grid from normal operations. In a three-month period in 2014, the California Integrated System Operator, CAISO, was required to curtail wind and solar generation in four instances for six hours to

77. Schatzki et al., *supra* note 71, at fig. V-9.

balance supply and demand on the system, curtailing 485 MW of wind and 657 MW of solar.[78]

When there is demand for power, ISO-NE requires the lowest marginal cost of power generation—wind, solar, and hydro power—to be the first dispatched and purchased at lowest cost. Energy storage single-handedly changes any negative-value result: since the New England system's peak demand is in the evening hours, storage not only retains the power for when it is needed and will be accepted by the system, but also arbitrages the power to earn premium-time value revenue.

Importantly, 39 states allow net metering of renewable distributed power. See Chapter 9. Net metering forces the utility to provide generous financial credit value for renewable power when it is surplus and flows to the utility, whether or not the utility wants that power at that time. The utility does not necessarily store this net metered power (although it could if it has utility-scale storage facilities); rather, it curtails its other power supply in order to retail the net metered power that enters its system from dispersed distributed sources. Costs of net metering subsidies are passed on in higher distribution rates to all its customers. This option to net meter surplus solar power in 39 states rather than have it curtailed becomes a key factor in the business model and can become a contentious state issue as policies evolve.

One size does not fit all: storage is technology specific. There is no means to store electricity per se.[79] Instead, storage converts electricity into chemical energy in batteries, physical energy potential as compressed air, greater reservoir capacity in hydroelectric pumped storage facilities, kinetic physical energy in flywheels, or thermal energy. Pumped-storage hydroelectric power stations are by far the most common form of energy storage currently in use. In the United States, there are 40 such projects accounting for 22 GW, or approximately 2.2 percent of U.S. net summer power capacity.

Lithium-ion batteries can provide energy storage for slightly more than $30 per MWh, amortized over their full-service life (assuming 6,000 discharge/recharge cycles per battery). At present, most grid-based lithium-ion batteries can only provide approximately four hours of warrantied discharge. Much larger iron-air batteries can store and then discharge power for as long as 100 hours, giving utilities four days of electricity to bridge renewable

78. *Id.*
79. *Id.*

power gaps that can occur in U.S. grids. Energy storage carries electricity through time, as transmission lines carry it through space—without these technologies, electricity must be used instantly when generated.

One final note as we exit this discussion of technology: a move to renewable power technologies maintains links to fossil fuels. Oil and gas form the physical building blocks of the materials for wind turbines and solar panels. Wind turbines would not exist without use of fiberglass and thermoset plastics made from fossil fuels. Solar PVs utilize Plexiglas made from fossil fuels. EVs utilize many kilograms of plastic and other petroleum-derived materials.[80]

Electric technology is changing. Because electric power is the most regulated sector of the U.S. economy, anticipating the effect of regulatory changes is at least as important as technology change and its impacts in the evolving U.S. electric business model. The next chapter examines changing federal and state energy regulatory orders and legal decisions within which the electric sector business model must operate to stay in front of the wave of power sector regulatory change.

---

80. Michelle Michot Foss, *The "Criticality" of Minerals for Energy Transitions. Hydrocarbons? Yes, Hydrocarbons*, RICE UNIV. BAKER INST. (Feb. 8, 2021), https://www.bakerinstitute.org/research/the-criticality-of-minerals-for-energy-transitions-hydrocarbons-yes-hydrocarbons/.

CHAPTER 13

Repowered Law and the New Business Model

Regulatory Changes Altering the Business Model

With plans now for electrification of the entire economy, deep decarbonization incorporates

- Major transformation in how the grid is managed by regulatory agencies
- Much more electric generation—With the Inflation Reduction Act and Infrastructure Investment and Jobs Act in place, the role of electricity is modeled to more than double or triple rapidly from approximately 17.5 percent of primary energy use to 40–50 percent of all energy use.[1]
- A larger increase (even larger than for generation) in electric generation *capacity* for various grids
  - with locational differences
  - with different internal sources of zero-carbon generation
- Much more transmission capacity to move power across ISOs, RTOs, and regions
- Long-term storage capacity for power

1. Electric power now is 12.9 quadrillion Btu/year of a total U.S. energy production of 73.5 quadrillion Btu/year. *See U.S. Energy Facts Explained*, U.S. Energy Info. Admin. (Aug. 16, 2023), https://www.eia.gov/energyexplained/us-energy-facts.

The Inflation Reduction Act of 2022 and the Infrastructure Investment and Jobs Act of 2021 Changes and Incentives

A new investment of almost half a trillion U.S. federal dollars approved by Congress through tax incentives and grants now changes the financial structure and incentives within the electric business model. The Biden administration and Congress recently enacted two unprecedented new federal laws that will accelerate changing the electric power sector and its business opportunities. The Inflation Reduction Act of 2022 (IRA) and the Infrastructure Investment and Jobs Act of 2021 (IIJA) together represent historic investments in the nation's energy system totaling more than $430 billion.[2] Electric capacity additions are forecast to be two times current levels, half comprised of nuclear and half of renewable energy, according to Electric Power Research Institute (EPRI) modeling.[3] Recent forecasts by EPRI and the Environmental Protection Agency (EPA) are for power sector CO_2 emissions to decline

- 75–79 percent by 2035[4]
- 80 percent by 2040[5]

The U.S. Department of Energy (DOE)'s preliminary assessment found that the IRA can help drive 2030 economy-wide emissions of carbon to 40 percent below 2005 levels.[6] This requires a rapid deployment of renewable and zero-carbon power generation. The DOE estimates that the clean energy provisions of the IRA combined with the IIJA could reduce greenhouse gas (GHG) emissions by approximately 1,000 million metric tons (MMT) (a gigaton). These and other climate and energy provisions of the laws raise the DOE-estimated total annual carbon reduction to nearly 1,150 MMT by 2030, which is equivalent to the combined annual carbon

2. *See* U.S. Dep't of Energy Off. of Pol'y, *The Inflation Reduction Act Drives Significant Emissions Reductions and Positions America to Reach Our Climate Goals* 3 (Aug. 2022), https://www.energy.gov/sites/default/files/2022-08/8.18%20InflationReductionAct_Factsheet_Final.pdf [https://perma.cc/37T4-JEM9].

3. John Bestine, Elec. Power Rsch. Inst., Presentation at Resources for the Future, IRA Symposium (Feb. 15, 2023).

4. *Id.*

5. Cara Marcy, Env't Prot. Agency, Presentation at Resources for the Future, IRA Symposium (Feb. 15, 2023).

6. U.S. Dep't of Energy Off. of Pol'y, *supra* note 2.

emissions from all U.S. homes.[7] The critical path state transmission barriers analyzed in Chapter 11 could delay or frustrate these goals.

The Key Focus: Electric Power

The DOE estimates that approximately two-thirds of the carbon sector reductions incentivized by the IRA and the IIJA will occur in the electric power sector, dwarfing all reductions made in the transportation, building space heating, industrial, and other sectors combined, as shown in Figure 13.1.[8] In context, while the power sector is responsible for a bit more than one-quarter of U.S. GHG emissions, a figure that has declined recently, these new federal laws are targeting the electric sector to shoulder a disproportionate two-thirds of the reductions in carbon emissions to 2030; Resources for the Future forecasts that the electric power sector will shoulder even more—75 percent—of U.S. carbon reduction.[9]

Figure 13.1[10]

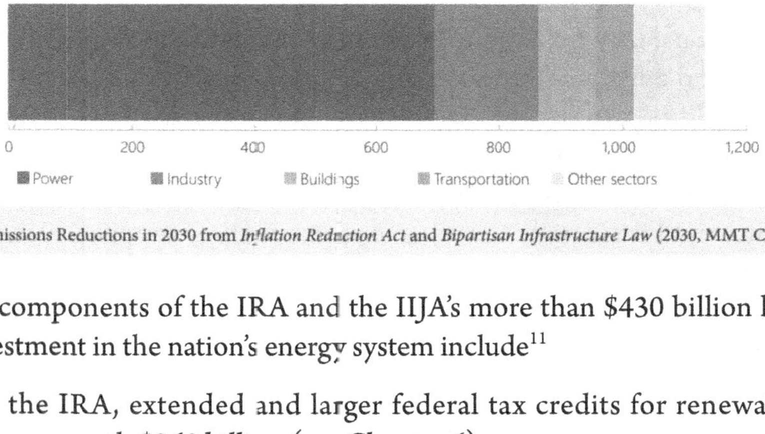

Estimated Emissions Reductions in 2030 from *Inflation Reduction Act* and *Bipartisan Infrastructure Law* (2030, MMT CO_2e)

The components of the IRA and the IIJA's more than $430 billion historic investment in the nation's energy system include[11]

- In the IRA, extended and larger federal tax credits for renewable energy worth $369 billion (see Chapter 6)
- In the IRA, a $5.8 billion Advanced Industrial Facilities Deployment Program subsidizing facilities to use advanced industrial technologies, including distributed cogeneration

7. *Id.*

8. *Id.*

9. RFF Live, *Inflation Reduction Act of 2022: Modeling Major Climate and Energy Provisions*, YOU TUBE (Aug. 12, 2022), https://www.youtube.com/watch?v=9G1kTm_1GVI.

10. U.S. Dep't of Energy Off. of Pol'y, *supra* note 2.

11. *Id.*

- In the IIJA, $3.5 billion in continued Weatherization Assistance Program funding for low-income renters and owners, Energy Efficiency and Conservation Block Grant Program, State Energy Program, money for efficiency loan funds, and Efficiency and Renewable Energy Grants for public schools, most of which programs support the electrification of buildings to supply all energy services
- In the IRA, $21 billion for climate-smart farms and ranches to make their operations more efficient, which can include methane recapture/use and self-generation of power[12]
- In the IRA, $3 billion for Climate Justice Block Grants and $27 billion for Greenhouse Gas Reduction for projects supporting communities with disproportionate energy burdens and pollution exposure—this includes $4 billion for Advanced Energy Project Credits directed to industrial or manufacturing facilities located in these communities and more than $10 billion for rural electric cooperatives to deploy low-carbon electricity[13]

See Chapter 6 for a more detailed analysis of the $369 billion of IRA tax credits and other provisions affecting the electric power sector.

In addition to the tax credits and grants extended in the IRA and the IIJA, the 2005 Energy Policy Act allowed municipalities to issue so-called socially responsible environmental, social, and governance (ESG)–certified tax-exempt bonds used to prepay for future energy supply, which could be deemed solar, wind, natural gas, or other power. Worldwide, in 2021 there were $481 billion in green bonds sold, some of which U.S. cities used to prepay for 30 years of renewable electricity or other energy (at a discount for this advance payment). ESG bond investments totaled $2.2 trillion in 2015, quadrupled in amount to $9.4 trillion in 2020, and almost doubled again in 2021 to $18.4 trillion.[14] This doubling rate resembles Moore's Law.

12. *Id.*

13. *Id.*

14. Christopher Helman & Matt Schifrin, *How Wall Street Banks Will Reap Billions from Tax-Free Renewable Energy Bonds*, Forbes (Dec. 7, 2022), https://www.forbes.com/sites/christopherhelman/2022/12/07/big-wall-street-banks-will-reap-billions-from-renewable-energy-bonds/?ss=energy&sh=11fd1e7977a1&sh=645ae9d677a1.

Recent Environmental Law Changes and Power Risks

After the *West Virginia v. EPA* Supreme Court decision in 2022, EPA promulgated a final rule in 2024 that could force the closure of every coal-fired power plant in the United States as well as most of the natural gas plants if each cannot cut its emissions by 90 percent between 2035 and 2040.[15] At the same time, the demand for electricity will skyrocket: the Biden administration proposed strict new automobile tailpipe pollution limits that require at least 54 percent of new vehicles sold in the United States by 2030 to be electric and as many as two-thirds of those vehicles to be electric by 2032.[16] In December 2022, the North American Electric Reliability Corporation (NERC), the nonprofit entity that advises regional grid operators about the reliability of the bulk power system, released a report that found that much of North America is at "elevated" or "high" risk of electricity shortfalls during extreme weather.[17]

In 2023, PJM, the largest regional transmission operator in 13 states in the northeastern United States, issued a report that found that several trends, including early retirements of coal plants, "present increasing reliability risks during the transition, due to a potential timing mismatch between resource retirements, load growth and the pace of new generation entry under a possible 'low new entry' scenario:"[18]

- The growth rate of electricity demand is likely to continue to increase from electrification coupled with the proliferation of high-demand data centers in the region.
- Thermal generators are retiring at a rapid pace due to government and private sector policies as well as economics.

15. *See* Robert Bryce, *Fire Sale* (July 24, 2023), https://robertbryce.substack.com/p/fire-sale; https://eelp.law.harvard.edu/2024/04/timelines-of-epas-final-rules-to-reduce-climate-changing-pollution-from-power-plants/#:~:text=Today%20the%20Biden%20administration%20released,operating%20the%20plant%20with%20CCS.

16. Tom Krisher & Matthew Daly, *AP Sources: EPA Car Rule to Push Huge Increase in EV Sales*, AP (Apr. 10, 2023), https://apnews.com/article/biden-electric-vehicles-epa-tailpipe-emissions-31bf8104f44d81b988249483f1a79117.

17. N. Am. Elec. Reliability Corp., 2022 Long-Term Reliability Assessment, https://www.nerc.com/pa/RAPA/ra/Reliability%20Assessments%20DL/NERC_LTRA_2022.pdf.

18. PJM, Energy Transition in PJM: Resource Retirements, Replacements, and Risks 1 (2023), https://www.pjm.com/-/media/library/reports-notices/special-reports/2023/energy-transition-in-pjm-resource-retirements-replacements-and-risks.ashx.

- Retirements are at risk of outpacing the construction of new resources, due to a combination of industry forces, including siting and supply chain, whose long-term impacts are not fully known.
- PJM's interconnection queue is composed primarily of intermittent and limited-duration resources. Given the operating characteristics of these resources, we need multiple megawatts of these resources to replace 1 MW of thermal generation."

The national transmission regulator, FERC; the regional ISOs such as PJM; and the national grid reliability agency, NERC, all are warning publicly of troubles ahead with the critically important U.S. electric grid.

State Partial Competitive Retail *De*regulation of Power

While ownership of most power distribution lines by geographically monopolized regulated utilities is still the norm, the electric power industry has moved in the opposite direction. There are now more stakeholders performing different tasks and services in the electric power industry than at any other time since electricity was first harnessed by Thomas Edison 145 years ago; many cities in the United States only have had electric service during the last 100 years.

The Changing Checkerboard, Stakeholders, Assets in Deregulated U.S. Electric Markets

Restructuring and deregulation of the retail electric power sector in one-third of the U.S. states now dramatically change the regulatory model for electric energy. Competition and deregulation of retail power sales were adopted partially or fully in 18 states, beginning in 1997 in Massachusetts and Rhode Island and then spreading to 13 states and the District of Columbia, as well as five other states partially (see Figure 13.2). For context, 19 U.S. states restructured prior to the electric sector deregulation debacle in California in 2000–2001, whereafter a half dozen states near California reversed course and returned to maintaining their regulated retail electric system models. See Chapter 14 for more analysis of these changes. Now, approximately two-thirds of the states retain traditionally structured geographic monopoly utility retail electric franchises.

Figure 13.2[19] Retail Electric Choice in U.S. States

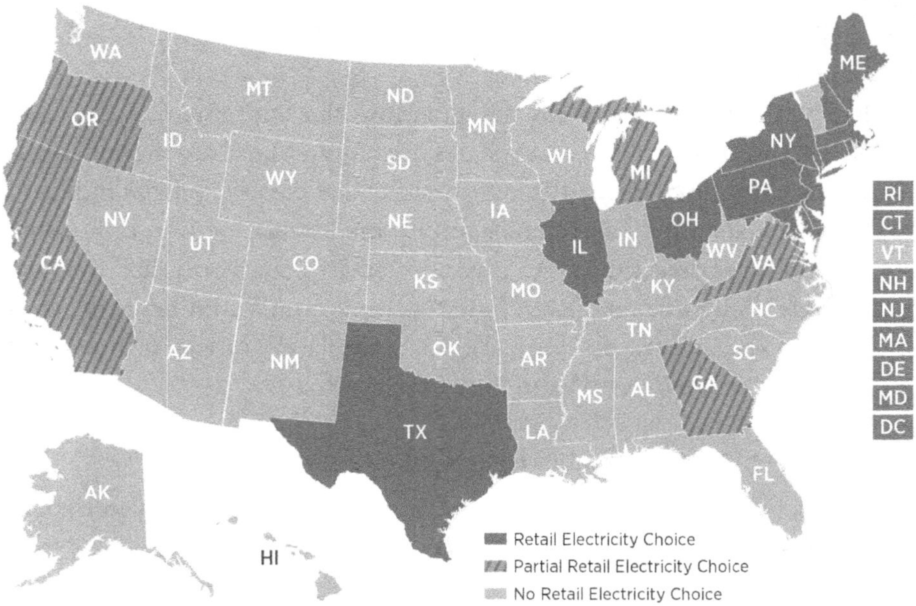

The approximately one-third of states with partially deregulated retail power includes every one of the most populated states except Florida, so the number of consumers with retail power choice is significant. Typically, full deregulation allows retail electric sales to be made by any party, including brokers, marketers, consumers, and independent power producers (IPPs), to any retail customers. While these unregulated entities include Qualifying Facilities (QFs) under PURPA (see Chapter 5), small QFs can experience difficulty competing against much larger IPPs in competitive markets. Who can compete, where, and how is distinct in each of the deregulated states, which elevates these regulatory state differences to render different opportunities and business risks in each state.

In a significant subset of the 18 states with totally or partially deregulated retail power, this deregulation also was accompanied by the state utility regulatory commissions causing their regulated monopoly electric utilities to sell

19. *Power Market Structure*, U.S. ENV'T PROT. AGENCY (Jan. 15, 2024), https://www.epa.gov/green-power-markets/power-market-structure.

their electric generation units to IPPs to spur more competition in power generation.[20] Thereafter, now since 2004, more new electric power generation facility capacity is constructed each year by IPP competing "merchant" companies than by regulated utilities.[21]

Reflecting these moves for deregulation, the Supreme Court noted, "Over the past few decades, many states, including Maryland, have deregulated their energy markets," utilities "purchase that electricity from independent power generators," and the electricity market has evolved to become a more "competitive interstate business and FERC's role has evolved accordingly."[22] Significant changes are resulting from a 21st-century set of major alterations in state and federal electric regulatory orders, technologies of choice, and stakeholder roles in the electric sector.

State Regulatory Enhancement of Business Cash Flow

The states have undertaken significant renewable energy policy initiatives in the past two decades, promoting sustainable energy policy using five legal and policy incentives:

- Net metering: in 80 percent of states—see Chapter 9
- Renewable Portfolio Standards (RPSs): in 65 percent of states—see Chapter 8
- Renewable System Benefit Charges: in 33 percent of states—see Chapter 3
- Carbon and GHG regulation: in 20 percent of the states—see Chapter 2
- Feed-in tariffs: in less than 10 percent of states—see Chapter 8. Of note: it is not legal for states to require regulated utilities to pay more

20. U.S. Energy Info. Admin., The Changing Structure of the Electric Power Industry 2000: An Update 106, https://grist.org/wp-content/uploads/2010/02/update2000.pdf.

21. "In the 1970s, vertically integrated utility companies (investor-owned, municipal, or cooperative) controlled over 95 percent of the electric generation in the United States. . . . [B]y 2004 electric utilities owned less than 60 percent of electric generating capacity. Increasingly, decisions affecting retail customers and electricity rates are split among federal, state, and new private, regional entities." Elec. Energy Mkt. Competition Task Force, Report to Congress on Competition in Wholesale and Retail Markets for Electric Energy 10 (2007), https://www.ftc.gov/sites/default/files/documents/reports/electric-energy-market-competition-task-force-report-congress-competition-wholesale-and-retail/epact-final-rpt.pdf.

22. Hughes v. Talen Energy Mktg., LLC, 136 S. Ct. 1288 (2016).

for wholesale renewable power than the PURPA Avoided Cost established pursuant to preemptive federal law (see Chapter 5).

Each of these state policies is a powerful stimulant to renewable energy deployment: each provides an additional financial inflow at the point of either project construction or generation of renewable electric power. For the evolving electric power business model, one must understand how each of these incentives operates, what stakeholders or what technologies qualify, for how long a period for additional cash flow, which options are mutually exclusive, the comparative advantages of each option, which are guaranteed as of right or can later be changed or terminated, which are embedded in statute and thus only changeable by the legislature, which are in agency regulations that can be unilaterally changed, and which are subject to termination through "sunset" provisions at a particular point in time. See Chapters 8 and 9.

Omitting Fuel Inputs

In addition to additional cash flow inputs, renewable technologies do not incur a key cost in the energy business model: the volatile cost of external fuel supply for power generation is not a factor for solar or wind power, the two renewable generation technologies increasing most rapidly now in the United States. For an example of recent fuel volatility, after the 2022 invasion of Ukraine stressed fossil fuel markets, the U.S. forward price of natural gas quickly tripled in mid-2022 to $9.00/MMBtu, after years in the vicinity of $3.00/MMBtu, and then decreased $4.00/MMBtu in one month from early June to early July 2022; during the same period, crude oil escalated to over $120 per barrel and then dropped dramatically.

Natural gas is linked to U.S. electric power: the largest share of natural gas consumption in the United States is no longer used for building space heating but for electric power production and has increased (37 percent) during the 21st century. U.S. natural gas production rose every year from 2005 until 2016, as prices declined.[23] For more on natural gas and liquefied natural gas markets affecting the future of electricity, see Chapter 12, "International Energy Inflation Impact."

23. *Natural Gas Explained: Use of Natural Gas*, U.S. Energy Info. Admin. (Apr. 28, 2023), https://www.eia.gov/energyexplained/natural-gas/use-of-natural-gas.php.

Fuel supply and price volatility are circumvented by most renewable energy power technologies, which capture only free insolation or wind. This changes risk parameters and inputs in the business model. There remain siting issues regarding all power generation technologies (see Chapter 10 regarding renewable technologies' much larger need for land per kWh generated and some barriers). Concerns have been expressed that state retail deregulation allowing competitive generation and subsidies for specific modular renewable technologies could usher in a new industry architecture, ultimately supplanting the centralized utility grid with a new decentralized, cellular topology.[24] Some commenters forecast that utilities could become more like phone companies in a new era of total competition:[25]

> As a result of these trends, PV [photovoltaic] could act as a disruptive technology that challenges the incumbent players in its industry. Many analysts have forecasted that the centralized utility model that has served most of the world for over 100 years could give way to new business operating paradigms.[26]

However, there is an important distinction to note: unlike phone communication now not needing traditional phone lines, today the electric utility grid remains essential, and there remains only one set of utility transmission and distribution lines. There is a prediction that the new utility business model will focus on outputs rather than inputs.[27] Under some hypothesized new business models, utilities would become neutral managers of grid infrastructure, brokers of new customer relationships, partners with service providers, or financiers of infrastructure. A study for the International Energy Agency forecasts a new era of "prosumers"[28] who will develop their own distributed PV solar power on site to cause a decentralized electric supply

---

24. Michael T. Burr, *Microgrid Milestones*, Pub. Utils. Fort. (Dec. 19, 2013), http://spark.fortnightly.com/fortnightly/microgrid-milestones.

25. Ronald L. Lehr, *New Utility Business Models: Utility and Regulatory Models for the Modern Era*, 26 Elec. J. 35, 40 (2013).

26. Wilson Rickerson et al., Int'l Energy Agency–Renewable Energy Tech. Deployment, Residential Prosumers: Drivers and Policy Options (Re-Prosumers) 12 (2014).

27. Lehr, *supra* note 25, at 50. Inputs are easily quantifiable in the form of costs of utility operation; outputs are more subjective elements.

28. Rickerson et al., *supra* note 26, at 13.

internationally and "revolutionize the utility sector just as personal computers and cell phones changed their respective industries."[29] Time will tell.

Independent "Merchant" Owners and Distributed Generation

The source and ownership of power generation assets are changing rapidly. Today, the global market for distributed generation is projected to reach $183.2 billion by 2025.[30] Some estimates are that there will be 1,182 GW of distributed generation operating in 2030.[31] This would represent approximately 10 percent of global installed power generation.[32] As regulatory markets in the United States have changed, baseload nuclear, coal, and gas-fired generation resources recently have struggled to recover their long-term capital and operating costs in a more competitive market. Independent "merchant" and traditional generators of fossil-fuel-fired electric power have been challenged with

- Recent relatively flat demand for electricity
- Federal and state regulatory policies promoting and increasing renewable generation featuring zero variable cost of operation given free access to renewable sun and wind
- Crimped financial returns in both the electric capacity and energy markets for merchant-owned, rather than utility-owned, fossil-fuel-fired power plants
- The IRA extension of the federal Production Tax Credit and Investment Tax Credit to benefit new renewable power generation (see Chapter 6)
- State-level RPSs, clean peak standards, or zero-emission credit programs, as well as carbon emission credit charges to fossil-fuel-fired carbon-emitting electric generation plants operating in the RGGI states and in PJM and ISO-NE in the eastern United States (see Chapters 2 and 8)

---

29. *Id.* at 5.

30. *See* Press Release, GlobeNewswire, The Global Market for Distributed Generation (DG) Is Projected to Reach US$183.2 Billion by 2025 (Nov. 4, 2020), https://www.globenewswire.com/news-release/2020/11/04/2119743/0/en/The-global-market-for-Distributed-Generation-DG-is-projected-to-reach-US-183-2-billion-by-2025.html.

31. *Id.*

32. *See id.*

Lawyers Confront the Critical Path Transmission Obstacle

Transmission interconnection recently has been elevated to be the critical path barrier to new distributed power. There could be an average four-year wait for additional National Environmental Policy Act Environmental Impact Statement compliance, as well as a multilayered multiyear wait while transmissions providers/utilities conduct studies on the impacts of individual interconnection requests for distributed power resources and any transmission upgrades they necessitate.

FERC recently promulgated its final Order No. 2023, attempting to streamline and accelerate the processing of interconnection requests. Through the dissemination of information and the geographic clustering of interconnection needs of multiple projects, FERC opens an important window for lawyers and stakeholders in the energy and land-use sectors. Pursuant to Order No. 2023, transmission providers must conduct one cluster study of transmission infrastructure per year. In Order No. 2023, FERC dispenses with the prior first stage of "Feasibility Studies" as part of an interconnection application and instead requires transmission operators to provide accessible, updated "heat maps" that show graphically where there is transmission system congestion that would require system upgrades to accommodate more power generation using the grid.

Order No. 2023 also encourages renewable power generation and energy storage resources to be developed on or near a common site, which could share a single interconnection point on the grid, whereby proximate energy storage could substitute for network upgrades. The order dispenses with the requirement for a 60-day material modification determination and creates a new exception for transmission providers that operate pursuant to fuel-based dispatch orders. A more informed, initiative-oriented, and proactive role for lawyers/stakeholders utilizes these additional tools accessing this critical path transmission interconnection obstacle.

Wholesale versus Retail Power Transactions

Electric power trading and transactions have changed. An increasingly larger share of U.S. power now proceeds through a wholesale power sale prior to its ultimate retail sale and consumption by consumers.[33] This extra transaction creates a wholesale sale that is not subject to any state regulation, controlled

33. *See* ELEC. ENERGY MKT. COMPETITION TASK FORCE, *supra* note 21.

by FERC at the federal level, and state regulators must incorporate federal decisions in their retail rates pursuant to the Filed Rate Doctrine (respecting the supremacy of federal regulation over state regulation), which Supreme Court decisions have enforced.

The utility system is changing, especially the following aspects:

- *Utility corporate goals*: 75 percent of U.S. electric customer accounts are served by either utilities boasting 100 percent carbon-reduction targets at the retail level or a retail utility subsidiary owned by a parent company with a 100 percent carbon-reduction target.[34]
- *Absolute amounts*: Zero-carbon sources produced twice as much U.S. power as did burning coal.[35]
- *Trends between 2015 and 2020*: Zero-carbon electricity generation grew by approximately 20 percent; coal-fired electricity generation declined by nearly 40 percent.[36]
- *States*: There are 22 states that have goals to achieve 100 percent clean energy use in their states in the next 25 years.[37] Such goals cover all centrally supplied power and distributed power generated on the consumer side of retail electric meters.

An increasing percentage of consumers will generate their own "distributed" power by either owning or renting generation assets, such as rooftop solar panels. Solar power generation enjoys comparatively quick construction time of only one to nine months, depending on the size of the facility. Depending on how a given state permits and/or regulates distributed power, it has the potential to provide benefits for both the power system and the consumer:

- The generator/consumer avoids all transmission, distribution, energy commodity, system benefit charge, and tax costs in the retail bill for the amount self-generated.

---

34. *Utility Carbon-Reduction Tracker: Utilities' Path to a Carbon-Free Energy System*, Smart Elec. Power All., https://sepapower.org/utility-transformation-challenge/utility-carbon-reduction-tracker/ (last visited May 17, 2024).

35. U.S. Energy Info. Admin., October 2022 Monthly Energy Review fig. 7.2, https://www.eia.gov/totalenergy/data/monthly/archive/00352210.pdf.

36. *Id.*

37. *Guide to 100% Clean Energy States*, Clean Energy States All., https://www.cesa.org/projects/100-clean-energy-collaborative/guide/ (last visited May 17, 2024).

- The generator can receive cross-subsidies in the form of RPS RECs, net metering credit value, system benefit charges, and carbon credits. See Chapters 8 and 9.
- Having more independent points of generation of electric supply increases power system diversity and reliability.[38]
- Utilizing on-site private power puts less pressure on an aging power distribution system than moving more power through it.[39]

Altering Regulatory "Grip"

These significant developments in power sector competition, replacing monopoly, change the business model, loosening the "grip" of certain regulators over the power system. For example, in the traditionally regulated states, regulators can compel or induce utilities to build additional generating capacity at any point, the costs of which can be passed on to consumers. In those states with deregulated retail sales and competition in power generation, regulators have no direct means to control or require any IPPs or independent generators to supply power or to build additional generating capacity. The costs of any overbuilding are incurred by the independent owners of the generation, not utility ratepayers, who are no longer a captive customer base.

Increased Power of ISOs and RTOs Operating under Different FERC Orders

Just as states have different electric sector regulations that affect the final product, subsidies, and rules, location matters when modeling evolving regulatory factors. FERC encourages distribution utilities to form and join independent system operators (ISOs) to coordinate wholesale power supply and regional distribution activities. It matters which regional transmission organization (RTO) or ISO one operates in geographically in changing power markets. Regional ISOs and RTOs are not state creations: they are quasi-public/

38. *See Distributed Energy Basics*, U.S. Nat'l Renewable Energy Lab'y. For more on engineering reliability of a changing grid, see National Academy of Engineering, https://www.nae.edu.

39. *Distributed Energy Resources*, ACEEE, https://www.aceee.org/topic/distributed-energy-resources#:~:text=Distributed%20energy%20resources%20can%20lead,risk%20of%20brownouts%20and%20blackouts (last visited June 25, 2024) ("Distributed energy resources can lead to a more reliable and resilient grid. Generation, demand response, and energy efficiency can all provide capacity during system peaks, reducing the risk of brownouts and blackouts.").

private entities. Their task is to manage wholesale transactions and power transmission, and they are federally regulated by FERC.

There are ISOs regulating wholesale power sales of utilities in all or part of 31 states and RTOs covering utility wholesale transactions in all or part of seven states in addition to those in which at least some utilities are also ISO-regulated. Figure 13.3 displays these. Each of these ISOs and RTOs is unique, operating under distinct FERC tariffs and orders individually submitted and FERC-approved in response to various FERC rules.

Figure 13.3[40] U.S. ISOs and RTOs

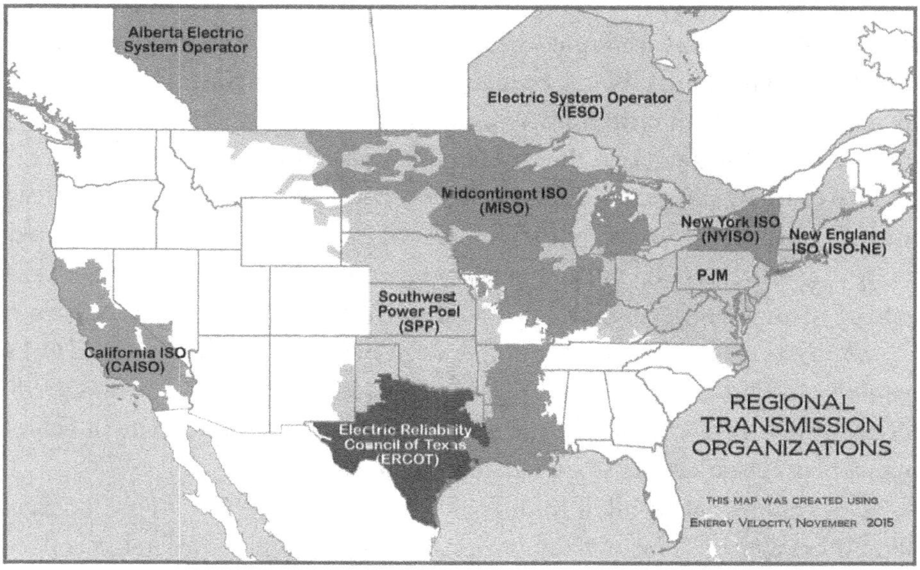

In deregulated U.S. states, power supply comes, goes, and operates by market forces. Each of seven different ISOs and RTOs across the United States administers the electric grid as well as the nondiscriminatory competitive operation of wholesale electricity markets.[41] Each RTO/ISO differently establishes participation models for electric resources and requirements for providing services to the grid, as individually approved in separate FERC

40. *Power Market Structure*, U.S. Env't Prot. Agency (Jan. 15, 2024), https://www.epa.gov/green-power-markets/power-market-structure.

41. *RTOs and ISOs*, Fed. Energy Regul. Comm'n (Jan. 17, 2024), https://www.ferc.gov/power-sales-and-markets/rtos-and-isos.

orders.[42] While all regions provide access to wholesale electricity markets for generators, customer demand response entities, and retail load serving entities, the variance in RTO/ISO participation models places different obligations on stakeholders today.[43]

As a recent example of similar rules but different ISO/RTO outcomes and factors: FERC Order No. 2222 (2020) required *all* ISOs and RTOs to allow aggregators of wholesale power to participate in wholesale power markets. Previously, FERC Order No. 841 (see "FERC Federal Orders on Storage") had required *all* ISOs and RTOs to allow electric power storage resources to participate in wholesale power markets. In 2021, NERC, the U.S. agency responsible for electric-grid reliability, expressed concern that the shift to increased renewable energy resources had the potential to threaten grid reliability. When challenged, FERC Order No. 841 was upheld by the D.C. Circuit as within FERC's authority.[44]

However, the devil is in the details: and in each ISO and RTO the operational details are different. FERC Order No. 2222 proposed eleven directives for ISOs and RTOs to utilize to break down barriers to smaller distributed energy resource (DER) participants from participating in an aggregate collective format. In certain situations, distribution system operators have the ability to override transmission system orders. Each ISO and RTO in response to Order No. 2222 submitted and had approved a significantly different system allowing distributed power aggregators to participate in evolving wholesale markets, as shown in Table 13.1.

Decoding what resulted in different ISOs/RTOs: FERC required that all of these aggregations must be no smaller than 100 kW after being collectively assembled. The four ISOs' maximum aggregation size varies from 1 to 20 MW. Neither RTO imposed a maximum size limit. Each ISO and RTO could decide in its submission to FERC whether to allow only a single node of interconnection by any particular applicant aggregator or to allow multiple nodes of interconnection of small DERs by an aggregator to be treated as an individual entity. The latter option allows a business to assemble strategically more resources to both satisfy the FERC-ordered 100 kW minimum size and not exceed each authority's maximum aggregated size limit.

---

42. Electric Storage Participation in Markets Operated by Regional Transmission Organizations and Independent System Operators, Notice of Proposed Rulemaking, FERC, Docket No. RM16-23-000, at 2 (Nov. 17, 2016).

43. *Id.*

44. NARUC v. FERC, 964 F.3d 1177 (D.C. Cir. 2020).

Table 13.1 FERC Order No. 222 ISO and RTO Key Provisions

ISO/RTO	Max Size Interconnection Allowed	Single/Multi	Effective Date
Cal ISO	1 MW	Multi	First approved 6/16/2022
NY ISO	20 MW	Single	First approved 6/16/2022
PJM ISO	5 MW	Single (energy markets)	
	5 MW	Multi (capacity and ancillary services markets)	
ISO-NE	5 MW	Multi	
MISO RTO	No limit	Single	
SPP RTO	No limit	Single	

Winners and Losers

Who Exercises Authority?

The Supreme Court notes that the electricity business market has evolved to become a "competitive interstate business."[45] The Supreme Court further noted:

> When combined with federal preemption law, one crucial result of these energy market regulatory reforms has been "a massive shift in regulatory jurisdiction from the states to FERC." . . . The upshot of these federal and state innovations in electricity regulation is that state regulators, despite their continued authority over rates charged directly to consumers, have much less actual authority over those rates than they did [earlier].[46]

Now, for more than a decade, more new power generation is constructed each year by IPP ("merchant") companies than by U.S.-regulated utilities.[47] As held by the federal court of appeals and affirmed by the Supreme Court:

---

45. Hughes v. Talen Energy Mktg., LLC, 578 U.S. 150, 154 (2016) (citing EPSA v. FERC, 577 U.S. 260, 267 (2016)).

46. Pub. Util. Dist. No. 1 of Snohomish Cnty., Wash. v. FERC, 471 F.3d 1053, 1066–67 (9th Cir. 2006), *aff'd in part and rev'd in part sub nom.* Morgan Stanley Cap. Grp., Inc. v. Pub. Util. Dist. No. 1, 554 U.S. 527 (2008).

47. Elec. Energy Mkt. Competition Task Force, *supra* note 21, at 10.

> Local utilities now obtain power largely through wholesale contracts subject to FERC's exclusive regulation, rather than through self-generated and transmitted power. . . . Although state regulators formerly took an extremely active role so as to ensure the just and reasonable retail power rates, FERC has exclusive jurisdiction over the wholesale rates that now drive the electric power market and, as a practical matter, largely determine the rates ultimately charged to the public.[48]

The Traditional Model

Utility Reduced Revenue

States allocate transmission and distribution (T & D) costs not by a fixed fee per customer but as a function of volume of electricity transmitted and for some large customers based on their maximum electricity demand. Distributed energy generators are able to supply some or all of their own electricity on site from their generation unit and for that do not incur significant T & D charges based on any significant volume of centralized power moved to them. As well, such self-generators with storage can control their maximum coincident peak system usage over time, which determines demand charges assessed to customers whose tariffs incorporate such charges.

The traditional business model for regulated utilities is to sell kilowatt-hours. One-third of states began the change when they partially deregulated and made retail power sales competitive. When fixed utility grid costs are allocated to a smaller volume of utility company sales due to an increase in on-site distributed power generation, by default, this increases the retail electricity price of each kWh.[49] Under a system of decoupled utility rates, utilities become energy-services providers, with energy efficiency being just one facet of their services, instead of being only merchants of power.[50] Business models must now evolve to incorporate and meet formidable challenges posed by fossil-fuel-fired emission externalities and climate change.[51] See Chapter 2.

---

48. *Pub. Util. Dist. No. 1 of Snohomish Cnty., Wash.*, 471 F.3d at 1066–67.

49. J. McMahon, *Steven Chu Solves Utility Companies' Death Spiral*, Forbes, Mar. 21, 2014; H.K. Trabish, *California PUC President: The Utility Death Spiral Is "Last Year's Hype,"* GreentechMedia.com, Jan. 29, 2014.

50. Katherine Ling, *Rising Temps Melt Electric Utilities' Business Models*, N.Y. Times (Sept. 10, 2009), http://www.nytimes.com/gwire/2009/09/10/10greenwire-rising-temps-melt-electric-utilities-business-72148.html.

51. Lehr, *supra* note 25, at 35.

New Business Model Public Losses

State governments receive significant revenue from taxes embedded in the typical retail utility bill. Local governments receive property taxes on utility poles, transformers, facilities, and wires on their streets, whose fair market value for taxation could be decreased as they handle fewer power transactions. Regulated utility companies pay taxes based on net income and on gross receipts.[52] As on-site distributed self-generation and competition account for more distributed power creation and supply, utility gross receipts decline, and state tax revenues decline correspondingly.

Changing Regulatory Treatment of Power Storage

There Are Two Sides of Every Meter

Electric power storage can be sited either behind the meter on the customer side of the retail meter or in front of the meter (FTM) on the transmission/distribution side of the meter. Thirty percent of all U.S. battery storage capacity installed through 2020 was distributed behind the retail meter. There still exist several regulatory challenges to FTM storage deployment, including interconnection costs of the storage resource, potential operational restrictions on charging and discharge imposed by distribution companies, low and uncertain wholesale market revenue opportunities in the different ISO and RTO systems, and the inability of FTM storage to monetize some of the transmission benefits created amid high and volatile capital costs.

Power Storage Tariffs

Stakeholders must understand the tariffs applicable to particular power storage system operations. Given that electricity can move at near the speed of light and be delivered through much of the continental United States, and that significant areas of the United States are in Opportunity Zones in which there are substantial federal tax benefits (see Chapter 6), power storage systems can be sited in a variety of differently regulated and/or subsidized areas of the United States.

52. Taxes imposed on utilities include the 9A corporate franchise tax, the gross receipts tax, and the sales/use tax. There also can be local taxes including business income/gross receipts taxes, sales taxes, and property taxes. Sheldon Silver & Paul Tonko, *The Electric Industry in New York*, sec. III, tbl. 3, http://assembly.state.ny.us/Reports/Energy/199710/#III.%20FACTORS%20AFFECTING%20ELECTRICITY%20COSTS; Marilyn M. Rubin, *A Guide to New York State Taxes* 9-4 (2011), https://www.researchgate.net/publication/293820300_A_Guide_to_New_York_City_Taxes_History_Issues_and_Concerns.

Electricity for charging storage facilities (as opposed to station service) in some jurisdictions may be accompanied by filed tariff "riders" imposing higher kWh charges, which compromise effective storage discharge cycling at different times of day to earn revenue. Alternative tariff design options could include a coincident demand charge (based on load during the system monthly peak hour(s)), which would have different business model impacts and design options. In 2021, two of four FERC commissioners at that time, including its chairperson, issued a letter stating there was a "strong case" that fixed charges in Alabama "may be violating the Commission's PURPA regulations, undermining the statute's purpose of encouraging Qualifying Facilities."[53]

In many regions, there is still lack of clarity regarding which wholesale or retail tariffs should be applied to distribution-connected storage participating in wholesale markets and whether those tariffs are jurisdictional to FERC or are within the responsibility of state Public Utility Commissions (see Chapter 4 for detail). There can be substantial net public benefits and positive externalities created from power storage that are not privately internalized and can justify market-based incentives to owners of storage systems. One such mechanism is the Massachusetts Clean Peak Energy Standard, which provides higher tariffs applied to transactions where electric storage increases system electric discharge reliability accompanying on-site distributed renewable energy supply.

State Regulatory Requirements for Energy Storage

In the eastern United States, several states promote energy storage. In Massachusetts, the new Solar Massachusetts Renewable Target program provides incentives and a financial "adder" creating a premium power sale price higher than federally mandated Avoided Cost rates for solar projects paired with colocated energy storage projects. See Chapter 5 on Avoided Cost. New York and New Jersey have energy storage goals and targets.

In the western United States, California adopted laws that require utilities to procure considerable amounts of energy storage resources, as well as revamped and extended interconnection requirements for small energy storage project interconnection, and provide consumer rebates worth an

53. *See Form 10-K, Sunrun, Inc.*, U.S. Sec. & Exch. Comm'n (2022), at 22, https://www.sec.gov/Archives/edgar/data/1469367/000146936723000030/run-20221231.htm.

estimated $800 million through 2026.[54] An Oregon statewide energy storage mandate was implemented requiring each electric company with 25,000 or more retail customers to procure storage systems with the capacity to store at least 5 MWh of energy.[55] The Washington Utilities and Transportation Commission issued a policy statement recognizing energy storage.[56] A Nevada statute assures the right to interconnect solar energy projects accompanied by energy storage systems.[57]

FERC Orders on Storage

FERC has issued orders affecting energy storage and project cash flow under an evolving business model.

FERC Order No. 841 required each RTO/ISO to revise its tariff to establish a participation model accommodating the physical and operational characteristics of electric storage resources.[58] FERC defined an "electric storage resource" as "a resource capable of receiving electric energy from the grid and storing it for later injection of electric energy back to the grid" on either the transmission or distribution systems; behind-the-meter storage resources that do not inject electric energy onto the grid are not included in the definition.[59] Any electric storage resource that injects electric energy back to the grid for purposes of participating in a FERC-regulated RTO/ISO market is deemed to engage in wholesale interstate commerce. FERC asserted jurisdiction over the "inbound" wholesale distribution service required to charge

---

54. *See* Jeff St. John, *California Passes Bill to Extend $800M in Incentives for Behind-the-Meter Batteries*, Greentech Media (Aug. 31, 2018), https://www.greentechmedia.com/articles/read/california-passes-bill-to-extend-incentives-for-behind-the-meter-batteries#gs.goUssmg.

55. H.B. 2193, 2015 Leg. Assemb., 78th Sess. (Or. 2015), https://olis.oregonlegislature.gov/liz/2015R1/Measures/Analysis/HB2193.

56. Mark A. Lazaroff & Maggie E. Curran, *State by State: A Roadmap through the Current US Energy Storage Policy Landscape*, n.26, Morgan Lewis (Mar. 4, 2024), https://www.morganlewis.com/pubs/2024/03/state-by-state-a-roadmap-through-the-current-us-energy-storage-policy-landscape#_ftn26.

57. Assemb. B. 405, 2017 Leg., 79th Sess. (Nev. 2017), https://www.leg.state.nv.us/App/NELIS/REL/79th2017/Bill/5487/Overview.

58. Electric Storage Participation in Markets Operated by Regional Transmission Organizations and Independent System Operators, 83 Fed. Reg. 9580, 9580 (Mar. 6, 2018) (codified at 18 C.F.R. pts. 35, 385).

59. *Id.* Storage resources possess unique attributes: bidirectional capability and the ability to both inject energy to the grid and receive energy from it.

battery storage by distributed storage resources that participate in FERC-jurisdictional energy and ancillary service markets.

FERC Order No. 792 amended FERC's pro forma interconnection agreements and protocols for Small Generator Interconnection Agreements (SGIAs) and Small Generator Interconnection Procedures to now include small energy storage resources.[60]

FERC Order No. 845 earlier amended the pro forma interconnection rules regarding Large Generator Interconnection Procedures for large generators and SGIA for small generators without providing specific requirements for energy storage resources.[61]

FERC Order No. 819 allows energy storage resources to provide further ancillary services, including primary frequency response service.[62]

Power Storage and Discharge Are Changing Business Models

In the business model, depending on the FERC-regulated regional ISO/RTO market and state regulatory requirements, battery energy storage system (BESS) assets can function in multiple different revenue-generating modes interchangeably and simultaneously. With the change in federal and state regulation, new BESS assets can now operate in a dual mode: they can serve conventionally as energy storage backup for generation and sale of energy when required by the system; where markets permit, they can supply paid ancillary services (reactive power, operating reserves, loss compensation, and frequency control) to the grid operator to support and balance the grid.

Terms for offering ancillary services will be controlled by the regulator overseeing other grid network services. In the alternative, BESS assets can be operated or dispatched as a generation alternative creating new power fed into the system from off-system storage assets. The role BESS assets play in power markets will depend on the business model applied, the ownership of the assets, and supporting or secondary market regulations or arrangements addressing variables such as power reserves. BESS assets can provide various

60. Small Generator Interconnection Agreements and Procedures, 78 Fed. Reg. 73,240, 73,241 (Dec. 5, 2013) (to be codified at 15 C.F.R. pt. 35).

61. Reform of Generator Interconnection Procedures and Agreements, 83 Fed. Reg. 21,342, 21,343 (May 9, 2018) (to be codified at 18 C.F.R. pt. 37).

62. Third-Party Provision of Primary Frequency Response Service, 80 Fed. Reg. 73,965, 73,966 (Nov. 27, 2015) (to be codified at 18 C.F.R. pt. 35).

services to both power generation and maintenance of the grid in an operational, uncongested, and balanced mode and manner.

Some U.S. ISOs offer forward capacity market long-term payments. There also are frequency response ancillary services for BESS assets, which can offer a substantial revenue component to participating BESS assets in markets that allow their participation. One of the distinguishing characteristics of battery storage is its capability to provide two-second quick-delivery power that competes with and often exceeds the speed of conventional quick-start power generation. Quick-delivery or quick-start energy services now become much more important with the major additions to the grid of weather-dependent intermittent solar and wind renewable power with their minimal marginal cost of operation, which change and favor order of grid asset dispatch.

The three most important revenue sources for BESS assets in the evolving electric power business model in which such assets can participate and be optimized to earn multiple power revenue streams are[63]

- Long-term capacity payments to provide reliability
- Energy supply managed by wholesale energy market arbitrage trying to maximize the difference between the wholesale cost of acquiring power to charge batteries and the wholesale or retail revenue from discharging stored power at peak times and operating battery storage in a manner to minimize power storage losses over time
- The largest potential revenue share from supplying ancillary services with very quick battery response times to support the grid operating with much-increased amounts of intermittent power

Moving forward, a successful business model will include consideration of how to incorporate and/or rapidly deploy "hybrid" generation resources combining solar or wind generation with colocated on-site or pooled energy storage. This raises complex questions for grid operations and for properly valuing business model economics:[64]

---

63. *Id.* Supplying BESS reserves increases supply, which can correct for system frequency drops or satisfy increasing consumption correcting for frequency rises over a range of response time durations and system needs. Value is driven by earning revenues from capacity payments for reserve providers, selling services in a balancing market, or obtaining regulated tariffs for these services.

64. Will Gorman & Joachim Seel, Batteries Included: Top 10 Findings from Berkeley Lab Research on the Growth of Hybrid Power Plants in the United States, Berkeley

- *Market drivers*: Solar hybridization is driven by tax credits and other benefits.
- *Configuration choices*: Market prices have incentivized shorter-duration batteries associated with PV solar generation.
- *Capacity value*: The capacity contribution of a hybrid renewable/storage system is less than the sum of its parts.
- *Ancillary services*: Ancillary service payments can yield significant additional revenue.
- *Distributed hybrids*: Growth of customer-sited PV+storage hybrid systems offers new business opportunities. Thirty percent of all U.S. battery storage capacity installed through 2020 was distributed behind the retail meter, much of that paired with solar PV systems. Only 6 percent of residential and 2 percent of nonresidential PV systems include any storage.[65]

Reprise: Location Matters; ISOs Are Not Identical

ISO-NE, controlling wholesale power dispatch and transmission system balance in the six New England states, provides the greatest amount of any of the ISOs of incremental revenue for ancillary services supplied by intermittent wind and solar power.[66] In the five ISOs and two RTOs, demonstrably larger incremental revenue per unit of ancillary service delivered is provided by pairing storage with solar projects than by pairing storage with wind projects.[67] This is in part because during most late afternoon and early evening hours during the peak demand period, fixed solar PV panel output is either nonoperational or generating at angles of insolation that do not achieve maximum capacity energy output. Therefore, storing PV power and shifting its reinjection to the power grid later during peak times at higher prices in the wholesale power market yield greater operational and financial value. Of

---

Lab (2022), https://eta-publications.lbl.gov/sites/default/files/berkeley_lab-_battery_included_-_top_10_hybrid_research.pdf.

65. Galen Barbose, Salma Elmallah & Will Gorman, *Behind-the-Meter Solar+Storage: Market Data and Trends*, Elec. Mkts. & Pol'y (Jan. 2021), https://eta-publications.lbl.gov/sites/default/files/btm_solarstorage_report_-_factsheet.pdf (6 percent of all U.S. residential PV systems and 2 percent of all nonresidential systems installed in 2020 included storage).

66. Gorman & Seel, *supra* note 64.

67. *Id.*

note, location in a particular ISO or RTO subject to different FERC orders, as illustrated earlier, matters in the evolving electric sector business model.

Understanding the market battery charge and discharge signals and aligning related incentive structures with grid needs are increasingly important as the hybrid power generation/storage sector grows. While all of these considerations are challenges, they also are opportunities. All of this changes the new business model.

Proximate Business Opportunities

The Biden-Harris administration and international climate agreements endeavor to make unprecedented reductions in power generation CO_2 emissions at heretofore unseen rapidity. These will likely focus primarily on the electric sector of the U.S. economy going forward. This speed of transition, when so many other elements of technology, stakeholders, and regulation are changing, is unprecedented. When this many elements of conventional electric power markets change under accelerated time pressures, the business model also must change to incorporate regulatory requirements to take advantage of opportunities.

Business Opportunity Created by Somewhat Overlooked Subsidy Opportunities

The G7 nations, in June 2022, pledged $600 billion over five years for middle-income developing countries, devoted to climate change (featuring renewable energy generation), health care, and energy market needs caused by the Russian invasion of Ukraine. This pledge from the G7 nations, at more than $100 billion/year, exceeds the $100 billion/year pledge of all three dozen developed nations as part of the Conference of the Parties to fund climate change mitigation and adaptation in all less developed countries beginning in 2020 and after (see Chapter 2). This also is more than the $11.6 billion annual U.N. budget or the $8 billion annual budget of the World Bank. The middle-income countries to which these pledged G7 funds will be directed for energy concerns harbor three-quarters of world population, contributing one-third of global GNP, and include most of the neighboring countries in the Americas and Caribbean.

The U.S. electric sector is the engineering and regulatory template for the power systems throughout the Americas, which adopted U.S. power at 120 volts with compatible appliance plug design, rather than E.U. and

Asian voltages and plug designs. The United States is the most affluent and advanced G7 country and nearest to the countries and territories located in Central and South America and the Caribbean. The U.S. Customs and Border Protection authority in 2021 refused to allow import of certain silica-based solar cell products manufactured in the Xinjiang Uyghur Autonomous Region of China because of allegations regarding forced labor in China, which is the world's dominant producer of solar energy products. These facts present new business opportunities for U.S. companies to assist these neighboring countries with electric power development.

Informed stakeholders must stay in front of this fast-evolving legal/regulatory curve of new regulation that now fundamentally reshapes the industry. We have already entered a period from now until 2050 where climate goals and regulatory requirements emerge as new meta law considerations for lawyers and their clients participating in the electric power industry. Part IV of this book highlights things not yet visible on the radar screen that lawyers must soon deal with. The next chapter analyzes massive new demands imposed on the electric grid as it becomes multidimensional, handling a multitude of expanding intermittent supply sources amid increasing power demand, and how this changes the legal challenges confronting attorneys.

PART IV

Looming Challenges

In this part of the book, we analyze major forces reshaping the future of environmental, land-use, and energy law between now and 2035. This future fundamentally alters the demand for and type of electric power, its environmental impacts, and the intensity of its land use. Each of these changes will be controversial, with both substantial support and opposition, and spawn major legal challenges in court and before state Public Utility Commissions (PUCs) and FERC. These new factors fundamentally change what the grid is and how it operates in a more multidirectional mode, the science behind environmental law, and the looming legal response in Washington, D.C. This part of the book looks beyond the current environmental and energy law radar screen to highlight and analyze

- The underanticipated physical remaking of the new grid—and the risk of a less reliable and resilient grid, the most important engineered system in the United States, that lawyers and their clients must navigate as well as mitigate amid changing law between now and 2035
- The significant statutory legal changes in energy and environmental law pending, but not yet enacted
- New science highlighting a new molecule that changes what, where, and how U.S. law will need to address the electric sector, environment, and climate change going forward

Read on.

CHAPTER 14

Toughening the Grid and Law

"The Earth is where we make our stand."

—Carl Sagan, *Pale Blue Dot: A Vision of the Human Future in Space*

"We make our stand" keeping the American power grid, one of the greatest engineering achievements in history, in balance and functional. The U.S. grid is being asked to do much more, with more complexity: the grid must operate multidirectionally with many more power supply inputs, without control over when it must accept intermittent and unpredictable amounts of new independent power supply, straddling an unprecedented legislative push to exclusively electrify the operation of the entire U.S. economy. The grid must accomplish this with legal control over the U.S. power grid divided between federal and state regulation, with states differing fundamentally as to whether they allow nonincumbent transmission grid competition or maintain monopoly legal rights of first refusal over new grid infrastructure. Law is bifurcated and time matters, as new grid infrastructure and upgrades are subject to National Environmental Policy Act Environmental Impact Reports, which typically delay projects for up to six years.

The part of the electric system that will change most between now and 2035 will be the power grid. The interconnected grid functions as one large complex machine with different regional moving parts. Going forward, the grid will need to be rapidly extended to more remote locations, creating much greater capacity, while handling intermittent power transmission that uses the system less consistently and less efficiently and incurs greater cost than traditional transmission use. This grid must interface legally and technologically with new electric power generation sources.

Maintaining the grid requires sophisticated technical skills along with strategic legal acumen to keep the grid in balance. The grid is an extraordinarily complex machine comprised of not only the approximately 7,300 power generation facilities but also 167,000 miles of very high-voltage power lines operating at 230 kV (kilovolts) and higher, plus millions of miles of low-voltage lines, plus the transformers, breakers, and cable to interconnect them with consumers, collectively operating as an energized instantaneous network:

> Today, the U.S. transmission and distribution system is a vast physical complex of interlocked machines and wires, with a correspondingly complex set of institutions overseeing and guiding it through policies, statutes, and regulations. The U.S. grid delivers approximately 3,857 terawatt-hours [or trillion watt-hours] of electrical energy from electric power generators to 159 million residential, commercial, and industrial customers. This is accomplished via 19,000 individual generators at about 7,000 operational power plants in the United States with a nameplate generation capacity of at least one megawatt (MW). These generators send electricity over 642,000 miles of high-voltage transmission lines and 6.3 million miles of distribution lines. Together with its electric generation component, the grid is sometimes referred to as the world's largest machine; in 2000, the National Academy of Engineering named electrification as the greatest engineering achievement of the 20th century.[1]

Technically, the electric grid must recalibrate and rebalance constantly, every second, 365 days of every year. The electric power system must constantly, every few seconds, balance supply with demand to keep the U.S. grid operational.

The grid technical challenges now are changing and becoming more legally complex. In terms of new generation, rapidly increasing solar and wind renewable power generation, which comprise the bulk of renewable power development, are intermittent resources not predictable in terms of when they will operate to supply sufficient power. To improve wind power predictability, there is a lack of empirical data because wind generation data from existing turbines is considered proprietary business secrets that are not typically shared or in the public domain. Regional solar insolation data is more available. If bulk power supply does not respond to instantaneous demand, with a deficiency of supply the grid can shut down and black out

---

1. *See* U.S. Dep't of Energy, Quadrennial Energy Rev. Rep., ch. III, at 3–4 (2015), http://energy.gov/sites/prod/files/2015/04/f22/QER_Ch3.pdf.

large areas of service. U.S. power grids are already strained,[2] and blackouts like those not long ago seen in Texas[3] and California[4] could become more common as climate change advances.[5]

While the engineering aspects of the grid, if properly designed, operate objectively as a machine pursuant to engineered protocols, the machine is not autonomous. The levers of the grid are moved pursuant to legal and regulatory orders, rules, and precedents. These are not as objective as the law of physics by which the engineered aspects of the grid operate. Pulling together the key intertwined threads in the earlier chapters of this book, recently, the Infrastructure Investment and Jobs Act and the Inflation Reduction Act each launched a decade-long investment in, and change of legal authority between state and federal government jurisdiction over, the national transmission grid and its regional subparts in order to strengthen the grid. See Chapter 6. Lawyers and their clients participate in and affect this grid operation.

This unprecedented federal legislation's investment in and subsidy of more renewable power generation is a first step, although not the essential step. The critical path to the current transition to renewable intermittent power generation is not technical—it is a legal challenge. This involves changing laws and regulations to expeditiously make and keep the grid more resilient and reliable as the sources of power generation change (see Chapter 2). In the U.S. market-driven economy, the energy business model must rapidly evolve to work within a new legal reality (see Chapters 12 and 13).

While strengthening the grid is an engineering undertaking at a projected cost of more than an additional $2 trillion by 2050 (see Chapter 11), the ultimate challenge is legal/regulatory to be managed by legal counsel. The grid from an *engineering* perspective is one set of wires and infrastructure, but *legally* the grid is divided into two differently regulated types of transactions over the same wires. Since FERC Order No. 888 a quarter

---

2. Nichola Groom & Tina Bellon, *EV Rollout Will Require Huge Investments in Strained U.S. Power Grids*, Reuters (Mar. 5, 2021), https://www.reuters.com/article/us-usa-weather-grids-autos-insight/ev-rollout-will-require-huge-investments-in-strained-u-s-power-grids-idUSKBN2AX18Y.

3. Justin Worland, *The Texas Power Grid Failure Is a Climate Change Cautionary Tale*, Time (Feb. 18, 2021), https://time.com/5940491/texas-power-outage-climate/.

4. Sammy Roth, *What Caused California's Rolling Blackouts? Climate Change and Poor Planning*, L.A. Times (Oct. 6, 2020), https://www.latimes.com/environment/story/2020-10-06/california-rolling-blackouts-climate-change-poor-planning.

5. John Schwartz & Ivan Penn, *Texas Power Grid, Strained Last Winter, Now Faces an Early Heat Wave*, N.Y. Times (June 15, 2021), https://www.nytimes.com/2021/06/15/climate/texas-heat-wave-electricity.html.

century ago, the same wires, regardless of the voltage at which they operate, at the same time handle power movement that is exclusively split between state and federal regulation, transaction by transaction. There is a Supreme Court "bright line" split separating federal jurisdiction over the transmission grid operation from state jurisdiction over the distribution grid operation (see Chapter 4). Moreover, the federal transmission grid is divided among three separate interconnections within the continental United States (see Figure 3.8).

Electric power is one of history's most important inventions, and it moves over critical 21st-century U.S. infrastructure. The portion of the grid legally allocated to federal regulation is delegated for almost 60 percent of the country to independent system operators (ISOs) and regional transmission organizations (RTOs), which are exclusively overseen pursuant to substantively different filed and approved orders of FERC. The regulatory structure is evolving rapidly, with some utilities in deregulated states and some not, with some utilities in ISOs/RTOs and others not, amid legally mandated rapid electrification of the U.S. economy while also attempting to address climate warming. See Chapters 2 and 3.

How large a legal and regulatory challenge does grid modification pose? In mid-2023, testifying before the U.S. Senate Energy and Natural Resources Committee hearing, the FERC commissioners, who regulate the U.S. transmission grid, ventured ominous forecasts of what the current rapid electrification of the entire U.S. economy and switch away from baseload electric power generation to more intermittent generation threaten:[6]

- FERC Acting Chair Willie Phillips: "We face unprecedented challenges to the reliability of our nation's electric system."
- FERC Commissioner Mark Christie:
  - "The United States is heading for a very catastrophic situation in terms of reliability."
  - "The arithmetic doesn't work. . . . This problem is coming. It's coming quickly. The red lights are flashing."
  - The grid is "heading for a very catastrophic situation in terms of reliability."

---

6. Ethan Howland, *FERC Commissioners Tell Senators of Major Grid Reliability Challenges, with Some Blaming Markets*, Utility Dive (May 5, 2023), https://www.utilitydive.com/news/ferc-grid-reliability-senate-energy-hearing/649523/#:~:text=DER-.

- FERC Commissioner James Danly:
  - There is a "looming reliability crisis in our electricity markets."
  - "FERC has allowed the markets to fall prey to the price distorting and warping effects of subsidies and public policies that have driven the advancement of large quantities of intermittent renewable resources onto the electric system."
  - "The subsidies available to renewable generators are so lucrative that, when participating in procurement auctions, they are able to offer at a price of zero instead of their actual cost. The market signal thereby created is that these new resources can be built for *free*, and thus the cost of power is also free."[7]

These admonitions warn about the legal and regulatory challenges of shuttering traditional baseload power sources in favor of intermittent generation. Not long after these admonitions about grid reliability, in September 2023, Michael Bloomberg announced that Bloomberg Philanthropies would provide an additional $500 million to the Beyond Carbon campaign with a goal to "shut down every last U.S. coal plant," "slash gas plant capacity in half, and block all new gas plants."[8] According to the Statistical Review of World Energy, natural gas and coal supplied 59.8 percent of all U.S. electric generation in 2022.[9]

Either technical model can be implemented. Whether it operates successfully is a legal and regulatory challenge. Operating within the legal system to remake the new grid in a more resilient and reliable mode is a significant challenge between now and the 2035 target date to do so. Following are the engineering and legal challenges, and repercussions, to keep the grid balanced and operational.

---

7. *Written Testimony of James P. Danly Commissioner, Federal Energy Regulatory Commission Before the Committee on Energy & Natural Resources United States Senate May 4, 2023*, https://www.ferc.gov/news-events/news/written-testimony-james-p-danly-commissioner-federal-energy-regulatory-0.

8. Press Release, Bloomberg Philanthropies, Michael R. Bloomberg Doubles Down with Additional $500M to Help End Fossil Fuels and Usher in a New Era of Clean Energy in the United States (Sept. 20, 2023), https://www.bloomberg.org/press/michael-r-bloomberg-doubles-down-with-additional-500m-to-help-end-fossil-fuels-and-usher-in-a-new-era-of-clean-energy-in-the-united-states/.

9. BP Statistical Review of World Energy 2022 (71st ed.), https://www.bp.com/content/dam/bp/business-sites/en/global/corporate/pdfs/energy-economics/statistical-review/bp-stats-review-2022-full-report.pdf.

Loss, Cost, and Legal Repercussions of Power Grid Failure

Legally, attorneys think strategically about how to minimize risk, mitigate damages, and put their clients in the best possible position. The power sector can be a complex maze to navigate. A shortage of electricity has dire social and political consequences; a blackout has been equated to a natural disaster.[10] Allowing rolling blackouts as a matter of policy, as occurred in California (ultimately leading to the recall of Governor Davis and the election of Governor Schwarzenegger as his replacement), is a very inefficient way to balance supply and demand differences (see California covered in more detail later in "California Deregulatory Grid Challenges").

The resiliency and reliability of the power grid, a most important and complex machine, decreased between 2015 and 2025. Major grid blackout events increased by over 60 percent between 2015 and 2020, with extreme weather events identified as the leading cause for such outages.[11] A small amount of this is expected traditionally: a typical U.S. electric customer experiences nearly six hours of outage annually, with at least two hours due to distribution system faults.[12]

There have been recent concerns that a cyber-directed or physical terrorist attack could bring down the regional grid and other systems that depend on electricity, such as telecommunications, computers and the internet, hospitals without cogeneration backup power supply, and national defense systems. If utility transmission towers or pipelines are physically destroyed or disrupted, it can take weeks to repair them.[13] Hackers utilized firewall vulnerabilities to cause blind spots across the U.S. grid for nearly ten hours in

---

10. Allen Williams, Jr., *The U.S. Electricity Sector: What after California?*, 14 Elec. J. 51, 52 (2001).

11. Elise Gout, *A Clean Power Grid Is a Reliable Power Grid*, Ctr. for Am. Progress (Feb. 24, 2022), https://www.americanprogress.org/article/a-clean-power-grid-is-a-reliable-power-grid/; René Marsh, *Energy Experts Sound Alarm about U.S. Electric Grid: "Not Designed to Withstand the Impacts of Climate Change,"* CNN (June 2, 2022), https://www.cnn.com/2022/05/31/us/power-outages-electric-grid-climate-change/index.html.

12. *See U.S. Customers Experienced an Average of Nearly Six Hours of Power Interruptions in 2018*, U.S. Energy Info. Admin. (June 1, 2020), https://www.eia.gov/todayinenergy/detail.php?id=43915.

13. Nat'l Acads. of Scis., Eng'g & Med., Enhancing the Resilience of the Nation's Electricity System ch. 3 (Nat'l Acads. Press 2017), https://www.nap.edu/read/24836/chapter/5.

2019.[14] The Russian invasion of Ukraine focused on cutting off electric supply, as well as occupying the Chernobyl nuclear power facility and others.

The Cost of Grid Failure

Even short and discrete regional grid failures create very substantial losses. The U.S. Department of Energy estimates power outages are costing American businesses around $150 billion per year.[15] Not every consumer attaches the same value to electricity at a given hour. For some industries, even a short blackout can ruin millions of dollars of production; for others, it is a minor inconvenience. Where loss of refrigeration is involved, or businesses involving digital services are affected, brief interruptions can cost hundreds of thousands or even millions of dollars for pharmaceutical, brokerage, and semiconductor companies.[16] For certain industries, the cost of a one-hour blackout can be many millions of dollars in lost production, lost orders, or lost information.[17] The U.S. Department of Energy reported the following costs for power outages for communication-dependent businesses: cellular communications, $41,000/hr.; telephone ticket sales, $72,000/hr.; airline reservations, $90,000/hr.; credit card operations, $2.58 million/hr.; and brokerage operations, $6.48 million/hr.[18]

---

14. *See* Brian Barrett, *Security News This Week: An Unprecedented Cyberattack Hit US Power Utilities*, WIRED (Sept. 7, 2019), https://www.wired.com/story/power-grid-cyberattack-facebook-phone-numbers-security-news/.

15. *See* Kristina Hamachi LaCommare & Joseph H. Eto, *Cost of Power Interruptions to Electricity Consumers in the United States (U.S.)*, OFF. OF SCI. & TECH. INFO. (Feb. 16, 2006), https://perma.cc/W3J9-53HE (commenting on a U.S. Department of Energy study that published cost-of-reliability estimates ranging from $150 to $400 billion per year); *Department of Energy Report Explores U.S. Advanced Small Modular Reactors to Boost Grid Resiliency*, ENERGY.GOV (Jan. 25, 2018), https://www.energy.gov/ne/articles/department-energy-report-explores-us-advanced-small-modular-reactors-boost-grid.

16. Joel N. Swisher, *Cleaner Energy, Greener Profits: Fuel Cells as Cost-Effective Distributed Energy Resources* 21, ROCKY MTN. INST. (2002), https://rmi.org/wp-content/uploads/2017/05/RMI_Document_Repository_Public-Reprts_U02-02_CleanerGreener.pdf.

17. *See* Asim Hussain, *A Day without Power: Outage Costs for Businesses*, BLOOMENERGY (Oct. 8, 2019), https://www.bloomenergy.com/blog/a-day-without-power-outage-costs-businesses. *See also* U.S. DEP'T OF ENERGY, STRATEGIC PLAN FOR DISTRIBUTED ENERGY RESOURCES 7 (2000). This study estimates that the value of a one-hour blackout to a brokerage firm is $8.5 million.

18. R. COWART ET AL., NAT'L RENEWABLE ENERGY LAB'Y, NREL/SR-560-32498, STATE ELECTRICITY REGULATORY POLICY AND DISTRIBUTED RESOURCES: DISTRIBUTED RESOURCES AND ELECTRIC SYSTEM RELIABILITY 10 (2002) (quoting U.S. DEP'T OF ENERGY, DISTRIBUTED ENERGY RESOURCE PROGRAM AND STRATEGIC PLAN (2000)).

Most system interruptions in the United States result from transmission and distribution difficulties within one-half mile of a customer.[19] Of note, distributed solar generation adds a modular element to increase electric grid resilience. As a vivid example of distributed power flexibility and resiliency, at the end of March 2022 as part of the Russian invasion of Ukraine, a missile damaged 416 photovoltaic (PV) panels as well as four inverters at a 3.9 MW solar facility in Ukraine's Kharkiv region. Half of the generating capability of the PV facility could be isolated and kept independently operational; one week later, staff had disconnected the damaged PV strings to keep operational 1.8 MW of power generation.

Texas Trouble Managing the Grid

On February 26, 2008, the ERCOT grid operator in Texas, the state leading in U.S. wind power deployment, was unable to compensate with sufficient backup power when there was an unexpected 80 percent drop in wind power production.[20] Texas officials ordered an investigation of rolling blackouts that affected the state's electric grid again in 2010 and 2011;[21] ERCOT tapped three connections with Mexico in 2011 to pull power from south of the border to compensate.[22] In February 2021, approximately 46,000 MW of power on a high-demand day were taken off the Texas grid due to power-generating failures stemming from winter storms, during which natural gas lines froze and inadequate winterization of the grid system led to repeated failures in transmission infrastructure.

Sixty-nine percent of Texas consumers—4.5 million customers—were without power and water for multiple days during subfreezing temperatures; water pipes burst, and city water-delivery systems could not operate without electricity for pumps.[23] By the end of the storm, 111 people were officially

---

19. Zerriffi, Dowlatabadi & Strachan, *infra* (citing H.L. Willis & W. Scott, Distributed Power Generation: Planning and Evaluation 15 (Marcel Dekker, Inc. 2000)).

20. *How Renewables Can Be Undermined by Intermittency*, 5 Elec. J. (2008).

21. Rebecca Smith, *Texas to Probe Rolling Blackouts*, Wall St. J., Feb. 7, 2011.

22. *Id.*

23. *See* Reese Oxner & Juan Pablo Garnham, *Over a Million Texans Are Still without Drinking Water. Smaller Communities and Apartments Are Facing the Biggest Challenges*, Tex. Trib. (Feb. 24, 2021, 6:00 PM CT), https://perma.cc/2T7C-95AV.

reported dead, primarily due to hypothermia during the blackouts, while the *Houston Chronicle* reported the number of dead as nearly 200.[24]

Blackouts occur in other developed countries. A blackout of power to 57 million people in Italy occurred in September 2003.[25] Just prior to this blackout, Italian officials pronounced that a U.S.-Canada-style blackout as occurred August 14, 2003, was "impossible" in Italy. However, Italy then imported 17 percent of its electricity from Switzerland and France, making it the most dependent on electricity imports of the major European countries (the next largest importer is Spain at 4 percent). Italy's blackout started with a problem in the Swiss interconnection, causing a system imbalance, resulting in a cascading failure. London, Denmark, and Sweden also experienced significant blackouts in 2003.[26]

Regional U.S. Grid System Failures

Even before recent changes, on July 2, 1996, there was an outage that affected Arizona, California, Colorado, Idaho, Montana, Nebraska, Nevada, New Mexico, Oregon, South Dakota, Texas, Utah, Washington, and Wyoming, as well as parts of western Canada and Baja California, affecting two million customers consuming approximately 12,000 MW for up to a few hours.[27] On

---

24. *See* Zach Despart et al., *Analysis Reveals Nearly 200 Died in Texas Cold Storm and Blackouts, Almost Double the Official Count*, Hous. Chron. (Apr. 2, 2021), https://www.houstonchronicle.com/news/houston-texas/houston/article/texas-cold-storm-200-died-analysis-winter-freeze-16070470.php.

25. *Italy Recovering from Big Blackout*, CNN (Sept. 28, 2003), https://www.cnn.com/2003/WORLD/europe/09/28/italy.blackout/index.html#:~:text=Officials%20told%20CNN%20the%20entire,at%20night%2C%20during%20severe%20storms.

26. *See* Markus Schläpfer & Hans Glavitsch, *Learning from the Past—Electrical Power Blackouts and Near Misses in Europe*, Springer (2006), https://link.springer.com/content/pdf/bbm%3A978-1-4020-4364-2%2F1.pdf.

27. A line shortage in a 345 kV line caused the inability to carry power away from a generating plant in Idaho, which caused a decline in frequency in the Western Interconnection, resulting in scattered customer outages. On August 10, 1986, an outage hit Arizona, California, Colorado, Idaho, Montana, Nebraska, Nevada, New Mexico, Oregon, South Dakota, Texas, and Utah, affecting 7.5 million customers consuming 28 MW for up to nine hours. This was triggered by a combination of random transmission line outages resulting in system oscillations when a 500 kV line shorted due to touching trees and led to overloads and cascading outages throughout the Western Interconnection accompanied by certain transmission mismanagement. On June 25, 1998, Minnesota, Montana, North Dakota, South Dakota, and Wisconsin, as well as parts of Canada, involving 152,000 customers with 950 MW of demand, lost power for up to 18 hours due to a lightning storm that struck a 345 kV line

August 14, 2003, a typical summer day, transmission capacity problems in Ohio caused significant parts of the Midwest, New York, and the mid-Atlantic region, involving 50 million customers, to lose power for up to a day.[28] This constituted the largest blackout impact in modern North American history.[29]

This blackout resulted when the Midwest ISO shut down an automatic grid monitoring system to fix a problem, and then human error caused operators to forget to reactivate it.[30] When lines to Canada from New York failed, New York suddenly had a surplus of 3,000 MW that would have been exported to Canada, equal to 11 percent of the actual demand on the New York system at the time, causing automatic shutoffs of power plants to prevent overloading these lines.[31] In this blackout:

- More than one hundred power plants, including nine of the nation's nuclear plants, were tripped offline to preserve their equipment when line capacity went down.[32]
- Reserve margins were adequate.
- The integrated grid as a whole was vulnerable.
- Fifty million people in eight states and two Canadian provinces experienced power failure.[33]

---

and de-energized it and overloaded lower-voltage lines, which were then de-energized, causing system protection to take lines out of service throughout the Mid-continent Area Power Pool (MAPP) region.

28. *See* J.R. Minkel, *The 2003 Northeast Blackout—Five Years Later*, Sci. Am. (Aug. 13, 2008), https://www.scientificamerican.com/article/2003-blackout-five-years-later/.

29. In this blackout, the overflow of power spread so quickly that protective equipment in various parts of the Midwest and New York were not able to isolate outages before they spread to neighboring areas. Other parts of the PJM grid were able to isolate power flows as the power started to deviate below 60 MHz.

30. *Task Force Lays Blame at Feet of FirstEnergy, MISO, Exonerates Other Actors in Blackout*, Elec. Util. Wk, Nov. 24, 2003, at 1, 10. Additional monitoring tools were not in place. No real-time data on the system failure was available for more than three hours. System operators were not adequately trained. *Id.*

31. *See* U.S.-Can. Power Sys. Outage Task Force, Final Report on the August 14, 2003 Blackout in the United States and Canada: Causes and Recommendations (2004), https://www3.epa.gov/region1/npdes/merrimackstation/pdfs/ar/AR-1165.pdf.

32. *Id.*

33. *See id.* at 11.

- Ten major airports were shut down and seven hundred flights nationwide were canceled.[34]
- Some people were without drinking water.
- 350,000 people were stranded on the New York City subway when the power went out with 19 trains in underwater tunnels at the time.[35]
- Ohio electric-powered pumping stations were unable to lift water out of Lake Erie, causing all residents to have to boil their water.[36]
- Certain sewage treatment plants, which are large consumers of electric power for pumps, aeration, and settling tanks operation, did not function during the outage, causing sewage discharges prior to treatment and increase in bacteria levels at discharge points.

With lack of grid resilience, there is cost. The August 2003 blackout cost the economy in a few hours as much as $6 billion.[37] New York City Controller Bill Thompson estimated the 29-hour blackout cost the city more than $1 billion in perishable goods and business—a $36-million-per-hour hit.[38] In addition to the comptroller's figure, then-Mayor Bloomberg estimated $40 million in lost tax revenue and $10 million incurred for overtime pay for city workers, including extra police officers on patrol and sanitation crews that worked through the weekend to pick up spoiled food.[39] The blackout

---

34. *Id.; see also* James Barron, *The Blackout of 2003: The Overview; Power Surge Blacks Out Northeast, Hitting Cities in 8 States and Canada; Midday Shutdowns Disrupt Millions*, N.Y. TIMES (Aug. 15, 2003), https://www.nytimes.com/2003/08/15/nyregion/blackout-2003-overview-power-surge-blacks-northeast-hitting-cities-8-states.html [https://perma.cc/R45N-9JZ3].

35. *See* David Teather, *Blackout Cost New York $36m an Hour*, THE GUARDIAN (Aug. 19, 2003), https://perma.cc/5LMK-U6D3.

36. *See Most Lights Back On in Cleveland*, CNN (Aug. 15, 2003), https://www.cnn.com/2003/US/08/15/blackout.cleveland/index.html.

37. *Blackout Adds to Long List of Utilities Woes*, BALT. SUN, Aug. 24, 2003. The Brattle Group estimated that the blackout cost businesses alone $6 billion, with $75 million compensated by business insurance, given that less than 10 percent of U.S. businesses purchased blackout insurance. Frank Graves & Lisa Wood, *Economic Cost of the August 14th 2003 Northeast Power Outage: Preliminary Estimate*, THE BRATTLE GRP., INC. (Aug. 18, 2003), https://perma.cc/QK4J-RVRW.

38. *See* Teather, *supra* note 35; Eric Herman, David Saltonstall & Corky Siemaszko, *New Yorkers Return to Work as Officials Assess Cost to Blackout*, KNIGHT RIDDER/TRIBUNE NEWS SERV., Aug. 19, 2003.

39. Herman, Saltonstall & Siemaszko, *supra* note 38.

cost the city's 22,000 eateries alone between $75 and $100 million in wasted food and lost business.[40]

The cost of the blackout, just in Ohio, was estimated at $1.1 billion by the Ohio Manufacturers Association.[41] The blackout cost Michigan about $1 billion, according to then-Governor (and now U.S. Secretary of Energy) Jennifer Granholm.[42] More than 70 manufacturing companies shut down, and state and local authorities spent about $20 million on emergency services.[43] The blackout also shut down water and sewage systems in Ohio, creating public health hazards for millions of people.[44]

Grid Regulation; Resilience

Each regional grid in the United States operates under different rules and regulations. Utilities make choices in their regional grid membership or isolation, where grid-specific regulation, orders, and law fundamentally affect grid resilience. In the eastern blackout of 2003, the Midwest ISO, a legal regulatory entity, violated its own reliability standards and rules and failed to prevent the cascade of outages across the Eastern Interconnection.[45] The relatively weak Midwest ISO did not have overarching regulatory authority to order operational changes or responses within the region; instead it had to call each generating plant owner and each utility to suggest operational changes for which it lacked authority.[46] Consequently, human error, loss of a line, and computer failures made contingency analysis of no value and set

40. *When the Lights Went Out, Many Businesses Were Left with No Choice but to Close Shop. And for Food Stores, Shelves Had to Be Emptied, Costing Owners Thousands of Dollars* (News 12 Westchester, Aug. 18, 2003).

41. *See* Elec. Consumers Res. Council, *The Economic Impacts of the August 2003 Blackout* (Feb. 9, 2004), https://perma.cc/G3PU-R3NG; Columbus (Ohio) Dispatch, Sept. 5, 2003.

42. *See* Jennifer Granholm, *Blackout Exposed Vulnerability of Nation's Electrical Power System*, Roll Call (Sept. 19, 2003), https://www.rollcall.com/2003/09/19/blackout-exposed-vulnerability-of-nations-electrical-power-system/.

43. *See* Sumana Chatterjee, *Government Investigating Sharp Rise in Gas Prices*, Charlotte Observer, Sept. 4, 2003.

44. *Id.*; *see Most Lights Back On in Cleveland*, *supra* note 36.

45. U.S.-Can. Power Sys. Outage Task Force, *supra* note 31; *Task Force Lays Blame at Feet of FirstEnergy, MISO, Exonerates Other Actors in Blackout*, *supra* note 30.

46. *See Blackout 2003: How Did It Happen and Why?*, 108th Cong. 1 (2003) (statement of Bob Taft), https://www.govinfo.gov/content/pkg/CHRG-108hhrg89467/html/CHRG-108hhrg89467.htm.

off a cascade of interruptions on high-voltage lines, tripping off 263 power plants.[47]

Here is the status of the legal fabric: the regulatory authority exercised by the North American Electric Reliability Corporation (NERC) and the ISOs and RTOs is voluntary, not mandatory, and lacks enforcement power.[48] The blackout of 50 million consumers in August 2003 illustrated that the interstate transmission system is at least as important to the nation as the interstate highway system or the interstate natural gas pipeline system. And there was not sufficient legal authority to pull the correct levers as needed at the correct time. Artificial intelligence, going forward, may improve the algorithm and response.

Technically, here is what happens: when power flows are reversed, there are severe frequency and load oscillations.[49] The shutdown of the grid system sometimes is necessary to prevent greater damage to the system hardware, which could take weeks or months to repair, rather than the temporary loss of service for a few hours.[50] The power system becomes a more complex machine when attempting to manage balancing intermittent power supply with demand for more electrification of the U.S. economy.

Electric power can supply either baseload power or backup/peaking power. Intermittent renewable resources cannot supply reliable baseload power, as they deliver a relatively low availability factor in the 10–50 percent range of hours during a day or month. Correspondingly, intermittent renewable resources without storage cannot serve as reliable backup/peaking power resources, because they are often unavailable at times when needed to supplement increased peak power demand. With much more intermittent power on the grid since it became more economically feasible after 2010, new standards to maintain resilience are changing. The Infrastructure Investment and Jobs Act, which attempts to build new power transmission infrastructure (see Chapter 11 for details), is critiqued by some who say that "[t]he US infrastructure bill doesn't go far enough to climate-proof the electric grid."[51]

---

47. K. Maize, *Analysis: The Hows and Whys of the Big Blackout*, ELEC. DAILY, Nov. 20, 2003, at 1.

48. Not only is there a 700-page NERC manual for grid operation, but additional state and regional rules are also imposed.

49. *See id.*

50. *See* NAT'L ACADS. OF SCIS., ENG'G & MED., *supra* note 13.

51. Tim McDonnell, *The US Infrastructure Bill Doesn't Go Far Enough to Climate-Proof the Electric Grid*, QUARTZ (Sept. 28, 2021), https://qz.com/2066074/how-the-us-infrastructure-bill-climate-proofs-the-electric-grid/.

California Deregulatory Grid Challenges

There are examples in this century of regulatory failures in managing the transmission system, markets, and electric supply. During the electric energy crisis in California during 2000–2001, with a regulatory failure over a few months, the price of electricity quadrupled. The state budget was decimated and the governor recalled and replaced by actor Arnold Schwarzenegger.

California itself is a huge economic engine. The retail value of the California electric market in 2000 was approximately $20 billion annually, with peak electric load of 53 GW and consumption of 264,000 GWh.[52] In 1998, California became the third state in the nation, after Massachusetts and Rhode Island, to restructure its electric sector, allow retail competition, and force or incentivize its investor-owned utilities to sell their generating assets to the highest competitive bidder. When A.B. 1890 to accomplish this was eventually enacted by the California legislature in September 1996, it passed by a unanimous vote, which was extremely unusual in a deeply divided legislature.[53]

The State Regulatory Straitjacket

In short, the California legislation capped the retail utility rate for each class of customer at an immediately discounted value of 90 percent of its current level for a period of approximately five years.[54] FERC approved the California plan.[55] As no new plants of any significant size were built in the western

---

52. Lawrence Berkeley Nat'l Lab'y, *The California Energy Crisis: A Brief Summary of Events*, II Env't Energy Techs. Div. News 2 (2001). Utilities supply approximately half of this load, with non-utility generators supplying approximately two-thirds of the remainder and importation from out of state supplying one-third of the remainder.

53. Act of September 24, 1996, Cal. Stat. 854 (codified at Cal. Pub. Util. Code §§ 330–398.5). John L. Jurewitz, *California's Electric Debacle: A Guided Tour*, 15 Elec. J. 10, 13 (2002).

54. *Id.*; A.B. 1890 § 368, 1996 Cal. Stat. 854, 1996 Cal. Legis. Serv. ch. 854, § 10 (West) (codified at Cal. Pub. Util. Code § 368, West Supp. 2003).

55. Pac. Gas & Elec. Co., 81 FERC ¶ 61,122 (1997); Pac. Gas & Elec. Co., 80 FERC ¶ 61,128 (1997). These FERC approvals transferred control of the utilities' transmission systems to the California ISO, designated transmission infrastructure, and approved the operation of the ISO and the Power Exchange. Supported by California officials and the PUC, the independent wholesale generators applied to FERC for and were granted market-based rates, typical of those granted in many other states. Duke Energy Morro Bay LLC, 83 FERC ¶ 61,317 (1998); Pac. Gas & Elec. Co., 81 FERC ¶ 61,122 (1997).

United States during the 1990s, California did nothing at the state level to facilitate addition of significant new generating facilities.[56]

Regulatory authorities required the utilities to buy a substantial amount of their power requirements on the "spot" market—day-to-day—rather than through forward-hedged long-term contracts.[57] The California restructuring legislation required each of the California investor-owned utilities to place all of its day-ahead power requirements for default service customers through the California Power Exchange on an hourly basis.[58] California's wholesale power prices jumped dramatically by 500 percent from the year before in late 2000 and were approximately ten times what they were in 1998; power shortages began in summer 2000 in California.[59]

In June 2000, due to hot weather, generation out of service, and increasing demand, the ISO declared a Stage II emergency, which resulted in power curtailment to certain nonfirm large retail customers.[60] During January and February 2001, the ISO declared Stage III alerts, leading to rolling blackouts in some utility service territories.[61] In January, the California utilities began defaulting on their payment obligations for wholesale power to the ISO and the Power Exchange.[62] On January 17, 2001, Governor Davis declared a state of emergency based on an "imminent threat of widespread and prolonged

---

56. Jurewitz, *supra* note 53, at 16.

57. *Id.* at 15.

58. A.B. 1890 (Cal. 1996).

59. *See* Paul L. Joskow, California's Electricity Crisis 1 (2001) (unpublished); the California restructuring order is *In re Proposed Policies Governing Restructuring California Electric Services Industry and Reforming Regulation*, 166 P.U.R.4th 1 (1995), as modified by decision 96-01-009 (1996). This created an ISO, which inherited operational control over the transmission systems of the three large investor-owned utilities in California. Also created was a California Power Exchange, which cleared all buy-sell transactions for wholesale power in the state, attempting to create a transparent spot market administered by the state-chartered Exchange. The Power Exchange was independent of the ISO. Southern California Edison Co. and Pacific Gas & Electric Co. were ordered "to voluntarily divest themselves . . . of at least 50% of their fossil generating assets." CHRISTOPHER WEARE, THE CALIFORNIA ELECTRIC CRISIS: CAUSES AND POLICY OPTIONS 1–2 (2003).

60. *See Subsequent Events—California's Energy Crisis*, U.S. ENERGY INFO. ADMIN., https://www.eia.gov/electricity/policies/legislation/california/subsequentevents.html (last visited June 26, 2024) (detailing Stage I, II, and III outages from January 2000 to August 2001).

61. A Stage III alert is declared when reserve margins fall to less than 1.5 percent, which they did on an almost daily basis during January and some of February 2001. WEARE, *supra* note 59, at 19.

62. Jurewitz, *supra* note 53, at 23–24.

disruption of electrical power."[63] During February 2001, the defaults rose to more than $12 billion, causing the Power Exchange to discontinue its operations in February and to declare bankruptcy on March 9, 2001.[64]

In response to ratepayer protest, the state ordered retail rates frozen at $0.055/kWh.[65] Many of the investor-owned retail utilities were purchasing power at substantially higher wholesale spot market prices but were allowed to pass on much less than this acquisition cost in retail rates under this retail rate cap.[66] In late 2000, the utilities were selling power to retail customers for less than 20 percent of what they were paying for it on the wholesale market.[67] The revenue-strapped regulated California distribution utilities were unable to pay on time for their wholesale power acquisitions because of dwindling cash resources. The utilities teetered on the verge of bankruptcy.

Blackouts and Stakeholder Bankruptcy

The first rolling blackouts in California since World War II occurred on January 17, 2001, and power supply emergencies were declared every day for the following 30 days.[68] The average California retail electric bill increased by 30–40 percent.[69] Rolling blackouts were imposed on consumers during the *off-peak* winter and spring months of 2001. This was and remains unprecedented in modern U.S. history.

In a matter of a few months, this created a $14 billion loss for the state purchasing power on behalf of its essentially insolvent investor-owned utilities[70] that would have to be subsidized and recouped over a decade by California taxpayers and ratepayers. From mid-January through September 2001, the California Department of Water Resources spent $10.7 billion to

63. Gov. Gray Davis, Proclamation by the Governor of the State of California (Jan. 17, 2001), https://docs.cpuc.ca.gov/published/FINAL_DECISION/20291-01.htm.

64. *CALPX Files for Bankruptcy, Blames Lawsuits*, EEI Energy News, Mar. 12, 2001, at 2.

65. A.B. 265 (Cal. 2000) (codified at Cal. Pub. Util. Code § 332.1 (West 2000)).

66. *See* Ahmad Faruqui et al., *Analyzing California's Power Crisis*, 22 Energy J. 37 (2001).

67. *See* Joskow, *supra* note 59, at 34 (utilities were paying approximately $400/MWh for power in the wholesale market while reselling it on the retail market for only $65/MWh).

68. Jurewitz, *supra* note 53, at 24.

69. *Most Californians Conserve Power*, Energy Rep., July 23, 2001, 2001 WL 8475156; Marie Bussing-Burks, *California's Failed Electric Power Industry Reforms*, Nat'l Bureau of Econ. Rsch. (Dec. 1, 2001), https://www.nber.org/digest/dec01/californias-failed-electric-power-industry-reforms. "[I]n June 2001 retail price increases averaging 30 to 40 percent went into effect." *Id.*

70. *See, e.g.*, Virginia Ellis, *8 State Power Contracts Seen as Bad Deals*, L.A. Times, Sept. 30, 2001, at B1.

purchase power on the spot market to supply customers' needs.[71] This wiped out the entire state tax surplus and led to the first recall of a sitting governor in modern history.

To pay for power, in March 2001, the California PUC finally and belatedly increased retail electric rates by 40–50 percent ($0.03/kWh), the largest increase in state history.[72] The enactment of emergency legislation did not end the problems. By early 2001, both Southern California Edison Co. and Pacific Gas & Electric Co. were effectively insolvent. PG&E, the nation's largest utility, filed for Chapter 11 bankruptcy protection in April 2001. The utility had incurred approximately $9 billion in purchased-power costs since June 2000, with no prospect in real time of recovering these past costs under the prior frozen rates.[73] The PG&E bankruptcy under Chapter 11 was meant to stem ongoing losses exceeding $300 million/month.[74]

The bankruptcies were broader. They impacted quasi-public entities. At the end of 2000, FERC terminated formerly approved tariffs of the California Power Exchange; by January, the Power Exchange was in bankruptcy.[75] The California ISO subsequently filed for bankruptcy protection. In September 2001, the California PUC voted to suspend retail electric competition in the state so as to prevent customers from leaving state-purchased power for less expensive and unregulated competitive independent suppliers.[76] There was not a scarcity of energy or of grid hardware or capacity; this was a regulatory legal failure of the California grid to procure and deliver power to California consumers. Contracts for power are legal instruments, and those also became a major issue.

California Contract Conundrum

Here was the legal response: the California state government in 2001 executed nearly $43 billion in long-term power contracts with wholesale suppliers to secure a long-term power supply for a significant share of California's

---

71. Jurewitz, *supra* note 53, at 24.

72. *Rate Hikes Ignite Widespread Protests, Yet Are Unlikely to Resolve Calif. Crisis*, Platts Elec. Util. Wk., Apr. 2, 2001, at 1.

73. *PG&E Files for Bankruptcy: "Regulators and Political Process Have Failed Us,"* Platts Elec. Util. Wk., Apr. 9, 2001, at 1–2; *see also* Jurewitz, *supra* note 53, at 25.

74. *PG&E Files for Bankruptcy: "Regulators and Political Process Have Failed Us,"* Platts Elec. Util. Wk., Apr. 9, 2001, at 1–2; *see also* Jurewitz, *supra* note 53, at 25.

75. Jurewitz, *supra* note 53, at 23.

76. *Id.* at 26; *CPUC Ends Direct Retail Access, Effective September 20*, Elec. Daily, Sept. 25, 2001, at 1–2.

future electricity requirements, on behalf of its insolvent utilities. Although California sought to lock in power supply before prices escalated more, this regulatory response made the system less reliable, pressuring wholesale suppliers to enter these contracts at the most inopportune time. The futures market in November 2000 was approximately $150/MWh; the August 2001 futures price had increased to $350–$550/MWh and even reached as high as $750/MWh when California was finalizing its massive contract deals in April 2001.[77] Shortly after California concluded executing these contracts, by July 2001, the August 2001 future electric market had receded to below $100/MWh.[78] This was inopportune in terms of price—and particularly doing so as a fixed price—which every lawyer must pay particular attention to, as price is always a material contract term in every contract for sale.

However, California also made missteps in each of the other material contract terms in these $43 billion of long-term contracts. For quantity—which always is a material contract term that must be carefully calibrated—a study by the Los Angeles Department of Water Resources indicated that almost a third of the power the state procured under these long-term contracts was unneeded, costing consumers almost $4 billion of wasted expense.

And California suffered again attempting to mitigate this excess in 2003 alone.[79] California lost millions selling excess power that it had purchased during 2001.[80] In July 2001, the state lost $46 million after selling surplus power for approximately 20 percent of the price it had paid for it.[81] It sold power to the Los Angeles Department of Water & Power for 0.5¢/kWh and then essentially gave it away to Canada on another occasion in late May.[82] Within six months prices had returned to precrisis levels, although California regulators had locked into uneconomic long-term contracts at the worst time at the highest prices.[83] The length of the contract terms—also always a material contract term—had been deliberately extended by California long-term at peak prices in a volatile short-term market over an extended period, which worked substantially to the state's detriment.

---

77. *See* Jurewitz, *supra* note 53, at 25.

78. *Id.*

79. *California Overbought Power, New Study Indicates*, EEI Energy News, Nov. 26, 2001, at 2; L.A. Times, Nov. 23, 2001, at pt. A, pt. 1, p. 1; Chi. Tribune, Nov. 25, 2001, at 18.

80. Paul Feist, *State Loses $25 Million in Power Plays*, S.F. Chron., Oct. 25, 2001, at A-19.

81. *Id.*

82. *Id.*

83. *California Power Prices Averaged Less Since Dereg., Analyst Says*, EEI Energy News, Apr. 14, 2003, at 9–10.

There is a lesson when California, the largest state with the fifth largest economy in the world, could not use its several energy regulatory agencies' extensive resources to keep its own grid operational even before today's complexity of distributed generation, cyber hacking, and multiple energy sector stakeholders. Grid resiliency and reliability are now the meta values that must be preserved. There is no electric power when the grid is not in balance.

"Fatboy" and "Deathstar": The Role of Other Stakeholders

It is of note that even the finite number of additional stakeholders during the 2001 California grid resilience crisis exacerbated and exploited the regulatory vulnerabilities. In spring 2002, it was revealed that Enron, Reliant,[84] Dynegy,[85] and CMS[86] had engaged in questionable wholesale power trading activities in the California market.[87] Enron engaged in practices that it dubbed "export of California power,"[88] "inc-ing load,"[89] "fatboy,"[90]

---

84. *Reliant, CMS Trading Chiefs Resign as Companies Deal with "Wash Trades,"* PLATTS ELEC. UTIL. WK., May 20, 2002, at 1, 5. CMS and Reliant engaged in "wash trades" during 2000 and 2002 where they sold power to each other at identical prices so as to deliberately inflate their trading volumes. The top officials at both companies were forced to resign after revelations about this practice. *Id. See also CMS Unloads Bill McCormick as CEO*, ELEC. DAILY, May 29, 2002, at 1.

85. The chair of Dynegy Corp., Chuck Watson, also was forced to resign over this "wash" trade scandal. *Dynegy Board Ousts Founder Chuck Watson*, ELEC. DAILY, May 29, 2002, at 1.

86. *Reliant, CMS Trading Chiefs Resign as Companies Deal with "Wash Trades," supra* note 84, at 2, 5. At CMS, the president of trading operations was forced to resign, and subsequently, the CEO of the parent company, William T. McCormick, was forced out over the scandal. *Id.* at 6; *CMS CEO Quits as Result of Wash Trading*, EEI ENERGY NEWS, May 28, 2002, at 2. CMS faced more than a half dozen class action suits as a result of the reported "wash" trading activity. CMS elected to write off approximately $1 billion of round-trip "wash" trades in 2001.

87. *FERC Expands Western Probe, Seeks Reports on Extent of "Wash" Trading*, PLATTS ELEC. UTIL. WK., May 27, 2002, at 3–4.

88. *"Fat Boy," "Get Shorty" and "Inc-ing": A Look at Enron Trading Practices*, PLATTS ELEC. UTIL. WK., May 13, 2002, at 7–8. Under this practice, Enron bought power on the California Power Exchange for export to higher-priced markets outside of California that were not subject to any price caps. The California Power Exchange price was capped at $2,500/MWh, and the California ISO had a real-time price cap of $250/MWh. A variation of this practice was called "Ricochet," which was the simple laundering of power. Under "Ricochet," Enron exported power from California to a control area outside of the state, paid a fee to "park" the power, and then sold it back to California so as to avoid the price cap. *Id.*

89. *Id.* This involved overscheduling load, which carried no significant penalties. While utilities typically underscheduled load, this extra power became valuable and received a premium price.

90. The "fat boy" scheme was an alternative to "inc-ing" load. Where load was overscheduled, that overscheduling was done in the day-ahead market. When there was surplus power left at the end of that period, the ISO would pay Enron for that surplus, which resulted from the overscheduled load

"Deathstar,"[91] "load shift,"[92] "scheduling energy to collect congestion charge II,"[93] "nonfirm export,"[94] "wheel out,"[95] and "get shorty"[96]—each of which is described in detail in this sentence's footnotes. Enron had created phantom

---

that did not materialize. In the real-time market, the ISO paid Enron the market clearing price for the surplus power.

91. In "Deathstar," Enron was paid for relieving congestion that may or may not have been fictitiously created. For Deathstar, Enron scheduled power to flow in the opposite direction of the flow of load, for which it received a premium counterflow payment from the ISO. Typically, Enron would schedule power across the congested Path 15 to the California-Oregon border and simultaneously schedule power back to the point of origin using less congested lines or out-of-state lines. The two amounts scheduled would cancel each other out, and Enron would not actually have to purchase any power net. By fictitiously moving power on paper, without transacting any net power, Enron arbitraged the appearance of where its power was flowing. *Id.* Rebecca Smith, *FERC Orders Power Suppliers to Pay Refunds*, WALL ST. J., Mar. 12, 2001, at A4.

92. *Id.* For "load-shift" Enron would overschedule load in one congested zone and underschedule load in another zone. This boosted the price the ISO would pay for relief in the congested zone, which price was exacerbated by the overscheduling. Enron would receive a premium price. When it turned out that the power was not really needed in the overscheduled and artificially inflated zone, after being paid, Enron could then balance its load by switching the power back to the other zone. No real transmission capability was needed because Enron knew in advance it would not have to actually move the power into the zone. This effectively increased congestion management costs to all participants. This was a basic maneuver to get paid for scheduling nonfirm power sales that Enron knew it would not need to make. It would benefit from congestion payments when it later cut the schedules. *Id.*

93. *Id.* For this, Enron scheduled a power flow in the opposite direction of the congestion, even when it was short of power to accomplish this flow. Enron would cover this obligation in the real-time market. When congestion payments were greater than the charge associated with the energy that did not have to be delivered, Enron made money.

94. *Id.* This was similar to the tactic of "scheduling energy to collect congestion charge II." In this case, the power sale was nonfirm and therefore contractually could be cut. Enron would set up counterflow with nonfirm energy export to a control area outside the state and was paid a congestion payment.

95. *Id.* In this, Enron would schedule power flow over a line going out of the state that it knew was completely constrained or unavailable. When the availability of that line was cut, Enron would get a payment for its denial of access, even though it did not intend to ship energy over that line. It benefited from receipt of this congestion payment.

96. *Id.* In this, Enron speculated on the ancillary services market by promising to provide such services or by selling nonfirm energy as if it were firm energy. Enron would sell these ancillary services in the day-ahead market and then cover this obligation in the actual market. Enron never had these ancillary services to sell and could not have covered this obligation had it been required to do so. This basically was a speculative ploy that the real-time market services would cost less if it had to cover than the price it received in the day-ahead market. Therefore, it was arbitraging the time value of power, having also manipulated markets to influence perceived trades. When it sold nonfirm energy as firm energy, Enron again counted on the fact that it would not have to supply this energy because markets were being manipulated as to the amount of power actually required.

congestion diminishing resilience on the California grid or along certain paths of the grid and then would be paid for relieving some of the value of the phantom congestion it had created.

Collectively, grid failure punctuated by the rolling California blackouts in 2001 cost Silicon Valley businesses an estimated $75 million a day; the rolling brownout in the first two weeks of January 2001 cost the state economy $2.3 billion due to production cutbacks and lost wages.[97] The 20 hours of outages are estimated to have reduced gross California state output by $21.8 billion and reduced household income by $4.6 billion more.[98]

The Importance of Legal Contracts

California Governor Davis demanded wholesale suppliers renegotiate the long-term deals he had previously made with them a few months before. A few months later in February 2002, the California PUC filed petitions with FERC to void 32 long-term power contracts that the state negotiated in 2001 with 22 different individual wholesale power suppliers, alleging that the contracts were negotiated in an anticompetitive environment and exceeded "just and reasonable" prices by $14 billion.[99] At that time, the $43 billion in contracts had a market value of approximately half the price at which they were negotiated.[100]

Despite each of these long-term contracts having been voluntarily entered into in the competitive market that California regulators had created, a FERC administrative law judge in December 2002 ruled that electricity suppliers had overcharged the since-defunct California Power Exchange and the California ISO by some $1.8 billion.[101] Disputes over the California crisis are still being litigated and settled today, more than two decades later.

---

97. Ann Deering, *The Expanding Energy Crisis: United States*, Risk Mgmt., May 1, 2001.

98. AUS Consultants, *Impact of a Continuing Electricity Crisis on the California Economy*, May 3, 2001, at ii; *see also* California Alliance for Energy & Economic Stability Study on the California Blackout, May 2001.

99. FERC Docket No. EL 02-60; *Wholesale Suppliers Plead with FERC to Uphold Calif. Long-Term Contracts*, Platts Elec. Util. Wk., Apr. 1, 2002, at 1.

100. Tim Reiterman, *State Disputes Long-Term Power Pacts*, L.A. Times, Feb. 25, 2002, at 1; James Steingold, *California Tries to Have Energy Deals Renegotiated*, N.Y. Times, Feb. 25, 2002, at A-17.

101. *Calif. Owes Suppliers, Rules FERC ALJ*, Elec. Daily, Dec. 16, 2002, at 1. FERC presiding judge Bruce Birchbaum ruled that the $1.8 billion in overcharges was offset by approximately $3 billion still unpaid by the purchasers to the suppliers. This decision was the culmination of a process of off-record negotiations, record hearings, and intervention by 100 active parties, amid political pressure.

Because power in one state affects other states, missteps also change the future of the electric power regulatory landscape in the region and/or across the nation. Of those 23 states plus the District of Columbia that began restructuring and partially deregulating their retail electricity markets at the end of the 20th century, the collapse in California caused six of them to change course: California suspended retail deregulation, and five other states, near to California and to Texas, delayed and then reversed the implementation of their in-progress electric system deregulation.[102] In addition to these reversals, with the collapse of the California deregulated energy markets in 2001, the progress toward deregulation in all other pending states was halted. For more on the current status of state deregulation, see Chapter 13.

The grid remains the most complex facet of the electricity system, involving a very complex engineered machine. There are many alternatives to generate electric power—all involve different prime movers and mechanisms to move electrons in metal conductors. Amid more competition in generation and a substantial increase in wholesale power, there remains only a single electric grid, comprised of the most important infrastructure in the United States. It requires constant rebalancing to deliver reliable power. It requires an evolving set of legal rules and regulations to operate resiliently. It is now in the process of rapid change. Legal rules and FERC and PUC orders will shape these changes.

The next chapter pivots to shine new light on the proposed federal initiative that could significantly change a century of law on how power is paid for and challenge many legal precedents governing how electricity is provided and regulated. It could alter the law of energy and environment fundamentally. The next chapter fills in the gaps on what these new laws could do, legal tripwires and challenges of proposed new laws, and how attorneys can prepare for such a legal pivot.

See also Let Down by FERC ALJ Ruling, Calif. Vows to Push For at Least $9 Billion, PLATTS ELEC. UTIL. WK., Dec. 16, 2002, at 1.

102. The five states that delayed were states either of major western power supply, including a source of electric supply to California (Nevada and Montana), or that bordered the other largest state to deregulate, Texas (New Mexico, Oklahoma, and Arkansas).

CHAPTER 15

Legal Tripwires Associated with a Green New Deal

What is on the horizon for future new law for U.S. power? The so-called Green New Deal, if and when it collects enough votes to be enacted, will be a different domestic energy initiative. In 2021, the U.S. population polled supported the Green New Deal by a 31-point margin.[1]

Even if it is enacted, it will take multiple years to implement, similar to the time needed for the recently enacted Infrastructure Investment and Jobs Act and the Inflation Reduction Act. See Chapter 6. More than timing, the substantive question is: can the Green New Deal avoid being challenged for violating U.S. law?[2]

This chapter sidesteps the pro-con policy debate surrounding the Green New Deal to analyze the fundamental legal issue of how it will fare under U.S. law and how stakeholders will adapt or challenge its legality. The Green New Deal is at the center of a national dialogue on U.S. policy. The Green New Deal combines "green" sustainable elements with its redistributive provisions—will these two policies achieve the sum of their parts?

Then-President Trump tweeted his opinion that the Green New Deal eliminates "all Planes, Cars, Cows, Oil, Gas & the Military."[3] He subsequently concluded: "[It will] kill millions of jobs, it will crush the dreams of the poorest Americans and disproportionately harm minority communities

---

1. Danielle Deiseroth & Lew Blank, *Voters Overwhelmingly Support the Green New Deal*, DATA FOR PROGRESS (Apr. 19, 2021), https://www.dataforprogress.org/blog/2021/4/19/voters-support-green-new-deal.

2. *See* Earl J. Ritchie, *What You Should Know about the Green New Deal(s)*, FORBES (Feb. 8, 2019), https://www.forbes.com/sites/uhenergy/2019/02/08/what-you-should-know-about-the-green-new-deals/#1dafd2332389 (noting that some versions of the Green New Deal incorporate "broad societal and governmental changes, such as income redistribution and reduction of the U.S. military").

3. Salvador Rizzo, *What's Actually in the "Green New Deal" from Democrats?*, WASH. POST (Feb. 11, 2019), https://www.washingtonpost.com/politics/2019/02/11/whats-actually-green-new-deal-democrats/.

.... I will not stand for it."[4] President Obama's Secretary of Energy, Ernest Moniz, voiced skepticism, raising the possibility that this legislation could not achieve its goals and would set back climate control objectives:

> I'm afraid I just cannot see how we could possibly go to zero carbon in the 10-year time frame .... It's just impractical. And if we start putting out impractical targets, we may lose a lot of key constituencies who we need to bring along to have a real low-carbon solution on the most rapid time frame that we can achieve ....[5]

The United States is a known top contributor to greenhouse gas (GHG) emissions among major countries.[6] There are federal and state legal tripwires that confront seamless implementation of a Green New Deal—

At the federal level:

- Binding Federal Energy Regulatory Commission (FERC) orders mandate that all power generation be dispatched or operated based on the value of the lowest competitive cost, which may or may not be "green" in a given year.
- Three recent decisions of the Supreme Court even before the *Loper Bright* 2024 Supreme Court decision in 2024 overruled *Chevron*, substantially limited traditional *Chevron* deference for executive branch agency regulations that fundamentally change electric sector operation or emissions affecting climate change, without clear direction from Congress for that change.

At the state level:

- Renewable energy resources are not evenly distributed among the states, with as much as a 4:1 state-by-state differential of available solar and other "green" power (see Chapter 3).
- Certain states have not favored policy supporting renewable power.

---

4. Joseph Zeballos-Roig, *President Donald Trump Used a Speech Aimed at Touting His Environmental Record to Declare War on Alexandria Ocasio-Cortez's "Unthinkable" Green New Deal*, Bus. Insider (July 8, 2019), https://www.businessinsider.com/president-trump-declares-war-on-aoc-green-new-deal-2019-7 (alteration in original).

5. Rizzo, *supra* note 3 (internal quotation marks omitted).

6. M. Crippa et al., Joint Rsch. Ctr., CO2 Emissions of All World Countries: JRC/IEA/PBL 2022 Report 12, tbl. 2, https://edgar.jrc.ec.europa.eu/booklet/CO2_emissions_of_all_world_countries_2022_report.pdf.

- A recent Supreme Court decision outlaws state regulations that attempt to attract certain types of power generation to their states when they participate in interstate power markets,[7] which most state utilities do.
- Energy regulatory law in many of the states prohibits redistributing wealth through differential pricing of retail electricity.

Energy is the principal sector through which climate issues will be addressed, given that the energy sector contributes more than half of all CO_2 emissions.[8]

Legally Distinguishing "Green" from "New Deal" in the Green New Deal

The Green New Deal features key goals for both its "green" sustainability and for "New Deal"–type measures as tracked by observers:

Green:[9]

- Cutting greenhouse-gas emissions dramatically by 2035 and to no power sector carbon emissions
- Meeting 100 percent of the power demand in the United States through clean, renewable, and zero-emission energy sources.
- "Building or upgrading to energy-efficient, distributed, and 'smart' power grids, and working to ensure affordable access to electricity."
- "Upgrading all existing buildings in the United States and building new buildings to achieve maximal energy efficiency, water efficiency, safety, affordability, comfort, and durability, including through electrification."

---

7. Hughes v. Talen Energy Mktg., LLC, 136 S. Ct. 1288 (2016).

8. U.S. Dept of Energy, EIA, ("In the United States, most (about 74%) human-caused (anthropogenic) greenhouse gas (GHG) emissions come from burning fossil fuels—coal, natural gas, and petroleum—for energy use. "), https://www.eia.gov/energyexplained/energy-and-the-environment/where-greenhouse-gases-come-from.php; U.S. EPA ("The largest source of greenhouse gas emissions from human activities in the United States is from burning fossil fuels for electricity, heat, and transportation."), https://climatechange.chicago.gov/ghgemissions/sources-greenhouse-gas-emissions#:~:text=The%20largest%20source%20of%20greenhouse,electricity%2C%20heat%2C%20and%20transportation.

9. Rizzo, *supra* note 3 (quoting H.R. Res. 109, 116th Cong. (2019)).

New Deal:

- "Guaranteeing a job with a family-sustaining wage, adequate family and medical leave, paid vacations, and retirement security to all people of the United States."[10] Representative Ocasio-Cortez's office later augmented this in an FAQ, stating that "the Green New Deal sought 'economic security for all who are unable or unwilling to work.'"[11] Others added: "We need to treat clean energy as a human right and a common good. We also need a just transition to provide resources to the low-income communities and communities of color most impacted by climate change."[12]
- "Providing all people of the United States with—(i) high-quality health care; (ii) affordable, safe, and adequate housing; (iii) economic security; and (iv) access to clean water, clean air, healthy and affordable food, and nature."[13]
- "Providing resources, training, and high-quality education, including higher education, to all people of the United States."[14]
- Representative Ocasio-Cortez's office provided an FAQ that added a proposal to build "high-speed rail at a scale where air travel stops becoming necessary."[15]

The items in the first section of the preceding list are "green" sustainable energy elements, while the items in the second section of the preceding list are more accurately categorized as redistributive social elements. This distinction is important if legal challenges occur.[16] The "green" elements predominately involve the electric power sector, and this is not by chance.[17] The consensus climate change mitigation plan, put together by former California Governor Jerry Brown and former New York City Mayor Michael Bloomberg, designates the electric sector of the economy—even

---

10. *Id.* (quoting H.R. Res. 109).
11. *Id.* (citation omitted).
12. *Green New Deal*, Green Party U.S., https://www.gp.org/green_new_deal (last visited May 23, 2024).
13. Rizzo, *supra* note 3 (quoting H.R. Res. 109).
14. *Id.* (quoting H.R. Res. 109).
15. *Id.* (citation omitted).
16. *See* Daniel Oberhaus, *The Real Challenge for the Green New Deal Isn't Politics*, Wired (July 9, 2019), https://www.wired.com/story/real-challenge-green-new-deal-isnt-politics/.
17. Rizzo, *supra* note 3.

though it contributes only approximately 28 percent of total GHG emissions annually—to eliminate 620 million metric tons (MMT) of carbon dioxide equivalent (CO_2e) of the total 1,020 MMT of CO_2e targeted for elimination, shouldering more than 60 percent of the total effort by 2025.[18] The Biden-Harris administration goes even further, imposing two-thirds of the responsibility to reduce GHG emissions on the electric sector.[19]

"Green" Power Grid Changes to Accommodate Renewable Power

The electric sector dominates emissions of the primary GHG, CO_2, and the second most important climate-changing molecule, CH_4 or methane (see Chapter 16), compared to all other sectors of the economy. Power plants emit approximately 40 percent of all anthropogenic CO_2 emissions in the United States.[20]

Power requires hard wiring to be delivered in a form usable by consumers. The electric power grid provides an essential service to constantly balance demand of power with supply necessary to keep the grid operational. See Chapter 14. Moving electrons cannot be efficiently stored as electricity for more than a fraction of a second before the energy is lost as waste heat. Supply of electricity must match the volatile demand for electricity over the centralized utility grid at all times to maintain electric system operation. Either too much or too little power during any few seconds can cause system instability.[21]

---

18. Bloomberg Philanthropies, Fulfilling America's Pledge 5–6, 19 (2018), https://www.bbhub.io/dotorg/sites/28/2018/09/Fulfilling-Americas-Pledge-2018.pdf; Sources of Greenhouse Gas Emissions, U.S. Env't Prot. Agency (May 15, 2024), https://www.epa.gov/ghgemissions/sources-greenhouse-gas-emissions.

19. U.S. Dep't of Energy, *The* Inflation Reduction Act *Drives Significant Emissions Reductions and Positions America to Reach Our Climate Goals* 3 (Aug. 2022), https://www.energy.gov/sites/default/files/2022-08/8.18%20InflationReductionAct_Factsheet_Final.pdf.

20. Standards for Performance of Greenhouse Gas Emissions for New Stationary Source: Electric Utility Generating Units, 77 Fed. Reg 22,392, 22,395 (Apr. 13, 2012) (to be codified at 40 C.F.R. pt. 60); *Overview of Greenhouse Gases: Carbon Dioxide Emissions*, U.S. Env't Prot. Agency (Apr. 11, 2024), http://www3.epa.gov/climatechange/ghgemissions/gases/co2.html.

21. Power Blackout Risks, CRO Forum 6 (2011), https://www.thecroforum.org/wp-content/uploads/2012/09/CRO-Position-Paper-Power-Blackout-Risks-1-1.pdf.

Wind and solar "green" power differ from many other forms of electricity generation in that their outputs are intermittent and thus are distinct from traditional forms of baseload power deployed in the United States.[22] Non-tracking solar photovoltaic (PV) panel technology and wind power demonstrate a relatively low capacity factor in the 10–50 percent range of hours during a week. The capacity factor calculates what percentage of the maximum "nameplate" power generation potential of the equipment is realized in operation.[23] The recorded U.S. annual wind capacity factor was 33.9 percent in 2014; the U.S. Energy Information Administration calculated the median wind capacity over a recent decade as 31 percent.[24] In the United Kingdom, the calculated wind capacity factor ranged from a low of 21.5 percent in 2010 to a high of 27.9 percent in 2013.[25]

Intermittent renewable power triggers a management issue for grid operation. In a three-month period in 2014, the California Integrated System Operator (CAISO) was required to curtail wind and solar generation in four instances for six hours to balance supply and demand on the system.[26] The oversupply of intermittent renewables curtailed 485 megawatts (MW) of wind and 657 MW of solar.[27] In Hawaii, solar panels produced more power than used.[28] Consequently, "[t]he energy [could] flow back to the substation . . . which [could] lead to reliability problems and possibly surges. And if crews are working in the area, there's a potential danger."[29] In response,

---

22. Victor Provenzano, *The Intermittency of Wind and Solar: Is It Only Intermittently a Problem?*, CleanTechnica (Aug. 12, 2013), https://cleantechnica.com/2013/08/12/intermittency-of-wind-and-solar-is-it-only-intermittently-a-problem/.

23. *See What Is Generation Capacity?*, U.S. Dep't of Energy, Off. of Nuclear Energy (May 1, 2020), https://www.energy.gov/ne/articles/what-generation-capacity.

24. Planning Engineer & Rud Istvan, *True Costs of Wind Electricity*, Climate Etc. (May 12, 2015), http://judithcurry.com/2015/05/12/true-costs-of-wind-electricity/.

25. *Id.*

26. David Howarth & Bill Monsen, *Renewables Face Daytime Curtailments in California*, Project Fin. NewsWire 12, 12–13 (Nov. 2014), https://www.projectfinance.law/media/1584/pfn_1114.pdf.

27. *Id.*

28. *See* Robert Fares, *3 Reasons Hawaii Put the Brakes on Solar—and Why the Same Won't Happen in Your State*, Sci. Am. (Dec. 15, 2015), https://www.scientificamerican.com/blog/plugged-in/3-reasons-hawaii-put-the-brakes-on-solar-and-why-the-same-won-t-happen-in-your-state/.

29. Anne C. Mulkern, *A Solar Boom So Successful, It's Been Halted*, Sci. Am. (Dec. 20, 2013), https://www.scientificamerican.com/article/a-solar-boom-so-successfull-its-been-halted/.

Hawaii eliminated its net metering program entirely in 2015, replacing it with two options: self-supply and grid supply.[30] See Chapter 9.

Supreme Court Deleverages Federal Regulatory Power over Electric Power and Its Climate Impacts

Any federal congressional action to approve the Green New Deal would invoke constitutional federal power over interstate commerce and the federal taxing power. Most, or even all, of it would be implemented by executive branch regulations that might be promulgated primarily by FERC and the EPA. Recently in a series of three decisions, the Supreme Court restricted the ability of federal agencies to implement law addressing climate change affecting the energy sector of the U.S. economy.

Utility Air Regulatory Group v. EPA: Limiting Executive Agency Discretion on Electric Power

In 2014, the EPA, implementing President Obama's Climate Action Plan, promulgated regulations to supplement provisions of the Clean Air Act to address the emission of GHGs from power plants.[31] The EPA estimated that compliance would cost private power generators up to $8.8 billion annually.[32] The U.S. Supreme Court in *Utility Air Regulatory Group v. EPA* overruled such exercise of EPA authority on electric generating plants and climate change, stating:

---

30. *See State Net Metering Policies*, NAT'L CONF. OF STATE LEGISLATURES (Nov. 20, 2017), https://www.ncsl.org/energy/state-net-metering-policies; Phil Cross, *Net Metering Skirmishes in Hawaii, California, Mississippi, Nevada*, PUB. UTILS. FORT., Feb. 2016, at 56; Mark Dyson & Jesse Morris, *Hawaii Just Ended Net Metering for Solar. Now What?*, RMI OUTLET (Oct. 16, 2015), https://rmi.org/hawaii-just-ended-net-metering-solar-now/. *See* Krysti Shallenberger, *Hawaii Regulators Nix Bid to Raise Caps on Grid-Supply Rooftop Solar Incentive*, UTIL. DIVE (Dec. 15, 2016), http://www.utilitydive.com/news/hawaii-regulators-nix-bid-to-raise-caps-on-grid-supply-rooftop-solar-incent/432464/; Heather Payne & Jonas Monast, *Valuing Distributed Energy Resources: A Comparative Analysis* 16, UNC CTR. FOR CLIMATE, ENERGY, ENV'T & ECON. (2018), https://law.unc.edu/wp-content/uploads/2019/09/derpaperfinal.pdf.

31. *See FACT SHEET: Clean Power Plan*, U.S. ENV'T PROT. AGENCY, https://archive.epa.gov/epa/cleanpowerplan/fact-sheet-clean-power-plan.html#print (last visited May 23, 2024).

32. *FACT SHEET: Clean Power Plan Benefits of a Cleaner, More Efficient Power Sector*, U.S. ENV'T PROT. AGENCY, https://archive.epa.gov/epa/cleanpowerplan/fact-sheet-clean-power-plan-benefits-cleaner-more-efficient-power-sector.html (last visited May 23, 2024).

> Were we to recognize the authority claimed by EPA in the Tailoring Rule, we would deal a severe blow to the Constitution's separation of powers. Under our system of government, Congress makes laws and the President, acting at times through agencies like EPA, "faithfully execute[s]" them. . . . The power of executing the laws necessarily includes both authority and responsibility to resolve some questions left open by Congress that arise during the law's administration. But it does not include a power to revise clear statutory terms that turn out to not work in practice.[33]

The U.S. Supreme Court held that the executive branch of government cannot refashion parts of congressional environmental statutes addressing climate change: "EPA's interpretation is . . . unreasonable because it would bring about an enormous and transformative expansion in EPA's regulatory authority without clear congressional authorization."[34] The Court struck the agency's interpretation of a statute applying to GHG emissions and climate change:

> An agency has no power to "tailor" legislation to bureaucratic policy goals by rewriting unambiguous statutory terms. Agencies exercise discretion only in the interstices created by statutory silence or ambiguity; they must always "give effect to the unambiguously expressed intent of Congress."[35]

This 2014 Supreme Court opinion limits the additional discretion that the EPA may exercise under any presidential administration to implement a "green" climate change statute addressing the electric power sector.

---

33. Util. Air Regul. Grp. v. EPA, 134 S. Ct. 2427, 2446 (2014) (alteration in original) (citations omitted). In ruling against the EPA's Tailoring Rule argument, the Court reaffirm[ed] the core administrative-law principle that an agency may not rewrite clear statutory terms to suit its own sense of how the statute should operate. EPA therefore lacked authority to "tailor" the Act's unambiguous numerical thresholds to accommodate its greenhouse-gas-inclusive interpretation of the permitting triggers. Instead, the need to rewrite clear provisions of the statute should have alerted EPA that it had taken a wrong interpretive turn.

34. *Id.* at 2444.

35. *Id.* at 2445.

Michigan v. EPA: Limitations on EPA Energy Sector Regulation

In 2015, the Supreme Court overturned executive environmental and energy regulations that did not consider costs before requiring action of the private electric power industry.[36] This decision was issued during the Obama administration, a year before the election of President Trump. This decision, for the first time in the history of U.S. jurisprudence, made the consideration of costs, even where not expressly required in the statute, a prerequisite to justify EPA energy sector regulation.[37] This alters traditional court *Chevron* deference to executive branch and EPA initiatives, particularly regarding EPA regulation of the energy sector regarding climate change.[38]

In this regulation of mercury emissions from power generation facilities, the EPA—without providing any statistical basis or medical proof—claimed long-term health benefits of $37–$90 billion annually.[39] What the Supreme Court noted about costs and benefits and their ultimate balance is of note for future disputes that could also embroil the Green New Deal or similar legislation:

> During oral arguments, several members of the Court were critical that the EPA's cost-benefit analysis for the MATS [Mercury Air Toxics Standards] rule—which attributed annually billions of dollars in annual public health benefits to the reduction of $PM_{2.5}$ and other pollutants—regulated under other sections of the Clean Air Act unrelated to the MATS mercury standards, "even though the agency could only quantify between $4 million and $6 million in benefits to reductions of hazardous air pollutants," a fraction of one percent of the "benefits."[40]

The Supreme Court overturned the MATS rule because the EPA is required to "consider cost—including, most importantly, cost of compliance—before deciding whether regulation is appropriate and necessary,"

---

36. Michigan v. EPA, 135 S. Ct. 2699, 2711–12 (2015).

37. *See id.* at 2708–10 (finding that the Court's precedent has never held that cost was necessary in an "appropriate and necessary" determination by an agency).

38. Chevron v. Nat'l Res. Def. Council, 467 U.S. 837, 844 (1984).

39. *Michigan*, 135 S. Ct. at 2706.

40. Patrick Ambrosio, *Supreme Court Remands EPA Mercury Rule for Failing to Consider Cost to Power Plants*, Daily Env't Rep. (BNA) (June 30, 2015).

because "[o]ne would not say that it is even rational, never mind 'appropriate,' to impose billions of dollars in economic costs in return for a few dollars in health or environmental benefits."[41] The decision in *Michigan* establishes at least two new limitations on such actions targeting energy industries or regarding climate change:

- A prerequisite cost consideration is now required for action regarding the power sector under the Clean Air Act.
- It is not yet clear what will be the Court's reaction when program costs far exceed benefits.

West Virginia v. EPA: EPA Cannot Regulate Electric Power Dispatch

In 2016,[42] the Supreme Court took an action that it had never taken before—indefinitely enjoined an entire federal regulation from its preamble to its final sentence before any substantive federal circuit court decision regarding any specific challenged section of the statute reached it on appeal.[43] Again, this involved an EPA regulation of the electric power sector involving the Obama administration Clean Power Plan (CPP).

A majority of U.S. states challenged the EPA regarding its CPP regulations, with the minority of states supporting the CPP.[44] The Supreme Court in 2022 in *West Virginia v. EPA* restricted federal regulatory power over electric power and dramatically increased the power of the plaintiff states to regulate electric power.[45] The Court held that existing federal law does not permit the EPA to attempt to regulate what or how electric generation facilities in the states generate electric power or to change the U.S. energy dispatch/delivery system, and the EPA admitted that it had no expertise in this area.[46]

This trio of recent Supreme Court decisions, with the *West Virginia* case yielding two decisions six years apart, substantially constricts the federal agency and executive branch regulation of electric power operations.

---

41. *Michigan*, 135 S. Ct. at 2707, 2711.

42. *See generally* West Virginia v. EPA, 136 S. Ct. 1000 (2016).

43. *See* Linda Tsang & Alexandra M. Wyatt, Cong. Rsch. Serv., R44480, Clean Power Plan: Legal Background and Pending Litigation in *West Virginia v. EPA* 14–15 (2017) (clarifying that the Court's split decision was rare without a lower court hearing the case on the merits).

44. *Id.*

45. West Virginia v. EPA, 142 S. Ct. 2587, 2606 (2022).

46. *Id.* at 2616.

Moreover, the degree of resiliency of the Supreme Court decision in *Massachusetts v. EPA*,[47] which initially permitted the EPA regulation of carbon emissions, also has been a subject of discussion in the Court since its issuance: in a concurring opinion in *American Electric Power Co. v. Connecticut*, Justices Alito and Thomas were receptive to reconsidering the *Massachusetts* decision.[48] In *Utility Air Regulatory Group v. EPA*, these justices argued that *Massachusetts* "was wrongly decided at the time."[49]

The Green New Deal purposefully and directly seeks to address the power sector in its "green" initiatives. Of note, the Court-stricken CPP in the *West Virginia* case was less of a change to the power sector than what was proposed in the Green New Deal.

Complicating Implementation of the Green New Deal

The legal precedent controlling federal and state jurisdiction over electric power treats all consumers equally while minimizing the cost of provision of electric power service. The "New Deal" elements of the Green New Deal would steer a new direction that could differently treat consumers using the same quantity and quality of power from identical sources of supply. These elements could confront significant legal challenges at both the federal and state levels.

The Supremacy Clause "Bright Line" Shifts Power Away from States

Sections 205 and 206 of the Federal Power Act (FPA)[50] empower FERC exclusively to regulate rates for the interstate and wholesale sale and transmission of electricity.[51] The U.S. Supreme Court held that Congress meant to draw a "bright line"—easily ascertained and not requiring case-by-case analysis—separating state and federal jurisdiction over power.[52] When a transaction is subject to exclusive federal jurisdiction and FERC regulation, state regulation is preempted as a matter of both federal law and the U.S.

---

47. 549 U.S. 497 (2007).

48. 564 U.S. 410, 430 (2011).

49. 573 U.S. 302, 343 (2014).

50. Energy Policy Act of 2005, 16 U.S.C. § 824d–e.

51. Pub. Util. Dist. No. 1 v. FERC, 471 F.3d 1053, 1058 (9th Cir. 2006), *aff'd in part, remanded in part sub nom.* Morgan Stanley Cap. Grp., Inc. v. Pub. Util. Dist. No. 1, 554 U.S. 527 (2008).

52. Fed. Power Comm'n v. S. Cal. Edison Co., 376 U.S. 205, 215–16 (1964).

Constitution's Supremacy Clause, according to a long-standing and consistent line of rulings by the U.S. Supreme Court.[53] See Chapter 4.

The entire suite of rates, terms, and provisions of any wholesale sale or transmission of electricity in interstate commerce is exclusively within federal jurisdiction and control—not state authority.[54] Under the FPA, FERC has "exclusive authority to regulate the transmission and sale at wholesale of electric energy in interstate commerce, without regard to the source of production."[55] The Filed-Rate Doctrine applies to and blocks efforts by state regulators to modify the terms of a FERC-mandated rate determination or cost allocation.[56] The Filed-Rate Doctrine, which preempts state law, applies with equal force in both federal and state courts.[57]

The Supreme Court in 1986, and again in 1988, 2003, and 2008, reaffirmed and enforced exclusive federal jurisdiction pursuant to the Filed-Rate Doctrine when states attempted to assert jurisdiction inconsistent with FERC's exclusive authority over wholesale-rate determinations.[58] If states impose a rate in excess of Avoided Cost (the wholesale value of power in the market) by either "law or policy," the "contracts will be considered to be void *ab initio*."[59] See Chapter 5 on Avoided Cost. States, however, retain authority over retail electric sales, because "FERC's jurisdiction over the *sale* of power has been specifically confined to the wholesale market."[60]

A federal court ruled that any state regulation of wholesale-power preferences and sales violated the U.S. Constitution.[61] Preemption of state

---

53. New Eng. Power Co. v. New Hampshire, 455 U.S. 331, 340–44 (1982); *see also* Entergy La., Inc. v. La. Pub. Serv. Comm'n, 539 U.S. 39, 49–50 (2003); *accord* Miss. Power & Light Co. v. Mississippi *ex rel.* Moore, 487 U.S. 354, 371–72 (1988); Nantahala Power & Light Co. v. Thornburg, 476 U.S. 953, 966 (1986); Mont.-Dakota Utils. Co. v. Nw. Pub. Serv. Co., 341 U.S. 246, 251–52 (1951).

54. *See New Eng. Power Co.*, 455 U.S. at 340.

55. *Id.*

56. *See Entergy La., Inc.*, 539 U.S. at 47.

57. *See* Ark. La. Gas Co. v. Hall, 453 U.S. 571, 581–82 (1981).

58. *See* Morgan Stanley Cap. Grp. Inc. v. Pub. Util. Dist. No. 1 of Snohomish Cnty., 554 U.S. 527, 531 (2008); *accord Entergy La., Inc.*, 539 U.S. at 41, 49–50; *Miss. Power & Light Co.*, 487 U.S. at 371; *Nantahala Power & Light Co.*, 476 U.S. at 963.

59. Conn. Light & Power Co., 70 FERC ¶¶ 61,012, 61,029–30 (1995); *see also* Indep. Energy Producers Ass'n v. Cal. Pub. Utils. Comm'n, 36 F.3d 848, 858–59 (9th Cir. 1994); S. Cal. Edison Co., 70 FERC ¶¶ 61,215, 61,676 (1995).

60. New York v. FERC, 535 U.S. 1, 20 (2002) (emphasis in original).

61. Entergy Nuclear Vt. Yankee, LLC v. Shumlin, 838 F. Supp. 2d 183, 243 (D. Vt. 2012), *aff'd in part, rev'd in part*, 733 F.3d 393 (2d Cir. 2013).

jurisdiction to regulate wholesale-power transactions, as well as dormant Commerce Clause violations resulting from state attempts to discriminate in their preference for in-state regulation of power moving in interstate commerce, resulted in the federal court's finding of unconstitutionality.[62]

Legal Limits on State Electric Power Rates

State courts in many of the states and territories over the last century have made binding decisions regarding equal protection of all consumers of retail electric power. The 50 states have split opinions about renewable energy versus traditional forms of electricity production and related costs of electric power.[63] States face a hurdle in implementing certain elements of the Green New Deal. The costs of construction and operation of key power infrastructure now are allocated on a neutral cost basis to all consumers in a user class. Seeking via the Green New Deal to shift costs from certain residential power consumers to other residential power consumers through different electric power rates may not be consistent with law in many states.

Discrimination in Electric Power Prices

Pursuant to legal principles at the federal level of regulation, Section 205 of the FPA prohibits utilities from granting for wholesale rates "any undue preference or advantage to any person or . . . maintain[ing] any unreasonable difference in rates . . . either as between localities or as between classes of service."[64] FERC regulations specify that it is illegal to discriminate in rates among customers of the same class.[65] There should be horizontal equity between different customer classes and vertical equity among customers who use different amounts of electricity within the customer class.[66]

The bulk of legal challenges to policies of differentiated retail utility rates has been based on the equal protection clause of the applicable state

62. *Id.* at 242–43.

63. Ellen Knickmeyer, *Amid Urgent Climate Warnings, EPA Gives Coal a Reprieve*, Associated Press (June 19, 2019), https://www.apnews.com/d48562a8d7ee4df1bceec0990205e5b3.

64. 16 U.S.C. § 824d(b).

65. Pub. Serv. Co. of Ind. v. FERC, 575 F.2d 1204, 1212 (7th Cir. 1978), *aff'd sub nom.* City of Frankfort v. FERC, 678 F.2d 699 (7th Cir. 1982); Wis. Mich. Power Co., 54 Pub. Util. Rep. 3d (PUR) 321 (Fed. Power Comm'n 1964).

66. *See* Am. Elec. Power Serv. Corp., 67 FERC ¶ 61,168, ¶ 61,490, *clarified*, 67 FERC ¶ 61,317 (1994).

constitutions.[67] State regulatory commissions must determine whether different customers have paid variable retail rate amounts for the same service under the same circumstances. Successful legal challenges have prevented states attempting to affect welfare policy through differentiated retail electric utility tariffs for different groups of power consumers. This could be done utilizing more direct state tax or spending policies financed from general state revenues to assist certain consumers. Following are examples of legal decisions from states in different areas of the country.

Pennsylvania's energy regulatory commission order requiring electric utility retail charges to be applied equally within the residential class was violated by the offer of a special rate to low-income and fixed-income customers, which constituted unconstitutional discrimination.[68] The commission was concerned about the spillover impact of decreased costs to the benefited group of consumers and the commensurate increased costs to similarly served customers.

Indiana law prohibited utilities from charging different rates for customers who receive "the same services under the same conditions."[69] Targeted lifeline rates that provided a below-cost electric rate for specific customers based on their level of income or demography were found to violate state statutes prohibiting undue discrimination.[70] The court held that it was discriminatory to charge customers different rates when they were "receiving the same service under the same circumstances."

The Colorado Supreme Court held that targeted lifeline rates for low-income customers were unconstitutional because they were unjustly preferential, discriminatory, and contrary to legal prohibition of preferential rates.[71] The court reasoned that the PUC is a nonelected body that cannot determine which customers could receive a special rate: "To find otherwise would empower the PUC, an appointed, nonelected body, to create a special rate for

67. *See* Mountain States Legal Found. v. Pub. Utils. Comm'n, 590 P.2d 495, 496–97 (Colo. 1979); *In re* Cent. Me. Power Co., 26 Pub. Util. Rep. 4th (PUR) 388, 430 (Me. 1978); Pa. Pub. Util. Comm'n v. Phila. Elec. Co., 91 Pub. Util. Rep. 3d (PUR) 321, 373 (Pa. 1971).

68. *See Pa. Pub. Util. Comm'n*, 91 Pub. Util. Rep. 3d (PUR) at 373.

69. Citizens Action Coal. of Ind., Inc. v. Pub. Serv. Co. of Ind., 450 N.E.2d 98, 101 (Ind. Ct. App. 1983).

70. *Id.*

71. *See Mountain States Legal Found.*, 590 P.2d at 498 (en banc).

any group it determined to be deserving."[72] The court expressed concern that other captive retail customers ineligible for such preferences were compelled to finance the lower rates.

The Maine PUC held that a reduced rate for elderly, low-income customers was unjust and unreasonable. The commission held that the reduced rate was an inappropriate "social judgment[]."[73] When Washington ordered utility companies to reduce the utility rates of distressed farmers,[74] the Washington Supreme Court held that the ability or inability to pay could not support a rate reduction for some ratepayers borne by other ratepayers paying for more than they consumed.

Certain states are exceptions to this rule of equal protection for consumers when selling identical electric power to members of the same consumer category (e.g., residential, commercial, industrial). The Public Service Commission of Utah concluded that lifeline rates were legal under state law and in the public interest.[75] Massachusetts is the only state in which a discounted rate for certain customers not provided to other customers has been upheld by its highest court.[76] In Massachusetts, utility companies provide a straight percentage discount for low-income customers. Aside from states that are exceptions, constitutions in several states and their common law interpretation require equal protection implemented through cost-of-service-based rates for all retail power consumers in a given category.

---

72. *Id.*

73. *See In re* Cent. Me. Power Co., 26 Pub. Util. Rep. 4th (PUR) 388, 430 (Me. Pub. Util. Comm'n 1978), *appeal sustained in part, denied in part sub nom.* Cent. Me. Power Co. v. Pub. Util. Comm'n, 405 A.2d 153 (Me. 1979). The commission stated:

> We cannot solve the nation's economic problems and we cannot solve ratepayers' financial problems. What we can do, however, is try to insure that those who buy electricity pay what it costs to generate and deliver that electricity to them, and that no one group of customers is subsidized at the expense of another. By doing this, we believe that all customers will be treated as fairly as possible; that they will be more able to choose wisely among competing energy technologies; that use of electricity will be neither promoted nor discouraged artificially; and that rates will, ultimately, be more stable than might otherwise be the case.

Id. at 429.

74. *See* State *ex rel.* Puget Sound Power & Light Co. v. Dep't of Pub. Works, 38 P.2d 350, 351–52 (Wash. 1934).

75. *See In re* PacifiCorp, No. 98-2035-04, 1999 WL 1489663 (Utah Pub. Serv. Comm'n Nov. 23, 1999).

76. *See* Am. Hoechest Corp. v. Dep't of Pub. Utils., 399 N.E.2d 1, 4 (Mass. 1980).

Separation of Powers

Of note, the Inflation Reduction Act's federal tax credits include a 10 percent bonus for domestic content requirements for steel, iron, or manufactured components of the project.[77] See Chapter 6. Under the Inflation Reduction Act,

- 100 percent of steel and iron (not including refinement of steel additives) used in a project must be "produced" in the United States,[78] and/or
- 40 percent of all manufactured products for projects and 20 percent for offshore wind projects (with percentages increasing over time) must be produced in the United States for the facility as a whole.[79]

Other countries have claimed that such domestic content provisions violate World Trade Organization (WTO) fair trade requirements.

If the Green New Deal reemerges to incorporate U.S. protectionist measures, it risks running afoul of WTO and other restrictions. The Green New Deal may confront significant hurdles to fully pass muster under U.S. state and federal law. State constitutions and precedent in many states ensure equal protection and equitable tariffs for all similarly situated residential retail consumers. When regulators allow any group of consumers to pay less than the cost of the commodity/service, neither those regulators nor the utility absorbs this unpaid cost. Instead regulators order that cost to be paid by other customers, who may have no choice in traditionally regulated states other than to buy that power from monopoly utility suppliers at rates above the cost of service.

As an alternative to "New Deal" provisions in the Green New Deal to redistribute wealth through retail rates that do not reflect the cost of service, wealth redistribution may be accomplished by raising taxes, which state law can allow to be progressively structured based on taxpayer income.

77. Inflation Reduction Act of 2022 § 13102(l) (to be codified at 26 U.S.C. § 48(a)(12)). For tax preferences for domestic content, see CHRISTOPHER D. WATSON & MOLLY F. SHERLOCK, CONG. RSCH. SERV., IN11983, PROPOSED TAX PREFERENCE FOR DOMESTIC CONTENT IN ENERGY INFRASTRUCTURE (2022).

78. Inflation Reduction Act of 2022 § 13102(l) (to be codified at 26 U.S.C. § 48(a)(12)).

79. *Id.* § 13101(g) (to be codified at 26 U.S.C. § 45(b)(9)(C)). See sections 13101(g), 13701(a), 13102(l), and 13702(a) of the IRA, respectively, for the domestic content bonus credit amount requirements under sections 45(b)(9), 45Y(g)(11), 48(a)(12), and 48E(a)(3)(B).

Redistributing income through retail electric rate discrimination rather than through progressive taxes could violate certain state rate law concerning precedent on equal protection in state constitutions.

There are some similar redistributional aspects in the Inflation Reduction Act, including:

- Electric vehicle purchase tax credits based on buyer income
- Residential energy efficiency tax credits based on income
- Increased Investment Tax Credits and Production Tax Credits for power suppliers located in certain distressed energy communities[80]

However, none of these is accomplished through changing or discriminating in retail rates for electricity. Rather, they provide different amounts of tax credits and grants to certain stakeholders supplying and providing electricity. Governments are allowed to provide different tax treatment or grants to different taxpayers.

It remains to be seen what provisions will remain in the Green New Deal when it reemerges for consideration and enactment. If the Green New Deal incorporates redistributional provisions through differentiated retail power rates required to be paid by consumers in the same category, especially when those consumers have no choice of competitive power supply, they may be legally challenged in various states.

Next we identify a newly reemerging molecule that from now on will become a significant factor in the production of electric power in the United States and the reduction of U.S. GHG emissions. It is unique in being deemed by the Supreme Court as a "pollutant" to be regulated by EPA and is simultaneously a valuable chemical commodity that can be monetized and traded to reduce climate change.

---

80. *Id.* § 13102(o) (to be codified at 26 U.S.C. § 48(a)(14)).

CHAPTER 16

Methane's Impact

Science matters. Discussion about potential power generation options now highlights a molecule elevated to more prominent status at the 2021 COP Glasgow climate meetings—methane (CH_4):

- Methane's short-term impact on climate was grossly underestimated.
- While the United States is not the world's largest emitter of carbon dioxide, trailing China by a huge margin, the United States is the world's largest emitter of methane.
- The electric power sector is closely associated with the emission of methane.

Traditional climate policy focused primarily on one warming chemical, carbon dioxide (CO_2), the most prevalent greenhouse gas (GHG).[1] Methane, the second most prevalent warming chemical, until recently was largely overlooked. Unlike recent CO_2 emission increases that are principally caused by increasing fossil fuel use in *developing* countries, recent increases in methane emissions are substantially a *developed* country phenomenon, with U.S. emissions constituting a stunning 30–60 percent of the recorded global growth in methane emissions since the beginning of this century.[2]

The 2021 atmospheric methane burden was 162 percent greater than preindustrial levels and 15 percent higher than during the period from 1984 to 2006. Atmospheric methane increased faster in 2021 than any time since

1. Marianne Fay et al., *Decarbonizing Development: Three Steps to a Zero-Carbon Future* 25, World Bank Grp. (2015); *see* Sustainable Dev. Sols. Network & Inst. for Sustainable Dev. & Int'l Rels., Pathways to Deep Decarbonization 2014 Report viii (2014), https://perma.cc/2PY2-DRHW.

2. Bobby Magill, *Study Ties U.S. to Spike in Global Methane Emissions*, Climate Central (Feb. 16, 2016), https://www.climatecentral.org/news/us-60-percent-of-global-methane-growth-20037 (noting Harvard study).

systematic recordkeeping began in 1983:[3] in October 2022, the World Meteorological Organization announced the largest annual surge in methane concentrations on record.[4]

National and International Goals

By slashing methane emissions, humans can avoid four times more warming by 2050 than through CO_2 decarbonization alone.[5] The power sector is under pressure to address methane. Things change in the United States because of the 2022 Inflation Reduction Act (IRA) and the 2021 Infrastructure Investment and Jobs Act (IIJA), which together include more than $20 billion of new investments to reduce U.S. methane emissions,[6] discussed in Chapter 6 as well as later. This changes the shape of future U.S. electric power generation. Flared and leaked gas in the oil and gas sector wastes 260 billion cubic meters of gas worldwide every year.[7]

The United Nations (U.N.) report from the Intergovernmental Panel on Climate Change (IPCC) concluded that in order to maintain world warming below an additional increase of 2°C, gas emissions must be

---

3. *See* Press Release, World Meteorological Org., More Bad News for the Planet: Greenhouse Gas Levels Hit New Highs (Oct. 26, 2022), https://perma.cc/MHR4-CLLX ("Since 2007, globally-averaged atmospheric methane concentration has been increasing at an accelerating rate. The annual increases in 2020 and 2021 (15 and 18 [parts per billion] respectively) are the largest since systematic record [sic] began in 1983.").

4. *See* Press Release, World Meteorological Org., Eight Warmest Years on Record Witness Upsurge in Climate Change Impacts (Nov. 6, 2022), https://perma.cc/A6DB-F22E (the 2021 annual increase in methane concentration was the highest on record).

5. *See* Gabrielle B. Dreyfus et al., *Mitigating Climate Disruption in Time: A Self-Consistent Approach for Avoiding Both Near-Term and Long-Term Global Warming*, 119 Proc. Nat'l Acad. Sci. 22, https://doi.org/10.1073/pnas.2123536119 (reporting that "[b]y 2050, the net avoided warming from the targeted non-CO_2 measures is 0.26 °C, almost four times larger than the net benefit of decarbonization alone (0.07 °C)"). Duke University, *Curbing Other Climate Pollutants, Not Just CO_2, Gives Earth a Chance*, Sci. Daily (May 24, 2022), https://perma.cc/6EDT-TUKZ (asserting that the simultaneous reduction of emissions of methane and other often-overlooked climate pollutants could cut the rate of global warming in half by 2050).

6. *FACT SHEET: President Biden Announces New Initiatives at COP27 to Strengthen U.S. Leadership in Tackling Climate Change*, The White House (Nov. 11, 2022), https://www.whitehouse.gov/briefing-room/statements-releases/2022/11/11/fact-sheet-president-biden-announces-new-initiatives-at-cop27-to-strengthen-u-s-leadership-in-tackling-climate-change/.

7. *Id.*

reduced 40–70 percent from their 2010 levels by no later than 2050.[8] A U.S. report also concluded that to limit the increase in temperature to 2°C above preindustrial levels, GHG emissions must be reduced by 80 percent below recorded 1990 levels by 2050.[9] The 2021 COP26 climate summit in Glasgow, Scotland, ended with more than 100 countries agreeing to cut emissions of methane by 2030; a year later at the 2022 COP27 in Sharm el-Sheikh, Egypt, the total increased to 130 nations.[10]

The Chemicals Compared

The short-lived global warming chemicals, including methane (CH_4), black carbon ("soot"), and fluorinated gases (F-gases, including hydrofluorocarbons (HFCs)), together in real time are responsible for about 40 percent of current net climate drivers forcing climate change.[11] This is 200–300 percent more warming impact than the approximately 16 percent share that officials have previously attributed to these short-lived chemicals.[12] Methane is deemed responsible for most of this much larger 40 percent share.[13] Methane is the second most pernicious warming chemical after CO_2, even *before* the new data discussed later, which elevates significantly its actual total impact in current time.[14] A significant portion of non-CO_2 warming emissions is related to fossil fuel used in traditional electricity generation.

---

8. Intergovernmental Panel on Climate Change, Climate Change 2014 Synthesis Report Summary for Policymakers 20 (2014), https://www.ipcc.ch/pdf/assessment-report/ar5/syr/AR5_SYR_FINAL_SPM.pdf [https://perma.cc/HCT3-GEX8]; *see also* Susan Solomon et al., *Irreversible Climate Change Due to Carbon Dioxide Emissions*, 106 Proc. Nat'l Acad. Sci. 1704 (2008).

9. James H. Williams et al., Sustainable Dev. Sols. Network & Inst. for Sustainable Dev. & Int'l Rels., Pathways to Deep Decarbonization in the United States xii (2015), https://perma.cc/4FZB-PX4M.

10. *Id.*

11. Cal. Env't Prot. Agency Air Res. Bd., Proposed Short-Lived Climate Pollutant Reduction Strategy 13 (2016), https://perma.cc/P8VV-D2VA.

12. *See, e.g.*, *Global Greenhouse Gas Emissions Data*, U.S. Env't Prot. Agency, https://perma.cc/52MP-3M8K (last visited May 29, 2024).

13. Cal. Env't Prot. Agency Air Res. Bd., *supra* note 11, at 7.

14. *See Overview of Greenhouse Gases: Methane Emissions*, U.S. Env't Prot. Agency (Apr. 11, 2024), https://www.epa.gov/ghgemissions/overview-greenhouse-gases#methane [https://perma.cc/5CHU-ZK22].

One can distinguish GHG sources: the three predominant GHGs—CO_2, nitrous oxide, and methane—are produced naturally and are also by-products of economic and human activities. The three more minor GHGs (HFCs, SF_6, and PFCs) are synthetic chemicals not occurring in nature, manufactured and eventually released by human activity. The Environmental Protection Agency (EPA) and the U.N. Framework Convention on Climate Change (FCCC) previously rated methane as exhibiting 20 to 30 times more warming capacity (the ability to trap infrared heat) per molecule than CO_2.[15] This calculation by federal and international agencies substantially underestimated the actual impact of methane on the environment in real time.

In fact, a gram of methane absorbs and retains in the atmosphere 70 times more infrared radiation than a gram of CO_2.[16] Therefore, in real time, the chemical properties of methane make it approximately 86 times more heat trapping than CO_2.[17] However, the EPA's and U.N. FCCC's assessment of chemical impact previously calculated all impacts normalizing and spreading them across 100 years regardless of actual impact in specific years; this spreading inaccurately dilutes methane's actual short-term impact over more years than it remains active. It results in assigning methane a cumulative heating value impact of only 28 to 36 times that of CO_2, even though its molecular warming impact is 86 to 105 times greater than CO_2.[18] The reality is that methane does all of its climate-warming damage in a more concentrated period of slightly more than a decade before chemically degrading and no longer retaining heat in the atmosphere.[19] Correctly adjusting for real time, research places the actual climate damage of a released methane molecule at between 86 and 105 times that of a CO_2 molecule.[20]

---

15. Stephen H. Schneider, Global Warming: Are We Entering the Greenhouse Century? 101 (1989).

16. Hem S. Ray, Elements of Creative Management 175 (2006).

17. Joe Romm, *How the EPA and New York Times Are Getting Methane All Wrong*, ThinkProgress (Aug. 20, 2015), https://thinkprogress.org/how-the-epa-and-new-york-times-are-getting-methane-all-wrong-eba3397ce9e5/ [https://perma.cc/C3YB-EVUD]. The IPCC Fifth Assessment Report now calculates that a molecule of methane, with its calculated lifetime of 12.4 years, exhibits a global warming potential of 86 times that of CO_2 (CO_2 has a value of one) when calculated over 20 years or 34 times that of CO_2 when calculated (inaccurately) over 100 years. *Id.*

18. Bill McKibben, *Global Warming's Terrifying New Chemistry*, The Nation (Mar. 23, 2016), https://perma.cc/2M9M-CPLF.

19. *See* Euan G. Nisbet et al., *Methane on the Rise—Again*, 343 Sci. 493 (2014).

20. McKibben, *supra* note 18.

More accurate methane emissions now are being recognized by world nations. The social cost[21] of one ton of CO_2 emissions in 2020 dollars is estimated by the U.S. government under the Biden administration as ranging from $14 to $152, depending on the discount rate applied; the president's discretion to set this value was upheld in late 2022 by a U.S. court.[22] The social cost of one ton of methane emissions in 2020 dollars is estimated by the Biden administration as ranging from $670 to $3,900, depending on the discount rate applied.[23] Thus, the estimated social cost of methane now is 24–48 times that of the same amount of CO_2 emitted to the atmosphere. These values can change in different presidential administrations.

Where does it come from? Sixty-two percent of methane emissions from 2007 to 2016 was anthropogenic (caused by people's use of energy) rather than naturally occurring.[24] Over a 20-year period, each ton of methane emitted to the atmosphere from energy or other uses examined later has the same warming effect as 84–87 tons of CO_2 emitted during the same time. The emissions of methane are accelerating and have been, and continue to be, underreported by nations covered by the Paris Agreement.

In addition to warming, methane in the atmosphere also contributes to tropospheric ozone formation, increasing the quantity of that warming chemical by a significant multiplier[25] and potentially depleting more stratospheric ozone that protects humans from ultraviolet radiation causing skin

---

21. The social cost of emissions for each of these chemicals includes the value of all climate change impacts, including (but not limited to) changes in net agricultural productivity, human health effects, property damage from increased flooding and other natural disasters, disruption of energy systems, risk of conflict, environmental migration, and the value of ecosystem services.

22. Clark Mindock, *Biden "Social Cost of Carbon" Climate Risk Measure Upheld by U.S. Appeals Court*, Reuters (Oct. 21, 2022), https://www.reuters.com/markets/commodities/biden-social-cost-carbon-climate-risk-measure-upheld-by-us-appeals-court-2022-10-21/.

23. *Id.*

24. Jeff Tollefson, *Scientists Raise Alarm over "Dangerously Fast" Growth in Atmospheric Methane*, Nature (Feb. 8, 2022), https://www.nature.com/articles/d41586-022-00312-2?utm_source=Nature+Briefing&utm_campaign=d6c58c6a9d-briefing-dy-20220208&utm_medium=email&utm_term=0_c9dfd39373-d6c58c6a9d-45437102.

25. U.N. Env't Programme & World Meteorological Org., Integrated Assessment of Black Carbon and Tropospheric Ozone: Summary for Decision Makers 57 (2011), https://perma.cc/8LJ7-BDX3; Ivar S.A Isaksen et al., *Atmospheric Ozone and Methane in a Changing Climate*, 5 Atmosphere 518, 518–19, 521, 528 (2014), www.mdpi.com/2073-4433/5/3/518/pdf (methane increases tropospheric ozone, a warming chemical, through a current feedback loop multiplier of 1.3–1.5).

cancers.[26] Methane, which is the primary molecule in natural gas, when burned, has an impact somewhat similar to that of other fossil fuels, although emitting only approximately half as much carbon as burning an equivalent heating value of coal, although when it escapes unburned, methane traps 86–105 times more heat in Earth's atmosphere than CO_2.[27] These characteristics make atmospheric methane an extremely potent GHG, giving it, molecule for molecule, as much as approximately 100 times more power to warm climate than CO_2.[28]

The New Math; the Methane Problem

Contrary to earlier EPA reports of decreased GHG emissions since 2010,[29] nationwide satellite data shows that U.S. methane emissions increased 30 percent between 2002–2014.[30] In terms of the historic role of methane since 1983, one-fifth of the increase in radiative forcing of climate warming by anthropogenic sources of GHGs is attributable to methane.[31] Figure 16.1 illustrates this phenomenon since 1983.

26. *See* Durwood Zaelke & Nathan Borgford-Parnell, Primer on Short-Lived Climate Pollutants 14–15 (Nov. 2013) (Inst. for Governance & Sustainable Dev. Working Paper), http://www.igsd.org/documents/PrimeronShort-LivedClimatePollutantsNovemberElectronicversion.pdf [https://perma.cc/L25B-2DFR].

27. McKibben, *supra* note 18.

28. U.S. Env't Prot. Agency, Methane Emissions and Opportunities for Control 20–21 (1990).

29. *E.g.*, U.S. Env't Prot. Agency, Inventory of U.S. Greenhouse Gas Emissions and Sinks: 1990–2014, at 2–21 (2016), https://www.epa.gov/sites/production/files/2016-04/documents/us-ghg-inventory-2016-main-text.pdf [https://perma.cc/G5JR-4GW2] [hereinafter EPA, 1990–2014 Inventory of Emissions and Sinks].

30. McKibben, *supra* note 18.

31. *Id.*

Figure 16.1[32] Global Average Methane Concentration Increases

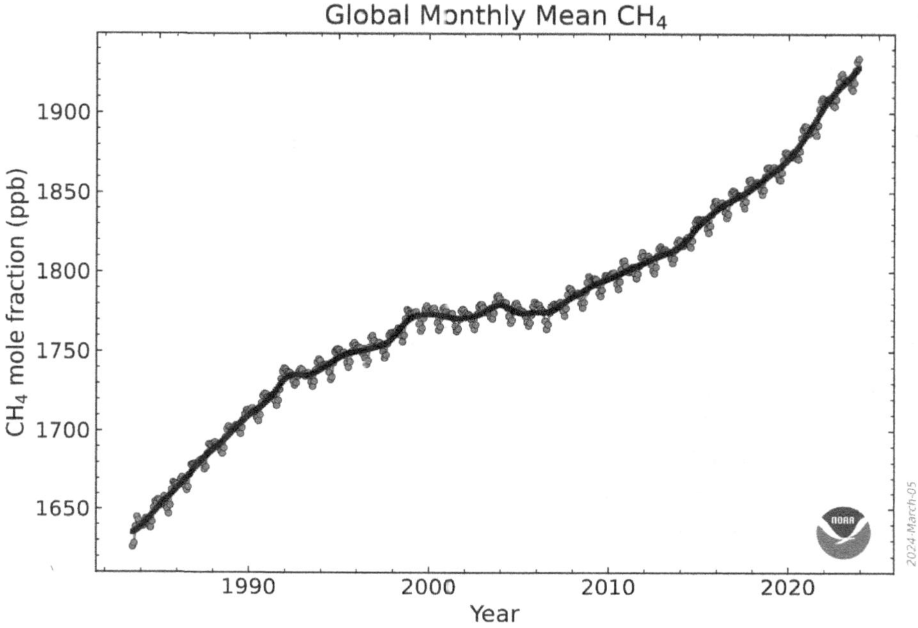

Methane molecules are distinct from all other GHGs in that they are not a waste product always to be discarded but can be repurposed as a valuable energy resource powering the modern economy via electric generation. The traditional common practice of flaring natural gas at the wellhead wastes the energy value of the gas, although at the same time it accomplishes a 95–99 percent reduction of the warming impact of the released methane gas because flaring natural gas converts the methane to CO_2, which is only approximately 1 percent as warming as methane, according to the most recent research.[33] Yet despite this impact, atmospheric methane increased faster in 2021 than any time since systematic recordkeeping began in 1983.[34]

---

32. *Trends in CH_4*, NAT'L OCEANIC & ATMOSPHERIC ADMIN., https://gml.noaa.gov/ccgg/trends_ch4/ (last visited May 29, 2024).

33. Morgan Kelly, *A More Potent Greenhouse Gas Than CO2, Methane Emissions Will Leap as Earth Warms (Nature)*, PRINCETON RSCH. (Mar. 26, 2014), https://blogs.princeton.edu/research/2014/03/26/a-more-potent-greenhouse-gas-than-co2-methane-emissions-will-leap-as-earth-warms-nature/ [https://perma.cc/R8Z2-9H2F].

34. *Trends in CH_4*, *supra* note 32.

Biden Administration Methane/Electricity Initiatives

Regulation and Policy

There are new opportunities to capture fugitive methane and utilize it for power production with incentives provided by new legislation and policy. Limiting warming to 1.5°C will require dramatic reductions in global methane emissions of at least 30 percent from 2020 levels by 2030, a goal that has been endorsed by over 130 countries representing over half of global methane emissions, including the United States, at recent meetings of the U.N. FCCC in Glasgow and in Egypt. In addition to this, the United States joined a Joint Declaration with the European Union and five other countries, reiterating its pledge to "reduce anthropogenic and collective methane emissions by at least 30 percent by 2030 compared to 2020 levels."[35] The Biden administration unveiled its Methane Emissions Reduction Action Plan (MERAP), which targets fossil fuel source emissions. MERAP targets emissions from the oil and gas industry, abandoned mines, landfills, and agriculture.[36] Among other initiatives, states will be required to develop plans to reduce methane emissions from existing sources—likely to impact 300,000 existing oil and gas well sites.

President Biden announced new initiatives in late 2022 at the U.N. Climate Change Conference, COP27, in Sharm el-Sheikh, Egypt, to strengthen proposed domestic methane standards to capture flared and leaked gas in the oil and gas sector that would reduce wasted energy and harmful methane emissions from its covered sources by 87 percent below 2005 levels by 2030. The 2022 Biden administration methane plan includes more than $20 billion

---

35. Madeline Bruning, *EPA Proposes Tougher Rules on Methane Leaks*, The Regul. Rev. (Nov. 30, 2022), https://www.theregreview.org/2022/11/30/bruning-epa-proposes-tougher-rules-on-methane-leaks/#:~:text=In%20addition%2C%20the%20United%20States,2030%20compared%20to%202020%20levels.

36. *Fact Sheet: President Biden Tackles Methane Emissions, Spurs Innovations, and Supports Sustainable Agriculture to Build a Clean Energy Economy and Create Jobs*, The White House (Nov. 2, 2021), https://www.whitehouse.gov/briefing-room/statements-releases/2021/11/02/fact-sheet-president-biden-tackles-methane-emissions-spurs-innovations-and-supports-sustainable-agriculture-to-build-a-clean-energy-economy-and-create-jobs/. *See also Executive Order on Tackling the Climate Crisis at Home and Abroad*, The White House (Jan. 27, 2021), https://www.whitehouse.gov/briefing-room/presidential-actions/2021/01/27/executive-order-on-tackling-the-climate-crisis-at-home-and-abroad/.

of new investments to reduce methane emissions from the IIJA, IRA, and annual appropriations.[37] The United States will require routine monitoring of emissions and leaks to continue at every well site in the country even after wells cease operation. For context, methane leakage from the oil and gas industry contributed approximately 4 percent of global GHGs and 28 percent of U.S. methane emissions, with the entire energy sector responsible for 41 percent of U.S. methane emissions.[38]

This is a significant revision of the 2021 proposed regulation, which included exemptions for smaller well sites. Although those wells are small, their leakage is significant: they produce only 6 percent of the nation's oil and gas but are suspected to create about half of the industry's methane emissions.[39] It is now possible to monitor emissions by drones and other remote third-party sensing devices. EPA's regulations were finalized in December 2023 and promulgated.[40]

The IIJA, which became U.S. law in 2021, allocated $4.7 billion for states to plug leaky and abandoned oil and gas wells. Included are guidelines for regulating methane emissions from existing oil and gas facilities, which are proposed under section 111(d) of the Clean Air Act. The EPA estimates these new initiatives will reduce 41 million tons of methane from 2023 to 2035.[41] Further, EPA's Regulatory Impact analysis estimates the value of the cumulative net climate benefits from the proposal, including the cost of compliance and savings from recovered natural gas, is $48–49 billion from 2023 to 2035.[42] See Chapter 7 detailing the new required consideration of costs to the power industry when enacting federal regulations.

---

37. *FACT SHEET*, *supra* note 6.

38. U.S. Energy Info. Admin., DOE/EIA-0573(2009), Emissions of Greenhouse Gases in the United States 2009, tbls. 17 & 18 (2011), https://www.eia.gov/environment/emissions/ghg_report/pdf/tbl17.pdf, https://www.eia.gov/environment/emissions/ghg_report/pdf/tbl18.pdf.

39. Bruning, *supra* note 35.

40. *See* Press Release, U.S. Env't Prot. Agency, Biden-Harris Administration Finalizes Standards to Slash Methane Pollution, Combat Climate Change, Protect Health, and Bolster American Innovation (Dec. 2, 2023), https://www.epa.gov/newsreleases/biden-harris-administration-finalizes-standards-slash-methane-pollution-combat-climate.

41. Press Release, U.S. Env't Prot. Agency, U.S. to Sharply Cut Methane Pollution That Threatens the Climate and Public Health (Nov. 2, 2021), https://www.epa.gov/newsreleases/us-sharply-cut-methane-pollution-threatens-climate-and-public-health [https://perma.cc/25SM-VNC2].

42. *See id.* The benefits are equivalent to $4.5 billion saved per year. *See id.*

The IRA

The IRA provides "carrots" and "sticks" regarding methane. In terms of "sticks," it will impose a fee on excess methane leaking from oil and gas wells, pipelines, and other infrastructure constrained by a maximum annual methane waste emission rate of 25,000 metric tons of CO_2e (carbon dioxide equivalent) (vented, released, or flared): the initial fee is $900 per metric ton of methane emitted, increasing to $1,500/metric ton after two years.[43] There is an exemption from this emissions charge if EPA regulations addressing methane emissions are in effect in all states and will "result in equivalent or greater emissions reductions as would be achieved" by the November 2021 proposed EPA rule.[44] See Chapter 6. The act also contains $1.5 billion for methane emission reduction programs:[45]

- $850 million to provide grants to facilities subject to the methane charge for such technology "improving and deploying industrial equipment and processes" that reduces methane emission[46]
- $700 million for "marginal conventional wells"[47]

These grants are in addition to the IIJA, which included $4.7 billion to plug leaking oil and gas wells. For the waste and agricultural sectors, in the IRA there are new credits for biogas, additional resources for monitoring, and funding to address agricultural animal "enteric emissions," which includes $21 billion for climate-smart farms and ranches to make their operations more efficient, which can include methane recapture/use and

43. Standards of Performance for New, Reconstructed, and Modified Sources and Emissions Guidelines for Existing Sources: Oil and Natural Gas Sector Climate Review, 86 Fed. Reg. 63,110 (Nov. 15, 2021). These regulations address methane emissions from the same categories of new and existing facilities that are subject to the methane charge. For more background on these issues, see Richard K. Lattanzio, Cong. Rsch. Serv., R42986, Methane and Other Air Pollution Issues in Natural Gas Systems (2020).

44. Inflation Reduction Act § 60113 (2022) (to be codified at 42 U.S.C. § 136(f)(6)(a)(ii)).

45. For more information, see Jonathan L. Ramseur, Cong. Rsch. Serv., R45472, Market-Based Greenhouse Gas Emission Reduction Legislation: 108th through 117th Congresses (2022); Jonathan L. Ramseur, Cong. Rsch. Serv., R47206, Inflation Reduction Act Methane Emissions Charge: In Brief (2022).

46. Inflation Reduction Act § 60113 (2022) (to be codified at 42 U.S.C. § 136(a)).

47. *Id.* (to be codified at 42 U.S.C. § 136(b)).

self-generation of distributed electric power.[48] There is $3 billion for Climate Justice Block Grants and $27 billion for Greenhouse Gas Reduction for projects supporting communities with disproportionate energy burdens and pollution exposure—this includes $4 billion for Advanced Energy Project Credits directed to industrial or manufacturing facilities located in these communities and more than $10 billion for rural electric cooperatives to deploy new clean electricity.[49] For more detail on the IRA, see Chapter 6.

Obama-Biden Administration

In 2016, under the Obama administration, EPA released new final Clean Air Act New Source Performance Standards regulations for landfills built or modified after July 17, 2014,[50] to be effective September 15, 2016. Existing landfills' requirements to capture and contain fugitive methane emissions would be lowered for the threshold of regulation from the then-current 50 metric tons, equivalent to 50 Mg (megagrams), of nonmethane organic compounds per year to 34 metric tons annually.[51] The same threshold for methane capture applied to existing landfills as was established for new landfills. In terms of scope of application, EPA estimated that 115 new landfills and 731 existing facilities would be required to install additional pollution controls to capture and reduce fugitive methane emissions by 334,000 metric tons at an annual EPA-estimated cost to the industry of $6 million in 2025.[52] This proposed methane regulation was suspended during the Trump administration.

---

48. U.S. Dep't of Energy, *The* Inflation Reduction Act *Drives Significant Emissions Reductions and Positions America to Reach Our Climate Goals* (Aug. 2022), https://www.energy.gov/sites/default/files/2022-08/8.18%20InflationReductionAct_Factsheet_Final.pdf.

49. *Id.*

50. *See* Andrew Childers, *EPA Tightens Landfill Standards to Reduce Methane*, ENERGY & CLIMATE REP. (BNA) No. 136, July 15, 2016 (citing 40 C.F.R. § 60.750–.759 (2017)).

51. *See id.* (citing 40 C.F.R. § 60.33c) (stating "[u]pdated controls would need to be installed within thirty months of meeting that emissions threshold").

52. *Id.* ("The Tier 4 system would exempt a landfill from installing the required pollution controls if it can demonstrate that surface emissions are below 500 parts per million for four consecutive quarters even if other monitoring methods would indicate the emissions threshold has been exceeded.").

Recaptured Methane and Additional Electricity Production

Captured methane offers opportunities for new power generation. Petroleum and natural gas were responsible for 28 percent of U.S. methane emissions, with the entire energy sector responsible for 41 percent of U.S. methane emissions, in 2009.[53] Electricity production, current transportation fuels (many of which policymakers plan to be electrified in the future), and commercial and residential heating that several states are planning to electrify by 2035 account for more than two-thirds of methane emissions. Where there is a methane release issue, there is an opportunity to capture this methane and utilize it to produce electric power and/or building heat.

Whether or not a match lights methane (or it enters a fuel cell) matters: released directly into the Earth's atmosphere, methane increases warming; captured and utilized as an energy source, methane produces power and/or building heat. Opportunities exist in each sector for control of anthropogenic methane emissions:

- Methane recovery systems at landfills capturing renewable waste-derived landfill gas (LFG) for electricity production
- Improvements in leak detection and containment in natural gas transportation systems
- Recovery of coal-bed methane from coal mining operations

The following sections highlight opportunities for capture and conversion of methane to electric power, which enjoy benefits under the federal IRA and several state programs:

- Federal PURPA Qualifying Facility status and exemptions from certain elements of regulation using LFG or other waste methane (see Chapter 5)
- Certain state Renewable Portfolio Standards (RPS) Renewable Energy Credit (REC) programs supporting and subsidizing renewable energy (see Chapter 8)
- Distributed power generation eligible for net metering (see Chapter 9)

---

53. U.S. Energy Info. Admin., *supra* note 38.

Landfill Methane Capture for Electric Generation

One source for distributed renewable power production is landfill gas, which is predominately methane that can be converted to renewable electric power recognized under federal, and some state, law. Landfills are the third largest source of U.S. methane emissions.[54] The amount of municipal solid waste (MSW) generated worldwide and the amount of potential methane emitted are expected to almost double to 2.2 billion tons annually from 2012 to 2025.[55]

The Source

Trash in landfills produces 17 percent of all anthropogenic methane.[56] Trash creates climate change emissions because its organic materials decompose to methane under anaerobic conditions.[57] The source of future methane formation in landfilled waste is the decomposition of organic materials in trash—paper, food scraps, and yard waste. More than half of the total amount of trash is organic matter that will degrade to release methane under anaerobic conditions.[58]

With the passage of time, bacterial decomposition of organic material in the absence of oxygen, volatilization of certain wastes, and chemical reactions within the landfill create quantities of methane gas.[59] Landfill gas chemically includes 45–60 percent methane, 40–60 percent CO_2, and smaller

54. *Basic Information about Landfill Gas*, U.S. Env't Prot. Agency (Apr. 25, 2024), https://www.epa.gov/lmop/basic-information-about-landfill-gas [https://perma.cc/E8KT-XH3U].

55. *See* Daniel Hoornweg & Perinaz Bhada-Tata, World Bank Grp., What a Waste: A Global Review of Solid Waste Management 8 (2012), http://documents.worldbank.org/curated/en/302341468126264791/pdf/68135-REVISED-What-a-Waste-2012-Final-updated.pdf [https://perma.cc/QGF3-WUPD].

56. Dave Fehling, *Garbage Gas: Is Methane Going to Waste in Texas?*, StateImpact (Dec. 4, 2012, 6:45 AM), http://stateimpact.npr.org/texas/2012/12/04/garbage-gas-is-methane-going-to-waste-in-texas/ [https://perma.cc/96X4-BQYS].

57. Agency for Toxic Substances & Disease Registry, U.S. Dep't of Health & Hum. Servs., Landfill Gas Primer: An Overview for Environmental Health Professionals 3–4 (2001), https://www.atsdr.cdc.gov/hac/landfill/pdfs/landfill_2001_ch2mod.pdf [https://perma.cc/72XJ-SJZX].

58. *See* EPA, 1990–2014 Inventory of Emissions and Sinks, *supra* note 29, at 7–18 (noting that in 2014, 20.2 percent of all waste sent to MSW landfills was food, 13.4 percent was paper and paper board, 7.6 percent was wood, and 7.4 percent was yard trimmings).

59. Agency for Toxic Substances & Disease Registry, *supra* note 57, at 3.

amounts of nonmethane organic compounds (NMOCs) and some other trace organic elements.[60] So the methane in LFG at 45–60 percent is significantly less than the approximately 99 percent methane in pipeline natural gas.[61]

Renewable Electricity Production versus Burning

The size of the U.S. landfill sector is significant: at the beginning of the 21st century, approximately 29 percent of U.S. anthropogenic methane emissions were released from all waste management,[62] more recently estimated to be 20 percent.[63] Landfills represent the source of 98 percent of this 8.1 million metric tons of methane emissions from waste management, by far the single largest subsource of waste sector methane releases.[64] At the beginning of the 21st century, approximately 4.9 million metric tons of these approximately 8 million tons of landfill methane annually were LFG captured at the source, and 2.5 million metric tons of this captured methane was used as energy, while the residual 2.4 million metric tons of the recovered LFG were flared with no application for energy use.[65] Stated in percentages of existing energy uses and remaining opportunities with both captured methane and yet to be captured methane: about half of methane is captured, but only a fraction of it is converted into electric power.

Methane can be captured and employed productively as a methane gas converted to electric power, collected and flared for no productive purpose, or left alone to migrate into the environment as a potent GHG.[66] The potential threshold opportunity is significant: of 989 open and closed

---

60. *Id.*

61. *See* Jonathan Martel et al., *Obama Administration Sharpens Focus on Reducing Methane Emissions*, 15 Daily Env't Rep. (BNA) No. 16, Jan. 26, 2016, at B-3.

62. *See* U.S. Env't Prot. Agency, EPA 430-R-05-003, Inventory of U.S. Greenhouse Gas Emissions and Sinks: 1990–2003, at 25, 261 (2005), https://www.epa.gov/sites/production/files/2015-12/documents/05cr.pdf [https://perma.cc/2ASF-MC8D] [hereinafter EPA, 1990–2003 Inventory of Emissions and Sinks]; U.S. Energy Info. Admin., *supra* note 38.

63. *See* EPA, 1990–2014 Inventory of Emissions and Sinks, *supra* note 29.

64. EPA, 1990–2003 Inventory of Emissions and Sinks, *supra* note 62, at 40. The remaining 2 percent of these emissions from waste management is associated with domestic wastewater treatment programs. *Id.*

65. Energy Info. Admin., *supra* note 38.

66. U.S. Env't Prot. Agency, EPA 430-B-96-0004, Turning a Liability into an Asset: A Landfill Gas-to-Energy Project Development Handbook 1–2 (1996), https://nepis.epa.gov/Exe/ZyPURL.cgi?Dockey=600008CZ.txt [https://perma.cc/Y49F-ETTS].

registered U.S. landfills, 574 would be large enough from an engineering perspective to generate enough emissions to be required to collect and control their methane in 2025, as explained more later.[67] When utilized, landfill gas is considered a carbon-neutral fuel, since its combustion releases carbon that was recently sequestered as CO_2 by maturing organic source materials (trees, crops, etc.) before degrading anaerobically in a landfill, where they would release methane to the atmosphere.[68]

Burning MSW, rather than landfilling it, is an alternative to eliminate a significant weight and volume of MSW and simultaneously produce electricity regarded as favored under the federal PURPA law. See Chapter 5. About 12 percent of MSW in the United States was incinerated in 2012,[69] and the heat produced during that incineration optionally could be used to produce steam for a steam-cycle turbine to produce electricity.[70] This is known as waste-to-energy (W-T-E); more than 100 facilities to produce W-T-E were sited in the last quarter of the 20th century. There was only one new W-T-E facility proposed, sited, and constructed in the United States in the 21st century. With difficulty siting new W-T-E plants, and some older plants closing, the number still operating had decreased to 75 plants in 2021.[71]

These remaining 75 U.S. W-T-E facilities now operate as a critical element of the U.S. waste management system. W-T-E power generation can be achieved at approximately $0.0457/kWh,[72] which is less expensive than

---

67. *See* Emission Guidelines and Compliance Times for Municipal Solid Waste Landfills, 80 Fed. Reg. 52,100, 52,118 (Aug. 27, 2015) (to be codified at 40 C.F.R. pt. 60) ("The Emission Guidelines in the baseline are estimated to require control at 574 of the 989 affected landfills in 2025 and achieve reductions of 57,300 Mg/yr NMOC and 9.0 million Mg/yr methane (226 million mt/yr CO_2e).").

68. Jennifer Weeks, *Landfills Expand Energy Output*, BIOCYCLE, Aug. 2005, at 51.

69. U.S. Env't Prot. Agency, *Municipal Solid Waste Generation, Recycling, and Disposal in the United States: Facts and Figures for 2012*, at 2 (2014), https://archive.epa.gov/epawaste/nonhaz/municipal/web/pdf/2012_msw_fs.pdf [https://perma.cc/MQ67-6NTK].

70. *Energy Recovery from the Combustion of Municipal Solid Waste (MSW)*, U.S. ENV'T PROT. AGENCY (Jan. 30, 2024), https://www.epa.gov/smm/energy-recovery-combustion-municipal-solid-waste-msw [https://perma.cc/F22V-99HD] (stating that U.S. incineration in the early 1990s was more than 15 percent of MSW).

71. *Energy Recovery from the Combustion of Municipal Solid Waste (MSW)*, U.S. ENV'T PROT. AGENCY (Jan. 30, 2024), https://www.epa.gov/smm/energy-recovery-combustion-municipal-solid-waste-msw#:~:text=Currently%2C%20there%20are%2075%20facilities,combustion%20of%20municipal%20solid%20waste.

72. U.S. ENV'T PROT. AGENCY, REGULATORY IMPACT ANALYSIS FOR THE PROPOSED REVISIONS TO THE EMISSION GUIDELINES FOR EXISTING SOURCES AND SUPPLEMENTAL PROPOSED NEW SOURCE PERFORMANCE STANDARDS IN THE MUNICIPAL SOLID WASTE LANDFILLS SECTOR

many forms of electric power supply. W-T-E waste management is favored by several municipalities, as it eliminates risk of long-term liability under the federal Superfund (CERCLA) law for eventual contamination remediation at landfills. The most significant deployment of W-T-E combustion facilities to handle MSW is in the New England region, where 35 percent of the waste stream is handled in this manner.[73]

Remaining potential. As of 2017, 634 MSW landfills in the United States had LFG-to-energy projects.[74] The EPA maintains a database of more than 2,400 U.S. landfills that can be surveyed as potential LFG-to-energy locations.[75] This EPA Landfill Methane Outreach Program tracks operating LFG projects in the United States and identifies more than 400 additional landfills as good candidates to capture and deploy their methane because of their size and methane generation characteristics.

Law Regulating Landfill Methane Management

Two federal laws affect the management of methane at very large landfills. Both of these regulations require management practices that potentially can lead to creation of renewable LFG electric generation and qualify for state RPS RECs (see Chapter 8). Both of these federal statutes contain in their text so-called savings clauses that allow state governments to enact more stringent standards and requirements than contained in the federal law.[76]

3–6 (2015), https://www3.epa.gov/ttnecas1/docs/ria/landfills_ria_proposed-nsps_2015-08.pdf [https://perma.cc/E7AC-W8SX].

73. Phil Simmons et al., *The State of Garbage in America*, BioCycle, Jan. 2004, at 27. This technology is used least in the Rocky Mountain and Midwest regions, and conversely, the areas where the largest percentage of waste is landfilled are the Rocky Mountain region, where 90 percent of the MSW stream is landfilled; the Midwest, where 75 percent of the waste stream is landfilled; the Great Lakes region of the Midwest, where 68 percent of the waste stream is landfilled; and the South, where 69 percent of the waste stream is landfilled. *Id.* at 33–34.

74. *Project and Landfill Data by State*, U.S. Env't Prot. Agency (Mar. 22, 2024), https://www.epa.gov/lmop/project-and-landfill-data-state [https://perma.cc/3744-W9GH].

75. *LMOP Landfill and Project Database*, U.S. Env't Prot. Agency (Mar. 22, 2024), https://www.epa.gov/lmop/landfill-gas-energy-project-data-and-landfill-technical-data (providing maps of locations and a costing methodology for determining the economic feasibility of development).

76. 42 U.S.C. § 7604; 42 U.S.C. § 6929.

The Resource Conservation and Recovery Act (RCRA)

The Resource Conservation and Recovery Act (RCRA) subtitle D establishes legal standards for MSW landfills that were active on or after October 9, 1993, to limit actual landfill methane emissions to the atmosphere.[77] RCRA mandates that all MSW landfills maintain an ongoing methane gas concentration of less than "25 percent of the lower explosive limit for methane . . . (excluding gas control or recovery system components)" and a concentration of less than the lower explosive limit for methane at the facility boundary.[78] Landfill operators or owners are required to monitor methane emissions on an ongoing basis to prevent or control any off-site migration, groundwater contamination, odors, and emissions of NMOCs.[79] What this "lower explosive limit" translates to is that methane gas is explosive at concentrations between 5 and 15 percent.[80]

Directions of Methane Travel

Since methane is lighter than air, it can move vertically or laterally through air. For vertical methane rise, all large landfills operating after 1991 must install a protective cover or cap to control fugitive methane vertical emissions.[81] Landfills constructed or modified in capacity after October 1993 are required by RCRA to install a lining between the landfill and the earth to retard lateral and subfill migration of gas and eliminate groundwater contamination.[82] It constitutes a RCRA legal "Imminent Hazard" when methane is released from landfills and migrates to occupied structures or underground utility conduits at concentrations of 10 percent or more of the lower explosive limit.[83] RCRA attempts to keep landfill methane on site, setting standards at the landfill property boundary for methane concentrations not to exceed the lower explosive limit for methane.[84]

---

77. *See* Resource Conservation and Recovery Act, 40 C.F.R. § 258.40.

78. *Id.* § 258.23 (defining "lower explosive limit" as "the lowest percent by volume of a mixture of explosive gases in air that will generate a flame at 25 degrees Celsius and atmospheric pressure").

79. Curtis A. Moore, *Existing Authorities in the United States for Responding to Global Warming*, 40 Env't L. Rep. 10185, 10203 (2010).

80. John Bell et al., *Landfill Gas Training* 15, Cal. Dep't of Res. Recycling & Recovery (Aug. 2005), https://perma.cc/BB7W-GZ3Z.

81. 40 C.F.R. § 258.40.

82. *Id.*

83. 310 Mass. Code Regs. § 40.0321.

84. 40 C.F.R. § 258.23.

Bringing the Standard Current

Landfills constructed, reconstructed, or modified after July 17, 2014, are permitted to release one-third of their methane emissions into the atmosphere at designated and monitored control points. Two-thirds of methane must be captured. Postclosure environmental monitoring is required.

Clean Air Act New Source Performance Standards

The Clean Air Act addresses emissions of designated criteria pollutants and hazardous emissions, in which methane is not included—nor was CO_2 formally so designated in the statute. Landfill gases include more than criteria and hazardous substances, which the Clean Air Act obligates operators of large landfill sites to monitor, collect, and dispose of. Large landfills with a design capacity greater than 2.5 million cubic meters must install a landfill gas collection system particularly targeting not methane but NMOCs[85] if they release more than 50,000 Mg of NMOCs per year.[86]

- The gas control system implemented must include an open flare design and a "control device capable of reducing NMOC emissions by 98 weight-percent."[87]
- Although NMOCs do not include methane, if NMOC gas is flared, methane also is destroyed.[88]

An owner of a large landfill must reduce NMOCs by 98 weight-percent, or to less than 20 parts per million (ppm) by volume, dry basis as hexane at 3 percent O_2.[89] If a landfill is not subject to the Clean Air Act section 111 New Source Performance Standards, separate rules apply.[90] The owner/operator must test the ambient level of methane concentration to ensure that level does not exceed 500 ppm above the background concentration.[91]

"In 2004, 64 percent of MSW landfills were owned by public entities while 36 percent were privately owned."[92] Because most private landfills

---

85. *Id.* § 60.752(b).
86. *Id.* § 60.752(b)(2).
87. *Id.* § 60.752(b)(2)(iii)(A)–(B).
88. *See id.* § 60.752.
89. *Id.*
90. *Id.* § 60.30(c).
91. *Id.* § 60.755(c).
92. U.S. Env't Prot. Agency, Municipal Solid Waste Landfills: Economic Impact Analysis for the Proposed New Subpart to the New Source Performance Standards 2-2

have already taken advantage of the additional incentives and revenues from installing LFG electricity generation projects, the majority of remaining LFG-to-electricity development projects are located at municipally owned landfills.[93] Cost-effective projects still exist, particularly now after enactment of the IRA.[94]

Municipal Sewage Treatment Methane Electric Generation

From Landfill Waste to Wastewater Waste

Municipal wastewater plants offer another significant opportunity for new renewable electric power generation options where fugitive methane is captured and converted to electric power or facility heat applications. U.S. wastewater treatment systems emitted 2 percent of national methane emissions.[95] U.S. wastewater treatment facilities process approximately 34 billion gallons of wastewater every day.[96]

Treatment of human wastewater creates methane from the decomposition of organic matter in the waste.[97] Methane released from wastewater treatment, although a smaller volume than methane released from landfills, also can be captured for electric power generation.[98]

(2014), https://www3.epa.gov/ttnecas1/regdata/EIAs/LandfillsNSPSProposalEIA.pdf [https://perma.cc/3V2M-UX3W]; U.S. Env't Prot. Agency, EPA-821-B-99-005, Economic Analysis of Final Effluent Limitations Guidelines and Standards for the Landfills Point Source Category 4-3 (1999).

93. *See Landfill Technical Data: Landfill Data Files* (.xlsx), U.S. Env't Prot. Agency (Mar. 2024), https://www.epa.gov/lmop/landfill-technical-data.

94. A study of shale gas wells in the United States found that capturing otherwise fugitive methane emissions can produce net profits in as much as 95 percent of instances. Francis O'Sullivan & Sergey Paltsev, *Shale Gas Production: Potential versus Actual Greenhouse Gas Emissions*, 7 Env't Res. Letters 1, 4–5 (2012), http://iopscience.iop.org/article/10.1088/1748-9326/7/4/044030/pdf [https://perma.cc/PB9Z-KZ88].

95. EPA, 1990–2014 Inventory of Emissions and Sinks, *supra* note 29, at ES-6.

96. *Sources and Solutions: Wastewater*, U.S. Env't Prot. Agency (May 6, 2024), https://www.epa.gov/nutrientpollution/sources-and-solutions-wastewater [https://perma.cc/GLJ4-EYTT].

97. *Municipal Wastewater Methane: Reducing Emissions, Advancing Recovery and Use Opportunities*, Global Methane Initiative (Jan. 2013), https://www.globalmethane.org/documents/ww_fs_eng.pdf [https://perma.cc/J3XX-8547].

98. *Id.*

An anaerobic digester collects the methane or "biogas" that bacteria converts when consuming wastewater organic material anaerobically.[99] The biogas produced from wastewater organic waste is comprised of about 60 percent methane, 40 percent CO_2, and approximately 0.2–0.4 percent hydrogen sulfide as a trace element.[100] The methane can be combusted for electricity or thermal energy.[101] Sewage methane also can be used in advanced fuel cell technologies to produce direct current renewable electricity or used as a feedstock to produce hydrogen for energy applications, both of which are incentivized by the IRA.[102]

Universal Location in Almost 50 Percent of U.S. Towns and Cities

These facilities are spread throughout every state. See Chapter 3 for the location of resources by state. There are approximately 16,000 publicly owned wastewater treatment facilities in the United States.[103] This is almost half of the approximately 35,000 towns and cities in the United States. Of these 16,000 treatment facilities:

- 1,269, or less than 10 percent, have anaerobic digesters on site to extract methane gas forming from organic material.
- Only 860, or less than 6 percent, employ the captured methane as a reusable energy fuel.[104]

Stated succinctly:

- Less than 10 percent of facilities are capturing valuable methane before they emit it to the atmosphere.

---

99. Michael Schirber, *Waste Not: Energy from Garbage and Sewage*, Live Sci. (Nov. 3, 2004, 4:00 AM), https://www.livescience.com/25-waste-energy-garbage-sewage.html [https://perma.cc/LXK8-D7DH].

100. Christopher Henry & Richard K. Koelsch, *What Is an Anaerobic Digester*, 7 Manure Matters 1 (2001).

101. *Gasification*, Biomass Energy Res. Ctr., https://perma.cc/F4WY-7QY7 (last visited May 31, 2024).

102. Steven Ferrey, *Converting Brownfield Environmental Negatives into Energy Positives*, 34 Bos. Coll. Env't Affs. L. Rev. 417, 433 (2007).

103. *Water and Wastewater Systems*, U.S. Dep't of Homeland Sec., https://www.dhs.gov/water-and-wastewater-systems-sector (last visited June 26, 2024).

104. *2017 Infrastructure Report Card: Wastewater*, Am. Soc. Civ. Eng'rs, https://www.infrastructurereportcard.org/wp-content/uploads/2017/01/Wastewater-Final.pdf [https://perma.cc/EN94-QZ8X].

- 94 percent of facilities are wasting methane energy they create by flaring it or ignoring capturing it rather than applying it productively as a fuel for electricity or thermal energy.
- 90 percent of all wastewater facilities emit their gas as climate-warming methane, rather than flaring it to destroy that methane emission.
- There is no legal requirement for wastewater treatment to capture methane.

Animal Waste Electric Generation

Along with trash and human wastewater, animals are a source of waste. In certain large animal agricultural facilities, there is an opportunity to capture fugitive methane to produce electricity. Anaerobic digesters can capture methane from agricultural animal waste and produce renewable electricity or heat, mitigating some of the nitrogen and phosphorus environmental impacts when waste is left on the land. To do so, manure is heated in an anaerobic tank, where bacteria break down chemical constituents[105] to create methane, which becomes a medium-Btu gas.[106] There are 225 anaerobic digesters in operation on farms across America.[107]

Financing

There is federal and some state financing for rural biogas-to-electricity generation projects. Federally, the section 1603 program provides grants to reimburse businesses for a portion of the cost of installing anaerobic digesters on farms.[108] The Rural Energy for America Program provides guaranteed loan

---

105. *Economics of Anaerobic Digesters for Processing Animal Manure*, LPELC (Aug. 4, 2022), https://lpelc.org/economics-of-anaerobic-digesters-for-processing-animal-manure/.

106. *Biogas, Anaerobic Digestion for Industry and Agriculture*, SCS Eng'rs, http://www.scsengineers.com/services/biogas-anaerobic-digestion-cng-energy-systems/biogas/ (last visited May 31, 2024).

107. U.S. Dep't of Agric., U.S. Env't Prot. Agency & U.S. Dep't of Energy, Biogas Opportunities Roadmap: Voluntary Actions to Reduce Methane Emissions and Increase Energy Independence 14 (2014), https://perma.cc/CK5P-6F3C.

108. *1603 Program: Payments for Specified Energy Property in Lieu of Tax Credits*, U.S. Dep't of the Treasury, https://home.treasury.gov/policy-issues/financial-markets-financial-institutions-and-fiscal-service/1603-program-payments-for-specified-energy-property-in-lieu-of-tax-credits (last visited May 31, 2024).

financing and grant funding for the construction of rural biogas facilities,[109] as does the U.S. Department of Agriculture's Environmental Quality Incentives Program, the Conservation Stewardship Program, and the Conservation Loan Program.[110] Nevertheless, biogas facilities development has progressed slowly.

Fossil Fuel Supply, Methane Loss, Efficiency Opportunities

From 2014 to 2024, U.S. natural gas production increased by more than one-quarter,[111] and U.S. oil production increased by more than 15 percent.[112] Almost one-third of America's methane emissions are estimated to be released from oil and gas production and distribution.[113] Methane is released in the fossil fuel gathering process, with new targeting of natural gas hydrofracking wells being drilled to liberate gas trapped in underground shale formations.[114] The Congressional Research Service concluded that "[i]n 2010, fossil fuels accounted for 78.0% of U.S. primary energy production,"[115] which, of note, is a smaller share than the 2012 average among all world

---

109. *Rural Energy for America Program Renewable Energy Systems & Energy Efficiency Improvement Guaranteed Loans & Grants*, U.S. Dep't of Agric. Rural Dev., https://www.rd.usda.gov/programs-services/energy-programs/rural-energy-america-program-renewable-energy-systems-energy-efficiency-improvement-guaranteed-loans (last visited May 31, 2024).

110. *Conservation Programs*, U.S. Dep't of Agric. Farm Serv. Agency, https://www.fsa.usda.gov/programs-and-services/conservation-programs/index (last visited May 31, 2024).

111. *U.S. Dry Natural Gas Production*, U.S. Energy Info. Admin. (Apr. 30, 2024), https://www.eia.gov/dnav/ng/hist/n9070us2A.htm [https://perma.cc/XM3U-YBEP].

112. *U.S. Field Production of Crude Oil*, U.S. Energy Info. Admin. (Apr. 30, 2024), https://www.eia.gov/dnav/pet/hist/LeafHandler.ashx?n=pet&s=mcrfpus2&f=a [https://perma.cc/H889-SGGU].

113. Tripp Baltz, *States Lead on Regulating Gas Flaring, Venting, Leaks*, 121 Daily Env't Rep. (BNA) No. 112, June 23, 2016, at B-5.

114. *See* Mark Fischetti, *Fracking Would Emit Large Quantities of Greenhouse Gases*, Sci. Am. (Jan. 20, 2012), https://www.scientificamerican.com/article/fracking-would-emit-methane/; Gayathri Vaidyanathan, *Methane Leaks from Oil and Gas Wells Now Top Polluters*, Sci. Am. (Apr. 16, 2015), https://www.scientificamerican.com/article/methane-leaks-from-oil-and-gas-wells-now-top-polluters/; ICF Int'l, Economic Analysis of Methane Emission Reduction Opportunities in the U.S. Onshore Oil and Natural Gas Industries 1-1 (2014), https://www.edf.org/sites/default/files/methane_cost_curve_report.pdf [https://perma.cc/3ZYF-TTV9].

115. Molly F. Sherlock, Cong. Rsch. Serv., R41953, Energy Tax Incentives: Measuring Value across Different Types of Energy Resources, at Summary (2012), https://www.hsdl.org/?view&did=722543 [https://perma.cc/4WQA-5D9J].

economies.[116] "The oil-and-gas industry is the largest emitter of methane, and the U.S. is the world's largest oil-and-gas producer . . . [,] responsible for about 10% of global methane emissions."[117]

Coal had been the dominant source of electricity production in the United States and in the world since the first harnessing of electricity 140 years ago.[118] Coal production accounts for approximately 9 percent of methane emissions, mostly from releases at newly opened mines.[119] Coal use for electricity production has decreased significantly and rapidly in the United States since 2007, from more than half of all electricity production to less than 20 percent now: the electric system now relies more on natural gas–fired technology than coal.[120] Figure 16.2 shows the increase in nonhydroelectric renewable energy use for power generation in the United States since 1776 and the U.S. Energy Information Agency projections for the future.

However, a significant portion of the underground natural gas pipeline distribution system is aged and subject to leakage of methane in the distribution of natural gas. Statewide in Massachusetts, nearly 40 percent of distribution mains and over 25 percent of services were installed prior to 1970 and are now more than 50 years old.[121] Costs of lost leaked gas of $20 billion per decade are passed on in gas rates to captive natural gas customers.[122] Lost gas also imposes risks: in the decade from 2002 to 2012, there were almost 800

---

116. Milena Gonzalez & Matt Lucky, *Fossil Fuels Dominate Primary Energy Consumption*, WORLDWATCH INST. (Oct. 24, 2013), https://perma.cc/6TRH-JFUB (stating that 87 percent of primary energy worldwide was from fossil fuels in 2012).

117. Eric Roston, *Obama Sets Stage for Huge Emissions Regs, Unless Trump Wins*, NEWSMAX (May 15, 2016, 8:13 AM), http://www.newsmax.com/Newsfront/obama-emissions-cuts-trump/2016/05/15/id/728888/ [https://perma.cc/47EG-JBA3].

118. John Muyskens et al., *Mapping How the United States Generates Its Electricity*, WASH. POST (Mar. 28, 2017), https://www.washingtonpost.com/graphics/national/power-plants/ [https://perma.cc/LR9G-4TTJ].

119. *Reducing Methane Emissions from the Oil and Gas Sector*, Ctr. for Climate & Energy SOLS., https://perma.cc/2YSC-ELV5 (last visited May 31, 2024).

120. *See What Is U.S. Electricity Generation by Energy Source?*, U.S. ENERGY INFO. ADMIN. (Feb. 29, 2024), http://www.eia.gov/tools/faqs/faq.cfm?id=427&t=3.

121. ENERGY & ENV'T ECON., INC. & SCOTTMADDEN INC., MASSACHUSETTS D.P.U. 20-80, THE ROLE OF GAS DISTRIBUTION COMPANIES IN ACHIEVING THE COMMONWEALTH'S CARBON GOALS 45 (2022).

122. DEM. STAFF OF H. NAT'L RES. COMM., AMERICA PAYS FOR GAS LEAKS 1 (2013), https://www.markey.senate.gov/imo/media/doc/documents/markey_lost_gas_report.pdf [https://perma.cc/9AK7-PV4C] (stating consumers in Massachusetts alone have paid up to $1.5 billion in extra charges from 2000 to 2011).

reported significant accidents on gas distribution pipelines, including several hundred explosions, which killed 116 people and caused more than $800 million in property damage.[123]

Figure 16.2[124]

Methane emissions are economically and legally distinct from CO_2 emissions; the former have resale value if captured, while the latter do not.[125] Captured methane can be sold to consumers as a substitute for burnable pipeline gas or used to generate what is deemed "renewable" electric power by both federal (see Chapter 5) and many state (see Chapter 8) laws and is eligible for additional refundable tax credit subsidies under the IRA (see Chapter 6). Going forward, it will be profitable, and to some extent required by law, to capture and utilize methane as a power generation source to prevent it from escaping to warm the climate.

Where there is challenge, there is opportunity. This theme resonates through many chapters in this book. The electric sector is changing dramatically—seize the opportunities!

---

123. *Id.*

124. Fossil Fuels Still Dominate U.S. Energy Consumption Despite Recent Market Share Decline, U.S. Energy Info. Admin. (July 1, 2016), https://www.eia.gov/todayinenergy/detail.cfm?id=26912.

125. Jayni Foley Hein, Inst. for Pol'y Integrity, Pol'y Brief No. 15, Capturing Value 7 (2014), http://policyintegrity.org/files/publications/Capturing_Value_-_Methane_Policy_Brief.pdf [https://perma.cc/B6LR-FQTH].